The Presidency
Then and Now

The Presidency
Then and Now

Edited by
Phillip G. Henderson

ROWMAN & LITTLEFIELD PUBLISHERS, INC.
Lanham • Boulder • New York • Oxford

ROWMAN & LITTLEFIELD PUBLISHERS, INC.

Published in the United States of America
by Rowman & Littlefield Publishers, Inc.
4720 Boston Way, Lanham, Maryland 20706
http://www.rowmanlittlefield.com

12 Hid's Copse Road
Cumnor Hill, Oxford OX2 9JJ, England

British Library Cataloging-in-Publication Information Available

Library of Congress Cataloging-in-Publication Data

The presidency then and now / edited by Phillip G. Henderson.
    p.   cm.
  Includes bibliographical references (p. 249) and index.
   ISBN 0–8476–9738–X (cloth : alk. paper). — ISBN 0–8476–9739–8
pbk. : alk. paper)
    1. Presidents—United States. 2. Presidents—United States—
History. I. Henderson, Phillip G., 1952–.
JK516.P657 2000
973'.099—dc21   99-38796
                                                    CIP

Printed in the United States of America

∞ ™ The paper used in this publication meets the minimum requirements of
American National Standard for Information Sciences—Permanence of Paper for
Printed Library Materials, ANSI/NISO Z39.48–1992.

To my wife, Mary Lou, and our sons,
John and Stephen

Contents

Acknowledgments

The idea for a book on *The Presidency Then and Now* began with a symposium that I organized for the journal *Perspectives on Political Science*, published by Heldref Publications in Washington, D.C. Forrest McDonald's chapter, "Presidential Character: The Case of George Washington," and earlier versions of the essays by Keith Whittington, Richard Ellis, and David Mayer (© David Mayer) appeared in the symposium for *Perspectives* as did my initial work on the policy wonk presidency. My colleagues were eager to join me in expanding our earlier discussions in the form of book chapters for the current volume. We have had the good fortune of adding several other colleagues to our joint enterprise: Mark Rozell, Shirley Anne Warshaw, Steve McKenna, Gary Gregg, Ray Tatalovich, Jay Avella, Graham Dodds, Scott Yenor, and Travis Cook. These scholars have provided valuable insights on such topics as executive privilege, presidential oratory, the evolution of the cabinet, early and modern media coverage of the presidency, the development of executive use of force doctrine, and the historical shift from congressionally centered government to presidentially centered government.

I wish to thank Steve Wrinn, executive editor at Rowman & Littlefield and fellow political historian, for bringing this project together with enthusiastic support and a record-breaking time for production. Though we trust that the broad historical perspective offered in this volume will have lasting value in the study of the American presidency, our discussion of current trends in the presidency, and particularly our assessments of Bill Clinton's presidency, resonate acutely in the here and now. I also wish to thank Julie Kirsch and Mary Carpenter of Rowman & Littlefield for skillfully managing the production of this volume.

Rowman & Littlefield graciously allowed Gary Gregg to adapt portions of his book, *The Presidential Republic,* for inclusion in chapter 5. Thanks also to *Presidential Studies Quarterly* for allowing Joseph Avella to adapt portions of a previously published article for inclusion in his discussion of presidential use of force doctrine in chapter 4.

I also wish to acknowledge the able assistance of my good friend and colleague, Stephen McKenna of the English department at the Catholic University of America. Steve not only provided valuable insight on the scope and content of the entire project but also gave generously of his time and expertise on the technical aspects of manuscript preparation. Special thanks also to my new colleague at the Catholic University of America, but longtime friend, Mark Rozell. Mark was instrumental both as a major contributor to the volume and as a sounding board for several of the chapters in the book and for guidance throughout the entire project.

I would like to thank my good friends Gary Greene and Aaron Hoffman for helpful suggestions on several of the chapters in the book and Laura Neidlinger for her technical assistance in manuscript preparation.

Finally, I would like to acknowledge the loving support of my wife Mary Lou and my sons John and Stephen. Thanks for allowing me to miss a few soccer games and swim meets to help meet deadlines on this project. And thanks, Cal Ripken, for saving your 3,000th hit until next season so that I may have the good fortune of being at "The Yard" when it happens!

Introduction

Phillip G. Henderson

When Woodrow Wilson studied for his doctorate in political science at Johns Hopkins University, a banner displayed in one of the reading rooms was inscribed with the words "History Is Past Politics—Politics Present History." True to the Hopkins tradition, *The Presidency Then and Now* is written with the intent of bridging the growing breach between history and political science by fostering a greater appreciation for the historical development of the American presidency from its inception at the Constitutional Convention in Philadelphia to its contemporary complexion more than two centuries later. This book is written not only for political scientists and students of the presidency but for historians and general students of American government who wish to have a broad overview of the origins, ongoing debates, and key political developments that have affected the presidential office over time.

In addressing such themes as past and present press coverage of the presidency; the origins, development, and changes in the role of the cabinet as an advisory institution; the evolution of "use of force" doctrine in national security policy and the rise of presidential primacy in this realm; the development of the doctrine of "executive privilege" and the Clinton administration's recent assertions of privilege in the context of past precedents, *The Presidency Then and Now* provides an important vehicle for taking the measure of the presidency today against the backdrop of deep historical insight provided by some of the nation's leading political scientists and historians. In addressing these and related themes, the authors seek to answer the following questions: Where have profound shifts taken place in the presidential office with regard to the doctrine of separation of powers and the nineteenth-century standard of a constitutionally circumspect and constrained chief executive? In what ways have dramatic changes in presidential campaigns and presidential oratory impacted the constitutional character of the institution? How does the scandal-driven journalism of the present compare with the partisan press of the early republic? What are some of the differences in philosophy and emphasis between liberal, activist-oriented presidency scholars of the post–New Deal era and early and modern twentieth-century conservative constitutionalists? In what ways has the public and political character of the institution changed and what are the consequences of these changes for American leadership? How has the recent trend toward a policy-centered and technocratic form of presidential leadership supplanted broad vision and historically informed judgment in the presidency? In answering these and other questions, the authors of *The Presidency Then and Now* set out to show how the past illuminates our understanding of the presidency in all of its modern manifestations.

The book opens with a chapter by the distinguished historian Forrest McDonald on "Presidential Character: The Example of George Washington." McDonald has written authoritative histories on the Washington and Jefferson presidencies, as well as several distinguished books on the American founding. His chapter provides timely insights into the ennobling qualities of Washington's leadership. Indeed, in a period in which soft-money campaign contributions, White House coffees, and formal bills of impeachment charging the president with perjury have dominated the headlines, it is as refreshing as it is informative to be reminded of the impeccable character of the nation's first president. "Virtuous leaders," McDonald posits, "are necessary, as examples and inspirations, to the preservation of the virtue of the citizens." As an exemplar for the ages, Washington set the stage for honor and esteem in private and public life on the belief that virtuous and dignified leadership is a cornerstone of republican government.

Constitutional law professor David Mayer follows with a discussion of Thomas Jefferson's efforts to bring the presidency into balance with the other branches of government through a strict adherence to the doctrine of separation of powers. Whereas Washington was scrupulously attentive to preserving his reputation and avoiding even the slightest appearance of impropriety, Jefferson was scrupulous in his adherence to constitutional principle and to the constitutionally ordained separation of powers. With the possible exception of Washington himself, Mayer writes, "Jefferson took the doctrine of separation of powers more seriously than any other president in American history." Mayer notes, for example, that Jefferson never exercised the use of the presidential veto during his eight years in office because of his belief that "on mere policy differences, presidents should defer to Congress" and his judgment that constitutional objections constituted the only legitimate ground for the use of the veto power. So scrupulous was Jefferson, in fact, that, despite his opposition to the bill creating the First Bank of the United States, he advised Washington that he should veto the bill only if his mind were "tolerably clear that it is unauthorized by the Constitution." In his letter to Washington, Jefferson wrote: "If the pro and con hang so even as to balance, a just respect for the wisdom of the legislature would naturally decide the balance in favour of their opinions." Hence, Jefferson seemed to share James Madison's sentiments in *Federalist* 51 that "in a republican government, the legislative authority necessarily predominates."

The Jeffersonian standard regarding the veto prevailed throughout the first forty years of the republic, for, as Mayer notes, the veto was exercised only ten times by the six presidents who served from 1789 until 1829. In contrast, Andrew Jackson vetoed twelve bills in eight years, more than all of his predecessors combined—and he made no pretense of needing a constitutional basis for the veto. In Jackson's view, mere policy disagreement was sufficient cause for exercising the veto. And, as Mayer notes, the Jacksonian view has prevailed in the modern era. Grover Cleveland vetoed 482 bills and Franklin Roosevelt vetoed over 600 bills during his extended stay in office. In light of similar expansiveness in the war power and in other realms in the modern era, the Jeffersonian legacy of strict adherence to separation of powers "as an effective check on presidential power" has, in Mayer's view, become "all but dead."

The discussion of separation of powers continues in chapter 3 by Mark Rozell, one of the nation's leading authorities on executive privilege. Rozell explores the development and evolution of executive privilege, including a detailed discussion of the Clinton administration's claim of executive privilege during grand jury proceedings in the Monica Lewinsky investigation. Rozell notes that the doctrine of executive privilege finds support in the Hamiltonian view of presidential power, and particularly Hamilton's argument in *Federalist* 70 that "Decision, activity, secrecy and dispatch will generally characterize the proceedings of one man in a much more eminent degree than the proceedings of any greater number."

Beginning with Washington's assertions of executive privilege involving a 1791 military expedition against Native Americans and in the famous instance involving the Jay Treaty, Rozell traces key precedents in the nineteenth and twentieth centuries that developed the doctrine of executive privilege. According to Rozell, historical precedents suggest that "the president's constitutional authority to withhold information must necessarily be limited to matters of national importance (e.g., diplomatic negotiations, national security) or to protecting the privacy of internal deliberations when it is in the public interest to do so." These considerations were not at play in Richard Nixon's claim of privilege in the Watergate tapes case. Rozell concludes that "Nixon did not use executive privilege during Watergate to protect the presidency and the nation; he did so to protect himself." Similarly, Bill Clinton failed to "make a compelling argument that the public interest would somehow suffer from the release of information about White House discussions over the Lewinsky investigation. Not only had he failed to do so; for months he even refused to answer basic questions as to whether he had formally invoked the privilege." Hence, Judge Norma Holloway Johnson ruled against President Clinton's claim of executive privilege. "There is little evidence," Rozell suggests, "that the Clinton White House undertook this drawn-out battle merely to make a principled stand on executive privilege. All evidence to date suggests that Clinton used executive privilege to frustrate and delay the investigation—all the while successfully convincing most of the public that the blame for the inquiry taking so long and costing so much belonged to the Office of Independent Counsel."

In chapter 4, Joseph Avella rounds out the discussion of separation of powers with a distinctively Hamiltonian bent in his defense of executive primacy in decisions to use military force abroad. Avella, a former navy captain with first-hand experience in the Office of the Secretary of Defense during the Persian Gulf War, suggests that there is much evidence to support the notion of presidential primacy in fateful decisions to use force. Avella argues that the Framers of the Constitution recognized that it is possible to *engage* in war without *declaring* war. This viewpoint coincides with Hamilton's assertion in *Federalist* 23 that the executive's ability to direct the operations of the armies that Congress has raised and the fleets it has built "ought to exist without limitation, because it is impossible to foresee or to define the extent and variety of national exigencies."

The contemporary dilemma, Avella suggests, is to reconcile presidential primacy in use-of-force decisions in such cases as Panama, Bosnia, and most recently the Clinton administration's decisions to bomb Iraq and Kosovo with the power of Congress to declare war. Avella argues that the War Powers Resolution of 1973 is a poor device for trying to achieve constitutional balance. He suggests that the executive branch in the aftermath of Vietnam has been more successful than Congress in structuring clear criteria and procedures for use-of-force decisions. The criteria for use-of-force decision-making developed at the Pentagon by Defense Secretary Caspar Weinberger and refined by Chairman of the Joint Chiefs Colin Powell and President George Bush are, in Avella's judgment, more practical than the War Powers Act. Avella concludes his chapter with a case study in which he applies the Weinberger/Powell/Bush "tests" to the Persian Gulf War with Iraq in January, 1991. Although one case study does not validate a concept, Avella cites related research to reach the conclusion that the use of the Weinberger tests as an analytical framework "provides remarkable correlation between compliance with the tests and overall success" of U.S. interventions. Avella further concludes that "the scales seem to point heavily in favor of presidential primacy as the most prudent and effective approach" to use-of-force policy.

Chapters 5 and 6 by Gary Gregg and Raymond Tatalovich, Scott Yenor, and Travis Cook present a formidable critique of the expansive, some would say grandiose, views of the presidency that were first articulated in the twentieth century by Theodore Roosevelt and especially Woodrow Wilson, but that date at least as far back as the era of Andrew Jackson. The liberal/progressive orthodoxy of such New Deal acolytes as Clinton Rossiter, Louis Koenig, and Richard Neustadt also finds a countervailing perspective in these chapters.

In "Whiggism and Presidentialism," Gregg traces the evolution of two distinct conceptions of presidential power in the nineteenth and twentieth centuries and discusses "the American ambivalence toward executive power—both loved and hated, trusted and feared." The essay juxtaposes the traditional Whig mistrust of executive power with the development of the modern plebiscitary conception of presidential power, and what Gregg refers to as the "cult of the presidency."

Gregg begins with an examination of Jackson's notion of presidentially centered representation and the Senate response posed by Daniel Webster and John C. Calhoun. The chapter shows how Jackson's concept of presidentially centered government became a guidepost for modern presidentialism in scholarship and in practice as manifested fully during Wilson's tenure as president. Likewise, Gregg shows how the Whig attacks on Jackson's leadership and the Whig defense of the traditional constitutional order serve as a model for critics of the modern plebiscitary presidency. Gregg's chapter provides a trenchant contrasting perspective to Richard Neustadt's work on the presidency. "Neustadt," Gregg notes, "demonstrates a Wilsonian dedication to the centralization of leadership and power in an activist presidency." Although he talks of a power to "persuade," Gregg writes, Neustadt "explicitly rejects a reliance on reasoned argumentation." What Neustadt's notion of persuasion boils down to is exploitation of "needs and fears" in the Washington community and reliance on "the coin of self interest."

In chapter 6, Raymond Tatalovich, Scott Yenor, and Travis Cook address "The Constitutionalist Presidency: Conservative Scholarship and Energy in the Executive." They demonstrate that the modern liberal conception of the presidency is centered on a highly personalized conception of power that contrasts sharply with twentieth-century traditionalists like William Howard Taft and Edward S. Corwin. These "conservative" constitutionalists held a constitutionally steeped conception of office in which "limited government, separation of powers, and faithful adherence to the Constitution and the rule of law take precedence over personal skill, political popularity, and the cult of personality." Whereas the liberal perspective engendered the view that the president as the voice of the people can do no wrong, Vietnam and Watergate revived, at least temporarily, the view that conservatives had long cherished of a balanced, constitutionally centered government in which the rule of law and the practice of governmental restraint prevail. But does the conservative conception of the presidency mean a weakened presidency devoid of precedent or prerogative? The answer, Tatalovich et al. note, is a resounding no. Even Taft, the premier constitutionalist of the twentieth century, fully acknowledged and promoted the vast, constitutionally rooted powers of the office. Not only was Taft a strong defender of the president's appointment and "absolute" removal powers, but also of the president's authority to use military force to defend U.S. citizens and property, which, Taft wrote, "grows not out of any specific act of Congress, but out of that obligation, inferable from the Constitution, of the government to protect the rights of an American citizen against foreign aggression." Anticipating the Supreme Court's eventual ruling in *Curtiss-Wright*, Taft argued that the president "and he alone is the representative of our nation in dealing with foreign nations." Despite these broad assertions of authority, however, Taft wrote that "the president can exercise no power which cannot be fairly and reasonably traced to some specific grant of power or justly be implied and included within such express grant as proper and necessary to its exercise."

Corwin, another prominent twentieth-century constitutionalist, went even further than Taft in championing a strong executive. "The fact is," Corwin wrote, "that what the Framers had in mind was. . . . the 'balanced constitution' of Locke, Montesquieu, and Blackstone, which carried with it the idea of a divided initiative in the matter of legislation and a broad range of autonomous executive power or 'prerogative.'" But it was Corwin who warned that "presidential power has been at times dangerously personalized." As a remedy to this problem, Corwin proposed that the president's cabinet be given greater institutional weight. He applauded Dwight Eisenhower for his efforts to institutionalize the presidency through increased utilization of the cabinet and recommended reforms to ensure that this process of consultation be continued in future administrations.

The importance of the cabinet as an institutional source of "independent advice" and as an extension of the president's institutional reach in the federal government is chronicled by Shirley Anne Warshaw in chapter 7. Notwithstanding Corwin's lofty aspirations for the cabinet, Warshaw notes that presidential utilization of the cabinet in the post-Eisenhower era has declined, not increased, and that the "independent advice" that had marked many of the early cabinets in American history is no longer pronounced. In the early years of the Republic most cabinet officers brought to the cabinet significant stature from distinguished careers in their states and from service in the new House and Senate. "In policy terms, members of the cabinet often considered themselves co-equals to the president," and, in fact, presidents gave great deference to the judgment of their cabinets. President

James Monroe, for example, upon consulting his cabinet, decided not to submit a paper to Congress detailing his opposition to signing laws providing for roads and other internal improvements. "The cabinet was divided" on the issue and "prevailed on Monroe not to send the document to Congress."

Warshaw notes that modern presidents, with the notable exception of Eisenhower, have turned increasingly to trusted confidants on the White House staff rather than the cabinet for policy advice and guidance. Franklin Roosevelt, for example, "ran as much of the government as he could on his own, relying on trusted loyalists rather than his cabinet to get things done." Eisenhower, in contrast, appointed "competent, proven administrators" to the cabinet and was not afraid to delegate considerable authority to his cabinet officers. Eisenhower also relied heavily on the cabinet for advice, although he did not return to the practice followed by Jefferson "on the gravest cases" of "taking the vote" of the cabinet "in which the President counts himself but one."

In the post-Eisenhower experience, Warshaw notes, presidents have been more concerned with the complexion and diversity of cabinet appointees than with the day-to-day operations of the departments. "The diversity that dominates the cabinet," Warshaw suggests, "has precluded the modern cabinet from being a body of great political or policy wisdom for the president." Instead, "every modern president has focused his policy making structure in the White House staff."

Chapters 8 through 11 focus on the changes that have taken place in press coverage of the presidency and in presidential rhetoric during and after election campaigns. In their chapter 8 essay, "The Press and the Presidency: Then and Now," Graham Dodds and Mark Rozell examine the evolving relationship between the national press and the presidency from a broadly historical perspective. The analysis is divided into three eras: (1) the era of the partisan press from the founding well into the nineteenth century where highly negative and commentary-laden coverage of the presidency was common; (2) the era of "objective" journalism from the early twentieth century through the McCarthy era; and (3) the modern era from the 1960s to the present, which has been characterized by a press reacting (some would say overreacting) to the failures and foibles of government from Vietnam to Watergate to the Monica Lewinsky story and beyond.

In chapter 9, Stephen McKenna examines the decline and near disappearance of historical narrative in presidential rhetoric. The use of expansive narrative in Western political oratory traces back to ancient, largely Ciceronian, rhetorical practices, which were still the dominant paradigm for thinking about the functions of public speech in eighteenth- and early-nineteenth-century America. As McKenna shows, earlier presidents saw the practice of historical and evidentiary narrative as an essential part of their rhetorical duties and as intimately tied to their conceptions of both republican democracy and executive leadership. In particular, the contextualizing power of narrative was a key means by which presidents demonstrated the continuity of the republic and the essential freedom of discourse in a democracy. Moreover, presidential narrative actively made audiences co-participants in a vivid and compelling national drama, and it thereby modeled a conception of citizenship framed by both mutual self-interest and historical consciousness. John Adams captured the essence of early nineteenth-century presidential oratory, McKenna notes, by showing "a conviction that civic fitness requires a historical view of the world, that leadership will be conducted in part through recourse to a contemplation of history in public speech, and that the rhetoric of republican democracy entails such free unfolding of events in public discourse." Twentieth-century "rhetorical" presidents, however, driven in part by the arrival and expansion of mass electronic media, have largely abandoned the practice of rhetorical narrative. With the notable exception of war rhetoric, presidential oratory has tended to cite history rather than trace it, to wield evidence rather than explore it. As a result, McKenna concludes, presidents since Teddy Roosevelt have increasingly conceptualized the nation as having superseded its own past. The ephemeral and, at times, self-serving rhetoric of modern presidents has dulled the once lively sense of historical continuity imparted in presidential speeches.

McKenna's examination of the form of presidential speeches is followed in chapters 10 and 11 by a discussion of the concept of the "rhetorical presidency" as pioneered in the work of Jeffrey Tulis and James Ceaser. The rhetorical presidency has become an instrumental device for drawing a qualitative distinction between nineteenth-century and twentieth-century presidential behavior. The nineteenth-century model of a restrained, constitutionally circumspect chief executive has given way in the twentieth century to a pattern in which chief executives are not only less sensitive to constitutional protocol, but more inclined toward highly personalized and direct appeals to voters, sometimes bordering on demagoguery.

Richard Ellis and Mark Dedrick, in chapter 10, "The Rise of the Rhetorical Candidate," assess the notion explicated by the rhetorical presidency school that dramatic changes have unfolded between the nineteenth-century and twentieth-century modes of behavior in presidential office seeking. Ellis and Dedrick argue that the dichotomy between a nineteenth-century "old way" and a twentieth-century "new way" has been exaggerated to some degree. They suggest that there was no single norm or constitutional "old way" that governed political behavior in a sharply differentiated way from the twentieth century. Rather, there were competing norms derived from divergent political cultures with signs of "old" and "new" coexisting at various junctures in American political history. Ellis and

Dedrick conclude their essay by pointing to a disturbing trend in which campaigns have become the model for governing. Today, those responsible for crafting the electoral strategy are brought in to shape governing strategy. Consequently, governance has become an extension of the campaign.

In "The Rhetorical Presidency, Presidential Authority, and Bill Clinton," Princeton political scientist Keith Whittington suggests that there is indeed a stark contrast between the contemporary era and the nineteenth-century canon of dignified, constitutionally informed restraint. Forums that had at one time been shunned as below the dignity of a presidential campaign, much less the office of the presidency, were highly alluring to Bill Clinton precisely because of their popular appeal. Whittington argues that Clinton's appearances on *Arsenio Hall*, MTV, the *Larry King Show*, and in various town hall forums "have broken new ground in contributing to a shift in political discourse away from reasoned deliberation and toward emotional reaction." Clinton's town hall meeting on health care, for example, featured tales of personal misfortune and despair over loss of health care insurance but offered "little in the way of useful information and debate." Whereas the Founders "sought to replace informal power based on individual charisma with formal power based on impersonal law," Whittington suggests that "the pursuit of public opinion has become the foremost goal" of the modern American presidency. In shifting the basis of presidential authority from constitutional office to personal popularity, Whittington suggests that the nineteenth-century ideal of presidential stature has lost much if not all of its meaning.

The assessment of contemporary trends in the presidency continues in chapter 12 with a discussion of the recent development of the "policy wonk" phenomenon in modern leadership. The policy wonk approach to leadership, as embodied in the presidencies of Jimmy Carter and Bill Clinton, can be characterized by a propensity to elevate the technical mastery of policy information and the detailed development of policy proposals over broad statesmanship and historically informed vision. Phillip Henderson examines several parallels between the Carter and Clinton presidencies, including the difficulty of prioritizing and focusing policies, the temptation toward micromanagement, the corresponding reluctance to delegate authority, and the marked tendency to place White House–centered policy development above legislative debate and purposeful deliberation by depoliticizing the policy process. From studying the Carter and Clinton examples, Henderson concludes that "the mastery of information and policy mechanics is far less consequential in shaping leadership than good judgment and a set of clear guiding principles. No matter how good a president or presidential candidate may be at advocating policies or showing good intentions, the lack of a clear vision and sense of strategy and purpose severely limits the capacity to lead and inspire."

Taken together, the twelve chapters that comprise *The Presidency Then and Now* offer the reader a historically steeped and at times provocative analysis, with the hope of fostering a greater appreciation for the office of the presidency as it was and as it is today. As McKenna notes in his chapter on presidential oratory, Calvin Coolidge inaugurated his term of office as president with words that are fitting to our enterprise: "It is necessary to keep the former experiences of our country both at home and abroad continually before us, if we are to have any science of government. If we wish to erect new structures, we must have a definite knowledge of the old foundations."

1

Presidential Character: The Example of George Washington

Forrest McDonald

The office of president of the United States could scarcely have been created had George Washington not been available to become its first occupant. Americans' distrust and fear of executive power was deep and longstanding, as was attested by the total absence of an executive branch in the Articles of Confederation and by the emasculated executives in the Revolutionary state constitutions. By the time of the Constitutional Convention of 1787, most of the delegates had been taught by experience that a government without an executive arm cannot be effective, but they remained so wary that more time was expended trying to devise a safe means of choosing the president than on any other subject. In the end, they settled on a single executive, but Article II, establishing the office—in sharp contrast to Article I, which establishes the Congress and itemizes its powers in meticulous detail—is a mere sketch of the executive power, in effect leaving Washington to fill in the details.[1]

Why Americans were willing to entrust the experiment to Washington's hands is well known. Quite simply, he had demonstrated that he was worthy of trust. He had served as commander in chief of the army for eight years, repeatedly rejecting proposals that he be granted dictatorial powers and spurning every suggestion that he dictate to the Congress; and when independence was won, he voluntarily laid down his sword and returned to private station. That action won him the admiration of the entire Western world, for it was generally assumed that successful commanders of revolutionary wars would follow the examples of Caesar and Cromwell, and set themselves up as tyrants.

Less known is how Washington became a man so deserving of trust. The answer is that he made himself such a man, by virtue of will, perseverance,

1

and long practice. In accomplishing that feat, he followed two separate but related courses. The first was to make a conscious effort, at all times, to merit and obtain respect and approval. He began this pursuit at an early age, dating at least from his adolescence, when he copied down 110 "Rules of Civility and Decent Behavior in Company and Conversation," and continued it throughout his life. In this regard, he was behaving as Adam Smith said, in *The Theory of Moral Sentiments*, that everyone did: Smith opined that men seek wealth or power not for its own sake but for the envy, admiration, or applause it elicits from others. Washington differed from most in craving the approval only of those he deemed to be wise, just, and honorable.

The other route was through the concept of character. In the eighteenth century the word "character" was not normally used to describe internal qualities, as it is in the twentieth. Rather, in its common signification it referred to reputation or public perception. A person had a character for meanness or prodigality, for taciturnity or volubility, for cautiousness or recklessness. But character also, among people in public life and in polite society, meant a persona that one deliberately selected and always wore: one chose a role, like a part in a play, and contrived to act it unfailingly, ever to be in character. When one selected a character with which one was comfortable, and after one had played it long enough and consistently enough, it gradually took on the quality of a "second nature" that superseded one's original base nature. One became, in other words, what one pretended to be.

Some readers may find it unsettling to be told that George Washington was on stage, acting a part, throughout his public career; after all, that is what we see in the sleaziest of modern politicians, and it is a kind of behavior that is endemic in electoral politics. But the effects, for good or ill, depend on the quality of the roles leaders play, the extent that the character itself (and not just the play-acting) becomes their second nature, and the quality of the audience to whom they play. When a modern president or presidential candidate panders to the dregs of society and portrays himself as a cross between Mr. Chips ("the education president") and Mother Teresa ("the president who feels your pain"), the discerning observer is properly disgusted. But that is not the way Washington played.

Instead, he acted a succession of characters, each grander and nobler than the last, to an ever-larger and more exalted audience that ultimately included all posterity. His first two roles, performed coterminously, were those of a prosperous gentleman farmer and a military hero. He chose those and had attained fulfillment in them before he was thirty years old. By the time he was forty he was leading Virginia's resistance to Parliament's encroachments on American liberty. At forty-three the role of commander in chief was thrust upon him (though he expected and willingly accepted it, albeit with some trepidation) and in that role he became the veritable embodiment of the Revolution. As early as 1777 he was being widely acclaimed as the father of his country. Along the way he developed a craving for Fame—the province of demigods, of mortals whose heroic services win them grateful remembrance in the hearts of generations unborn—and by 1783, when he sheathed his sword, his Fame seemed secure.

Only when he became persuaded that America's experiment in republican government might fail without him in the presidency did he agree, reluctantly, to take the office. His character as president—in both the eighteenth- and twentieth-century meanings of character—ensured that the experiment would not fail.

* * * *

The magnitude of Washington's achievement in his acts of self-transformation can perhaps best be appreciated in light of the eighteenth century's model of the human psyche, the theory of the passions. Passions were not ardent feelings, but drives for self-gratification; reason was not their master, but their servant. In any given person, some passions were naturally stronger than others, and as one went through life, a single "ruling" passion tended to overcome the rest. Among men in public life, ambition (the love of power or glory) and avarice (the love of money or possessions) were the most common ruling passions.

As a young man Washington was strongly driven by both those passions, and he was willing to do anything within the limits of the code of a Virginia gentleman to satisfy them. He sought wealth with considerable avidity, diligently maximizing his profits by supervising the work on his plantations and keeping careful records (neither of which most planters did), diversifying into crops other than tobacco and into manufacturing, and marrying a wealthy widow for good measure. What is more, he speculated in lands on a colossal scale, often engaging in what might be called insider trading, using knowledge gained through his capacity as surveyor; and he lobbied for and obtained lands granted as bounties to veterans of the French and Indian War.

The driving force of ambition was equally evident in young Washington. He pursued his craving for glory by genuine heroics, but he got the opportunity through political influence: he was made a major at the age of twenty and a colonel at twenty-three. He was assisted by some shrewd (or lucky) public relations strokes. He kept a journal of his harrowing expedition to the back-country in 1753, which chronicled awesome tribulations and triumphs over adversity, and the governor saw to it that the journal was published in Williamsburg and London; his survival of the encounter in 1755 in which General Edward Braddock and the other British officers were killed was likewise widely reported, making him a hero throughout the colonies. Tellingly, after his first taste of combat he wrote a letter to a younger brother in which he said, "I heard the bullets whistle, and, believe me, there is something charming in the sound."[2] That, too, was published in the several colonies and London: everybody knew who this audacious young colonel was.

Ambition then led Washington to seek electoral office, again in accordance with the conventions of the time and place. He carefully avoided campaigning directly, paying obeisance to the pretense that the office calls the man; but, to win a seat in the Virginia House of Burgesses, he had friends work diligently on his behalf, kept meticulous records of who voted for whom, and hired poll workers. He spent lavishly on entertainment for prospective voters, outlaying £25 to £50 per election. Most of the money went to ply the electorate with liquor: in 1758, Washington's agent supplied the 391 voters with 28 gallons of rum, 50 gallons of rum punch, 34 gallons of wine, 46 gallons of beer, and 2 gallons of cider royal—more than a quart and a half per voter.

But although such practices, like the ways he pursued wealth, may have been appropriate to the roles Washington played as a young provincial, they were entirely unsuitable on the larger stage he occupied from 1774 onward, and he changed his act accordingly. He refused to accept any salary for his services as commander in chief. It is true that he had an expense account, but during the course of the war his net loss—from neglect of his private business affairs and from debtors who wrote off their obligations to him in depreciated paper currency—came to some £15,000, an amount equal to about $5 million in 1997 dollars. After the war he was embarrassed when several states, most pressingly Pennsylvania, tried to express their gratitude by granting him large tracts of land. These grants he invariably refused, although he encouraged the states to reward other veterans with land grants. The most awkward situation regarding compensation arose when the legislatures of Maryland and Virginia incorporated companies to build canals connecting the Potomac and James Rivers with the Ohio and voted Washington 150 shares in the ventures. He ardently desired that the canals be built and had proposed such works before the Revolution, but he did not think it proper to profit from them. He fretted that refusing the shares would be regarded by the public as "an ostentatious display of disinterestedness or public virtue."[3] Washington resolved the problem by accepting the shares but, in due course, quietly turning them over to educational institutions.

His return to the public arena caused him great discomfort and was certainly not actively sought by him. In 1783, when he disbanded the army and resigned his commission, he declared that he was taking "leave of all the employments of public life" and that the resignation itself was the "last solemn act of my official life."[4] Because of that pledge, he was loath to attend the Constitutional Convention of 1787, despite his fears, incited by Shays' Rebellion and widespread political misconduct, that the country was degenerating into anarchy. Indeed, as late as the end of March, just six and a half weeks before the convention was scheduled to meet, he was still determined not to go.

The decision to serve as president was one of the most difficult of his life. He genuinely did not want the job; he thoroughly enjoyed retirement at Mount Vernon, and he sincerely doubted his ability to fill the office successfully. On the other hand, there was duty, if duty called. What aggravated the problem was that he could not properly discuss the situation with anyone, lest that "be construed into a vain-glorious desire of pushing myself into notice as a candidate."[5] Apparently David Humphreys, a former aide-de-camp who happened to be staying at Mount Vernon, first broached the subject with Washington. But it was another aide-de-camp, Alexander Hamilton, whose persuasion was decisive. Hamilton initiated an exchange of letters in which he argued that, because Washington had signed and urged the ratification of the Constitution, he had in effect pledged to do everything he could to breathe life into it. "It is to little purpose to have introduced a system," Hamilton insisted, "if the weightiest influence is not given to its firm establishment, in the outset."[6] The clincher was an appeal to Washington's love of Fame: "it would be inglorious in such a situation not to hazard the glory however great, which he might have previously acquired."[7] In other words, Washington could not continue to be the father of his country if the country did not continue to exist.

Washington's actual installation in office was delayed by his characteristic concern with propriety. In December of 1788 the presidential electors met in their states, as the Constitution required, and cast their ballots unanimously for Washington. The results were reported in the newspapers, and anyone else would have set out for New York, the temporary capital. Washington thought it would be unseemly to leave until he was officially notified, which could not take place until Congress counted the votes. For various reasons, Congress was slow in obtaining a quorum, and the result was that Washington was not sworn in until April 30, 1789, nearly two months after the scheduled inauguration date. (Washington insisted that his pay be docked accordingly, so his annual salary of $25,000, instead of yielding him $200,000 in eight years, yielded $196,121. He had asked that he be paid no salary, but Congress took the position that the Constitution mandated a "fixed compensation" for the president.)

* * * *

Sublimation of the baser passions, ambition and avarice, into the noble craving for Fame was virtually absolute with Washington. Overcoming his temperament, however, was another matter, for he was a man of violently explosive temper. He recognized his weakness and struggled against it throughout his life. The wife of a British minister to the United States wrote that he controlled his natural disposition "on publick occasions, but in private & particularly with his Servants, its violence sometimes broke out." Said Jefferson, "His temper was naturally irritable and high toned; but reflection and resolution had obtained a firm and habitual ascendancy over it. If ever, however, it broke its bounds, he was most tremendous in his wrath."[8] Gouverneur Morris made a similar observation, but cast it in admiring colors when he wrote that "few men of such steady, persevering industry ever existed, and perhaps no one who so completely commanded himself. Thousands have learned to restrain their passions, though few among them had to contend with passions so violent." He added, "But the self-command to which I allude was of a higher grade. He could, at the dictate of reason, control his will and command himself to act."[9]

His outbursts almost always came behind closed doors, but they were not always entirely in private. For example, there was the occasion in 1789 when he attempted to deal directly with the Senate. For some time, negotiations between government commissioners and certain Indian tribes had been under way, and it had become necessary to provide the commissioners with further instructions. The Constitution vests the president with the power to make treaties, "with the Advice and Consent of the Senate" (Art. II, Sec. 2). Washington took that passage literally, and one Saturday morning he and Secretary of War Henry Knox entered the Senate chamber just as the body was beginning its deliberations. Knox handed various papers to Washington, who handed them to Vice President John Adams, who read them to the senators. Carriages were rolling noisily by outside, and nobody could make out what was being said. Confusion and debate ensued, during which Washington "wore an aspect of Stern displeasure." Desultory motions to postpone the proceedings were made. Washington grew steadily angrier, then "started up in a Violent fret" and roared, *"This defeats every purpose of my coming here."* He cooled somewhat "by degrees," but finally stalked out "with a discontented Air." Senator William Maclay of Pennsylvania recorded in his diary that "had it been any other, than the Man who I wish to regard as the first Character in the World, I would have said with sullen dignity," that "the President wishes to tread on the Necks of the Senate."[10] That was a misreading of Washington's action: he simply could not suffer fools gladly. He removed himself from the possibility of future personal confrontations with the Senate by a less literal interpretation of the Constitution.

Washington also lost his temper frequently in response to attacks upon him in the press. Shortly after his first inauguration he wrote to Edward Rutledge about the praise that was being lavished on him and the resulting high hopes for the new government. He was afraid, he wrote, that the people "will expect too much from me." He feared that if the outcome of public measures fell short of the public's "sanguine expectations, they will turn the extravagant (and I may say undue) praises which they are heaping upon me at this moment, into equally extravagant (though I will fondly hope unmerited) censures."[11] The censures began to come by the start of his second term, and although they were unmerited, they were extravagant beyond what Washington could have imagined. The press of the 1790s was as vicious as yellow journalism would be a century later or partisan infighting would be two centuries later, and the repeated personal attacks stung Washington deeply. Again and again he interrupted cabinet meetings to launch a tirade against one newspaper printer or another.

Nonetheless, Gouverneur Morris's judgment was essentially accurate. Washington's lifelong struggle to control his temper both strengthened his will and had the therapeutic effect of enabling him to relieve some of the awesome pressures under which he labored. (No other president had half so much expected of him, and none demanded more of himself.) Furthermore, the outbursts never lasted long, and, with one exception—the occasion when Washington, faced with evidence of Secretary of State Edmund Randolph's treason, signed the Jay Treaty despite misgivings—the temper tantrums did not interfere with his policy judgments.

Toward the end of his second term, Mrs. Henrietta Liston, the wife of the British minister, said to him that she could read in his face the pleasure he anticipated from his forthcoming retirement. "You are wrong," he replied, "my countenance never yet betrayed my feelings."[12] That was not quite accurate, but it was true as far as the general public was concerned, and for purposes of presidential leadership public perception was what mattered.

* * * *

Washington was acutely aware, both intuitively and from long experience, of the importance to any position of leadership, and especially the presidency, of what has come to be called public image. Physical appearance is the first attribute of image, and in that respect he was truly blessed. He was slender and tall—six feet three inches and perhaps two hundred pounds when he became president (in a nation of citizens who tended to be short and fat)—with powerful shoulders, an erect bearing, and easy, graceful movements. Observers regularly described him as regal or majestic. Abigail Adams, a seasoned veteran of receptions at Versailles and the Court of St. James, gushed upon seeing him, as had Sheba upon meeting King Solomon, "The one half was not told me!" He moved, she said, "with a grace, dignity, and ease that leaves Royal George far behind him."[13]

As in other things, however, he augmented nature with art, which is to say he was extremely careful about the way he dressed, suiting his attire to his station and to the situation. When he attended the Continental Congress before being made commander in chief, he wore a splendid blue and buff uniform that he had designed himself. At his first inauguration he wore a well-tailored suit, but one obviously made of homespun American cloth, not British. That gesture was patriotic, not plebeian; it is impossible to imagine Washington appearing in public in an eighteenth-century equivalent of blue jeans or a sweatsuit.

But the crucial part of a public image is what is perceived to lie beneath the physical, and in this respect, as in most, Washington was careful in what he projected. He embodied all the desirable virtues of a president—morality, strength, integrity, steadfastness, sense of purpose, vision, intelligence, initiative, sensitivity to the nation's love of country, and so on—but there was more. He understood that the presidency is inherently dual in nature, partly executive but also partly ritualistic and symbolic, and that the latter part is quite as important to the well-being of the nation as the former. He perpetuated, for example, the British and early state practice of delivering a brief formal greeting to the legislative and receiving an answering address from that body. Such practices, he believed, were reassuring because they were familiar. Again, he was fastidiously concerned with what was proper, not in any narrow diplomatic sense of protocol, but from the profound insight that any departure from propriety constituted or could lead to a departure from morality. The proposition may be illustrated by a number of examples that may seem small but were crucial to establishing the presidency and the federal republic on firm and durable ground.

During his first few months in office, Washington devoted a good deal of attention to determining just how he should deal directly with the public. His rented house was overrun with visitors, a few on business, most there simply to gawk. Inquiring as to what had been the practice among presidents of the old Continental Congress, he was told that they had been "considered in no better light than as a maître d'hôtel," whose table "was considered as a public one."[14] Thoroughly miffed, he announced that he would receive visitors two afternoons a week, would return no calls, and would accept no invitations. That approach elicited howls of protest that the president was shutting himself off from the people "like an eastern Lama" instead of behaving as their elected servant. Then Washington questioned several trusted advisers including the *Federalist* authors James Madison, Alexander Hamilton, and John Jay, seeking suggestions regarding a policy that would strike a balance between "too free an intercourse and too much familiarity," which would demean the dignity of the office, and "an ostentatious show" of aloofness, which would be unsuitable in a republic.[15] Rules were devised: dinners every Thursday for government officials and their families on a rotating basis, hour-long levees for men on Tuesday afternoons, and tea parties for men and women on Friday evenings. At the public functions, anyone who was respectably dressed could attend. (Even on that limited basis, his liquor bill for entertainment ran to $2,000 in 1789.)

After the adjournment of the first session of Congress, Washington decided to make a goodwill tour of New England so that the people might see the living embodiment of their new government. During the trip he was able to establish several subtle points of federal–state relations. One concerned Rhode Island, which had not yet ratified the Constitution. Although the state was still nominally a member of the union under the Articles of Confederation, Washington was not an officer of that union and therefore had no relationship with it; he therefore refused to make Rhode Island a part of his tour. The second concerned Massachusetts. At Cambridge, the local militia asked him to review its troops. He declined "otherwise than as a private citizen," because the troops were under state command, not federal. The third involved Governor John Hancock of Massachusetts, a vain and pretentious man who had entertained hopes of becoming president himself as long as Virginia's ratification of the Constitution had been in doubt. When Washington reached Boston, Hancock invited him to stay in the governor's mansion. Washington refused the invitation but agreed to have dinner with him on the assumption that Hancock would acknowledge the subordinate position of state governors by paying the president a courtesy call. But Hancock, who was notorious for using attacks of gout, real or feigned, in service of his political ends, sent Washington a message claiming that he was gout-stricken and unable to leave home. Washington flatly refused to see him except in Washington's own lodgings; the next day, the governor, his foot heavily swathed in bandages, called upon the president.

Then there was the matter of religion as it related to the presidency. Washington was a deeply religious man who believed in the efficacy of prayer. He was firmly convinced that God intervened in human affairs and had chosen America for His special blessings. As he wrote to the Hebrew congregations in Philadelphia, Newport, Charleston, and Richmond in January of 1790, and repeated on other occasions, "The power and goodness of the Almighty were strongly manifested in the events of our late glorious revolution and his kind interposition in our behalf has been no less visible in the establishment of our present equal government."[16] As strongly, he believed that the Almighty had guided him in his great achievements. And, although he believed that every man was accountable to God alone for his religious opinions "and must be protected in worshipping the Deity according to the dictates of his own conscience,"[17] he also thought that public expressions of piety and thanksgiving were both appropriate and necessary. Thus in his general orders to his troops in 1775 he announced that he "requires and expects, of all Officers, and Soldiers, not engaged on actual duty, a punctual attendance on divine Service, to implore the blessings of heaven upon the means used for our safety and defence"[18]; and as president he declared days of national thanksgiving and prayer. When he took the constitutionally prescribed oath of office to preserve, protect, and defend the Constitution of the United States, he added the words "so help me God" at the end—a practice that every subsequent president has followed.

Public worship and professions of piety, in Washington's view, had incalculable instrumental as well as spiritual value. As he said in his Farewell Address, "Of all the dispositions and habits which lead to political prosperity, Religion and morality are indispensable supports. . . . The mere Politician, equally with the pious man ought to respect and to cherish them." And he added, "let us with caution indulge the supposition, that morality can be maintained without religion. Whatever may be conceded to the influence of refined education on minds of peculiar structure," he went on, "reason and experience both forbid us to expect that National morality can prevail in exclusion of religious principle."[19]

The only restraint on the mixing of politics and religion that Washington believed to be necessary was that no discrimination should be made for or against any particular sect or denomination, inasmuch as that would be tyrannical. He therefore did not object, in principle, to laws "making people pay towards the support of that which they profess, if of the denomination of Christians; or declare themselves Jews, Mahomitans or otherwise," in which cases they would be exempt from the taxes.[20]

*   *   *   *

Remaining to be considered is the matter of Washington's historical consciousness. All presidents, or almost all, are historically conscious in the sense that they are concerned with what the history books will have to say about them in future, but modern presidents tend to regard current popularity as a clue to what history's judgment will be—as is attested by their preoccupation, often amounting to obsession, with opinion polls and approval ratings. Washington labored under no such illusion: he shared with the authors of the *Federalist* the understanding that in the short term the people are frequently mistaken, and that it is the obligation of leaders as well as the design of the constitutional order to restrain the implementation of wrong-headed popular whims. He was therefore willing to take unpopular actions when necessary for the health and well-being of the republic, in the implicit faith that posterity would judge him favorably. When he marched into western Pennsylvania at the head of 12,900 militia troops to suppress the Whiskey Rebellion, for example, he was scarcely currying favor among the multitudes, yet he was doing what was right.

But there is historical consciousness in the broader sense of knowing and understanding what has gone before, and in this respect Washington was head and shoulders above most modern presidents. Clinton, early in his presidency, was quoted as saying that he would not recommend the study of American history because it was largely a record of racism, sexism, and exploitation. (On the eve of his second term, he said that "the last time I read the Constitution it said government of the people, by the people, and for the people.") His immediate predecessor was wont to snarl contemptuously, "That's history." Washington, though lacking much formal education and being by no means a bookish man, was nonetheless knowledgeable about history. He had read a great deal concerning ancient Rome, and he was thoroughly versed in the Whig interpretation of English history, especially the constitutional struggles of the seventeenth century. In addition, he read biographies of eminent statesmen. Inquiring as to a job applicant's suitability, he queried the man's "depth in the science of Politicks, or in other words, his acquaintance with history and his *general* knowledge."[21]

From all this Washington acquired practical lessons in statecraft. He learned that a free citizenry must watch its governors warily, being ever alert to the arrogance and abuses of power to which even the best rulers are prone, but he also learned that weak governments can be as dangerous to liberty as excessively powerful ones. He learned that the founders of republics lived in the grateful remembrance of posterity and that those who undermined or destroyed republics lived in infamy. He learned that republics are the freest of governments and, at the same time, the most fragile, depending as they do on the virtue of their citizens. And most importantly, he learned that virtuous leaders are necessary, as examples and inspirations, to the preservation of the virtue of the citizens. He earned his place in history by being that virtuous leader, and in the doing he ensured the perdurance of the American republic—at least, so far.

2

Thomas Jefferson and the Separation of Powers

David N. Mayer

In his draft of the Kentucky Resolutions of 1798, Thomas Jefferson declared, "Free government is founded in jealousy, and not in confidence; it is jealousy, and not confidence which prescribes limited constitutions, to bind down those whom we are obliged to trust with power." After further noting that the Constitution had "fixed the limits" of political power, he concluded, "In questions of power, then, let no more be heard of confidence in man, but bind him down from mischief by the chains of the Constitution."[1] As I have argued in my study of Jefferson's constitutional thought, this statement nicely sums up the essence of Jefferson's theory.[2] As a radical Whig who considered government an inherent threat to liberty,[3] Jefferson respected the safeguards provided by written constitutions to help keep government limited to its proper bounds—and "to bind down from mischief" the officers of government, including especially the President of the United States. To Jefferson, one of the most important safeguards, or "chains," of the Constitution was the principle of separation of powers.[4]

With the possible exception of George Washington (whom Jefferson, as Washington's secretary of state, advised on constitutional questions), Jefferson took the doctrine of separation of powers more seriously than any other president in U.S. history. His conception of the presidency was shaped by the doctrine—indeed, by a virtually pure form of the doctrine—that led Jefferson to an understanding of presidential powers quite different from the dominant view today. The Jeffersonian presidency in many respects was far less powerful than modern presidencies: the veto power and the war power were more constrained; the president was more purely an executive officer who deferred to Congress on policy questions, even in foreign policy and international relations; and much of the "pomp and circumstance" of the presidency, such as the annual State of the Union address, was absent. In only two respects was the Jeffersonian presidency more powerful than modern ones: Jefferson as president asserted the power to interpret the Constitution with authority equal to that of the Supreme Court in certain situations; and following his retirement, Jefferson theorized that, in times of national emergency, the president might exercise extraordinary powers not granted by the Constitution.

In practice, neither of these "strong" points of the Jeffersonian model has survived into the twentieth century, while in each of the other respects where the Jeffersonian model was relatively "weak," the power of the presidency has grown to astonishing levels. From a Jeffersonian point of view, modern presidents are no longer bound "by the chains of the Constitution," and separation of powers, as an effective check on presidential power, is unfortunately all but dead today.

Separation of Powers and Jefferson's View of the Presidency

Separation of powers theory was a critical aspect of early American constitutionalism, and Jefferson came closer than any of his contemporaries to a pure version of doctrine. Arguing that it received "its most complete and its most impressive intellectual expression" in Jeffersonian republicanism, M. J. C. Vile has summarized "the pure doctrine" this way:

> It is essential for the establishment and maintenance of political liberty that the government be divided into three branches or departments, the legislature, the executive, and the judiciary. To each of these three branches there is a corresponding identifiable function of government, legislative, executive, or judicial. Each branch of the government must be confined to the exercise of its own function and not allowed to encroach upon the functions of the other branches. Furthermore, the persons who compose these three agencies of government must be kept separate and distinct, no individual being allowed to be at the same time a member of more than one branch.[5]

Although commonly assumed to have been derived from Montesquieu, who was perhaps its most famous exponent, the doctrine was formulated in seventeenth-century English constitutionalism as the theory of the "mixed" or "balanced" constitution articulated by various political writers. As Vile has observed, however, separation of powers in its pure form is virtually incompatible with the theory of mixed or balanced government, which "was based upon the belief that the major interests in society must be allowed to take part jointly in the functions of government, so preventing any one interest from being able to impose its will upon the others." In contrast, the theory of separation of powers "in its pure form, divides the functions of government among the parts of government and restricts each of them to the exercise of its appropriate function."[6]

Jefferson was an early exponent of separation of powers theory, as his criticisms of the Virginia Constitution of 1776 in his *Notes on the State of Virginia* demonstrate. Jefferson regarded it as a fundamental defect that the constitution concentrated so much power in the legislature. Noting that "all the powers of government, legislative, executive, and judiciary," though in theory assigned by the Virginia Constitution to separate and distinct departments, in fact "result[ed] to the legislative body," he argued that such a concentration of power was "precisely the definition of despotic government." It did not matter that the legislators were elected by the people: "An *elective despotism* was not the government we fought for; but one which should not only be founded on free principles, but in which the powers of government should be so divided and balanced among several bodies of magistracy, as that no one could transcend their legal limits, without being effectively checked and restrained by the others."[7]

When he received a copy of the first volume of John Adams's *Defence of the Constitutions of the United States,* Jefferson wrote the author that "the first principle of a good government" was the separation of powers—"a distribution of its powers into executive, judiciary, and legislative, and a subdivision of the latter into two or three branches." Significantly, his first favorable reaction to Adams's *Defence* was prefaced by this remark. "It is a good step gained," he wrote to Adams, "when it is proved that the English constitution, acknowledged to be better than all which have proceeded it, is only better in proportion as it has approached nearer to this distribution of powers. From this the last step is easy, to shew by a comparison of our constitutions with that of England, how much more perfect they are."[8]

Gradually, over time, Jefferson's adherence to separation of powers evolved into a virtually pure version of the doctrine. Although his theory fell short of the "pure" version described above (because he also accepted the necessity of some checks and balances in a constitution), nevertheless Jefferson came closer to the pure version than any of his contemporaries except John Taylor of Caroline.[9] Jefferson's experience with the U.S. Constitution helped shape his devotion to the principle of separated powers: first as a commentator on the document during the ratification debates, while he was serving as minister to France, then as a member of President Washington's cabinet and as a leader of the Republican opposition during the turbulent decade of the 1790s, and finally, as president himself for two terms, from 1801 to 1809.

The Framers of the United States Constitution drew upon both separation of powers and the opposite theory of checks and balances in allocating the powers of the federal government. Separation of powers is the primary device, as the overall structure of the Constitution indicates. The first three articles of the Constitution are devoted to the three basic functions of government, each of which is assigned to a separate branch: thus, Article I, Section 1 provides, "All legislative Powers herein granted shall be vested in" Congress; Article II, Section 1 provides, "The executive power shall be vested in" the President; and Article III, Section 1, "The Judicial power of the United States shall be vested in" the Supreme Court and other federal courts. Notwithstanding these general provisions, however, the Framers also put in the Constitution numerous "checks and balances," as exceptions to the general rule of separation of powers. For example, the president is given a limited veto power over legislation (the "presentment clause" of Art. I, Sec. 7), and the Senate is given a share in the executive powers of appointments and treaty-making (the "Advice and Consent" clauses of Art. II, Sec. 2). That such checks and balances are exceptions to the general rule of separation of powers is underscored by their placement in the Constitution: the presidential veto is not found in Article II, among the presidential powers, but in Article I, because it concerns the exercise of legislative power; similarly, the Senate's "Advice and Consent" power is not mentioned among the provisions dealing with Congress in Article I, but instead is placed in Article II, among the executive powers. By complementing separation of powers with such checks and balances, the Framers sought to structure the government—as James Madison put it in *The Federalist Papers*—"as that its several constituent parts may, by their mutual relations, be the means of keeping each other in their proper places."[10]

Late in the fall of 1787, when he first saw copies of the proposed Constitution, Jefferson was ambivalent. Although he saw "a great mass of good" in the document, he also perceived "a bitter pill, or two."[11] The "good," in Jefferson's eyes, included both separation of powers and checks and balances; he wrote James Madison that he liked "the organization of the government into Legislative, Judiciary and Executive" and liked as well "the negative given to the Executive with a third of either house"—in other words, the presidential veto power.[12] The "bitter pill, or two," to Jefferson, were the two chief defects he cited in his letter to Madison: first, the absence of a bill of rights, something that "the people are entitled to against every government on earth"; and second, the lack of term limits for the president, whom he feared would become "an officer for life," essentially an elective monarch.[13]

Although he persisted in his call for a bill of rights—ultimately supporting ratification of the Constitution when it became apparent that a bill of rights would be added to the Constitution by way of amendment after its ratification—he decided not to press his objection to the perpetual eligibility of the president for reelection. Jefferson's concern about the lack of term limits for the president was not shared generally by the American people, who seemed to have unlimited confidence in George Washington, whom everyone expected would be elected. Washington later justified that confidence by setting the precedent of voluntary retirement after two terms, a precedent that Jefferson later happily followed. Nevertheless, during the debate over ratification of the Constitution, Jefferson predicted that amendment of the Constitution to impose term limits would occur after "inferior characters" succeeded Washington "and awaken us to the danger which his merit has led us into."[14]

Jefferson's desire for "rotation in office," or term limits, particularly with regard to the office of president, reflected his underlying fears about abuse of power in the executive branch. Recognizing that the absence of a separate executive, independent of the Congress, was a fundamental weakness in the national government under the Articles of Confederation, Jefferson nevertheless feared that in strengthening the executive branch, the Framers of the Constitution might have gone too far. Although he agreed with Madison that "the tyranny of the legislatures," state and federal, was "the most formidable dread at present," Jefferson also predicted that executive tyranny "will come in its turn," but at some "remote period."[15]

Jefferson's tenure as Washington's secretary of state helped to refine his understanding of separation of powers under the governmental system that had been created by the Constitution. What was significant about Jefferson's experience as secretary of state was that the office was so directly associated with the presidency: the secretary of state was the president's spokesman, subordinate and responsible to the chief executive by law.[16] As such, it was part of the province of his office, working with Washington, to arrive at a practical definition of the scope of presidential powers and thus to help keep clear the lines along which powers were separated. Those lines he maintained with scrupulous regard during his own presidency.

It has been observed that the constitutional separation of powers was "reflected and accentuated" in the residential and social pattern of the governmental community in Washington during Jefferson's administration. Legislators lived and worked on Capitol Hill, spatially separated from executives, who lived and worked in the neighborhood of the President's House; members of the federal judiciary, when in town, also lived and worked on Capitol Hill, but associated almost exclusively with one another. Thus the separation of powers became "the separation of persons."[17]

The geographical metaphor is apt, for Jefferson as president sought to keep his constitutional distance from the Congress. He could hardly have done otherwise without opening himself to charges of hypocrisy (by his enemies) or backsliding (from his friends and followers), for the Republicans in the 1790s had been sharply critical of what they perceived as Federalist attempts to institute an English monarchical and ministerial system. Consequently, early in his administration, Jefferson declared that he would abandon "all those public forms and ceremonies which tended to familiarize the public idea to the harbingers of another form of government."[18] These included the weekly "levees," or formal receptions, that had taken place at the executive mansion during his predecessors' administrations as well as the annual speech to Congress, which to Jefferson was too reminiscent of the King's opening of Parliament. In sending a written message to Congress rather than delivering it in person, he broke with the precedent that George Washington had set and started a tradition that lasted more than a century.

The Jeffersonian tradition ended with Woodrow Wilson, who returned to the practice of delivering the annual message in person. (In this, as in so many other ways, Wilson essentially destroyed the Jeffersonian presidency.) Jefferson probably would be appalled at the spectacle of the modern presidential State of the Union address. The ritual—with both houses of Congress assembled in the House chamber in wait on the president, whose presence is loudly announced and greeted with two separate standing ovations—is certainly reminiscent of the British monarch's opening of Parliament. The presence of the Supreme Court justices at such a highly political event, one that may very well concern legislation that will come before the Court, further violates strict separation of powers principles.

Jefferson also held a quite narrow view of the executive power, strictly speaking. On one occasion he wrote, "I am but a machine erected by the Constitution for the performance of certain acts according to the laws of action laid down for me." Although this statement ought not be considered outside its context, it may justly be regarded as an expression of Jefferson's attitude regarding the exercise of power, generally.[19] For example, when Jefferson as president refused to follow the practice of his predecessors, Washington and Adams, to designate a day of national prayer, fasting, or thanksgiving, he explained his position by noting that Congress was prohibited by the First Amendment from acts respecting religion and that the executive was authorized only to exercise their acts.[20] He also argued that the First Amendment prohibited the president from even merely recommending a day of fasting or prayer because the president could not "*indirectly* assume to the U.S. an authority over religious exercises which the Constitution has directly precluded them from."[21] These arguments reveal much not only about Jefferson's understanding of the First Amendment—his famous statement that it erects a "wall of separation between Church and State"—but also about his understanding of the presidency. His arguments assume that executive power was limited in its exercise both by constitutional restraints and by law.

The Veto Power

Jefferson viewed the veto power narrowly. His understanding—shared generally not only among the Founders' generation but also among virtually all the presidents before the twentieth century—was that use of the veto should be confined to unconstitutional legislation. On mere policy differences, he believed that presidents should defer to Congress, the branch of government in which the Constitution vested the legislative power. The veto was intended to be a preliminary line of defense against unconstitutional laws before they were put into effect. Unlike the absolute veto power of the British monarchs, however, the presidential veto is limited; it may be overridden by a two-thirds vote of both houses of Congress. Thus, it was not intended as an absolute check—for unconstitutional legislation could still be passed if sufficient majorities existed in Congress—but as an additional safeguard. The veto power explains in part why presidents take an oath "to preserve, protect, and defend" the Constitution.

In the conclusion of his famous opinion on the constitutionality of the bill chartering the first Bank of the United States, Jefferson advised President Washington that he veto the bill only if his mind were "tolerably clear that it is unauthorized by the constitution." He there described the President's veto power as "the shield provided by the constitution to protect against the invasions of the legislature 1. the rights of the Executive. 2. of the Judiciary. 3. of the states and state legislatures." Although Jefferson himself was quite certain that the bank bill was a case involving a right remaining exclusively with the states, and therefore "one of those intended by the constitution to be placed under [the President's] protection," he also suggested that the President to some extent should defer to the legislature. "If the pro and con hang so even as to balance" the President's judgment, which presumably was the case with the bank bill, when Washington had before him Secretary of the Treasury Alexander Hamilton's favorable opinion balanced against the negative opinions of Jefferson and others, "a just respect for the wisdom of the legislature would naturally decide the balance in favour of their opinion."[22] Not surprisingly, the President signed the bill.

When Washington did follow the advice of his secretary of state, and exercised the first of only two vetoes while in office, it concerned a congressional apportionment bill. Jefferson had argued that the bill was clearly unconstitutional because it violated the provisions that representatives shall be apportioned among the states according to their respective numbers and that the number of representatives shall not exceed one for every 30,000. Jefferson had urged that the bill be vetoed even if it could be saved from the constitutionality problem by an "inconvenient exposition" of the language of the Constitution. He thus took a somewhat broader view of the scope of the veto power, believing, Dumas Malone has argued, that it was "high time that the presidential veto should be used, in order to give assurance that the President was guarding the Constitution."[23] Still, Jefferson tended to see constitutional objections as the only legitimate ground for the use of the veto power.

In his two terms as president, Jefferson cast no vetoes at all. His predecessor John Adams also cast no vetoes, nor did Adams's son John Quincy Adams; and James Monroe vetoed only one piece of legislation, on constitutional grounds. The only early president to exercise the veto power with any frequency was James Madison, who vetoed seven bills, all on constitutional grounds. Thus in the forty-year period (1789–1829) covered by the first six presidential administrations, there were a total of only ten vetoes. Andrew Jackson's presidency marked an important change in use of the veto power, both in its frequency and in its rationale. Jackson's famous veto in 1832 of the bill rechartering the Second Bank of the United States cited not only constitutional grounds but also policy concerns. During his eight years in office, he vetoed twelve bills—more than all his predecessors combined—thereby earning the nickname "King Andrew," given him by his political opponents, who called their party "Whig" to emphasize their fears that Jackson was transforming the presidency into a monarchy.[24]

Most of Jackson's successors during the nineteenth century generally returned to the early tradition of limited use of the veto. Even Abraham Lincoln, a strong president who exercised extraordinary powers during the Civil War, cast only two regular vetoes. "As a rule I think the Congress should originate as well as perfect its measures without external bias," Lincoln wrote, showing that he, like the early presidents, was reluctant to substitute his judgment on policy matters for that of Congress.[25]

After the Civil War, the number of presidential vetoes increased dramatically, but the majority of vetoes were cast against private bills, granting pensions to Civil War veterans who claimed service-related disabilities but whose claims had been rejected by the Pension Bureau. Ulysses S. Grant, believing many of these claims to be fraudulent, vetoed forty private bills; Grover Cleveland vetoed 482. Forrest McDonald has noted that Cleveland's "veritable orgy" of vetoes was striking—Cleveland used the veto power more than twice as much as his twenty-one predecessors combined—but concluded that almost two-thirds of the bills vetoed during the Constitution's first two centuries were private bills, not public.[26] These vetoes often were premised on higher law principles, for private bills generally violated the longstanding but unwritten constitutional principle that it was wrong for the government to tax some citizens for the benefit of others.

In the twentieth century, use of the veto power decreased again until the presidency of Franklin Roosevelt, when the power again underwent a radical change. William McKinley vetoed only two public bills; Theodore Roosevelt, fifteen; William Howard Taft and Woodrow Wilson, each more than twenty. Roosevelt, in his twelve years in office, vetoed over six hundred bills, despite the fact that he had huge Democratic majorities in Congress who usually gave him what he wanted. As McDonald observes, Roosevelt used the veto "as a method of cracking the whip, to keep Congress subordinate if not subservient." Thus Roosevelt initiated the modern presidents' practice of using the veto as a political tool, a practice pursued by Roosevelt's immediate successor, Harry Truman, and utilized since by virtually every other president, Democratic or Republican.[27]

When modern presidents use the veto in so blatantly political a manner, they do more than simply engage in partisanship; they also seriously undermine the constitutional separation of powers. Profligate use of the veto also, in effect, transforms the simple majority vote required by Article I for passage of legislation in Congress to a two-thirds majority requirement, the majority needed to override a presidential veto—working a change in the constitutional procedures for enacting legislation. Modern presidents essentially have turned on its head their eighteenth- and nineteenth-century predecessors' understanding of the proper scope of the veto power; although they are quite willing to use the power illegitimately, to impose their policy preferences on Congress, they are surprisingly unwilling to use it legitimately, to guard against unconstitutional legislation, choosing instead to defer to the federal judiciary on constitutional questions. Considering not only his views of the veto power but also his views on constitutional interpretation, discussed below, Jefferson would be shocked at this development. Even his nemesis, Alexander Hamilton, who generally viewed executive power in much broader terms than did Jefferson, had agreed in the *Federalist Papers* that the veto was intended to give the president a "shield" against unconstitutional legislation.[28]

Equally distinct from Jefferson's practice is the extent to which modern presidents openly challenge Congress on policy matters. Although Jefferson has been credited with establishing a strong model for presidential leadership in his informal dealings with members of Congress,[29] in all of his formal dealings with Congress—particularly in his annual messages and in confidential messages dealing with foreign policy—Jefferson took an extremely deferential tone. He customarily spoke only in generalities, both in describing problems that ought to command the attention of the "Supreme Council of the nation" and in suggesting the solutions that they should adopt.[30] Indeed, one of the unfortunate consequences of Jefferson's excessive deference to Congress was the failure of the Embargo in his second term: proceeding under the fiction that the policy was Congress's, not the administration's, Jefferson never adequately explained it so as to gain public support.

Foreign Policy and the War Power

Jefferson recognized that Article II, Section 1 of the Constitution vested "the executive power" in the president and that diplomacy was generally an executive matter. Nevertheless, he recognized that Congress could not be excluded from policy-making altogether; and in certain areas where powers were shared between the legislative and executive branches, he considered presidential discretion to be quite limited. Accordingly, he distinguished the transaction of business with foreign nations from the making of foreign policy. The former was wholly executive;[31] the latter, although executive in theory, was in certain important aspects—most notably, the making of treaties—assigned jointly to the president and the Senate, by an exception to the general rule specified in the Constitution. Moreover, Jefferson also recognized that Article I vested in the two houses of Congress "All legislative powers herein granted," including the powers to declare war and to make appropriations. Reading the Constitution as a whole, he sought to give equal effect to all its provisions. This effort led him to see further limitations on the exercise of executive discretion, to ensure that the prerogatives of Congress not be undercut in practice by actions taken by the president alone.

His position regarding President Washington's 1793 Neutrality Proclamation makes clear Jefferson's understanding of the limits of executive powers in the realm of foreign policy. Jefferson was concerned that the proclamation not bind the United States in such a way as to undercut the power to declare war, vested alone in Congress by Article I, Section 8 of the Constitution—a deliberate decision of the Framers to give, in his words, an "effectual check to the Dog of war by transferring the power of letting him loose, from the Executive to the Legislative body, from those who are to spend to those who are to pay."[32] Although he had no objection to the precise wording of Washington's proclamation, which scrupulously avoided use of the word neutrality and simply declared the actual state of things to be that of peace, he considered a presidential declaration of neutrality to be tantamount to a declaration of no war, which was as much beyond the competence of the executive as a declaration of war. As chief executive, the President could issue a declaration clarifying the state of the law; however, he could not determine policy.[33]

Unlike modern presidents, who assert the power as commander in chief of the U.S. armed forces to send troops anywhere in the world without the consent of Congress, Jefferson as president was respectful of Congress's exclusive power to declare war, which he understood to mean the power to authorize the deployment of U.S. military force in all situations except those that were purely defensive. Thus, when U.S. Navy ships fought in the Mediterranean against pirates from the Barbary states of North Africa, Jefferson—recognizing that the Constitution gave Congress alone the power to declare war—publicly took the position that until Congress authorized offensive measures, the navy could engage only in defensive actions. His position—described by one modern commentator as "one of the most restrictive interpretations of executive war powers ever uttered by an American president"[34]—has been frequently cited to support a restrictive view of executive war powers.[35]

Under the circumstances, Jefferson arguably did not need authorization from Congress because the Bey of Tripoli had declared war on the United States; hence, orders from Jefferson's secretary of the navy to the commander of the Mediterranean squadron, Commodore Richard Dale, concerning this contingency could have been put into effect. Moreover, the majority of Jefferson's cabinet members advised him that if a state of war existed, American ships could be authorized "to search for and destroy the enemy's vessels wherever they can find them."[36] However, when one of the ships under Dale's command, the schooner *Enterprise*, encountered a Tripolitan cruiser and defeated it in battle, the captain of the *Enterprise* merely disabled the vessel, releasing it and its crew, because the *Enterprise* was engaged in a supply mission.

In his first annual message to Congress, Jefferson attributed the release of the captured Tripolitan vessel to constitutional rather than tactical considerations:

> Unauthorized by the Constitution, without the sanction of Congress, to go beyond the line of defense, the vessel, being disabled from committing further hostilities, was liberated with its crew. The legislature will doubtless consider whether, by authorizing measures of offence, also, they will place our force on an equal footing with that of its adversaries.[37]

In presenting the facts this way, Jefferson undoubtedly was inviting Congress to authorize offensive measures, and Congress responded with legislation explicitly authorizing the president to capture and make prizes of Tripolitan vessels. As in 1793 when he questioned the propriety of Washington's issuance of a proclamation of neutrality, Jefferson sought not to have the executive branch act unilaterally in any way that might compromise the power, assigned exclusively to Congress by the Constitution, to declare war. Thus he publicly took the position, as controversial in his own time as it is in ours, that the president lacked the power to act offensively against a nation that had both declared and made war on the United States.

The extremely limited nature of Jefferson's position is underscored by the criticisms of Alexander Hamilton, writing in the *New York Evening Post* as "Lucius Crassus." Hamilton agreed that it was the province of Congress, when the nation was at peace, to change that state into a state of war; but when a foreign nation declared or made war on the United States, he argued, a declaration by Congress, if not trifling, was at least unnecessary.[38]

As in so many other constitutional questions, the Hamiltonian position has been dominant in the twentieth century. Modern presidents assert broad commander in chief powers and, accordingly, refuse to comply with the provisions of the 1973 War Powers Act. Not only the Vietnam and Persian Gulf wars, but also U.S. military actions in such diverse places across the globe as Grenada, Panama, Somalia, and Bosnia have been undertaken by recent presidents without the congressional authorization required by the 1973 Act.[39] Defending these as United Nations–authorized "police actions," some scholars even have asserted that under the "new world order" of the U.N. Charter, congressional declarations of war, together with other constitutional checks on presidential military power, have become obsolete.[40] Moreover, the Supreme Court since the 1930s has held that presidential discretionary power in the realm of foreign affairs is virtually unlimited, a complete rejection of the Jeffersonian view.[41]

Constitutional Interpretation and Executive Prerogative

In two respects, however, Jefferson's rather strict theory of separation of powers resulted in a presidency that, theoretically, was stronger than the modern presidency: his "tripartite" doctrine, challenging the role of the Supreme Court as ultimate arbiter of constitutional questions; and his doctrine of extraordinary executive powers, or executive "prerogative." What scholars have designated as Jefferson's "tripartite" doctrine—his assertion that the president had the power, equal with that of the other two branches of the federal government, to interpret the Constitution—was fully developed in Jefferson's mind by the time of his presidency. He explained his doctrine in a letter written to Abigail Adams in 1804, defending his actions in discontinuing prosecutions and pardoning offenders under the Sedition Act:

> You seem to think it devolved on the judges to decide on the validity of the sedition law. But nothing in the Constitution has given them a right to decide for the Executive, more than to the Executive to decide for them. Both magistracies are equally independent in the sphere of action assigned to them. The judges, believing the law constitutional, had a right to pass a sentence of fine and imprisonment, because that power was placed in their hands by the constitution. But the Executive, believing the law to be unconstitutional, was bound to remit the execution of it; because that power has been confided to him by the constitution.

The Constitution, he concluded, "meant that it's co-ordinate branches should be checks on each other" and that, accordingly, to give the judiciary the right to decide questions of constitutionality "not only for themselves in their own sphere of action, but for the legislative and executive also in their spheres, would make the judiciary a despotic branch."[42]

Jefferson had seemed not at all troubled by the fear of conflicts arising from the departments' divergent interpretations of the Constitution. In part this was because, in Jefferson's day, for all practical purposes, the legislature and the executive continued to determine for themselves whether or not they were acting within the bounds of the Constitution. If a difficult conflict arose between two or more branches, it could be resolved by the only truly ultimate arbiter of constitutional questions—the people, acting in their elective capacity. By their periodic choosing of officers for two of the three departments of national government, the people, Jefferson believed, have an opportunity to "reintegrate" the Constitution, by demonstrating their approval or disapproval of those branches' interpretation of it.[43]

Jefferson, though not an advocate of "frequent and untried changes in laws and constitutions," nevertheless denied that he was a man who looked at constitutions with "sanctimonious reverence . . . like the ark of the covenant, too sacred to be touched."[44] Accordingly, he favored revisions of laws and constitutions, as the needs arose. His view was clearly distinct from that of Chief Justice John Marshall, who in his famous opinion in *McCulloch v. Maryland* argued that the Constitution was "intended to endure for ages to come." Jefferson, with his Whig heritage of distrust of law and government, looked to the people rather than to the courts when he thought of adapting the Constitution, or of determining the application of its provisions, to new circumstances. Always suspicious of men in power, Jefferson was particularly reluctant to entrust so important a role as the interpretation of the federal Constitution to any one body of men—especially to a Supreme Court dominated, as it then was, by John Marshall. Hence he preferred that constitutional difficulties remain unresolved, or that the mode of resolving them remain awkward and uncertain, than that absolute confidence be placed in the Court.

In the early 1820s, during the Virginia campaign against the claim that the U.S. Supreme Court was the ultimate arbiter of constitutional questions,[45] Jefferson again emphasized that the ultimate arbiter was the people themselves. As he wrote one correspondent in 1820, "I know no safe depository of the ultimate powers of the society but the people themselves; and if we think them not enlightened enough to exercise their control with a wholesome discretion, the remedy is not to take it from them, but to inform their discretion by education. This is the true corrective of abuses of constitutional power."[46]

Not only the "chains of the Constitution," strictly speaking, but also the elective power of the people, to which the president was ultimately responsible, provided a check on the exercise of presidential powers, in Jefferson's view. This ultimate check on presidential power applied not only to ordinary powers but also to extraordinary, or "prerogative," powers. After his retirement from the presidency, Jefferson recognized the principle of executive prerogative; that is, the idea that in certain extraordinary circumstances, the president has the right—indeed, the obligation—to depart from a strict adherence to the written law. He developed this doctrine of emergency power to justify the Louisiana Purchase, perhaps the most significant action of his presidency, about which Jefferson had deep constitutional qualms.

Critics of Jefferson, both past and present, have cited the Louisiana Purchase as an example of Jefferson's failure, as president, to consistently adhere to his doctrine of strict interpretation of federal powers. Rather than showing his hypocrisy, however, the entire episode of the Louisiana Purchase illustrates the seriousness of Jefferson's constitutional scruples.[47] Jefferson understood the importance of the Purchase; it secured New Orleans and control of the Mississippi and was therefore vital to the interests of the United States. Although his treasury secretary, Albert Gallatin, presented Jefferson with arguments supporting the constitutionality of the Purchase, Jefferson remained sufficiently troubled to draft a constitutional amendment explicitly making the Louisiana territory part of the United States. No important adviser or supporter of Jefferson apparently urged either the necessity or the practicality of such a constitutional procedure, however. Indeed, Jefferson's close friend, Senator Wilson Cary Nicholas, argued strongly against it, saying that a declaration from Jefferson that the treaty exceeded constitutional authority would lead to its rejection by the Senate, or at least to the charge of his willful breach of the Constitution.

Jefferson's reply to Nicholas's letter, stating in particularly striking terms his lingering constitutional scruples, has been one of the most often quoted of Jefferson's writings on constitutional matters:

> When an instrument admits two constructions, the one safe, the other dangerous, the one precise, the other indefinite, I prefer that which is safe & precise. I had rather ask an enlargement of power from the nation where it is found necessary, than to assume it by a construction which would make our powers boundless. Our peculiar security is in possession of a written Constitution. Let us not make it a blank paper by construction.

Conceding the likelihood that the Framers' enumeration of powers was "defective"—for "this is the ordinary case of all human works"—he urged, "Let us go on then perfecting it, by adding by way of amendment to the constitution, those powers which time & trial show are still wanting." In the present case, he concluded, it was "important . . . to set an example against broad construction by appealing for new power to the people."[48]

When Jefferson finally dropped the matter and acquiesced in the Louisiana Purchase despite the lack of a constitutional amendment, he did so not because he had given up strict construction but because he was following his advisers' recommendation not to press the constitutional problem, realizing that it could jeopardize a treaty so vital to the nation's security. "What is practicable must often control what is pure theory; and the habits of the governed determine in a great degree what is practicable," he noted. Jefferson took solace in what he regarded as the "good sense" of the people not to permit this one precedent to destroy the whole edifice of enumerated powers upon which constitutional limitations on the federal government rested. Indeed, a common-sense resolution of his constitutional qualms was suggested by Thomas Paine, who reassured Jefferson that "the cession makes no alteration in the Constitution; it only extends the principles over a larger territory, and this certainly is within the morality of the Constitution, and not contrary to, nor beyond, the expression of intention of any of its articles." If a new power had been added by construction to those powers assigned by the Constitution to the federal sphere, it was only the power to add to the domain of what Jefferson aptly called the "empire for liberty."[49]

The fact that, despite these assurances, Jefferson remained troubled about his constitutional scruples—for years after his presidency—only underscores the degree of his scrupulous regard for the "chains of the Constitution." Unable to square the acquisition of Louisiana and its incorporation into the Union with his theory of federal powers, Jefferson came to regard it as an extraordinary action of executive prerogative—he, as president, going beyond the strict limits of the law, for the good of the country. Even then, he still hoped for an "act of indemnity" by the nation, one that "will confirm & not weaken the Constitution, by more strongly marking out its lines."[50] The "act of indemnity" to which he referred was, of course, an amendment to the Constitution.

In a revealing letter written in 1810, when he was no longer president, Jefferson discussed the question, "whether circumstances do not sometimes occur, which make it a duty in officers of high trust, to assume authorities beyond the law." It was a question, he wrote, which was "easy of solution in principle, but sometimes embarrassing in practice." He then stated the principle, in a famous passage that subsequent generations of historians, political scientists, and other commentators have frequently cited out of context:

A strict observance of the written laws is doubtless one of the high duties of a good citizen, but it is not *the highest*. The laws of necessity, of self-preservation, of saving our country when in danger, are of higher obligation. To lose our country by a scrupulous adherence to written law, would be to lose the law itself, with life, liberty, property and all those who are enjoying them with us; thus absurdly sacrificing the end to the means.

Exercise of extraordinary powers, pursuant to these "unwritten laws," was not for governmental officers "charged with petty duties," he emphasized. "Where consequences are trifling, and time allowed for a legal course," the written law must be adhered to; otherwise, "the example of overleaping the law" would be "of greater evil than a strict adherence to its imperfect pro-visions." Only a high government official, like the president, might justifi-ably act beyond the written Constitution—acting at his "own peril" and throwing himself on "the justice of his country"—and only when extraordi-nary circumstances impose upon him this "higher obligation."[51]

Jefferson's doctrine of "higher obligation" probably derived from the idea of John Locke, with whom the notion of "the executive power," as conceived in modern constitutionalism, originated. In his *Second Treatise*, Locke identified as part of the executive power a discretionary power he called "Prerogative" and defined as the power to act "for the publick good, without the prescription of the Law, and sometimes even against it."[52] Like the power described by Locke, the doctrine of executive prerogative ex-pounded by Jefferson in 1810 concerned extraordinary acts required, liter-ally, to save the nation—where, as he put it, "the safety of the nation, or some of its very high interests are at stake." The fact that he posited such a doctrine underscores the degree to which Jefferson regarded the president, in all but the most extraordinary of cases, to be bound "by the chains of the Constitution."

Conclusion: The Presidency, Unbound

Neither Jefferson's "tripartite" doctrine of constitutional interpretation nor his theory of executive prerogative has survived into the twentieth century. A few of Jefferson's "strong" nineteenth-century successors—notably, An-drew Jackson and Abraham Lincoln—followed his doctrine in challenging Supreme Court opinions with which they disagreed; but since the end of the Civil War, American presidents generally have accepted the Supreme Court's role as ultimate arbiter of constitutional questions. Similarly, Jeffer-son's doctrine of executive prerogative has largely been ignored by his suc-cessors in the White House, even during the exigencies of wartime, in part because the Supreme Court has interpreted executive power, in times of peace as well as war, so broadly.[53] Ironically, it has proved unnecessary to theorize extraordinary executive powers because modern presidents' ordi-nary powers are so vast.

Jefferson's presidency exhibited instances of the exercise of executive powers that were unparalleled; yet it also simultaneously exhibited a sense of caution in exercising questionable powers—a concern by the executive over the constitutionality of its own actions—that also probably has not been matched in American history. "Let no more be heard of confidence in man, but bind him down from mischief by the chains of the constitution," he declared in 1798. His conception of a presidency bound strictly by the constitutional system of separation of powers, complemented by the additional safeguards provided by checks and balances, has been supplanted by a view under which presidents have virtually unlimited discretion to fully utilize all powers given them by the Constitution, whether in Article II (as, for example, the commander in chief power) or in Article I (the veto power). Modern presidents, engaged in all sorts of actions Jefferson would regard as "mischief," in domestic as well as foreign policy, act as if they are no longer bound by the chains of the Constitution, leaving the electoral power of the people and Congress's power to impeach as the only checks against abuse of power.

3

Executive Privilege: From Washington to Clinton

Mark J. Rozell

In 1998, in response to demands from the Office of the Independent Counsel to produce testimony from White House aides who may have had discussions with the president regarding the Monica Lewinsky investigation, the Clinton administration refused to comply and claimed executive privilege as the legal justification for so doing. Although often a controversial power, *executive privilege* is the right of the president and high-level administration officials to refuse to divulge information to those who have compulsory power: usually the Congress, but also in some cases the courts and special prosecutors (or independent counsels). Executive privilege may take the form, for example, of the president blocking an administration official from testifying before a congressional committee, or the president's White House counsel refusing to divulge to Congress or a special prosecutor the contents of internal White House memoranda.

The Clinton White House invoked longstanding principles in defense of the use of executive privilege in the Lewinsky investigation. Bill Clinton's legal team argued that since the early years of the Republic it has been widely recognized that presidents have a right of secrecy and that the power to compel testimony or documents is not absolute. They argued, as did the constitutional Framers over two centuries before, that secrecy was necessary to the conduct of the presidency.[1]

During this controversy, Independent Counsel Kenneth Starr gave a speech televised live by CNN on the doctrine of executive privilege. In that speech, Starr too invoked longstanding constitutional principles to bolster his claim that the Clinton White House had misused executive privilege. He specifically mentioned the very different actions of President George Washington when confronted with unwanted demands for White House information and indirectly suggested that Clinton's claims of privilege could not measure up to the standards established by the nation's first president.

When a federal judge's ruling rejected Clinton's claim of executive privilege in the Lewinsky investigation, White House Counsel Charles Ruff declared victory and then dropped the issue.[2] But that happened only after months of legal and political wrangling during which both sides claimed to be acting most appropriately according to the longstanding constitutional principles of the Republic.

Of course it is not unusual for political and legal combatants to both claim that they are the proper heirs of the principles of the American founding, or that they are acting in a way similar to what the Founders would have done. In some cases, properly invoking the principles of the founding is a valuable argumentative device that lends credibility to a claim. But in some instances, the invocation stretches credibility and, in the case of a dispute over access to White House information, has the potential to establish the kind of bad precedent that distorts the original meaning of constitutional powers.

The Clinton White House claim of executive privilege in the Lewinsky investigation was a clear misuse of that presidential power. Although the White House legal team presented credible arguments in favor of protecting the principle generally, they ultimately tried to apply executive privilege in the kind of case never intended to be covered by that doctrine. To properly understand why this use of executive privilege was deeply flawed requires an examination of the foundations of executive privilege and its earliest uses. In what follows, I describe and analyze the origins and earliest uses of executive privilege and then trace the evolution of that presidential power to the modern era. Executive privilege—then *and* now—is a legitimate presidential power, but one that is limited and subject, like other presidential powers, to challenge.

The Origins of Executive Privilege

Although not mentioned in the Constitution, executive privilege clearly is a legitimate presidential power.[3] That doctrine has its origins in the ideas of the leading thinkers of modern constitutionalism and in the writings of the Framers of the American Constitution. It also draws support from the actions of the earliest presidential administrations.

As part of their preparation for the Philadelphia Convention of 1787, the Constitutional Framers studied political theory and history. James Madison, for example, prepared a history of republican governments. The ideas of leading European philosophers weighed on the minds of the American

Constitutional Framers. An assessment of the Framers' intentions therefore requires an examination of the ideas of the most influential thinkers of modern constitutionalism—John Locke and Baron de Montesquieu.

Locke and Montesquieu emphasized restrained governmental powers and individual rights, which certainly had much to do with the appeal of these two thinkers to the American Constitutional Framers. Locke, in his *Second Treatise of Government*, offered a threefold distinction of governmental powers: the legislative, the executive, and the "federative."[4] Although on the surface Locke's emphasis on legislative supremacy seems unequivocal, he invests a considerable amount of power in the executive branch. For example, he places the "federative power"—the power to make war, peace, treaties, and alliances—solely within the realm of the executive.[5] Locke's chapter, "Of Prerogative," is the most revealing. In times of emergency, when the legislature is not in session, or where the laws are silent, he proposes giving the executive "the power of doing public good without a rule."[6] For Locke, the "supreme law" of the land is preservation of society. Only the executive can act with power and "despatch" in emergencies. Whereas the legislative has supreme law-making powers during normal times, the executive has the power to take extraordinary, even extra-legal, actions in emergencies.

Montesquieu also was concerned with the problem of reconciling freedom and coercion. Montesquieu more clearly formulated the proposition that power can only be checked by power than did earlier thinkers. Liberty, he wrote, can best be protected by preventing any one power from holding the authority to formulate and to execute the laws. He devised a governmental triad—legislative, executive, and judicial powers—as a means of preventing any one arm of the government from becoming tyrannical.[7]

Although Montesquieu favored limited government, he did not advocate weak government. He empowered the executive—the "monarch"—to act with a degree of discretion necessary in emergencies, even if such actions are not specifically granted by the legislature. In the end, Montesquieu allowed for a strong executive, independent of direct pressures from the "popular will," capable of acting with force and discretion.

The Constitutional Framers

Taking their cues in part from these two thinkers, the Framers sought to preserve both liberty *and* power in devising our constitutional scheme. In fact, Alexander Hamilton makes it clear in the *Federalist Papers* that effective government is most conducive to the maintenance of liberty. The notion of checks and balances, and the doctrine of separation of powers, were devices intended to enhance liberty, while maintaining "energy" in the executive.

Before discussing the Framers' views of executive power—an important foundation for establishing the legitimacy of executive privilege—it is helpful to note that the delegates conducted the Constitutional Convention in secret. They did not officially record the debates of the Convention. The official journal of the Convention listed only the formal motions and roll-call votes by state. Only the delegates had access to that journal. Madison attested that, "no Constitution would ever have been adopted by the Convention if the debates had been public."[8] In *U.S. v. Nixon* (1974), the Supreme Court noted that the secret Convention proceedings evidence the Framers' recognition of the need for governmental secrecy.[9]

Furthermore, it is important to emphasize the differences between the legislative and the executive articles of the Constitution. The legislative article contains the words "herein granted" in referring to the legislature's powers and specifies that branch's most important duties (e.g., to declare war, raise and support armies, provide and maintain a navy, regulate commerce, appropriate funds). The executive article provides a general grant of power with relatively few specifics. Many of the president's powers are not defined and enumerated, allowing the chief executive to exercise a broad scope of responsibilities under various circumstances. Under their general grant of authority—"The Executive Power shall be vested in a President of the United States of America"—presidents historically have exercised numerous powers not specified in the Constitution (e.g., issuing proclamations, making executive agreements with foreign nation-states, removing executive officials from office, adopting emergency measures in wartime).

Two passages from the *Federalist Papers* support executive branch secrecy. The classic statement is in Hamilton's *Federalist* 70: "Decision, activity, secrecy and dispatch will generally characterize the proceedings of one man in a much more eminent degree than the proceedings of any great number; and in proportion as the number is increased, these qualities will be diminished." John Jay, who had served as the secretary of foreign affairs under the Articles of Confederation, wrote in *Federalist* 64 that "secrecy" and "dispatch" were characteristic of the executive branch. He recognized the inability of a deliberative assembly to be entrusted with diplomatic secrets: "There are cases where the most useful intelligence may be obtained, if the persons possessing it can be relieved from apprehensions of discovery. Those apprehensions will operate on those persons whether they are actuated by mercenary or friendly motives; and there doubtless are many of both descriptions who would rely on the secrecy of the President, but who would not confide in that of the Senate, and still less in that of a large popular assembly."

The key members of the Committee of Style at the Constitutional Convention—Alexander Hamilton, Rufus King, Gouverneur Morris—shaped the language of Article II to allow the executive to exercise vast powers.

The vesting clause, the lack of any enumeration of duties in the commander in chief clause, and many silences about such powers as war, diplomatic powers, and control over executive departments, all leave the president with a vast reserve of unspecified authority. Article II "gives the president a power that has never been defined or enumerated and, in fact, cannot be defined since its scope depends largely on circumstances."[10]

James Wilson played a prominent role in drafting Article II. He served on the Committee of Detail and wrote the final version of the first draft. When it came to the subjects of executive power and secrecy, Wilson was unequivocal. He too recognized the necessity of an executive power characterized by the ability to act with secrecy and dispatch. Wilson's law lecture notes are consistent with the view of the *Federalist Papers*.

> In planning, forming, or arranging laws, deliberation is always becoming, and always useful. But in the active scenes of government, there are emergencies in which the man . . . who deliberates is lost. Secrecy may be equally as necessary as dispatch. But, can either secrecy or dispatch be excepted, when, to every enterprise, mutual communication, mutual consultation, and mutual agreement, among men of perhaps discordant views, of discordant tempers, and discordant interests are indispensably necessary? How much time will be consumed, how little business will be done. . . . If, on the other hand, the executive power of government is placed in the hands of one person, who is to direct all subordinate officers of that department, is there not reason to expect, in his plans and conduct, promptitude, activity, firmness, consistency, and energy.[11]

Chief Justice John Marshall wrote in *Marbury v. Madison* (1803) that "the president is invested with certain important political powers, in the exercise of which he is to use his own discretion, and is accountable only to his country in his political character, and to his own conscience."[12] Elsewhere Marshall commented that the president is the "sole organ of the nation in its external relations, and its sole representative with foreign nations."[13] Justice Joseph Story acknowledged that the president "is compelled to resort to secret and unseen influences, to private interviews, and private arrangements, to accomplish his own appropriate purposes."[14]

In Raoul Berger's view there is no constitutional basis for executive privilege. Berger believes that the Framers "patently modeled" Congress after the British Parliament. He points out that both the colonial legislatures and the British Parliament were able to compel disclosure of executive information.[15] For Berger, "history, the traditional index of constitutional construction, discloses that a sweeping power of legislative inquiry had been exercised by the Parliament and by the colonial legislatures."[16] He concludes that the modern Congress must have the same limitless power of inquiry as entrusted to the British Parliament.[17]

The problem with this argument is the assumption that the power of the executive in a presidential system can be equated with that of a parliamentary system. Yet, as James W. Ceaser writes, "under a presidential system the essential executive force is never extinguished or in doubt; under a parliamentary system the executive force cannot be guaranteed (and in practice has not been)."[18] Berger's argument also rests on the belief that the power of inquiry in a governmental system based on the separation of powers is as unquestioned and extensive as the power of inquiry in a system that rejects the concept of separation of powers. Although Congress indeed needs information to conduct inquiries, the Supreme Court has ruled that the congressional power of inquiry has limits.[19] Yet, the Court also has determined that in cases of inquiry into possible criminal actions, the executive has to release pertinent information.[20]

Although the philosophical and constitutional underpinnings of executive privilege are substantial, the legitimacy of that presidential power is strengthened by the evidence of its exercise by the early presidents. The intentions of the Framers are illuminated by what these men did when they put their ideas into practice.

Executive Privilege Then: Washington, Jefferson, and Madison

The first presidential administration established the most important precedents for the exercise of executive power. George Washington understood the crucial role that the Founders played in establishing precedents for future generations. As he wrote to James Madison on May 5, 1789, "as the first of everything, in our situation will serve to establish precedent, it is devoutly wished on my part, that these precedents may be fixed on true principles."[21] In his actions as president, Washington acted in accordance with a Hamiltonian view of executive power.

More specifically, several of Washington's actions established precedents for the exercise of what is now known as executive privilege. The first such action concerned a congressional request to investigate information relating to the failure of a November 1791 military expedition by General Arthur St. Clair against Native Americans. The House of Representatives established an investigative committee on March 27, 1792, "to call for such persons, papers and records, as may be necessary to assist their inquiries."[22] The investigating committee requested from the president documents regarding St. Clair's expedition.

Washington convened his cabinet to determine how to respond to this first ever request for presidential materials by a congressional committee. The president wanted to discuss whether any harm would result from public disclosure of the information and, most pertinently, whether he could rightfully refuse to submit documents to Congress. Along with Hamilton, Henry Knox, and Edmund Randolph, Thomas Jefferson attended the April 2, 1792, Cabinet meeting, and he later recalled the group's determination.

> We had all considered, and were of one mind, first, that the House was an inquest, and therefore might institute inquiries. Second, that it might call for papers generally. Third, that the Executive ought to communicate such papers as the public good would permit, and ought to refuse those, the disclosure of which would injure the public: consequently were to exercise a discretion. Fourth, that neither the committees nor House has a right to call on the Head of a Department, who and whose papers were under the President alone; but that the committee should instruct their chairman to move the House to address the President.[23]

Washington eventually determined that public disclosure of the information would not harm the national interest and that such disclosure was necessary to vindicate General St. Clair. Although Washington chose to negotiate with Congress over the investigating committee's request and to turn over relevant documents to Congress, his administration had taken an affirmative position on the right of the executive branch to withhold information.

On January 17, 1794, the U.S. Senate advanced a motion directing Secretary of State Edmund Randolph "to lay before the Senate the correspondence which have been had between the Minister of the United States at the Republic of France [Morris], and said Republic, and between said Minister and the Office of Secretary of State."[24] The Senate later amended the motion to address the president instead of Minister Morris. Significantly, the amended version also "requested" rather than "directed" that such information be forwarded to Congress.[25]

Believing that disclosure of the correspondence would be inappropriate, Washington sought the advice of his cabinet as to how to handle the Senate's request. On January 28, 1794, three of Washington's cabinet members expressed their opinions.

> General Knox is of the opinion, that no part of the correspondence should be sent to the Senate. Colonel Hamilton, that the correct mode of proceeding is to do what General Knox advises; but the principle is safe, by excepting such parts as the president may choose to withhold. Mr. Randolph, that all correspondence proper, from its nature, to be communicated to the Senate, should be sent; but that what the president thinks is improper, should not be sent.[26]

Attorney General William Bradford wrote separately that "it is the duty of the Executive to withhold such parts of the said correspondence as in the judgment of the Executive shall be deemed unsafe and improper to be disclosed." On February 16, 1794, Washington responded as follows to the Senate's request: "After an examination of [the correspondence], I directed copies and translations to be made; except in those particulars, in my judgment, for public considerations, ought not to be communicated. These copies and translations are now transmitted to the Senate; but the nature of them manifest the propriety of their being received as confidential."[27]

Washington allowed the Senate to examine some parts of the correspondence, subject to his approval. He believed that information damaging to the "public interest" could constitutionally be withheld from the Congress. The Senate never challenged the president's authority to withhold the information.[28]

In 1796, John Jay had completed U.S. negotiations with Great Britain over issues unsettled from the American Revolution. Because many considered the settlement unfavorable to the United States, Congress took a keen interest in the negotiations. Not only did the Senate debate ratification of the Jay Treaty; the House set out to conduct its own investigation. The House passed a resolution requesting from Washington information concerning his instructions to the U.S. Minister to Britain regarding the treaty negotiations. That resolution raised the issue of the House's proper role in the treaty-making process. Washington refused to comply with the House request and explained:

> The nature of foreign negotiations requires caution, and their success must often depend on secrecy; and even when brought to a conclusion a full disclosure of all the measures, demands, or eventual concessions which may have been proposed or contemplated would be extremely impolitic; for this might have a pernicious influence on future negotiations, or produce immediate inconveniences, perhaps danger and mischief, in relation to other powers. The necessity of such caution and secrecy was one cogent reason for vesting the power of making treaties in the President, with the advice and consent of the Senate, the principle on which that body was formed confining it to a small number of members. To admit, then, a right in the House of Representatives to demand and to have as a matter of course all the papers respecting a negotiation with a foreign power would be to establish a dangerous precedent. . . . [T]he boundaries fixed by the Constitution between the different departments should be preserved, a just regard to the Constitution and to the duty of my office . . . forbids a compliance with your request.[29]

The House of Representatives debated Washington's refusal to disclose the documents. The House took no substantive action other than passing two non-binding resolutions—one asserting that Congress need not stipulate any reason for requesting information from the executive; the other proclaiming that the House has a legitimate role in considering the expediency with which a treaty is being implemented.[30] Our chief constitutional architect, then Representative James Madison, proclaimed on the House floor, "that the Executive had a right, under a due responsibility, also, to withhold information, when of a nature that did not permit a disclosure of it at the time."[31]

Washington never included the Senate in the negotiation stage of the Jay Treaty. During the ratification stage, the Senate voted to keep the treaty secret, as Hamilton wrote, "because they thought it [the secrecy] the affair of the president to do as he thought fit."[32] The Senate minority opposed to ratification listed seven objections to the treaty. None cited Washington's decision to not seek Senate advice.[33]

Even so strong a defender of popular sovereignty as Thomas Jefferson recognized the legitimacy of executive branch secrecy. As president, he classified his correspondence as either public or secret. He withheld correspondence deemed secret from both the public and Congress.[34] For example, in 1807 President Jefferson denied a congressional request to provide information about the Aaron Burr conspiracy. Burr had been involved with a secessionist conspiracy, resulting in treason charges.[35]

Most relevant to the executive privilege debate, a January 1807 House resolution requested that the president "lay before this House any information in the possession of the Executive, except such as he may deem the public welfare to require not to be disclosed."[36] Congress had acknowledged the president's right to exercise a discretion to withhold information. Jefferson replied by announcing Burr's guilt and asserting a need to withhold information about the other alleged conspirators: "In this state of the evidence, delivered sometimes, too, under the restrictions of private confidence, neither safety nor justice will permit the exposing of names, except that of the principle actor, whose guilt is placed beyond question.[37] Jefferson also had written to the U.S. District Attorney conducting the Burr prosecution that it was "the necessary right of the President of the United States to decide, independently, what papers coming to him as President, the public interest permit to be communicated, and to whom."[38]

James Madison withheld information from Congress about French trade restrictions against the United States, which eventually led to widespread support for war against Great Britain.[39] Madison, and then later President James Monroe, withheld information from Congress regarding the U.S. takeover of the Florida territory.[40] On February 16, 1816, the Senate Committee on Foreign Relations issued a report stating: "If it be true that the success of negotiations is greatly influenced by time and accidental circumstances, the importance to the negotiative authority of acquiring regular and secret intelligence cannot be doubted. The Senate does not possess the means of acquiring such intelligence. It does not manage the correspondence with our ministers abroad nor with foreign concerns here. . . . The President . . . manages our concerns with foreign nations and must necessarily be most competent to determine when, how and upon what subjects negotiation may be urged with the greatest prospect of success."[41]

There are important common threads to the Framers' writings and these early exercises of executive privilege. First, presidents do not possess an unlimited right to withhold information. Rather, Congress has the right of inquiry and may request the production of materials and testimony. Second, the president's constitutional authority to withhold information must necessarily be limited to matters of national importance (e.g., diplomatic negotiations, national security) or to protecting the privacy of internal deliberations when it is in the public interest to do so. Third, the legislative power of inquiry, though substantial, is not absolute.

The early presidents took important actions to establish the legitimacy of executive privilege. The uses of that doctrine by their successors are so numerous that it is impossible to provide a full accounting here.[42] The key point is that successive presidents and congresses routinely accepted the legitimacy of this presidential power until its exercise became controversial in the mid-twentieth century. A brief description of key events in the modern evolution of executive privilege offers an understanding of why this presidential power today no longer attracts widespread acceptance.

Executive Privilege and the Modern Presidents

The Eisenhower administration represents an important period in the development of the doctrine of executive privilege. Eisenhower's administration invoked that doctrine on over forty occasions. The most important controversy concerned the Army–McCarthy hearings. During testimony the Army Counsel John Adams mentioned that he had a conference with top White House aides in the Attorney General's Office. Congressional investigators sought information on what transpired in those conversations. Dwight Eisenhower intervened with a letter on May 17, 1954, to Secretary of Defense Charles Wilson instructing employees of that Department not to testify.

> Because it is essential to efficient and effective administration that employees of the Executive Branch be in a position to be completely candid in advising with each other on official matters, and because it is not in the public interest that any of their conversations or communications, or any documents or reproductions, concerning such advice be disclosed, you will instruct employees of your Department that in all of their appearances before the Subcommittee of the Senate Committee on Government Operations regarding the inquiry now before it they are not to testify to any such conversations or communications, or to produce any such documents or reproductions. This principle must be maintained regardless of who would benefit by such disclosures.[43]

Other executive branch officials used Eisenhower's letter as the justification for their refusals to testify before Congress. United Nations Ambassador Henry Cabot Lodge, for example, refused to testify to Congress on the basis that he was a White House adviser. Eisenhower replied affirmatively: "The position you propose to take is exactly correct. I would be astonished if any of my personal advisors would undertake to give testimony on intimate staff counsel and advice. The result would be to eliminate all such offices from the presidential staff. In turn, this would mean paralysis."[44]

Senator Joseph McCarthy (R-Wis.) denounced Eisenhower's order as an "iron curtain" and exclaimed that, "this is the first time I've ever seen the executive branch of government take the fifth amendment."[45] Despite some other criticism of the president for defining executive privilege too broadly, the *Washington Post* agreed that the president's constitutional authority to withhold information from Congress "is altogether beyond question."[46]

All of Eisenhower's successors have used executive privilege, none so controversially as President Richard Nixon. The Nixon administration's official policy toward executive privilege did not differ fundamentally from those of his predecessors. In a memorandum outlining executive privilege procedures the president made it clear that the "scope of executive privilege must be very narrowly construed" and that it could only be asserted with "specific presidential approval." In a separate White House memorandum Nixon added that "this Administration will invoke this authority only in the most compelling circumstances and after a rigorous inquiry into the actual need for its exercise."[47]

Yet in practice President Nixon used executive privilege extensively and at one point the attorney general, Richard Kleindienst, expanded the doctrine by stating that the president had the authority to prevent any federal employee from testifying before Congress, for whatever reason. Nixon further claimed that every member of the executive branch was covered by the doctrine of executive privilege and that only the president himself had the authority to determine the scope and limits of his own powers. Even though the administration's guidelines on the use of executive privilege stated that the administration would comply with "reasonable" congressional requests for information, the president made it clear that only he and the attorney general were the appropriate arbiters of reasonableness. In effect, Nixon's standard held that even under a separation of powers system, the president's interpretation of his own authority cannot be questioned by another branch. The most extreme statement of this principle was former President Nixon's assertion in a 1977 interview that "when the president does it, that means it is not illegal."[48]

During the Watergate scandal executive privilege became especially controversial in light of the president's efforts to conceal White House wrongdoing. On July 16, 1973, former assistant to H. R. Haldeman, Alexander

Butterfield, testified before the Senate Watergate Committee that the president had tape-recorded conversations in the Oval Office and in the Executive Office Building. The committee requested the tapes, as did the special prosecutor, Archibald Cox. Nixon claimed executive privilege and refused to comply with the requests of the committee and the special prosecutor. Cox went to a federal court to have a subpoena issued for recordings of specific conversations. Judge John Sirica issued the subpoena, which Nixon refused to comply with, again claiming executive privilege. Nixon appealed Sirica's ruling and the U.S. Court of Appeals of the District of Columbia upheld the ruling. Nixon responded by having Cox fired—the notorious "Saturday Night Massacre"—and set off such a firestorm of protest that the president had to turn over the disputed tapes to Sirica.

In April 1974, the new special prosecutor, Leon Jaworski, requested sixty-four additional White House tapes. Nixon again claimed executive privilege. This time Sirica demanded that the tapes be turned over to him for in camera inspection. Nixon's attorney appealed the order to the court of appeals and Jaworski requested from the Supreme Court a *writ of certiorari* prior to the court of appeals' ruling.

In the landmark 1974 case *U.S. v. Nixon* (418 U.S. 683) the Supreme Court ruled that the president must turn over the tapes, setting forth the sequence of events leading to Nixon's resignation. During oral argument in that case, the president's attorney argued that Nixon did not have to comply with the special prosecutor's subpoena. Jaworski countered that executive privilege could not be used to cover up criminal conduct. The Court declared that executive privilege is "constitutionally based," yet added that the president's claim of privilege had to be balanced against the Court's need for information in a criminal case. The Court sided with Jaworski and ruled that the need for information in a criminal investigation had to override the president's claim of privilege.

The *Nixon* case is particularly important in the development of executive privilege. That case firmly reaffirmed the legitimacy of that power, yet made it clear that executive privilege is not an unlimited, unfettered prerogative as Nixon had claimed. The Court reaffirmed the right of Congress to challenge the exercise of executive privilege and the authority of the judiciary to say what the law is, as well as to challenge this presidential power. Yet Nixon persisted in his claim that his actions were motivated by national security and protecting the presidency—even after the publication of the White House transcripts and the *Nixon* case revealed the sham, even after he had been forced to resign the presidency.

Nixon did not use executive privilege during Watergate to protect the presidency and the nation; he did so to protect himself. A major effect of his actions was to discredit for many a legitimate, necessary presidential power. Nixon gave executive privilege a bad name and therefore made it difficult for his successors to properly use this power.

Nixon's immediate successors, in fact, avoided using the "phrase executive privilege" whenever possible. Presidents Gerald Ford, Jimmy Carter, Ronald Reagan, and George Bush made very sparing use of executive privilege, and an examination of archival materials reveals that in some cases these presidents purposefully devised strategies to conceal information without saying "executive privilege."[49] Ford's and Carter's advisers suggested that it was best to use statutory justifications for withholding information, or some other executive power, so that the president would not immediately be characterized as engaging in Nixonian tactics by claiming executive privilege. The Reagan administration also sparingly used executive privilege and, in most cases, simply backed down from its claims when challenged in Congress and the media. The Bush administration masterfully devised strategies for withholding information while avoiding executive privilege by claiming other presidential secrecy powers.

The Clinton presidency marks another important stage in the development of executive privilege. Clinton broke with the practices of his immediate predecessors and chose to make extensive use of executive privilege. The Clinton White House claimed executive privilege when Congress investigated the "travelgate" scandal, U.S.–Haitian policy, federal anti-drug policies, and on other occasions. But no use of executive privilege has stirred up as much controversy since Watergate as Clinton's attempt to use that doctrine to shield information from the independent counsel investigating the Lewinsky scandal allegations that the president may have committed perjury or engaged in a cover-up of a sexual relationship with a young White House intern.

Clinton's Failed Claim of Executive Privilege

Over time, executive privilege came to mean that presidents may withhold information regarding weighty matters of national importance: for example, national security or internal White House deliberations over official governmental matters. How does President Clinton's use of executive privilege in the Lewinsky investigation measure up to the legal standards that have been developed to control its applications? There was obviously no national security justification for withholding information about presidential and staff discussions over how to handle the Lewinsky matter; yet Clinton's White House counsel tried to make the argument that by harming "the president's ability to 'influence' the public," the investigation undermined his ability to lead foreign policy.[50] Nonetheless, the White House case for executive privilege ultimately hinged on the claim that the president had the right to protect the privacy of internal deliberations.

As Judge Patricia Wald's decision so correctly stated in the Mike Espy case (*In Re: Sealed Case*, 1997), presidents are entitled to candid, confidential advice. The executive privilege extends to presidential advisers because they must be able to deliberate and discuss policy options without fear of public disclosure of their every utterance. Without that protection, the candor and quality of presidential advice would clearly suffer.

The Clinton administration maintained that Wald's decision justifies any claims of privilege on behalf of discussions between the president and his aides, between and among aides, and even between the first lady and an aide. As a general principle, it is correct that such discussions can be covered by the privilege, although extending such protection to the first lady is very controversial.[51]

Executive privilege for the first lady is unprecedented and, regarding her deliberations during the Lewinsky investigation, quite likely a real stretch of the doctrine. To properly cover the first lady with a claim of executive privilege, it would have to be established that (1) she has an official position in her husband's administration; (2) in such a capacity, she has played an active role in those matters and participated in some of those official discussions that led to a claim of executive privilege; and (3) such discussions concerned matters that actually deserve the protection of the privilege.

The key issue is whether the White House discussions indeed had anything to do with official governmental business as opposed to being merely deliberations over how to handle political strategy during a scandal. Judge Norma Holloway Johnson ultimately ruled against Clinton's use of executive privilege in the Lewinsky investigation, and although much of her reasoning gave credibility to some debatable White House arguments, she correctly determined that the balancing test weighed in favor of Independent Counsel Starr's need for access to information crucial to a criminal investigation.[52]

For the White House position instead to have prevailed, Clinton needed to make a compelling argument that the public interest would somehow suffer from the release of information about White House discussions over the Lewinsky investigation. Not only did he fail to do so; for months he even refused to answer basic questions as to whether he had formally invoked the privilege.

Once Judge Johnson ruled against Clinton, the White House mercifully dropped its flawed claim of executive privilege. In an obvious face-saving gesture, White House Counsel Ruff declared victory because Judge Johnson, in ruling against the president, had nonetheless upheld the legitimacy of the principle of executive privilege and therefore had preserved this presidential power for Clinton's successors.

The doctrine of executive privilege certainly did not need this kind of help. Notwithstanding Raoul Berger's largely discredited thesis, executive privilege already stood as an unarguably legitimate presidential power, although one clearly tainted in the public mind by the Watergate episode.

Reestablishing the good reputation of executive privilege required a much more compelling circumstance for its exercise than a personal scandal; for example, military action.

Furthermore, there is little evidence from this episode to suggest that the Clinton White House undertook this drawn-out battle merely to make a principled stand on executive privilege. All evidence to date suggests that Clinton used executive privilege to frustrate and delay the investigation, all the while successfully convincing most of the public that the blame for the inquiry taking so long and costing so much belonged to the Office of the Independent Counsel.

For months, the Clinton White House did a masterful job of presenting its case before the court of public opinion. By summer 1998, the president's approval ratings remained strong, and most of the public had tired of the scandal and had become convinced that Starr lacked the objectivity to conduct a fair investigation.

With the White House winning the public relations battle and dropping its claim of executive privilege, many observers may reasonably ask why this dispute—and the politically motivated effort to delay its obvious resolution—mattered. It mattered because executive privilege embodies the principle that no one is above the law—not even a president who might otherwise be seen as a great foreign policy leader (Nixon) and not even a president who is perceived as a major contributor to a thriving economy (Clinton). White House efforts to obstruct and delay for the sake of some perceived political advantage cynically undermined both the privilege and the principle. Regarding executive privilege, Clinton's legacy appears not to be that of a president who reestablished this necessary power, but rather, like Nixon before him, one who gave executive privilege a bad name.

4

The President, Congress, and Decisions to Employ Military Force

Joseph R. Avella

Of all the decisions made by American presidents, none are more serious than those involving a military option. Presidents have exercised military options to solve crises, resolve conflict, or simply ease human suffering. More than any other, these decisions place Americans at direct personal risk. When writing his memoirs, Harry Truman said that committing military troops to Korea was the hardest decision of his presidency, even more so than the decision to use the atomic bomb. Fifteen days before leaving office, President George Bush noted in a speech at West Point: "Any president has many functions . . . none . . . is more important than his role as commander-in-chief."[1]

During this century, presidents have employed force for two world wars, three limited wars, and numerous interventions under both combat and other-than-combat scenarios. Former Chairman of the Joint Chiefs Colin Powell wrote in 1993:

> We cannot tell where or when the next crisis will appear that will demand the use of our troops. But we can say that in the last three years, our troops have acted in the Philippines (twice), Panama (three times), El Salvador, Liberia, Iraq (three times), Somalia (twice), Bangladesh, Zaire, Cuba, the former Soviet Union, Angola, and Yugoslavia. We could also mention our troops' involvement in UN actions from Western Sahara, Cambodia, and Bosnia-Herzegovina.[2]

Whether the president has the constitutional power to commit military force to missions short of all-out war unilaterally, or whether he must seek congressional approval has been one of the most contentious issues in the history of the Republic. Not only has it been the subject of confrontation between the two branches of government, but it also has been widely debated in the media, and in legal and academic circles. Arguments both pro and con have been put forth in almost every venue. Supporters of the president's authority point to the need for secrecy and dispatch in such circumstances. Those who argue for congressional primacy suggest that the seriousness of the decision requires open deliberation by the representatives of the people.

The issue has also been the subject of political posturing. During the presidencies of Ronald Reagan and George Bush, Senate Republican Leader Bob Dole firmly supported the president's power to commit military force. During the Clinton administration, however, Dole argued the reverse, stating that such power should be shared with the Congress. Well-known Democrat Arthur Schlesinger followed a similar course when he supported the use of force in Korea without formal declaration of war by fellow Democrat Harry Truman in 1950. Yet in 1990, he argued against a similar right for President Bush during Operations Desert Shield and Desert Storm.

Military forces have been used to support foreign policy in a wide range of mission scenarios, some very benign with little or no risk of combat. Perhaps the best example of this benign use is forward presence. America regularly bases troops in Europe and Asia or positions naval battle groups in areas of interest. The purpose is simple: to signal commitment to allies or to provide deterrence against regional conflict. Another benign example is humanitarian assistance. In 1991, at the conclusion of the Persian Gulf War, returning troops were diverted to Bangladesh to conduct relief operations in the aftermath of a devastating typhoon and ensuing floods. Yet even these benign missions can result in hostility and loss of American life as occurred in Lebanon in 1983 and Somalia ten years later.

Typically, however, the debate over executive or legislative primacy centers on military missions where the use of "violent" force is contemplated or expected. While it was the intent of Congress to preclude a second Vietnam in passing the War Powers Resolution of 1973, the resolution itself may not be constitutional, and may not be workable even in a structural or practical sense.

The executive branch has also recognized the need to avoid another Vietnam. Unlike the imposing, rigid, and somewhat ambiguous provisions of the War Powers Resolution, however, the executive approach has focused on structuring the decision process to ensure that clear and unambiguous criteria or "tests" are met. This approach was first articulated by former Secretary of Defense Caspar Weinberger in 1984,[3] and later refined by Bush and Powell in the 1990s after the Persian Gulf War.

The discussion that follows examines some of the key theoretical and practical considerations that have shaped the historical development of the doctrine on use of force in the United States. This discussion includes three elements: an assessment of the intent of the Framers of the Constitution concerning shared power; the congressional concern over executive power and the resultant problems in the War Powers Resolution; and the viability of the executive approach to use of force decisions as devised by Weinberger et al.

Framers' Intent[4]

Many debates took place among the Framers concerning distribution of power in foreign policy, national security, and warmaking between the executive and legislative branches. It is clear that the Framers agreed that there should be no absolute seat of power; history had shown that concentrated police and military power were instruments of tyranny. Dispersing power was, therefore, a high priority. This was achieved by dividing power across the three separate branches of government.

Despite the apparent consensus on a distribution of power, the Framers of the Constitution had a variety of concerns and motives. Some wanted to limit the legislative branch while others sought to avoid recreating George III's absolute power. In avoiding both, the Framers created a seemingly vague document that grants overlapping and sometimes contradictory military powers to both branches. It might be said that the Framers were willing to trade military and diplomatic efficiency to preclude either branch from consolidating authority and achieving absolute power.

The result has been a continuous confrontation between the two branches. Actual practice has been more the result of the politics of the day than the consequence of an interpretation of the Constitution by the judiciary. Former Secretary of State William P. Rogers noted that the exercise of war powers is a political process that requires cooperation and mutual trust between the president and the Congress.[5] Aggressive Congresses pushed reluctant presidents into an undeclared war with France in 1798 and declared wars with Great Britain in 1812 and with Spain in 1898. Presidents conducted wars without formal declaration in Korea, Vietnam, and the Persian Gulf.

Did the Framers purposely intend this continuing power struggle as a means to ensure there would be no consolidation of authority and corruption of power, or is the Constitution murky because they simply could not agree on a precise allocation of control over military power? This section examines the thinking of the Framers together with subsequent interpretations by various scholars, and seeks some understanding of why the Constitution is as unclear as it is.

At the center of the debate are two often-quoted sections of the Constitution. Supporters of the primacy of the legislative branch point to Article I,

Section 8, which states that Congress "shall have power . . . To declare war." Supporters of the authority of the executive branch point to Article II, Section 2, which states that "The President shall be Commander in Chief." One would think that these two statements are clear: Congress has the power to *authorize* and the president the power to *execute* war. This may be what Alexander Hamilton was thinking when he elaborated on the president's role as commander in chief in *Federalist 69*. Hamilton likened the power of the president to the king of England but to a lesser degree. The president's power "would amount to nothing more than the supreme command and direction of the military and naval forces, as first general and admiral of the Confederacy; while that of the British king extends to the declaring of war and to the raising and regulating of fleets and armies"[6]

Unfortunately, matters are not so clear and straightforward. Presidential scholar Donald L. Robinson notes that the original language of Article I, Section 2 empowered the Congress to *make* war.[7] However, once it was agreed that the president was to be commander in chief, the "authorize *and* execute" implication of the word *make* had to be narrowed. The change in wording was offered by James Madison and the change was made in order to provide the executive the power to repel sudden attacks.[8]

Robinson further notes that later, in Article I, Section 10, the Constitution states that "No state shall, without the consent of the Congress, . . . engage in war, unless actually invaded or in such imminent danger as will not admit of delay." Robinson makes two points about this provision. The first is to recognize, in general, that under the Constitution it was possible to *engage* in war without *declaring* it and, specifically, that states were empowered to do so under certain conditions. The second was that presidents might likewise *engage* in war without congressional declaration, specifically when the nation was being invaded or in "imminent danger." Constitutional scholar Clinton Rossiter shared this view when he noted that the president would "lead the government in its foreign relations, peaceful and hostile."[9]

The notion of engaging in hostile action without a formal declaration of war is reflected in the Militia Acts of 1795 and 1807, which empowered the president to call state militias into federal service without declaration of war. Congress followed the same course when authorizing force, but not declaring war, with the Tonkin Gulf Resolution in 1964 and authorizing force in the Persian Gulf War as discussed below.

Hamilton may have provided an argument in support of this view of executive authority. In *Federalist 23*, he includes among the authorities essential to the common defense the need to direct the operations of the armies that Congress has raised and the fleets it has built, a function that clearly falls under the authority of the president as commander in chief. Hamilton goes on to say that "These ought to exist without limitation, because it is impossible to foresee or to define the extent and variety of national exigencies. . . . "[10]

History validates Robinson's assertion that war could be waged without declaration. According to a Library of Congress study, there have been over two hundred cases where the United States has used armed forces between 1798 and 1983. Many of these cases involved the simple introduction of troops to protect U.S. citizens, or the enforcement of maritime law against pirates, and the like. Only five instances involving use of force were declared wars, and in four of the five, the declaration came after hostilities had begun. Thomas Jefferson set the precedent of presidential action without congressional authorization when he dispatched the fledgling U.S. Navy to challenge the Barbary pirates in 1801. Woodrow Wilson landed Marines at Veracruz in 1914, ordered General John Pershing to enter Mexico and capture Pancho Villa in March 1915, and landed troops in Haiti in 1915 and the Dominican Republic in 1916—all without congressional authorization.

The debate raises two hypothetical questions: What defines "war" in such a manner that requires Congress to declare it? And are there military measures short of war that do not require a declaration and that might fall within the power of the president to both authorize and execute?

War can be defined as a nation prosecuting its rights by military force. Under this meaning, it was war when Congress formally declared war to begin U.S. participation in World War I in 1917, even though hostilities had not yet commenced. It was also war when President John F. Kennedy executed the Cuban Quarantine in 1962.[11]

In 1625, the political thinker Hugo Grotius noted that a declaration of war contained many legal functions unrelated to the use of armed force. Grotius said that war turned neutrals into belligerents, permitted belligerents to intern their enemies, and allowed them to take possession of the enemy's property until the end of the war. Enemy merchant vessels were subject to seizure in port, capture at sea, and potential sale in prize court.[12]

The Framers included the power to "grant Letters of Marque and Reprisal, and make rules concerning Captures on Land and Water" in the same clause (Art. I, Sec. 8) as the power to declare war.[13] All other congressional war powers are in separate clauses, giving rise to the proposition that in the declaration clause the Framers were more concerned with the legal aspects of war, and making them applicable to the relations between states, and noting the legal impact of a declaration on personal status and property rights.

Grotius is not the only reference for this kind of interpretation. In ancient Rome, declarations of war had religious as well as political meanings, and references to ancient Rome were abundant in contemporary eighteenth-century writings.[14] Since the Roman Empire, states in general have often declared war for legal reasons that have had nothing to do with military action and, conversely, states have engaged in hostilities without any declaration of war. One study of conflict in Europe and America between 1700 and 1870 identified 107 cases of hostilities that began without declarations of war and only ten that did.[15]

It is entirely reasonable to assume that the Framers were aware that war was not always "declared" simply to authorize commencement of hostilities or to use military force. And it is also reasonable to ascertain that certain of the Framers were influenced by the thinking of Grotius, just as others were influenced by Edmund Burke or John Locke. Indeed, one Jefferson biographer, Willard Randall, noted that the works of Grotius were "very popular in Virginia."[16] Madison refers to Grotius specifically in *Federalist* 20, and Hamilton paraphrases him in *Federalist* 84. Constitutional scholar Jacob Cooke has noted that the writers of the Federalist essays were familiar with the political writings of their times and included Grotius's *Law of Nature and Nations* among them.[17]

To the earlier two questions concerning the Framers' intent (did the Framers purposely intend the power struggle, or is the constitutional language unclear because they could not agree?), one must now add another: Did the Framers recognize that a declaration of war was a legal action, and did they therefore construct the language and form of the Constitution to restrict the power to authorize it to Congress, while at the same time acknowledging a president's option to use military force short of war to achieve national objectives?

An early Supreme Court decision supports this appraisal. In an 1800 opinion rendered in the *Eliza* case, the Court acknowledged a difference between formal declared war and a more confined version. The decision stated that in the declared version, the whole nation was at war, but it also stated that limited hostilities not in declared form may exist as well.

When Jefferson dispatched the Navy to confront the Barbary pirates the following year, it was only twelve years after the ratification of the Constitution. Thirty-eight of the original fifty-five members of the 1787 Convention were still alive. Three were serving in Congress, and one was serving on the Supreme Court. Had either the 1800 *Eliza* decision or Jefferson's order to the Navy in 1801 been inconsistent with the Framers' intent, one might expect restricting legislation to be enacted at that time. No such legislation resulted.

The community of international law has apparently embraced the *Eliza* interpretation. William Bishop of the University of Michigan Law School has written that war in the technical sense should be distinguished from such use of force as reprisals, intervention, and collective security measures.[18] In support of this observation, Bishop cites John Bassett Moore, who said that "force may be employed by one nation against another, . . . and yet no state of war may arise." Bishop goes on to say that war occurs by formal declaration or by acts of force that either party regards as war. In either case, continuing reference is made to the "legal status of war" as different from mere employment of military force.[19] Such language can also be found in war declarations themselves. On April 6, 1917, Congress passed a joint resolution that noted "the state of war between the United States and the Imperial Government . . . is hereby formally declared." The use of the term "state of war" implies a condition, not an event. This conforms very closely to Grotius: "Cicero styled war a contention by force. But the practice has prevailed to indicate by that name, not an immediate action, but a state of affairs."[20]

In the *United States v. Curtiss-Wright Export Corporation et al.* decision of 1936,[21] the Court certified the authority of the president with respect to external affairs. The decision quoted John Marshall in a March 7, 1800, speech before the House of Representatives: "The President is the sole organ of the nation in its external relations." It further noted that on February 15, 1816, the Senate Committee on Foreign Relations reported that "The President is the constitutional representative of the United States with regard to foreign nations."[22]

In 1950, the administration cited constitutional authority as commander in chief to justify President Truman's action in committing troops to Korea. The document cited eighty-five cases in which the president acted as commander in chief and without congressional authority.[23]

Over the years, the evolution of the legal and political authorities by which the United States approaches war also would appear to be based on these legal opinions. Under current legal authorities, a declaration of war is accompanied by a broad range of emergency powers that mobilize the resources of the entire nation to the war effort. In keeping with Article I, Section 8, only Congress has authority to so obligate the nation. At the same time, however, lesser emergency powers are granted the president without need for a declaration of war. The authority granted by the Militia Acts to call the state militias into federal service without a declaration of war still applies. The president may also suspend budget laws and permit the Department of Defense to spend more money than appropriated by Congress in any fiscal year (41 USC § 11). While not to the same extent as Congress, the president has broad powers to react to crisis, solely under his authority as commander in chief.

In sum, then, two matters seem settled. The Framers clearly acknowledged the broad legal aspects of a war declaration and as such granted this power only to the Congress. On the other hand, they also recognized that there were occasions during peacetime when it was necessary to apply military force to realize national objectives. This power falls to the president as commander in chief.

Congressional Concern: The War Powers Resolution Case

The War Powers Resolution (hereafter, "the resolution") was passed over Richard Nixon's veto in 1973. Enacted after Vietnam, the resolution has been considered unconstitutional by every chief executive from Nixon to Bush. In vetoing it, Nixon noted that Congress attempted to "take away . . . authority which the President has properly exercised for almost 200 years." Yet no president has called for a test of its constitutionality in the courts.

The resolution states that the constitutional power of the president as commander in chief to introduce armed forces into actual or potential hostilities is limited to situations where there is: "(1) a declaration of war, (2) specific statutory authorization, or (3) a national emergency created by attack upon the United States, its territories or possessions, or its armed forces."[24]

Opponents of the resolution assert that it limits actions to doing nothing on one hand, or all-out war on the other. There is no local use of force.[25] Proponents argue that the resolution facilitates a "functioning partnership between the president and the Congress."[26] Indeed the resolution itself purports to ensure that "the collective judgment of both the Congress and the President will apply."

One might argue pro or con that the structure of either the executive or legislative branch is or is not more appropriate to the exercise of this authority, but no matter one's position, the fundamental question is this: Is it practical on a day-by-day basis that decisions to use military force are to be made by the Congress *and* the president? In the absence of any other statutory framework or reference, only the resolution provides anything resembling a procedure for making such decisions.

As noted earlier, proponents of the resolution point to creating a "functioning partnership" between the president and the Congress. Because the primary reason for the existence of a military is deterrence, the first practical question concerns the ability of the military to function in that role. How effective is the deterrent value when it can only be used as a result of a "collective" decision? Does it really deter an aggressor to know that Congress and the president need to agree before force may be used? Would the retaliatory missile strikes ordered by the Clinton administration against the Bin Laden terrorist camp, or the Reagan administration's air strikes against Libya, have occurred in as timely or surgically a manner if they had to come from a collaborative decision? Is it not more the case that those who undertake aggression would view the requirement for such a partnership as a weakness, not a strength?

A second practical question arises because even in the closest of partnerships, there is disagreement: Who arbitrates disagreements between the functioning partners? What is the procedure if Congress wants to take military action and the president does not, as occurred with France in 1798? The resolution makes no provision for such an eventuality. Presumably, Congress would now have to declare war. In the opposite case, if the president makes a unilateral decision without Congress as Truman did involving Korea in 1950, and the Congress disagrees, the resolution does provide for a concurrent resolution binding the president to withdrawing troops [50 USC §1544(c)]. Yet concurrent resolutions in the form of a legislative veto have been determined to be unconstitutional.[27] So who arbitrates the final decision? One might expect the courts to fill that function, yet the courts have already been asked and have chosen to stay out of the debate.[28] The question bears repeating: Who arbitrates the final decision when the partners disagree? Under the circumstances, it would appear nobody does.

The War Powers Resolution outlines three specific conditions under which the president alone might commit military forces into hostility or conditions of imminent hostility. It does not provide for other situations such as fulfilling treaty obligations, and still others are omitted. One is the rescue of American citizens abroad, as, for example, in the evacuation of Americans from Liberia and Somalia in 1991. Another involves increasing force levels in response to actual or potential violence against Americans in foreign nations. A third is participation in peacekeeping missions. Finally, there is the potential use of force within our own borders—suppressing civil disturbance and insurrection. The resolution addresses none of these, and indeed some, such as peacekeeping and deployed forces, did not exist at the time the Constitution was written. The resolution later states that: "The President in every possible instance shall consult with Congress before introducing United States Armed Forces into hostilities or into situations where imminent involvement in hostilities is clearly indicated . . ." (50 USC §1542).

Three specific questions concerning the above immediately come to mind. First, what constitutes "consult with Congress?" Does it mean that the president should meet with the bipartisan leadership, as Truman did in the early days of the Korean War? Does it mean that he needs only to inform the Speaker of the House and the President pro tempore of the Senate as Reagan did after sending troops to Grenada in 1983? Or does it mean that he should send a letter of intent or a proposal, and permit Congress to assign it to a committee, as called for in "Reporting requirements" and "Congressional action" (50 USC §1543 and 1544)? The first two cases imply that the entire Congress may be bound by the decision of a few. That raises a question in itself. And even after the president consults, who makes the final decision? Where does ultimate responsibility rest?

Second, while "introducing . . . into hostilities" is clear, how does one predict "imminent involvement?" When Air Force jets were ordered to overfly the Presidential Palace in Manila in December 1989 to support the government of Corazon Aquino against an attempted coup, was it "imminent involvement" in hostilities? Or was it simply "showing the flag" and demonstrating resolve to shore up the government? If the insurgents had shot at the jets, the conditions into which they were ordered to fly would have been "imminent involvement," but only in retrospect. How can anyone foresee all exigencies?

Third, what are the conditions required for something to be "clearly indicated?" Without any definitive requirements, it would seem that such an evaluation would be highly subjective. When the United States introduced troops onto Saudi Arabian soil after Iraq's invasion of Kuwait, many recognized a potential for skirmishes between Iraqi and U.S. troops. Does this constitute a situation in which "imminent involvement in hostilities is clearly indicated"? If this was "clearly indicated" but no hostility occurred, at worst it was a safe course of action. What about those conditions when it is not "clearly indicated," but occurs later, as in Somalia?

The text also presents broader concerns. In a review of the overall language, there is a general reference to Congress's "constitutional responsibility with respect to committing the nation to war" [50 USC §1543(b)]. The specific discussion, however, centers around terms such as "hostilities," and introduction of forces into the "territory of a foreign nation . . . equipped for combat" (50 USC §1543). From this one can infer that the Congress acknowledged no difference between the broad aspects of a declaration of war and other occasions during peacetime when it is necessary to use force to achieve a national objective. Did they mean to assert that World Wars I and II were legally and constitutionally the same as the Panama Intervention of December 1989 or the Aquino Palace overflight?

There are some operational considerations as well. The first is time. In April 1965, Lyndon Johnson ordered Marines ashore in Santo Domingo at the urgent request of the Ambassador to reinforce the Embassy guard and provide security for evacuating American citizens. Rebel forces had taken control of the city and there was a recognized danger to foreigners. Under such circumstances, it was clear that "imminent involvement" of the Marines in hostilities was "clearly indicated." Was it the intent of Congress that Johnson had to consult with Congress before any action was taken? Under the circumstances, there was no time for Congress to approve or disapprove the action. Any such requirement to delay would probably have led to civilian casualties or deaths. What if the Congress had said "no"? Would the Congress be liable for any casualties or deaths?

A second operational consideration is surprise. To reduce vulnerability, military forces are introduced into conditions where hostilities are "clearly indicated" or "imminent" with the highest attention to achieving surprise. Surprise provides the opportunity to strike at a time or place for which an adversary is unprepared, and it conceals capabilities and intentions so an adversary is unable to respond effectively. Seeking clearance to act from Congress diminishes, if not eliminates, the chance to achieve it.

A third operational consideration is security. The attempted raid to free the hostages in Tehran required maximum security in planning and execution to achieve success. Although it might again be argued logically that in undertaking such missions, "imminent involvement" in hostility was "clearly indicated," what guarantees were there to ensure the secrecy required could be maintained?

Despite these operational difficulties, Congress clearly had a valid concern that a president might gradually build up involvement in a war without congressional approval or constraint. In passing the War Powers Resolution, the intent of the Congress was to avoid another Vietnam, where Congress and the nation were presented with an undeclared war that involved hundreds of thousands of troops and experienced well over 50,000 fatalities. Yet, in a practical sense, it could be argued that Congress already had the power to stop such a war, prior to passage of the War Powers Act.

Each year of the Vietnam War Congress voted defense appropriations knowing that a significant part would finance the war's continuance or expansion. Those same conditions exist today: No president could gradually build up American involvement without congressional knowledge *and* approval provided in the annual defense appropriation. Using their constitutional power of the purse, Congress could have legislated at any time during Vietnam that defense spending in that theater should have been used only for withdrawal of troops and for protection of American lives and property. In truth they were not and are not powerless to end U.S. participation or to provide limits on any involvement. In Vietnam, Congress simply chose not to take forceful action until very late in the war.

The Executive Response to Vietnam:
New Criteria for Use of Force Decision-Making

Also driven by the Vietnam experience, a number of responsible executive branch officials have in recent years attempted to outline the circumstances and means by which the United States reaches a decision to use force. These "tests" are designed for a broad spectrum of operations that include threats against U.S. interests or policy, or involve humanitarian objectives. Earlier, other officials had approached this issue at various times: Washington's farewell address, Wilson's conditions for U.S. entry into World War I, and Dean Acheson's 1950 speech about Asian defense perimeters.

These efforts evolved into a more rigorous set of conditions when Defense Secretary Weinberger outlined specific criteria for the use of military

force in his National Press Club speech in 1984. Since then, a number of senior officials have articulated their views on the requirements to be satisfied
when choosing force. In addition to Weinberger, George Bush and Colin
Powell, among others, have presented their personal views or administration policy in speeches, articles, and policy documents.

Weinberger

On November 28, 1984, Secretary of Defense Weinberger spoke at the National Press Club and outlined six major tests to be applied when weighing
use of U.S. combat forces abroad.[29] Beginning in 1989, when U.S. forces invaded Panama, it has been a regular occurrence for potential and actual
military operations to be evaluated in light of what has since become
known as "the Weinberger doctrine."

The six tests can be described by their broad descriptions: vital interest,
clear intention of winning, clear political and military objectives, reassessment and reevaluation after force has been applied, assurance of support
of Congress and the people, and last resort. These should not be treated
simplistically, however, as the six alone do not reflect the extent of Weinberger's requirements. For example, when articulating the need for vital interest, Weinberger noted (in direct reference to Acheson's 1950 speech) that
the United States should not declare beforehand that "a particular area is
outside our strategic perimeter." The obvious implication is that vital interests are fluid. What is vital today may be peripheral tomorrow, and vice
versa. The assessment of vital interest must reflect current analysis, and not
necessarily be based purely on historical relationships or situations. To the
broad descriptions noted above, Weinberger qualified and expanded each
test, resulting in a much more detailed list. This list, presented in a chronologically consistent order, includes:

1. The circumstances and occasion are vital to our national interests at
   the time of decision.
2. Use of force is *a* last resort.
3. Actions will be governed by clear political and military objectives, with
   supporting campaign strategies and adequately sized and equipped
   forces.
4. Force will be applied with a clear intent of winning. Available means
   will be matched to desired ends.
5. The decision should ideally have the support of the people and the
   Congress. These will be based on candor and openness, and be
   marked by continuing dialogue.
6. Interests, objectives, strategies, and forces should be subjected to ongoing reassessment and reevaluation.

Powell's Elaboration

In the Winter 1992/93 issue of *Foreign Affairs*,[30] Chairman of the Joint Chiefs of Staff Colin Powell sought to define a new national military strategy that was aimed at accomplishing a range of missions broader than the U.S. military had known before and without the single threat of communist power that had guided earlier doctrine. Despite expressing an aversion for fixed, "cookie-cutter" criteria or tests, Powell did support the concept of presenting a list of questions to be addressed in the decision process. As such, Powell developed his own list of questions.

Comparing Powell's criteria to Weinberger's reveals many similarities. It also reveals some differences. Powell called for an evaluation of "costs and risks" that are not reflected in the Weinberger list, for example. He also sought analysis of the *consequences* of military action. No such criterion exists in the Weinberger list.

Bush's Fine Tuning of the Weinberger/Powell Criteria

Fifteen days before he was to leave office, Bush spoke to the cadets at West Point.[31] The speech included reference to the need for "judgment" in using force and, like Powell, an aversion to any fixed set of rules. But the speech did include a number of factors for consideration.

Bush explained that force was not always the answer with *vital* interests but may be the answer with *important* interests, and made reference to the use of force to stem the human tragedy of Somalia. This reflects a willingness to commit force for missions not in the vital interest of the United States, but in the general interest of humanity and thereby carrying their own unique importance. Examples of these include humanitarian assistance, peacekeeping, and the like. Bush also added another caveat for public and congressional support when he added an international dimension, to include participation in concert with other nations if possible. Bush did make it clear, however, that if necessary the United States will act alone.

Consolidating the criteria for using force from the Powell article and the Bush and Weinberger speeches yields the following, more comprehensive list of factors that decision-makers can take into account in use of force decisions:

1. The circumstances and occasion are vital to our national interests at the time of decision, or they support a broader humanitarian context.
2. Use of force is *a* last resort, or, due to extenuating circumstances, the only resort.
3. Actions will be governed by clear political and military objectives, with supporting campaign strategies, adequately sized and equipped forces, and an established and achievable endpoint.

4. Force will be applied with a clear intent of winning. Available means will be matched to desired ends, and both costs and risks deemed acceptable.
5. The decision should ideally have the support of the people, the Congress, and the international community—to include multilateral participation when possible. These will be based on candor and openness and on continuing dialogue.
6. Interests, objectives, strategies, and forces should be subjected to ongoing reassessment and reevaluation.
7. The consequences to military action are acceptable.

"Testing the Tests"—The Persian Gulf War

In the 1990s, the most significant event involving use of force has been the Persian Gulf War. As a validation of the consolidated "tests," the approach and conduct of the war are assessed below in light of the Weinberger/Powell/Bush criteria.

At 2 AM local time on August 2, 1990, Iraq invaded Kuwait. Later that day, Eastern Daylight Time, an emergency session of the U.N. Security Council (UNSC) voted 14-0 (Yemen did not participate) on Resolution 660 to condemn Iraq and demand withdrawal of its troops from Kuwait. Besides voting for the UNSC resolution, the Soviet Union announced an arms embargo of Iraq. President Bush, in a speech to the Aspen Institute, called the invasion "brutal aggression." The U.S. House and Senate also passed resolutions condemning Iraq. On August 3, the Iraqi army pushed toward the Kuwait–Saudi border and President Bush warned Iraq not to invade Saudi Arabia. Saddam Hussein pledged withdrawal from Kuwait in two days. On August 4, U.S. Naval Forces were dispatched to the Red Sea and the North Arabian Sea. Satellite photos indicated Iraqi forces in Kuwait were being reinforced, not withdrawn. On August 5, President Bush briefed the White House press corps about diplomatic initiatives taking place around the world to isolate Iraq.

On August 6, Saudi King Fahd invited coalition forces to Saudi Arabia to reinforce its defenses and requested U.S. military assistance. President Bush ordered Army, Air Force, and Marine Corps units to Saudi Arabia. Saddam Hussein announced his seizure of Kuwait was "irreversible." The UNSC voted 13-0 (Cuba and Yemen abstained) on Resolution 661 calling for broad economic sanctions against Iraq. On August 7, the first elements of U.S. military forces began deployment to Saudi Arabia. On August 8, Bush articulated the U.S. political objectives in deploying the troops: immediate, complete, and unconditional withdrawal of all Iraqi forces from Kuwait; restoration of Kuwait's legitimate government; security and stability of Saudi Arabia and the Persian Gulf; and safety and protection of the lives of American citizens abroad.[32]

1. *The circumstances and occasion are vital to our national interests at the time of decision, or they support a broader humanitarian context.* With the takeover of the Kuwaiti oil fields, Iraq would exert direct control over 20 percent of the world's known oil reserves.[33] Its ability to further threaten Saudi Arabia presented a risk that nearly 40 percent of the world's reserves might be dominated by Saddam Hussein. While such dominance was a matter of survival for Japan and Western Europe, it was not quite as significant for the United States. However, the potential for economic turbulence in this country, as had occurred during the oil embargoes of 1973 and 1979, could arguably be considered vital.

    The United States had no security assistance agreement with Saudi Arabia, but the threat to security posed by the million-man Iraqi army in an area already declared vital in 1980 by President Carter was formidable. It may be debatable whether this alone should be considered a vital interest, but after September 13, when Saddam Hussein threatened terrorist attacks against the United States, safety of American citizens also became a consideration, resulting in an overall evaluation of vital appropriateness.

    On August 8, 1990, President Bush announced the deployment of forces to Saudi Arabia in a speech from the Oval Office. He outlined the guiding principles of U.S. policy and noted the fact that the "sovereign independence of Saudi Arabia is of vital interest to the United States." Not only did Bush note the vital interest, but at two points in the speech he detailed why: "I am determined to protect the lives of American citizens abroad. . . . Our country now imports nearly half the oil it consumes and could face a major threat to its economic independence."

2. *Use of force is a last resort, or, due to extenuating circumstances, the only resort.* Immediately after the invasion of Kuwait, the UNSC voted to demand withdrawal of Iraqi troops. At the same time, President Bush ordered an immediate embargo of all trade with Iraq, and, together with other nations, announced economic sanctions to include freezing Iraqi assets. Although Saddam Hussein's immediate reaction was to declare that Iraqi forces would soon withdraw, he in fact declared the seizure irreversible on August 6. Saddam Hussein had rebuffed political and economic pressure, and would continue to do so throughout the period of the coalition force buildup before the hostilities began in 1991.

    As the test indicates, there may be times when "other avenues" cannot be pursued and the military option must be undertaken immediately. Such was the case here. There was an immediate risk that Iraqi forces would turn south into Saudi Arabia. Although it will no doubt be debated whether Saddam Hussein had the capability to totally overrun this country, most military strategists would agree that all that was necessary was for him to take a fifty-mile wide strip of the Saudi Arabian Persian Gulf coast to the Qatari border (including the ports of Dhahran and Al Jubayl) and he would essentially preclude (or at least make extremely difficult) the ability to respond with significant force. Some level of military action was required immediately.

3. *Actions will be governed by clear political and military objectives, with supporting campaign strategies, adequately sized and equipped forces, and an established and achievable endpoint.* President Bush declared the U.S. political objectives on August 8 (see page 61). In later speeches and press conferences, he continually reiterated them with statements like "this will not stand," and his call for Iraq's "immediate and unconditional withdrawal" from Kuwait. The political objectives provided a clear indication of what the United States sought to achieve in deploying military force.

Military objectives flowed as the continuing attempts at "other avenues" failed. The initial military objectives were to deter Iraq from further aggression, and, should deterrence fail, to defend the Saudi peninsula. Also included were the building of the military coalition and integrating the forces into operational plans, and the enforcing of the economic sanctions (the maritime interdiction) prescribed by UNSC resolutions 661 and 665.[34]

Later, the objective would remain deterrence, but was expanded to include preparations for offensive actions, if required. In January, after the U.N. deadline passed, the objective became the forcible removal of Iraqi forces from Kuwait, initially by air bombardment. On February 24, 1991, ground expulsion operations began. Military objectives for the offensive operations included attacks on leadership and command/control sites, gaining and maintaining air superiority, interdicting supply lines, destroying production and storage facilities for weapons of mass destruction, destroying the elite Iraqi Republican Guard forces in the theater of operations, and liberating Kuwait City.

During the defensive phase (August 1990 to January 1991), campaign plans were designed to delay further attack by Iraqi forces, while inflicting increasing damage with coalition airpower. Major population centers would be evacuated if coalition forces were required to fall back. Ultimately, with stretched lines of supply under continuing air attack, the Iraqi army would be defeated before they could reach the port city of Al-Jubayl. During the offensive phase (January to February 1991), campaign plans were designed to exploit Iraqi weaknesses and attack the centers of gravity. The war itself was divided into four phases: executing a strategic air campaign, achieving air superiority in the theater of operations, preparing the battlefield, and conducting the offensive ground campaign. Each phase had its own specific campaign objectives which supported the overall plan.

U.S. intelligence officials and operations planners had estimated that the Iraqi forces arrayed against the coalition early in 1991 numbered some 540,000 troops, supported by more than 4,200 tanks, over 2,800 armored personnel carriers, and approximately 3,100 artillery pieces. Coalition forces roughly equaled Iraqi totals at the start of the air campaign. The plan called for air operations prior to the ground war destroying or neutralizing half the Iraqi forces. If these results were achieved, the two-to-one force advantage, together with superior weapons technology and the mobility of the attacking force versus the static defensive posture of the Iraqis, would more than exceed the normal requirements for the ratio of attackers to defenders.[35]

Coalition ground forces included nine U.S. divisions, a British division, a French division, and four Arab/Islamic division equivalents. Sufficient planning and training time prior to launching the offensive ensured these were more than adequately matched to the mission.

The political objectives also provided the requirements for endpoint. The first of these—immediate, complete, and unconditional withdrawal—and the second—restoration of Kuwait's legitimate government—provided very specific answers to the question, "When is the operation over?"

Ultimately, the coalition forces would undertake offensive military operations to remove the Iraqi army from Kuwait forcibly and to restore the Kuwaiti government. Throughout the interim period, from August 1990 to February 1991, any of the imposed political or economic measures—e.g., the UN sanctions, or the maritime interception operations—could have precipitated the Iraqi withdrawal and the restoration of the government. The objectives provided the endpoint no matter which means were ultimately successful.

4. *Force will be applied with a clear intent of winning. Available means will be matched to desired ends, and both costs and risks deemed acceptable.* While the world was kept up-to-date daily on the status of military deployments and the number of forces in the Gulf, three actions did occur, which perhaps more than others provided concrete evidence of compliance with the first part of this criterion. In the first, on August 12, the first seventeen ships of the Ready Reserve Fleet (RRF) were activated. The RRF consists of militarily useful roll-on/roll-off and break-bulk cargo ships that the United States had begun pur-

chasing and storing in the 1970s to bolster the aging fleet of World War II–era cargo ships. Maintained at various sites by the U.S. Maritime Administration, the ships were designed to be ready for sea in short periods, depending on the individual readiness status of the vessel. The Persian Gulf War was the first case since program inception whereby these vessels were activated for actual use. Manned by civilian merchant mariners, the ships delivered 22 percent of the unit cargo for U.S. forces.

In the second action, on August 17, the Commander of the U.S. Transportation Command activated the Civilian Reserve Air Fleet (CRAF). CRAF is a program in which commercial airlines agree to make aircraft available for Department of Defense deployments in exchange for peacetime military business. Sixteen civilian airlines provided thirty-eight wide-bodied jets for use in the initial deployment. Ultimately, CRAF provided seventy-six aircraft, and air carriers volunteered additional aircraft and crews as they became available in the commercial schedules.

Finally, on August 22, President Bush authorized the first-ever use of the legal authority provided him in Title 10 to call up units and members of the Selected Reserve. By the time the ground war began, over 220,000 reservists were serving on active duty in support of the overall effort. In total, nearly 250,000 reserve personnel were involved in the Gulf War mobilization.

Concerning costs and risks, when forces were initially deployed, the risk was primarily centered on the Iraqi army continuing along the Persian Gulf coast and taking the key Saudi ports that would ultimately be used for the deployment. For about three frightening weeks in August 1990, U.S. forces deploying into the Gulf were highly vulnerable and subject to attack, with little chance to hold a determined foe. As the forces continued to build, it became clearer that Saddam Hussein had no immediate designs on Saudi Arabia and the risk diminished. When the war actually began, sufficient forces were available to carry out the objectives, and the major risk was Iraq's arsenal of weapons of mass destruction. Coalition forces were as prepared as a modern army could be and orders from the president were "to take every necessary step to prevail as quickly as possible, and with the greatest degree of protection possible for American and allied servicemen and women."[36] Notwithstanding the well-documented intelligence failure in properly evaluating Saddam Hussein's intentions in July 1990, before he invaded Kuwait, the key decision-makers knew of the challenges the coalition forces faced and deemed the operation worth the costs and risks.

5. *The decision should ideally have the support of the people, the Congress, and the international community—to include multilateral participation when possible. These will be based on candor and openness and on continuing dialogue.* It has been noted that the most critical factor in mobilizing the Congress and the general public to support intervention has been the ability of the president to seize the initiative and direct the content and the outcome of the debate.[37] Congress is sometimes reluctant and the public often suspicious of a president's motives. The president sits at the center of U.S. foreign policy. He sets the agenda, drives the debate, and precipitates action. President Bush did all that with his August 6 remark, "this will not stand," and Congress and the public responded.

The initial action by Congress in condemning Iraq's aggression provided initial support for the administration's actions. Later, when Congress voted to authorize the president to use force, it did so only by a 250–183 vote in the House and a 52–47 vote in the Senate, indicating perhaps diminished support. At the same time, continually favorable opinion polls reflected high public satisfaction with the way the president was handling the Gulf Crisis. This latter data provided a high degree of assurance that, once begun, any war would enjoy public support.[38]

By virtue of the twenty-eight nations that sent military personnel and participated in the coalition, and the many other nations that contributed funds and/or supplies, international support was also present.

Dialogue had been established and maintained with both the Congress and the public from very early in the crisis. From August 2, 1990, through January 15, 1991, Secretary of Defense Dick Cheney appeared in person over twenty times on the major television networks. During the same period, secretaries Baker and Cheney appeared before Congress over ten times.[39]

Frequent briefings for the media were held at the White House and at the Departments of State and Defense. CNN and the major networks provided almost continuous coverage of events in the Gulf and the aforementioned briefings. Debate in Congress was covered by C-Span as is normal, but what was not normal was the number of citizens who watched the unfolding events.

Media representatives stationed in the war zone were restricted from unlimited access to U.S. forces and operations. Many accused the military of "force-feeding" information and attempting to "control" the press. The permanence of this debate—access to information in an open society versus the need for security—was only reinforced in the Gulf War. While the media may have had their feathers ruffled, there is no evidence that the general public shared their anxiety.

6. *Interests, objectives, strategies, and forces should be subjected to on-going reassessment and reevaluation.* After the initial use-of-force decision in August 1990, there were at least three additional decisions—augmenting forces in November 1990, commencing the air phase of the war in January 1991, and commencing the ground war in February—that can be viewed as an outcome of a reassessment and reevaluation process. The decisions that followed the original were based on changes to the original strategy and the result of analyses conducted at the time.

History may never uncover whether the November decision to increase the size of the force to one with offensive capability was made to forcibly extract Iraqi forces from Kuwait, or whether it recognized that Iraq would never think the coalition serious if the capability was not present. Attempts at resolving the crisis by diplomatic and economic sanctions continued. Congressional debate continued over whether or not direct military action would be required, but never wavered from the desire to reverse Iraq's aggression. Public support for the president remained high (and actually increased, based on opinion polls). The immediate military objective of protecting Saudi Arabia from attack had been achieved. On the other side, Iraq was showing no willingness to budge from its takeover of Kuwait. The presence of military force was still required, but as Iraq continued to resist, the potential for ultimate military action appeared to increase. The reassessment and reevaluation yielded no change other than that of increasing forces in readiness to forcibly remove Iraqi forces from Kuwait, should it prove necessary.

In January, there was no change in the level of interest. Iraq continued to resist diplomatic and economic sanctions, and appeared even more hard-lined over retaining Kuwait. Some analysts even believed that Saddam Hussein really did not believe that the coalition was serious about taking military action. The United Nations' "pause of goodwill" had expired. Congress had authorized President Bush to use force and the public was solidly behind the effort. Although there were not sufficient forces available in theater to begin a ground offensive, any further delay could be construed as a sign of weakness. While the coalition continued to be united, the risk of rift was always present. The use of air power provided a means to begin the actual military operation, with hopes that Iraq might capitulate once they saw their chances of retaining Kuwait to be futile. Ground and support forces were continuing to arrive. As in November, the result of the reassessment and reevaluation came in the category of military objectives.

In February, interest still remained, last resort was no longer an issue, the political and military objectives continued, congressional and popular support was high, and the forces required to do the job had been provided. There remained only a change to the campaign plan—the introduction of ground forces—to satisfy the military objective.

7. *The consequences to military action are acceptable.* At the time of the original decision, the immediate objective was protection of the sovereignty of Saudi Arabia and its oil fields. The immediate risk (already noted) was that the Iraqi army would continue along the gulf coast, annexing a fifty-mile wide strip that terminated at the border of Qatar and the United Arab Emirates. By August 6, Iraq had overrun Kuwait and had some eleven combat divisions in the operational theater. Forces were being resupplied, a possible indication that they might continue south into Saudi Arabia.[40] Had that been Iraq's original intent, taking a military option and inserting U.S. troops was a high-risk proposition and could exacerbate the problem.

At the very least, achieving the immediate political objective of preserving Saudi sovereignty meant a long-term military presence. Meeting the longer-term objectives of forcing an Iraqi withdrawal and restoring the Kuwaiti government—whether by political/economic means, or by force if necessary—meant a significant expenditure of precious resources, and possibly blood.

When it came to war, many voices argued successfully for limited and expedient war aims. These individuals, with Joint Chiefs Chairman Powell as their spokesman, wanted no part of objectives that called for an extended occupation of Iraq or a hunt to apprehend Saddam Hussein. They seriously doubted whether—to use Powell's terms—"lots of little Jeffersonian democrats would have popped up to run for office."[41]

On the regional level, the limited war aims precluded an evisceration of Iraq and creation of a power vacuum that would strengthen Iranian or Syrian influence in the area. Iraq still had some twenty combat divisions north of the Euphrates river, outside the Kuwait theater. To have pursued more aggressive war aims would have required an extended campaign against these forces. Allowing them to survive the war would preserve the regional military balance while destroying the prior Iraqi superiority.

Clearly all the "tests" were met. Also clearly, one analysis alone does not validate a concept. Prior analyses have shown, however, that using the tests as an analytical framework provides remarkable correlation between compliance with the tests and overall success of the intervention—success being defined as meeting all political objectives.[42]

Conclusion

Discussions of the Framers' intent and the practical considerations involving use of the War Powers Resolution listed heretofore outline the case against congressional involvement in decisions to use military force short of full-scale war. And when taken together with the apparent validity of using "tests" as an executive framework for use-of-force decisions, the scales seem to point heavily in favor of presidential primacy as the most prudent and effective approach.

Indeed it should be the president, as commander in chief, who decides whether or not to use military force as an instrument of foreign policy. Nevertheless, Congress appears determined to play a role in the decisions concerning the use of military force, insisting that the combination of constitutional powers was what the Framers desired. If that is so, the War Powers Resolution is a poor example of legislation to achieve that purpose. Extensive modifications are necessary. Some examples include first defining what constitutes "war." Second, the Resolution should acknowledge a greater list of circumstances under which the president may act unilaterally. It should also clarify and streamline the collaborative process, making it as simple as possible and eliminating the legislative veto provisions of the current law. Further, to support this responsibility, Congress should establish a continuous emergency response capability similar to that which exists throughout the executive branch. It is only when changes such as these are made that the Congress will structurally and practically be able to assume a participatory role in decisions to use military force short of a declaration of war. Until they do, it cannot be anything other than the president's decision.

5

Whiggism and Presidentialism: American Ambivalence toward Executive Power

Gary L. Gregg II

The Founding Fathers had established a "system" of representative government. They did not center power and responsibility in one institution, level, or branch of government. Federalism and the separation of powers scheme created a complex republic in which public officials in each branch would perform important functions as representatives of the people; both would be legitimate and independent servants of the political sovereign. But this conception of divided and balanced representative government was not the traditional one that preceded the Constitution's writing either in practice or in theory. Nor has it been the understanding that has prevailed at all times in the American experience under the Constitution. Indeed, with regard to the presidency, ours is a history of ambivalence toward executive power—both loved and hated, trusted and feared.[1] This chapter explores the two seductive positions that lay at the extremes from the balanced and compound understanding of presidential power found in the Constitution and best explicated in *The Federalist Papers*.

On one extreme is the traditional Whig mistrust of executive power. To proponents of the Whig school of thought, representation is only possible in a numerous and locally elected legislative body. Such an institution should be the vital center of free government. At the other extreme is the doctrine of presidentially centered government that finds the people's will best expressed in the unitary and nationally elected executive authority. Such a presidentially centered conception of the office underlies the writings of Woodrow Wilson on the presidency. It also undergirds the practice of the modern plebiscitary presidency, and the "cult of the presidency" literature best expressed in Richard Neustadt's 1961 classic, *Presidential Power.*

This chapter explores some of the historic manifestations of these two positions on presidential–congressional power in America, and particularly focuses on the development of the political theory that underlies each of these positions. As will become clear, at the heart of both positions is a particular understanding of legitimate political representation and its needs. Throughout American history there has been perennial disagreement about what level or branch of government can best provide political representation, and these debates will be central to the pages that follow.

Beginning with the controversy over the Second Bank of the United States during Andrew Jackson's presidency, I will explore some of the most important conceptions of the presidential office and the values and ideas that underlie them. I begin with the Jackson presidency because it marked a real crisis point in our history under representative government. In the president's arguments and those of his Senate critics, we are starkly confronted with examples of two distinct understandings of the presidency and the representative process. The presidentially centered conception of representation that found expression in Andrew Jackson's presidency has informed much of the theory and practice of twentieth-century American governance. Jackson's notion of a centralized chief executive found a powerful echo in the writings and practice of Woodrow Wilson, which will also be explored. The "cult of the presidency" literature of mid-century also resembled Jackson's understanding and has itself greatly contributed to the underlying theory of the contemporary plebiscitary presidency. The best example of this literature is surely the writings of Richard Neustadt, which are explored later in the chapter.

But Jackson's understanding of the presidency and the political system did not go unopposed. His critics, especially those in the Senate, set down a forceful line of attack against Jackson's understandings of the constitutional order. They explicated a congressionally centered understanding of the political system that would find resonance down to the current hour. Below I also trace these ideas and end the chapter with a discussion of two important twentieth-century manifestations of this whiggish conception of representative government.

But why are these various understandings of the presidency important? Isn't it "mere theory" we are exploring? To a great extent, the presidency has been the office the people have wanted it to be. As Barbara Hinckley has demonstrated, the presidency's "open" character makes it uniquely susceptible to becoming what people expect. This symbolic circle is closed with the realization that presidents and other political leaders, teachers, and writers all affect our expectations of the presidency and its incumbents. As

Hinckley puts it, "By degrees almost imperceptible, as one kind of symbol replaces another, the office is transformed."[2] It is with this realization that we must be concerned with the symbolic representation of the office given by presidents, academics, and popular culture through American history. It is not "mere theory" we are exploring but the actual and fundamental limits and possibilities of our political institutions.

Jackson versus Congress and the Crisis of Representation

The clash between these two opposing views on the place of representation in the government can be seen in its most acute form in the early years of the fifth decade under the Constitution. The 1830s, and especially the election of 1832, were marked by an enthusiasm for democracy and the rule of the people that had not previously been seen in America. In the election of 1832 both major parties for the first time adopted the more democratic convention system for choosing presidential candidates and further encouraged the participation of the masses in politics. The Democrats and the National Republicans lavished wild praise upon the people for their wisdom and virtue. All had come to accept the notion that the masses should rule—an acceptance that did much to encourage the further democratization of American politics in the years to come.[3]

It is no accident that such a clash between Congress and the presidency would coincide with the great democratization of the American political ethos that occurred in the 1830s. Such a new revolutionary celebration of the mass electorate and their right to rule more directly would almost surely necessitate a rethinking of the institutions of popular control and their relationship to one another. The great clash would come when more than one institution would claim completely to represent the people—thereby claiming to be the guardian of their interests and the holder of their newly legitimized power.

Jackson's election in 1828 arguably made him the first popularly elected president in U.S. history, a fact that strengthened his conviction that as president he bore a direct mandate fresh from the source of all political sovereignty.[4] Indeed, in his "First Annual Message," Jackson urged amending the Constitution to further reduce the space between the president and the public by allowing them to directly choose their chief magistrate.[5] In office, Jackson's assertion as the people's representative came to a head in his conflict with Congress over the Second Bank of the United States. Robert Remini has called Jackson's veto of the bank bill on July 10, 1832, "the most important veto ever issued by a president."[6] Before Jackson, presidents generally held to a very narrow interpretation of the veto power: it was to be employed only when the president believed a piece of legislation to be unconstitutional. Notwithstanding this tradition, Jackson held the president to be empowered to reject any bill he felt would not be in the nation's interest, and, in his eight years in the presidency, he vetoed more bills than had been vetoed in the forty previous years combined.[7]

Jackson's conflict would not come with the House, as the Democrats held a substantial majority in that body. Rather, the Senate, where the Whigs led by Henry Clay and Daniel Webster were stronger and formed an alliance with southern Democrats like John C. Calhoun, would offer the strongest resistance to the expansive view of presidential power that was based on Jackson's conception of representation. The hostilities between the Senate and the president that followed Jackson's veto of the bank bill, his subsequent dismissal of the secretary of the treasury, and his removal of public funds from the Bank of the United States without congressional approval, provide an illuminating case study regarding the intellectual foundations of the presidential-centered and congressional-centered perspectives on representation and executive power.

After months of consideration, on March 28, 1834, the Senate passed a resolution chastising the president for actions that they found unconstitutional and despotic. They resolved that "the President, in the late Executive proceedings in relation to the public revenue, has assumed upon himself authority and power not conferred by the constitution and laws, but in derogation of both." President Jackson responded to the Senate on April 15 with a long and detailed protest of that body's actions that he "respectfully requested" be placed in its journals (it was read to the Senate on the seventeenth of that month). The themes and doctrines found in Jackson's message of protest and the heated responses from the Senate floor provide extraordinarily rich representations of the two polar predilections under discussion here.[8]

Jackson argued that he was duty-bound to make such a protest because of the oath he had taken to "preserve, protect, and defend the constitution of the United States" and because it was particularly the place of his office to defend the fundamental law. Although he couched arguments in language maintaining the traditional balance between the institutions of government, all of which are "the servants of the American people" with a "common superior," Jackson's language and doctrines are really more radical for the time than he let on.[9] What he actually articulates is an understanding of the presidency that places the president as the undisputed sovereign in the executive aspects of government, while at the same time forging a powerful link between the officeholder and the American people. Each of these ideas made the congressional Whigs cringe with a fear of monarchical despotism.

Jackson writes that the "executive power is vested exclusively in the President, except that in the conclusion of treaties and in certain appointments to office, he is to act with the advice and consent of the Senate."[10] But what role would the Senate here play in wielding these limited executive powers? At least in the realm of appointments—of most concern in the controversy—the Senate was to be "*merely* a check upon the Executive power of appointment."[11] Moreover, the Senate's confirmation power could not be used, in Jackson's view, to infringe on the president's "right to employ agents of his own choice to aid him in the performance of his duties, and to discharge them when he is no longer willing to be responsible for their acts."[12] With this assertion, Jackson not only diminishes the role of Congress in the actual governance of the country's business by directly limiting the Senate's place in the choice of governmental officials, but ultimately places all *responsibility* for the executive branch upon himself as president.

The basis of Jackson's understanding is that as president he "is the direct representative of the American people."[13] In fact, while Jackson carefully builds a case for his responsibility directly to the people and thereby his title of their representative, he also endeavors to undermine any claim the Senate and its members have as representatives in their own right in a democratic republic. While the president has been chosen by the people and is responsible to them, Jackson finds the Senate to be chosen by electors other than the people and elected for extended terms—making them not directly responsible to and not representative of the people.

> If the censures of the Senate be submitted to by the President, the confidence of the people in his ability and virtue, and the character and usefulness of his administration will soon be at an end, and the real power of the Government will fall into the hands of a body holding their offices for long terms, not elected by the people, and not to them directly responsible.[14]

The members of the Senate "represent, not the people, but the States," and their extended tenure, Jackson argues, leaves them but remotely responsible even in that capacity.[15]

But Jackson goes even further to outrage the Whigs in the Senate and to offend their sentiments on the representational morality of free government. The president employs his theoretical understanding of his place to maneuver himself closer to the people themselves by going over Congress's head directly to them. In claiming the support of the public, the president claimed an electoral mandate stemming from the last election and "the solemn decision of the American people."[16] He also quoted at length from state resolutions urging their officials in Washington to work against the rechartering of the bank—thereby castigating those Senators who did not act "in accordance with the sentiments of the legislatures."[17] Indeed, it was immediately understood in Congress that this "protest" was primarily

meant for public consumption, to garner public support and sympathy for
Jackson against Congress. Immediately upon the protest having been read,
Senator George Poindexter rose to his feet to condemn the president's im-
prudent appeal to the public.

> This effort to denounce and overawe the deliberations of the Senate may
> properly be regarded as capping the climax of that systematic plan of opera-
> tions which for several years past has been in progress, designed to bring this
> body into disrepute among the people, and thereby remove the only existing
> barrier to the arbitrary encroachments and usurpations of executive power.[18]

The Whigs Respond

The Whigs in the Senate wasted no time and spared no words in responding to Jackson's message of protest. Henry Clay, Daniel Webster, and the
other opponents of the president saw in his actions no less than a declaration of war against the Senate and the constitutional system of representative government itself. Senator Preston told his colleagues on May 6, 1834:
"This protest of the poor old man, is, throughout, war to the knife, and the
knife to the hilt, against the Senate."[19] In their speeches can be found many
of the most important doctrines and values that underlie the whiggish understanding of congressionally centered government and their consummate
fear of the ambitious executive.

To the Whigs in the Senate, the current battle with Jackson was but one
in the age-old contest "to rescue liberty from the grasp of Executive
power."[20] Webster told the Senate on May 7 that, "On the long list of the
champions of human freedom, there is not one name dimmed by the re-
proach of advocating the extension of Executive authority; on the contrary," he went on, "the uniform and steady purpose of all such champions
has been to limit and restrain it."[21] The danger was clear and present. Jackson's quest for power and his claim to be *the* representative of the people
might well lead, it was feared, to an American president's repeating
Napoleon's repetition of the declaration of Louis XIV: "I am the state!"[22] A
new dictator was making his move with appeals to being the legitimate expression of the nation's will.

In the conflict between the Senate Whigs and President Jackson, we can
note several important differences that animated their various stands on the
issues of power and representation in the American regime. They, in one
way or another, and to one degree or another, have remained important elements in related debates up to the current hour.

First, and perhaps most importantly at the time, Jackson and his opponents in Congress held to vastly different fundamental views on the nature
of representation. The first essential question of representation must always

be: who is it that is to be represented? On this count, the two sides disagreed widely. To Jackson, "the people" were to be represented; a "people" of the United States of America who were scattered over an extended republic and yet were more than capable of possessing a single mind—an interest that transcended the various boundaries within the nation. Jackson, as the single head of government, fashioned himself the direct representative of this people—in his unity was embodied the essential unity of the nation.

To one degree or another, Jackson's opponents held to a different understanding of the entity worthy of representation in a free government. There was more than a mass national populace to be represented, if that was even possible at all. While the membership of the House represented the people in their local communities, "The members of the Senate are representatives of the States" said Webster, "and it is in the Senate alone that the four-and-twenty States, as political bodies, have a direct influence in the Legislative and Executive powers of this Government."[23] South Carolina's Calhoun made the case for the representation of the people of the individual states even more clearly in his challenge to the Jacksonian doctrine.

He [Jackson] tells us again and again, with the greatest emphasis, that he is the immediate representative of the American people. He is the immediate representative of the American people! I thought the President professed to be a State rights man . . . that he believed that the people of these States were united in a constitutional compact, as forming distinct and sovereign communities; and that no such community or people, as the American people, taken in the aggregate existed. I had supposed . . . that the American people are not represented in a single department of the Government; no, not even in the other House, which represents the people of the several States, as distinct from the people in the aggregate . . . yet he claims to be not only the representative, but the immediate representative of the American people. What effrontery! What boldness of assertion![24]

The American people are not just some undifferentiated mass, Jackson's opponents argued. Rather, the American nation is comprised of variety that equally deserved representation. Besides, Calhoun argued, the president, despite his claim to be close to the people, was not elected directly by them. The legislatures that elected himself and the rest of the Senate, Calhoun reasoned, are actually more representative of the people than is the electoral college. Hence, the people are closer to the Senate than to the president.

Along with variety and complexity within the body to be represented in government, Webster and the others also argued for complexity within government as opposed to what they perceived to be Jackson's quest for simplicity and concentration. Here the Whig opponents of Jackson were reiterating Publius's doctrine that tyranny was the accumulation of all powers in the same hands, regardless of the methods by which those hands came to their position of authority.[25] The Whigs believed they were fighting to defend the constitutional system that had established a system of separated powers and checks and balances to limit the ability of any one aspect of government to make encroachments upon the public liberty.[26] "Nothing is more deceptive or more dangerous," Webster cautioned, "than the pretense of a desire to simplify government. . . . The simplest governments are despotisms;" he went on, "the next simplest, limited monarchies; but all republics, all governments of law, must impose numerous limitations and qualifications of authority, and give many positive and many qualified rights."[27] On the contrary, the spirit of presidentially centered representation that Webster saw as Jackson's agenda, and that would later guide the thought of individuals like Woodrow Wilson and Richard Neustadt, sharply contends with the Madisonian notions of complexity, fortifications, auxiliary checks, and limitations that the spirit of liberty seemed to demand. The emphasis is rather upon overcoming these barriers in the name of presidential representation of "the people as a whole." To the Whigs, simplicity in government was the doorway to despotism; to Jackson and later to Wilson, it was the pathway to an invigorated democracy.

Two other closely related themes were articulated by the opponents of Jackson's assertion of presidential power and representation. First, they made a direct challenge to the president's claim to be "responsible" to the people, on the basis of which he could claim his special representational role. And second, they made a direct and unambiguous challenge to the president's attempt to forge a special relationship with the American people. They realized that these two elements of the president's program would, if successfully developed into accepted constitutional doctrine, undermine Congress's place in government and legitimacy with the American people. The complex republic would be replaced by a simplified government by executive.

In his protest, Jackson as president claimed to occupy the sole place of responsibility in the executive branch of government. But to whom is the president responsible? Jackson asserted that the president is "elected by the people and responsible to them," not only for his own actions, but for the activities of the other executive officers as well.[28] To this claim the president's opponents raised a number of objections. Calhoun objected that the president's responsibility is not limited to the people, but extends to the legislature as well. That is, where the legislative department's mission was a deliberative one that would end with the passage of legislation, the president's was limited to ascertaining what that law was and then carrying it into effect. In this capacity, Calhoun argued, the president is to be responsible to Congress as much as to those who indirectly participated in his election. With this argument, Calhoun articulated the basic assumption of those who have historically taken the congressionally centered view of representative government.[29]

Daniel Webster rose to his feet on May 7, 1834, to lay down a direct challenge to the underlying premises of Jackson's doctrine of responsibility—a doctrine that encapsulates the foundation of the modern conception of the plebiscitary presidency. What does the president mean that he is "responsible," Webster asked rhetorically. He then noted two possible types of responsibility. First, the president could mean legal responsibility. But clearly this is not the doctrine of his protest, for the president is not saying that he is impeachable or otherwise punishable for the actions of others in the executive branch. On such a basis then, the president could not claim that all are his personal agents.

The avenue of responsibility that Jackson does assert is the one running directly between himself as president and the American people. As Webster puts it, the president's claim is no more than "merely responsibility to public opinion."[30] In explaining Jackson's conception of the office, Webster also describes with amazing accuracy the conception of responsibility that has guided the presidency in our own day. "It is a liability to be blamed; it is the chance of becoming unpopular, the danger of losing a re-election. Nothing else is meant in the world. It is the hazard of failing in any attempt or enterprise of ambition."[31] To Whig thought, such "responsibility" is no real responsibility at all. Indeed, such weak and ineffectual chains have historically been broken by ambitious executives and even turned into weapons to be used against popular legislatures. In a spirit that would be rekindled by critics of the "imperial presidency" in the current century, Webster reminds his colleagues and the nation of the dangers to free government from a popular executive who believes his mandate superior to the restraints of the Constitution and the rule of law.

> It is precisely the responsibility under which Cromwell acted, when he dispersed Parliament, telling its members, not in so many words, indeed, that they disobeyed the will of their constituents, but telling them that the people were sick of them, and that he drove them out "for the glory of God, and the good of the nation." It is precisely the responsibility upon which Bonaparte broke up the popular assembly of France. I do not mean, sir, certainly, by these illustrations, to insinuate designs of violent usurpations against the President; far from it; but I do mean to maintain that such responsibility as that with which the protest clothes him, is no legal responsibility, no constitutional responsibility, no republican responsibility; but mere liability to loss of office, loss of character, and loss of fame, if he shall choose to violate the laws and overturn the liberties of the country. It is such a responsibility as leaves every thing in his discretion, and his pleasure.[32]

One might also note the grounds here for another challenge to the plebiscitary presidency of the twentieth century. Although no president has had "designs of violent usurpations," one might find a systematic design for the peaceful usurpation of the legislature's role in the deliberative process of government involved in the presidential strategy of "going public" to pressure Congress to do the president's will.

This indeed is an important aspect of the Senate's whiggish attack on Jackson's protest. They believed it to be a "breach of privilege" that the president would venture to interfere in the relationship between the Senate and their constituents by charging them "with acting contrary to the will of those constituents."[33] Though appeals of this sort have become routine in the modern presidency, Webster declared with outrage at the time that not even an English sovereign "since Cromwell's time, dared to send such a message. "[34]

But why did Jackson attempt to wedge himself between the people and their elected representatives in Congress? The president's opponents well understood that in a democratic republic popularity and claims of representation mean power. What they saw Jackson attempting is what since Woodrow Wilson has been the standard presidential tactic in modern America—the attempt to "excite the sympathy of the people, whom he seeks to make his allies in the contest."[35] Calhoun saw a particularly ominous sign in the president's strategy.

> But why all this solicitude on the part of the President to place himself near to the people, and to push us off to the greatest distance? Why this solicitude to make himself their sole representative, their only guardian and protector, their only friend and supporter? The object cannot be mistaken. It is preparatory to farther hostilities—to an appeal to the people; and is intended to to [sic] prepare the way in order to transmit to them his declaration of war against the Senate, with a view to enlist them as his allies in the war which he contemplates waging against this branch of the Government.[36]

We can summarize some of the basic assumptions underlying the Whig sentiment on presidential representation in a few, perhaps overly simplified, observations. First, republican self-government demanded the central place of governmental power and leadership reside in the popular legislature. Congress was the first branch of government. Second, the emphasis is placed on representation through deliberation, which is the role of the legislature, rather than through action and activity, which is more available to the executive magistrate. Third, the entity to be represented is a diverse and varied people with similarly different interests and opinions. Only a locally elected legislature, elected from either districts or states, can possibly represent such a public—the unitary executive can represent only the ephemerally existent mass national public. Fourth, the dedication is to complex government and divided powers rather than to simplicity as the best guarantor of public liberty and good government. Such a dedication was particularly manifest in a deep-seated historical mistrust of executive power, whether found in a hereditary monarch or an elected president.

This conflict between President Jackson and the Senate was not simply for power over governmental actions concerning the Bank and the public revenues. It was more widely a fight over the rights and duties accorded to representatives in the American Republic. It was about the place of the various branches of the national government and the place of the American people in the governing of the nation. The Jacksonian presidency affected those that would follow to the point that though the Whigs elected presidents dedicated to congressional supremacy in the years that followed, even they would not completely live up to the Whig doctrines.[37] Indeed, Jackson's conception of the presidency would come to dominate the literature and the practice of the office in the twentieth century. But the whiggish defense of the traditional constitutional order would continue to inspire critics of presidentially centered government as well.

The Plebiscitary Presidency[38]

The doctrine of presidentially centered representation certainly has antecedents before the twentieth century. Besides the presidency of Andrew Jackson, one might, for instance, point to Abraham Lincoln's centralization of authority and power in the presidency during the Civil War. As a congressman, Lincoln had denounced the vigorous use of executive power. "Were I President," he had said, "I should desire the legislation of the country to rest with Congress, uninfluenced by the executive in its origin or progress, and undisturbed by the veto unless in very special and clear cases."[39] His actions as president, however, including the suspension of habeas corpus, the expansion of the military without consent of Congress, and the spending of millions of dollars of the public money without congressional appropriation, have led some to characterize him as a dictator.[40] In his actions the president seemed to be exercising a type of emergency representation of the "people" of the Union, a "people" that was perhaps even a higher "people" than found in the Constitution itself.[41] As Richard Loss has put it, "He temporarily made the presidency dominant over Congress and the Supreme Court, overrode individual rights and set a precedent for the future."[42]

But the precedent Lincoln set, it must be kept in mind, need not have extended beyond emergency times that posed considerable threat to the constitutional order. As president during the greatest crisis in the history of the Republic, Lincoln took all representation unto himself in the name of preserving republican government itself—a temporary cessation of the balanced constitutional republic, not its complete abandonment. During such extraordinary times, as Lincoln believed, it may very well be that one institution is the more legitimate holder of the people's will and power: "often a limb must be amputated to save a life; but a life is never wisely given to save a limb."[43] It was his belief that the oath he took to protect the Constitution, as he put it, "imposed upon me the duty of preserving, by every indispensable means, that government—that nation—of which that constitution was organic law."

Wilson and the American Presidency

What would develop decades after Lincoln would be the application of this same spirit to the regime during non-crisis times—amputation of the constitutional system of representation in the name of ordinary public policy, not national survival.[44] It is probably no accident that the foremost expositor of this representational role of the presidency lived both in the world of academia and in the White House as president himself. Woodrow Wilson, political scientist and twenty-eighth president of the United States, elaborated a theory of the presidency and its role in American politics that was systematic and revolutionary. He, above all others, systematized and developed the view of the president as *the* center of representation in the American political system. While Lincoln's actions were taken in a time of extraordinary national emergency, Wilson would articulate a doctrine of government that prescribed the centralization of representation and power in the presidency during the everyday course of public policy.

Wilson's early views of American government were set forth in his important work *Congressional Government*, which first appeared in 1885. In it he outlined a picture of our constitutional system, under which Congress necessarily predominated and the presidency was a clearly subordinate and ineffectual office.[45] This understanding of the American political system changed starkly decades later when he wrote his second book, *Constitutional Government*. The most important shift in Wilson's conception of the political system from his earlier work to his later *Constitutional Government* is the replacement by the executive of the representational duties of Congress and hence the president's central place in the regime.

The change in Wilson's thought is readily apparent even upon first glance at his two volumes. Representing his new thinking on the presidency, the executive moves from the back of his first volume to the first institution to be considered in the second. This change seems important beyond merely the ordering of the chapters. To wit, the logic of *Congressional Government* follows that of the Constitution itself—the House being the first institution, then the Senate, and finally the executive office—while the ordering of *Constitutional Government* follows Wilson's new logic of the system with the presidency predominant and the "center" of national leadership and representation.[46] In this change in the form of his writings on American government, we can also see the result of Wilson's theory of constitutionalism. To Wilson, the Constitution was not a document of constant or stable meaning. Neither did it establish a stable and constant political order consistent with the doctrine of checks and balances (although such a "mechanical theory" was the understanding of the Founders, Wilson concedes). Instead, Wilson puts together a conception of the constitutional order that rejects the Founders' intentions and even the very idea of an established constitutional order. By rejecting the "literary theory" of the Constitution, Wilson stitches together a "living Constitution" that is based on the idea of constant adaptation and change by the system to the needs of its environment. The constitutional institutions and the constitutional order that regulates them are subject to fundamental change and growth to "express the changing temper and purposes of the American people from age to age."[47]

But Wilson, who would become the first president to criticize the Constitution, goes even further toward withdrawing from the constitutionalism of the Founders.[48] Not only does the government change with the evolution of the American people and the political needs of the nation, thereby naturally changing from its original principles established in a different time,[49] but he also finds the very ideas and intent of the Framers to have been fundamentally flawed and untenable from the beginning. The Founders attempted to establish the unestablishable, to found a government on the Newtonianism of the Whig theory of politics with separate institutions operating "upon a theory of checks and balances which was meant to limit the operation of each part and allow to no single part or organ of it a dominating force."[50]

To Wilson, active political leadership was essential to any government and it must be lodged somewhere so as to bring all the organs of government into concert. Montesquieu's "gravitational theory" of politics, upon which the American Founders based their Constitution, must be doomed because, "No living thing can have its organs offset against each other as checks, and live."[51] To Wilson, Charles Darwin must replace Isaac Newton as the basis of politics because

> Government is not a body of blind forces; it is a body of men, . . . with a common task and purpose. Their cooperation is indispensable, their warfare fatal. There can be no successful government without leadership or without the intimate, almost instinctive, coordination of the organs of life and action. This is not theory, but fact, and displays its force as fact, whatever theories may be thrown across its track.[52]

The politics of the Founders, the constitutionalism embodied in *The Feder-alist*, was just such a theory thrown across the track of Wilson's political re-ality. The Constitution is to have no meaning and hence no protections but "the spirit of the age."[53]

The importance for the American presidency is that, following the logic of such a "living constitution," the office has "been one thing at one time, another at another."[54] To Wilson, the Founders might have intended the president to be "only the legal executive," with a veto that "was only his 'check' on Congress," without the function of promoting good law, as it was only "empowered to prevent bad laws."[55] And yet, these constitutional chains were unable to prevent the president from largely escaping (or at least greatly expanding) the tethers of "theory" that bound him. They could not prevent his becoming the "unifying force," the "guide of the nation," and its chief political representative. The Darwinian forces of changing cir-cumstances shaping the Constitution, with the responses of individual of-ficeholders, have made the president more of a political leader and less of an executive officer.[56] As "No one else represents the people as a whole," the president has become the center of representation in the American sys-tem; a position that gives him the ability, if power is wielded skillfully and if he rightly interprets the national thought, to become irresistible. Inde-pendent of any constitutional grant of authority, or of constitutional con-straints, it is the president's direct relation with public opinion that empowers him as the center of government. The *zeitgeist* has replaced the Constitution as the source of institutional position, power, and influence.[57] The constitutional *forms* of representation, according to Wilson, have been rightfully outgrown and replaced by the fluctuating nexus between mass opinion and the sitting president.

Central, then, to the president's position as *the* national representative is his place in speaking for and to the nation. In Wilson's earlier book, the legislative assembly was to perform the teaching function but that respon-sibility is transferred to the executive in *Constitutional Government.*

> The nation as a whole has chosen him, and is conscious that it has no other political spokesman. His is the only national voice in affairs. . . . His position takes the imagination of the country. . . . When he speaks in his true charac-ter, he speaks for no special interest. If he rightly interpret the national thought and boldly insist upon it, he is irresistible.[58]

As a rhetorical teacher, the president is not only the mouthpiece for the opinion of the people but, a "President whom it trusts can not only lead it, but form it to his own views."[59] Here the result also is the undermining of the constitutional (and representational) authority of the other branches of government. If the president can win the public to his view, he writes, "the leadership is his whether the houses [of Congress] relish it or not. They are at a disadvantage and will probably have to yield."[60]

Wilson's own position on presidential power comes even more clearly into relief as he writes that the president is "at liberty, both in law and conscience, to be as big a man as he can."[61] The Constitution will not set the limit to presidential power, but the only limit will be the officeholder's own capacity; "and if Congress be overborne by him, it will be no fault of the makers of the constitution,—it will be from no lack of constitutional powers on its part, but only because the President has the nation behind him, and Congress has not." The presidency is essentially formless, holding the position that facilitates leadership but nearly completely dependent upon the ambitions and talents of the occupant. "His office," writes Wilson, "is anything he has the sagacity and force to make it."[62] Wilson's is not an "empty" theory of the presidential vessel, however. The outcome he wants is clearly to have an active president leading the nation and "whipping" the individual organs of government into a "vital synthesis" that would negate the Founder's system of checks and balances and the spirit of the separation of powers.[63] He criticizes those "Presidents [who] have deliberately held themselves off from using the full power they might legitimately have used" for failing in just such an endeavor.

In sum, with Wilson we have the establishment of a new doctrine of presidential power, a doctrine that would have fundamental importance for the political regime in the twentieth century. Wilson elevates the presidency to the center of political leadership and representation in the American system. To do so, he rejects any type of "fixed" meaning for the Constitution and specifically undermines the "original intent" of the Founders. In so doing, Wilson also marks the end of the constitutional "people," the constitutional majority seen in *The Federalist*. The public are reduced to being merely the transient majority of a given moment in history; the only "people" to be given representation in the Wilsonian system are the temporarily empowered numbers. For instance, consider the following statement from Wilson's 1912 presidential campaign on his relationship to the people.

> I have often thought that the only strength of a public man consisted in the number of persons who agreed with him; and that the only strength that any man can boast of and be proud of is that great bodies of his fellow citizens trust him and are ready to follow him. For the business of every leader of government is to hear what the nation is saying and to know what the nation is enduring. It is not his business to judge *for* the nation, but to judge *through* the nation as its spokesman and voice.[64]

With a direct link to this public opinion that the other institutions of government lack, the president is able to dominate the government in the name of the "nation as a whole." Moreover, Wilson's idealized president provides the efficient synthesis of the political institutions and powers that the original "theory" of the Constitution made separate. By so elevating the presidency, Wilson correspondingly reduces the legitimacy of the other representative institutions. There is room in Wilson's thought for but one expression of popular self-governance, one locus of representation.

Though risking hyperbole, it might not be terribly far from the mark to liken Wilson's doctrine of presidential government to the reversal of the Whig revolution of 1689. Here parliamentary supremacy was recognized over the king. The more numerous legislative body elected by the people alone could represent them, it was believed. In Wilson the tide is turned with the people's direct and exclusive link to the single man in the White House as their only national representative. Wilson's was not a constitutional revolution in the strictest sense; it was a revolution in the understanding of the idea of representative government. It was not based in a formal transference of power, but one that found its sanction in a skillful and ambitious incumbent in league with the people.

Neustadt and the Political Science Presidency

This view of presidentially centered representation was systematically legitimated by Wilson, and was subsequently institutionalized with the Depression- and war-era presidency of Franklin Delano Roosevelt. Such is not the whole story, however. Wilson's doctrine of presidentially centered representation also became the dominant symbolic representation of the office in the scholarly and popular literature on the modern presidency, thus reinforcing the doctrine in the popular mind as well as legitimating it for incumbents. Though such a view can be seen at least tangentially in the near gushing praise of the office from scholars like Clinton Rossiter,[65] it was with the publication of Richard Neustadt's *Presidential Power*[66] in 1960 that such a view came to dominate the literature and thereby shape our expectations for the office and its incumbents.

In Neustadt's pathbreaking study we see the general doctrine of presidential representation found in Wilson further developed with practical advice to the would-be power wielder in the White House. Neustadt demonstrates a Wilsonian dedication to the centralization of leadership and power in an activist presidency whose powers are completely dependent on the relationship between the individual incumbent and the public. The Constitution, we are told, offers the president merely the "vantage points" from which he can attempt to cultivate power. Indeed, in passages rich with symbolism for the presidentially centered theory of government, Neustadt reduces all other public actors to the status of presidential "constituencies." The public, his partisans, foreign peoples, let alone Congress and executive officials are not independent and co-equal entities. Rather, they are all, the legislature included, dependent on the president as the represented are dependent on their empowered representative.[67]

In this system of "separated institutions *sharing* powers," it is particularly the president's responsibility to unite the fragments of power that the Constitution partially distributed.[68] Like Wilson, Neustadt seems to reject both the Framers' understanding that there exist different kinds of power as well as their dedication to the necessity of maintaining at least a significant degree of independent distribution between the branches.[69] Seeing governmental power as an "undifferentiated mass,"[70] Neustadt's prescription is for the active presidential channeling of that power into the president's own hands. The presidency is to become the home of representation as the president ambitiously builds and guards his power and influence over the rest of the government.

The "pursuit of presidential power," Neustadt writes, "is good for the country as well as for him."[71] Elected "by the nation," the president is unmatched by any other officer for judging potential public measures. "Our system affords nobody a better source of clues," Neustadt writes, and he adds, "In the sphere of validity [of public policy] our system can supply no better expert than a President intent on husbanding his influence."[72] Will all such presidents represent wisely? Neustadt writes that "because the President's own frame of reference is at once so all-encompassing and so political, what he sees as a balance for himself is likely to be close to what is viable in terms of public policy." The president is the central legitimate representative authority, Neustadt asserts, because the public good and the good of the individual incumbent are inescapably linked in a union of mutual needs and aspirations. "What is good for the country is good for the President, and vice versa."[73] In such striking clarity, we see the delegitimization of the other representative branches that is an inescapable part of a presidentially centered system of representative government.

And how is the president to whip the government into a unified actor for progress and policy? Where Publius held the president's role to be one of facilitating discourse, Neustadt rejects any such role on behalf of reason or deliberation. Though the central lesson of his volume is that presidential power is "the power to persuade," Neustadt explicitly rejects a reliance on reasoned argumentation. Rather, to persuade Congress and other actors to do his will, a president must rely on "the coin of self interest,"[74] through the exploitation of "needs and fears."[75] Presidential persuasion is not about the merits of public policy reasonably discussed in the legislature and among the branches. Rather, the president's object should be "to induce as much uncertainty as possible about the consequences of ignoring what he wants. If he cannot make men think him bound to win, his need is to keep them from thinking they can cross him without risk, or that they can be sure what

risks they run."[76] In Neustadt's formula for presidentially centered government, the complex representation of the Constitution is reduced to representation by one man in the name of the public interest and the public's
other bodies are diminished to the status of hurdles the president must seek
to overcome.

Neustadt's work also demonstrates that a Wilsonian presidentially centered scheme of representation is not completely dependent on presidential mass rhetoric. In fact, Neustadt nearly completely ignores (at least in his
original formulation) the role of presidential rhetoric.[77] And yet he still
maintains Wilson's close interaction between the officeholder and his constituents, though he ascribes to the people perhaps less influence than did
Wilson. In Neustadt's formulation, the relation between the public and the
president seems twofold. First, as we have seen, the public good is nearly
indistinguishable from the good of the president; hence their interests completely merge to the point where his quest for personal power is the highest form of representation of the national interest. Second, the president's
personal power is to some degree affected by his prestige with the public
because the other players in Washington are concerned with public opinion. Here we see the rational defense of the same basic formulation of presidential plebiscitary representation that inspired Wilson and that was
carried to its zenith in practice by FDR.

Neustadt's prescriptive formulations have inspired other students of the
office, presidential aides, and presidents themselves since 1960.[78] Indeed,
this Neustadtian/Wilsonian view of the presidency is the one that came to
dominate most public and academic circles from the 1950s at least until
Vietnam and Watergate, and it is a view that is still prevalent in various
forms today. This cult of the presidency, or as political scientist Thomas
Cronin called it, the "textbook presidency," was based on the premise that
the individual in the presidency was the only officer who could save the
nation from the changing fortunes of modern life and whose character was
unsoiled by the flaws of the rest of humanity.[79] As Cronin has put it, this
textbook presidency "describes and extols a chief executive who is generally benevolent, omnipotent, omniscient, and highly moral."[80] For our purposes we can note five major ingredients in the conception of presidentially
centered government that can be found particularly in the thought of Wilson and Neustadt.

1. There is a need to rectify the errors of the checks and balances and
   separation of powers system established by the Founders. The "deadlock" and "checking" must be overcome in favor of unity and a "vital
   synthesis" in government. An energetic presidency is the only office
   capable of overcoming this flawed or anachronistic "theory" of the
   Constitution.

2. Action is clearly favored over deliberation. Here Wilson and Neustadt largely reject the legislative and deliberative republic in favor of governmental activism under presidential direction. The energetic executive is not needed to facilitate the deliberative process of representation; rather, he is needed to make his will the government's and thereby to unite the parts of the government in a holy synthesis for progress. Moreover, this progress is implicitly defined in terms of an egalitarian and statist agenda.

3. The Madisonian majority of locally elected officials meeting in the seat of government to come to policy choices should be superseded by "the voice of the people as a whole," a truly national majority that the president alone adequately represents. The president is formulator of national policy and he must mold the pluralistic legislature to a more homogeneous view of the common good and national purpose. Democracy comes to be viewed here in terms of a plebiscitary choice by a national majority between two competing programs forwarded by presidential candidates—"the people," the national majority less inhibited by "lesser representatives," should get their wishes.

4. A great emphasis is placed on the presidential role of providing representation by being the nation's "teacher." Through mass or popular rhetoric, the president is to influence and/or shape and express public opinion; thereby "activating" that public opinion to pressure Congress (overcoming the separation of powers "problem"), while he also uses the office as a place for FDR's "moral leadership." As Cronin has shown, this view of the office as one of "instructing the nation as a national teacher and guiding the nation as national preacher," became a central part of the elite orthodoxy of the 1950s and 1960s.[81] Beyond his doctrinal contribution to the rhetorical presidency, Wilson brought mass speech to the forefront of our politics by reviving the dormant practice of delivering the state of the union address to Congress in person and in his speaking tour on behalf of the League of Nations.[82]

5. Presidential power is conceived in "realistic" terms rather than in formal or constitutional terms. That is to say, the "theoretical" limits to the office found in the text of the Constitution and the intent of the people who ratified it are less important (perhaps of no consequence at all) than the "real life" experience of that office and the expanded power that has come with that experience. Closely connected here is the emphasis on the characteristics, style, and leadership ability of the individual president as determinants of power, rather than the constitutional characteristics of the office. In essence, the constitutional institution of the presidency (and, necessarily the other institutions as well) is essentially formless; primarily it is the occupant's talents that

set the boundaries to presidential power, boundaries that should be cast wide to allow for the needed activism of the office.

Whiggism in the Twentieth Century

Several forces at work in the twentieth century have contributed to the institutionalization of the presidentially centered model of representation both in practice as well as in the century's guiding ideas—its *zeitgeist*. The growth of the United States as a world leader, the revolution that came with nuclear weapons and the threat of instant Armageddon, the growth in government power and activism, and the centralizing force of national radio and television all contributed in important ways to the rise of the modern presidency. Also important, however, were the ideological underpinnings of this new presidency.

As seen in Wilson and Neustadt, the strong presidency model of the twentieth century was undergirded by the ideological demands of liberalism. From the activist presidency of Roosevelt on through the presidency of John F. Kennedy and into that of Lyndon Johnson, liberal politicians and opinion leaders were the primary torch bearers in the "cult of the presidency." Here they found both the means to support their dedication to direct democracy as well as the most effective instrument for achieving their policy goals.[83] "Influenced in large part by world events," says Cronin of these liberal pundits, "they supported a strong presidency because they believed that a strong presidency would best serve their values."[84]

Although such a tendency to invest in the office of the presidency great power and leadership capacities has been the ruling paradigm of this century, the old whiggism has not completely resigned itself to the tomb of lost causes. Rather, we have seen two distinct and important periods of critical reconsideration of the governing understanding of the presidency and Congress during the century. Both were, to varying degrees, inspired by a fear of what was understood to be the dangerous path the nation had embarked upon, as well as by a genuine theoretical rethinking of the needs of democratic government. The first is found in the whiggish intellectual and popular writings of the conservative movement at mid-century; the other with the liberal reaction to the "imperial" presidencies of Johnson and Richard Nixon in the early 1970s.

Whiggish Conservatism at the Mid-Twentieth Century

Conservatives have traditionally maintained a healthy distrust of concentrated governmental power.[85] During the mid-twentieth century two major phenomena especially raised the ire of the right on this score—the decline of traditional federalism and the growth in the presidency that came with the New Deal and the Second World War. In the flow of power from the state capitals to Washington, the right saw the end of local differences and cultures, and the seeds of tyranny. The further concentration of the expanded power of the federal government into the president's hands caused conservatives additional concern.[86]

Starting with a reaction to the presidency of the New Deal, conservative opinion leaders and politicians embraced congressional power as the authoritative representative body and as the only check on the modern presidency, which they conceived to be a dangerous tool of the big government left (both of the liberal and the socialist variety). Conservatives of the period running roughly from the 1930s into the 1960s put forth several important arguments against the presidentially centered governmental system that seemed triumphant in America. Many of these arguments are the same as were put forth a century earlier by the Whig critics of Jackson.

First, at perhaps the most fundamental level, conservatives expressed a vigorous jealousy of concentrated power and simplicity in government. Whereas many liberals saw a concentration of power and leadership as the best means toward the achievement of an activist political agenda, conservatives saw the beginnings of tyranny and the end of justice. As Russell Kirk put it in 1954,

> Intelligent conservatives, from Burke to Adams to our time, have looked upon power as a most dangerous thing; for though unchecked power means complete freedom for the powerful man, it means abject servitude for his neighbors. . . . Thus the conservative, reading the lessons of history, has sought to hedge about power with strong restrictions, and to divide authority among groups and institutions, that concentrated power may reside nowhere.[87]

Second, mid-twentieth century conservatives tended to conceive of representation in a way more similar to the old whiggism of Webster and Calhoun than to the liberal appeals to the representation of "the nation as a whole." Indeed, some of their writings at times seem lifted straight from that older understanding of America and representative government. James Burnham, in his 1959 classic *Congress and the American Tradition*, provides a perfect example of this mode of thought. Contrasting the "loosely set gelatin" of "the masses" with the "varied unity of a living organism" that is "the people," Burnham argues that only the former can be represented in the presidency.

> The people cannot be represented by or embodied in a single leader precisely because of the people's diversity. Their representation, if it is to be more than a masquerade, must have some sort of correspondence to their di-

versity. The political will of the people must therefore be projected through a multiplicity of representatives and representative institutions, both formal and informal. Only in this way can the irreducible variety of the people's interests, activities and aspirations find political expression.[88]

A legislature comprised of numerous and diverse individuals could alone adequately represent the people of the United States.

Third, conservatives made an argument that went directly to the heart of the plebiscitary model of democracy that had supported the expansion of executive power in the twentieth century. Against the "democratization" of American politics and the national idea-system, and the plebiscitary nature of presidential representation that accompanied it, conservatives tended to support the much-maligned "Madisonian" majorities found in the legislature.[89] The best expression of this conception of representative government was put forward by Willmoore Kendall in his famous "Two Majorities" essay in which he argued in favor of the inherent soundness of the Madisonian majority that was intended to govern under the Constitution.[90] Conservatives emphasized deliberation and discussion in government rather than action and efficiency.

Conservatives of this period also tended to prefer the rule of constitutional and statutory law to what they saw as arbitrary and potentially tyrannical rule by executive decree.[91] And their jealousy of executive power often was closely wrapped up with what amounted to an isolationist foreign policy among many conservatives.[92] For much of the political right at the time, an interventionist foreign policy was closely connected to the rise of the strong, dominant presidency and the expansion of government at home.[93]

For these reasons conservatives following the presidency of FDR came to a whiggish embrace of congressional representation. Only in the legislature could there be found adequate representation of the people, they argued. Centering power and leadership in the presidency was a dangerous step toward "caesarism" and the demise of the traditional liberties that the original model of the separation of powers made possible. They embraced Congress as the first branch of government much as the Whigs of the nineteenth century had.

Such an intellectual embrace of the legislative body also became manifest in reform efforts forwarded by conservative and moderate Republicans of this period. Two of the most important were proposed constitutional amendments designed to prevent the presidency from growing out of republican bounds. On 5 August, 1954, conservative Senator John Bricker (R–Ohio) proposed the so-called "Bricker Amendment" that would have restricted the president's ability to enter into executive agreements and treaties with foreign powers. An even more overtly whiggish reform came with the passage of the Twenty-second Amendment to the Constitution in 1951. The limiting of presidential terms in the amendment had roots in whiggish thought as old as the Constitution itself. Indeed, as David Mayer notes in chapter 2, Thomas Jefferson argued that the lack of a term limit on the president was a major deficiency in the Constitution.

The 1970s—Liberalism at a Crossroads

As we have seen, the general trend in liberal power prescriptions during the twentieth century has been to embrace centralization of power and leadership in the institution of the presidency. In part, at least, this tendency was fueled by the dedication of many on the left to "democratization" of American life. They assumed that the president, as the only nationally elected official, was the only one truly capable of representing the people of the United States. In part this tendency also was due to the perceived need to centralize governmental authority to overcome paralysis and deadlock, which was considered the result of the traditional separation of powers system. Associated with this tendency was the institutional partisanship that stemmed from having liberal Democrats in the White House exercising leadership on behalf of a progressive agenda.

Much of the "cult of the presidency" came to an end in the early 1970s. In the aftermath of Vietnam and Watergate, a reevaluation of liberal power prescriptions occurred. In its wake, many who had formerly embraced the presidency of Neustadt and Wilson turned against a strong chief executive and embraced a resurgent Congress. The national legislature was again looked upon as a legitimately representative institution rather than one that simply functioned as a reactionary hurdle in the way of progressive presidents. The attack leveled against the presidency during the 1970s was another manifestation of the Whig theory of representative government that has periodically waxed and waned as an important force in American political history.[94]

The very language of the politicians, pundits, and scholars who brought the attack on the office is reminiscent of earlier Whig rhetoric. Particularly important was the challenge to the presidency's republican character. The unitary and independent nature of the American presidency has always made it susceptible to critics who would liken it to monarchy and kingship. This indeed has been the tactic of whiggish partisans of the legislature since the earliest days of the Republic. The most famous anti-strong presidency book of the 1970s was Arthur Schlesinger's *The Imperial Presidency,* with all its allusions to a monarchical office.[95] Another example of this literary attack is George Reedy's *The Twilight of the Presidency.* In this work Reedy paints a picture of the White House as a royal court that waits upon and insulates "the American monarchy" from national reality.[96] Other writers used phrases like a "Frankenstein monster" to describe the office.[97]

Similar to the response of the conservatives in the mid-twentieth century, much of the whiggish attack on the presidency in the 1970s centered on what was seen as the abuse of foreign policy powers by recent incumbents. As Schlesinger put it, the view was that "the American President had become on issues of war and peace the most absolute monarch (with the possible exception of Mao Tse-tung of China) among the great powers of the world."[98] Saul K. Padover said the president had, for all practical purposes, become "a dictator in international affairs."[99] Such whiggish opinion and scholarship has, according to James Ceaser, led to many in Congress acting "as if that institution performs its proper duty in a separation-of-powers system when it ties the executive's hands and attempts to guide much of the nation's foreign policy through the instrument of law."[100]

Such congressional responses to presidential power were manifest in several important pieces of legislation passed during the 1970s. The Congressional Budget Act of 1974 was an attempt to give Congress a larger role in the budgetary process. In response to Nixon's massive impoundments of funds, Congress also passed legislation in 1974 to curb the president's power in this area. Perhaps most importantly, in 1973 Congress passed the War Powers Resolution in an attempt to limit presidential control over military operations and to place Congress back at the center of the national security process.

Certain tendencies with regard to representative government underlay the anti-presidency writings of the 1970s, much like the writings of their whiggish predecessors. This can easily be seen in the cries of "imperialism," "monarchy," and "creeping caesarism." As *The New Republic* opined, the assumption was that the presidency had assumed so much power as to contradict "the principles of democratic government . . .", as the presidency "is not as compared with Congress, an institution of participatory democracy."[101] The fact should not be lost, however, that much of this literature was inspired, at least in part, by less lofty principles.

The origin of the presidentially centered understanding of representative government in America was inspired at least in part by liberal presidents pursuing an activist and progressive political agenda; the reaction against the presidency during the 1970s was led by liberals unhappy about the foreign policy of Lyndon Johnson and the foreign and domestic activities of his Republican successor, Richard Nixon. This type of "institutional opportunism," it should be noted, has not been a malady limited only to liberal Democrats. Starting with the Nixon presidency, some conservatives began to embrace presidential power in domestic politics as well as in the struggle against imperial communism.[102] Conservative Dartmouth Professor Jeffrey Hart in 1974 argued in *National Review* that it was time for conservatives to embrace executive hegemony while a conservative Republican was in the White House and perhaps in a position to undo some of the liberal sins of his predecessors.[103] This trend accelerated significantly during the presidency of Ronald Reagan, with many conservatives becoming nearly gleeful at the self-destruction of Congress and exceedingly jealous of presidential prerogatives.[104]

Conclusion

The whiggish distrust of executive power, especially unified executive power, led to an understanding of representation that basically excluded the presidency from any share in it. The whiggish doctrine of representation leads to a power prescription weighted heavily in favor of Congress and to the delegitimization of any energetic and independent executive authority. With the emphasis on the legislature, deliberation is valued as much as is political action.

On the other hand, the modern model of representation (Wilson's and Neustadt's) rejects government by deliberation in favor of governmental activism. To this end an energetic presidency is needed, not to facilitate the deliberative process of representative government but to make his will the government's and thereby to unite the separate institutions of government in a vigorous activism in the name of the public good. Under such a model, the other elected representatives of the people, combined in the two houses of Congress at the other end of the avenue, are reduced at best to the handmaids of the president and at worst to outright obstacles in the way of progress and the march of the people's will through their government. The complex representation of the Constitution is replaced by the unitary representation of presidential leadership, with the other institutions loosing legitimacy and their constitutional prerogatives subverted in the name of majority rule.

The two understandings represent dangerous ends of the spectrum of representative government. Their coming to the fore at one time or another in American history has led to our unhealthy tendency to swing from prescriptions for presidential power to calls for congressional supremacy and back again. The swing during the 1960s and 1970s from the "cult of the presidency" to the fear of "the imperial presidency" represents one recent example of the dangerous instability with which these two perspectives leave us.

A particular problem with both these positions is that they lend themselves so easily to institutional opportunism and partisanship. As we have seen, these two understandings of representative government offer deliciously inviting fruits to those bent on implementing certain policy goals and values. Our history of fluctuation between these two understandings has made it even easier to embrace one institution over the other in the name of policy, efficiency, or democratic rule. Politics is about the struggle over means and ends of public policy, and it is on this level that ideological struggles are meant to take place. The problem arises when these struggles ascend to the realm of constitutionalism and the institutional system established in our fundamental law.

Arguments on behalf of congressional representation and a legislatively centered federal system have led to corresponding arguments in favor of a resurgent presidency to "whip" Congress into line in the name of the people. This is the pulse of our understanding of representative government in America. Originating in the centuries-old philosophical and practical debates on free government and fueled by the immediate policy goals of our politicians, pundits, and scholars, these two arguments have periodically pulled America toward one extreme or the other. We might well wish to consider whether or not a more stable understanding of political representation and representative institutions in place of this pulse would render better service to the American republic.

6

The Constitutional Presidency: Conservative Scholarship and Energy in the Executive

Raymond Tatalovich, Travis Cook, and Scott Yenor

In this chapter we will assess twentieth-century "conservative" conceptions of the presidency against the backdrop of the "liberal" activist orientation that dominated the study of the presidency throughout the 1960s and beyond. By conservative, we speak not in a strictly partisan or ideological sense, but rather in terms of a constitutionally steeped conception of office in which limited government, separation of powers, and faithful adherence to the Constitution and the rule of law take precedence over personal skill, political popularity, and the cult of personality. In this sense, it could be argued that much of the groundwork for modern "liberal" conceptions of the presidency was laid by Republican President Theodore Roosevelt, whereas the "conservative" constitutionalist reaction to Roosevelt was best articulated by his hand-picked Republican successor, William Howard Taft.

Edward S. Corwin illustrates the difficulty of classifying twentieth-century thinking on the presidency. Corwin was hired personally by Woodrow Wilson to teach at Princeton University and wrote in support of Wilson's presidency and Franklin Roosevelt's New Deal policies and Court Packing Plan. Yet Corwin's conception of the presidential office was steeped in a constitutional understanding of its origins and development that fits well with Taft's traditionalist, constitutionally oriented school of thought. If not wholly "conservative," Corwin was undoubtedly more comfortable with Taft's conservative conception of the presidency than with modern Neustadtian notions of an intensely personalized, power-seeking, and aggrandizing presidency. Indeed, Corwin's work so frustrated Richard Neustadt's more grandiose expectations as to what the office of the presidency should be that Neustadt took up the task of providing his now famous alternative conception of presidential power. As will be shown below, Corwin, unlike Neustadt and other modern writers, did not elevate personal skill or charisma over the constitutional foundations of the office, though he did acknowledge that the precedents of "popular" crisis-driven presidents are left for all presidents to draw on.

In the traditional sense of conservatism, we are speaking of a balanced tripartite system of government in which each branch has significant power. Conservatives like Corwin (or Taft for that matter) do not necessarily hold a restrictive view of presidential power and may, as Corwin did, subscribe to broad notions of prerogative authority. Nor are conservatives inherently opposed to broad assertions of executive authority, as for example, Taft's support for the concept of executive privilege and broad power over appointment and removal of executive officers. We will begin with a brief discussion of the modern conception of presidential power that came to dominate the literature on the presidency in the 1960s and beyond. The "glorification" of the office of the presidency, and more to the point, of individual activist presidents, that dominated the scholarly perspectives of Richard Neustadt, Louis Koenig, Wilfred Binkley, and others during the 1960s, shaped what was perhaps the most prolific and highly influential collection of books ever written on the American presidency.

We will then step back to the beginning of the twentieth century to examine the classic debate over expansive and conservative conceptions of the presidency that found expression in the writings and comments of Theodore Roosevelt and Taft, respectively. Though both Republicans, Roosevelt and Taft were at polar extremes in their philosophical views of the presidential office. In many ways, Roosevelt represented the modern "liberal" thinking of an invigorated and highly personalized conception of presidential power. Taft, on the other hand, epitomized the classical conservative thinking of deference to the Constitution and to the rule of law. Despite this conservative orientation, however, we will show that Taft in some areas held a more Hamiltonian view of presidential power than might commonly be presumed.

The chapter will continue with a discussion of the academic writing of the distinguished constitutionalist, Edward S. Corwin, and of one of Corwin's contemporaries, C. Perry Patterson. Both Corwin and Patterson were wed to a traditional/constitutional view of office and both, but especially Patterson, became alarmed with the personalization of the presidential office in the mid-twentieth century.

Finally, we will conclude with a discussion of the diverse spectrum of "conservative" thought on the presidency as reflected in the considerable overlap between many Reagan-era conservative intellectuals and their liberal activist counterparts of the 1960s era. Both goups of intellectuals came to celebrate the primacy of presidential leadership and lament the frustrating intrusions of what they perceived as meddlesome Congresses.

The Liberal Bias of 1960s Perspectives on the Presidency

In 1971, political scientist William Andrews wrote an insightful essay critiquing the "bumper crop" of books that appeared on the presidency in the decade of the 1960s. Political scientists and historians had "burst forth with a veritable barrage of elaborate encomiums to the American presidency," Andrews noted.[1] "Some of the most distinguished members of the profession tied themselves in knots explaining why the presidency was superior to Congress and should, therefore, wield commensurately greater power."[2]

Of the eleven major books written on the presidency in the 1960s, the authors reached near unanimous accord that "the presidency was the seat of virtue and the principal seat of power in our governmental system. Because of its virtue," they contended, "its power almost inevitably would be wielded for the welfare of the nation." The literature of the 1960s "allowed for no other national political or governmental leadership than the President's. So far as Congress entered the picture at all, it followed the president."[3] Herman Finer went so far as to describe the presidency as "the incarnation of the American people in a sacrament resembling that in which the wafer and the wine are seen to be the body and blood of Christ."[4]

Scholars in the 1960s lamented that the power of the presidency "was exceeded by the requirements of our national problems. Therefore, they urged that its authority be increased and suggested ways to do so." Louis Koenig, for example, proposed political and institutional reforms "to make the presidency stronger and more capable of meeting its responsibilities."[5] Maximizing the power of the presidency and of the national government was the primary focus of Richard Neustadt's *Presidential Power*. "The more determinedly a President seeks power, the more he will bring vigor to his clerkship. As he does so he contributes to the energy of government."[6]

The glorification of the presidency extended well beyond domestic affairs into the realm of foreign and national security policy. Dwight D. Eisenhower's deference to Congress in asking for resolutions authorizing potential American intervention in the Quemoy-Matsu crisis of 1955 and in the Middle East in 1958 "was attacked as an abdication of responsibility and as a dangerous precedent for the erosion of presidential authority." Eisenhower was faulted by Clinton Rossiter for his "modest conception of the Presidency."[7]

Vietnam and Watergate changed scholarship on the presidency in the 1970s, though not dramatically or permanently. Even *Imperial Presidency* author Arthur Schlesinger Jr. refused to "renounce the idea of an affirmative Presidency or surround the President with hampering restrictions."[8] Why had there been such adulation of the presidency in the scholarship of the 1960s? Andrews is quick to point out that much of the pro-presidency bias was rooted in a partisan political consensus. All of the 1960s writers, Andrews noted,

> were deeply touched by and, in most cases deeply involved in the New Deal of the 1930s. They elevated that experience into a general constitutional theory without really considering, with reference to fundamental principles, the extent to which it was generalizable. They were, in a very real sense, victims and perpetrators of what [Thomas] Cronin has called the "Franklin Roosevelt halo-effect." This resulted partly from national experiences in which they shared, but, even more, from their very special involvement in those experiences.[9]

The liberal/Rooseveltian bias that dominated the textbook presidency of the 1960s is easy to explain given the political background of the major authors of that generation. Koenig, for example, held four different appointments in the Roosevelt and Truman administrations. Neustadt, whose father had served in the Roosevelt administration, had himself served for eight years in the Roosevelt and Truman administrations, including service as a special assistant to the president. Rexford Tugwell, the author of *The Enlargement of the Presidency,* served as one of Roosevelt's elite "Brains Trusters" and as the president's principal adviser on agricultural economics. Francis Heller, the author of *The Presidency: A Modern Perspective,* assisted Harry Truman in preparing his Memoirs and served on the Board of Directors of the Harry S. Truman Institute.

In the discussion that follows we will chart the earlier twentieth-century alternative to the modern, personality-centered school of thought on the American presidency that became the accepted paradigm of academics during the 1960s and beyond. We will assess some of the distinguishing characteristics of pre-1960s writing on the presidency and explain how earlier "conservative" thinking informs our understanding of the office and its powers.

Taft and Early Twentieth-Century Conservatism

After losing his bid for reelection to the presidency in 1912, William Howard Taft accepted the position of Kent Professor of Constitutional Law at Yale University. It was there that Taft authored a significant and revealing treatise on presidential power entitled *Our Chief Magistrate and His*

Powers. Even the title of Taft's book had a legal ring to it, reflecting the fact that the preponderance of Taft's pre-presidential career—twenty years to be exact—had been in legal and judicial positions.[10]

"Coming from such a legalistic–judicial background," Taft biographer Donald Anderson writes, "it is little wonder that he became the most judicial of our presidents and, paradoxically, one of the most political of our Chief Justices."[11] Taft came to the presidency "without ever having run for a major legislative or judicial office." His career, Anderson notes, "had not required the development of skills in campaigning or in manipulating public opinion, or as Taft himself would have expressed it, 'playing to the gallery.' "[12]

Anderson ascribes to Taft's conservative legacy four key principles: a strong belief in constitutional democracy and the "rule of law"; a firm commitment to the doctrine of separation of powers; a strong belief in parties as essential instruments of democracy; and a vigil against the dangers of radical majoritarianism.[13]

With regard to the first principle, Anderson notes, "Taft believed deeply in the 'rule of law' rather than the rule of men. For many today, the 'rule of law' has become merely a cliché, but, for Taft, it was his religion; it was his life!" Its effect on Taft's perspective cannot be overemphasized, Anderson suggests.

> He may have worshipped Law too deeply for his own public good (certainly Roosevelt and the Progressives thought so), but his public record cannot be properly understood without recognizing the critical role this belief played in guiding his public career. The "rule of law" meant, of course, constitutional democracy, always with the emphasis upon the word "constitutional" rather than the word "democracy." Democracy was only tolerable if it was restrained through appropriate constitutional devices to prevent majorities from abusing their powers.[14]

The second component of Taft's conception of office, his respect for the constitutional separation of powers and checks and balances, was equally essential. Yet, while Taft is correctly associated with the so-called constitutional or literalist conception of the presidency, "he was not, in fact, an advocate of a weak presidency." As Anderson writes: "He believed in a strong presidency, operating, however, in a balanced system with equally strong legislative and judicial branches." A presidency that dominated the other two branches of government "was not desirable in his view; in fact, it was a long term threat to our liberties."[15] Anderson adds: "If Taft is our only president to have spent more time worrying about the power and prestige of the judiciary than of the presidency itself (and he was!), it is not because he was somehow too weak, but because he was alarmed by progressive threats to the maintenance of a strong independent judiciary. . . ."[16]

This is not to suggest that Taft in any way subordinated executive authority to that of the judiciary or the legislature. Taft thought, for example, that the "great problem that is forcing itself upon the attention of the American people is the method of restraining the extravagance of legislatures and of Congresses." In championing the need for an executive budget, Taft believed that "the Chief Executive, because he is the one whose method of choice and whose range of duties have direct relation to the people as a whole and the government as a whole, is most likely to feel the necessity for economy in total expenditures."[17]

Taft also was a strong defender of the president's power of appointment, and of removal, of executive officers (as later elaborated in his ruling as Chief Justice in the case of *Meyers v. United States*). The Framers of the Constitution, Taft wrote, gave the president "the power of absolute removal, and they placed in his hands the control of the action of all those who took part in the discharge of the political duties of the executive departments.[18]

In warmaking, Taft likewise defended presidential authority. Congress can declare war, "but with the army and the navy," Taft wrote, "the President can take action such as to involve the country in war and to leave Congress no option but to declare it or to recognize its existence." The use of military forces in Central America to defend U.S. citizens and property, Taft suggested, "grows not out of any specific act of Congress, but out of that obligation, inferable from the Constitution, of the government to protect the rights of an American citizen against foreign aggression. . . ."[19]

Taft's view of the president's foreign affairs powers in general was quite broad. Echoing Hamilton's refrain about presidential prerogative (and anticipating the Supreme Court holding in *Curtiss-Wright Export Corporation v. United States* some twenty years later), Taft argued that the president "and he alone is the representative of our nation in dealing with foreign nations. When I say he alone, I mean that it is he to whom the foreign nations look."[20]

The third principle guiding Taft's thinking on the presidency, the notion that political parties were "critically important to the survival of popular government," also carried great weight. As Anderson notes:

> Without parties, Taft believed there could be no effective way in which the people could transform their private opinions into public policy. His whole public career is a testament to his loyalty to the Republican Party and its principles. He believed that citizens would have to subordinate their own personal views to those of the larger party organizations if they were to be effective in realizing their most important goals. . . .
>
> . . . When Taft saw progressive Republicans challenging the traditional norms of party loyalty and refusing to subordinate themselves to the larger organization and its way of doing things, a falling out with them was inevitable.[21]

Finally, Taft believed that unqualified majoritarianism would impede the deliberative process and was, consequently, both unsafe and unwise. Taft believed that "the Voice of the People is nearer to the Voice of God than any other human decision."[22] But as Anderson notes,

> The catch was that the Voice of the People had to be channeled and refined through our constitutional system, including an independent judiciary with the power of judicial review, before decisions approximating the ideal of justice could emerge. To the extent that progressives threatened to short circuit the deliberation required by our institutions, Taft believed their proposals for more direct democracy would inevitably bring popular disappointment and disillusionment with the political process.[23]

Given Taft's acceptance of a broad scope of presidential authority as established through constitutional provision and precedent, why is Taft viewed as a "conservative" relative to the progressive Theodore Roosevelt? The answer rests largely in Taft's complete disdain for the sweeping assertions of executive authority made by Roosevelt. The early twentieth century intellectual debate between Taft and his presidential mentor captures the essence of the different conceptions of presidential power that continue to shape philosophical debate on the scope of presidential power at the end of the twentieth century.

Taft's constitutional-literalist conception of the presidency provides a marked departure from the populist "stewardship theory" of leadership coined by Roosevelt. As Roosevelt put it in his autobiography:

> The most important factor in getting the right spirit in my administration, next to the insistence upon courage, honesty, and a genuine democracy of desire to serve the plain people, was my insistence upon the theory that the executive power was limited only by specific restrictions and prohibitions appearing in the Constitution or imposed by the Congress under its constitutional powers. My view was that every executive officer in high position, was a steward of the people bound actively and affirmatively to do all he could for the people, and not content himself with the negative merit of keeping his talents undamaged in a napkin. I declined to adopt the view that what was imperatively necessary for the nation could not be done by the president unless he could find some specific authorization to do it. My belief was that it was not only his right but his duty to do anything that the needs of the nation demanded unless such action was forbidden by the Constitution or the laws.[24]

As a legalist and constitutionalist, Taft could not accept the sweeping pretensions of power outlined in Roosevelt's stewardship theory. In his famous reply to Roosevelt, Taft wrote:

The true view of the executive function is, as I conceive it, that the president can exercise no power which cannot be fairly and reasonably traced to some specific grant of power or justly be implied and included within such express grant as proper and necessary to its exercise. Such specific grant must be either in the Federal Constitution or in an act of Congress passed in pursuance thereof. There is no undefined residuum of power which he can exercise because it seems to him to be in the public interest. . . . The grants of executive power are necessarily general in terms in order not to embarrass the executive within the field of action plainly marked for him, but his jurisdiction must be justified and vindicated by affirmative constitutional or statutory provision, or it does not exist.[25]

In arguing that there was no undefined residuum of power that presidents could exercise when it seemed to them to be in the public interest, Taft was, in a sense, bucking the intellectual tide that already had begun to take hold in the thinking of his successor, Wilson. Yet, Taft remained steadfast in his conservative conception of office. Taft viewed the notion that presidents should "play the part of a Universal Providence and set all things right" as an unsafe doctrine that could threaten individual rights.[26] The president, Taft observed, "cannot make clouds to rain and cannot make corn to grow; he cannot make business good."[27] In his most pointed attack on Roosevelt, Taft had this to say:

One who so lightly regards constitutional principles and especially the independence of the judiciary, and who is so naturally impatient of legal restraints, and of due legal procedure, and who has so misunderstood what liberty regulated by law is, could not safely be entrusted with successive Presidential terms. I say this sorrowfully, but with the full conviction of truth.[28]

Former President Calvin Coolidge introduced a more practical perspective into the classic debate on the scope of presidential authority waged between Taft and Roosevelt. In summarizing the essential elements of both arguments, Coolidge interjected a pragmatic twist, stating that while the president exercises his authority in accordance with the Constitution and the law,

He is truly the agent of the people, performing such functions as they have entrusted him. The Constitution specifically vests him with executive power. Some Presidents have seemed to interpret that as an authorization to take any action which the Constitution, or perhaps the law, does not specifically prohibit. Others have considered that their powers extended only to such acts as were specifically authorized by the Constitution and the statutes. This has always seemed to be a hypothetical question, which it would be idle to attempt to determine in advance. It would appear to be better practice to wait to decide each question on its merits as it arises. Jefferson is said to have entertained the opinion that there was no constitutional warrant for enlarging the territory of the United States, but when the actual facts confronted him he did not hesitate to negotiate the Louisiana Purchase. . . .[29]

However, "for all ordinary occasions," Coolidge suggested, the powers "assigned" to the president "will be found sufficient to provide for the welfare of the country. That is all he needs."[30]

Coolidge's astute observations capture the philosophical dimension of the debate between Taft and Roosevelt, while recognizing a more expedient and practical dimension to presidential decisions. However, these philosophical differences had significant impact on policy and on presidential pronouncements concerning policy. Barbara Hinckley notes, for example, that the contrast between Taft's and Roosevelt's conceptions of office is reflected in their inaugural addresses. Theodore Roosevelt's portrayal of the government, according to Hinckley, "is centered in a president who speaks so completely for the nation and the American people that they do not need to be mentioned separately." Taft's depiction of government, on the other hand, "is more complex and dispersed among many different actors."[31] Congress, for example, receives four mentions in Taft's inaugural address. The Constitution is the subject of four sentences, and the executive departments and commissions are referred to six times by Taft. Roosevelt's inaugural address, in contrast, contains far fewer references to other parts of the government. Tellingly, Franklin Roosevelt mentions even fewer non-presidential actors than his cousin Theodore. Indeed, Hinckley finds that FDR's inaugural addresses have fewer mentions of non-presidential actors than any president of the twentieth century (through 1990).

Franklin Roosevelt's sole reference to the Constitution, which occurs in his first inaugural address, is framed in the context of the possible need to take "extra-constitutional actions to meet the emergency" at hand. He speaks of the people "as a trained and loyal army willing to submit their lives and property to a leadership aimed at a larger good."[32]

Hence, in contrast to Taft's conception of power "carefully limited by a written Constitution," Franklin Roosevelt speaks of a broad, potentially "extra-constitutional" power "given by the people to an individual leader, who accepts it without condition."[33]

Corwin and the Mid-Twentieth-Century Constitutionalists

Corwin is perhaps the most noteworthy of the twentieth-century constitutionalists writing on the American presidency. In Corwin, we find elements of the conservatism of Taft, particularly in the defense of a tripartite system of separation of powers and in the rejection of highly centralized and intensely personalized notions of presidential leadership. Yet Corwin, even more than Taft, was Hamiltonian in his defense of broad, constitutionally rooted presidential authority and of an expansive notion of prerogative. "The fact is," Corwin wrote, "that what the Framers had in mind was . . . the 'balanced constitution' of Locke, Montesquieu, and Blackstone, which carried with it the idea of a *divided initiative in the matter of legislation and a broad range of autonomous executive power or 'prerogative'"* (italics in original).[34]

Corwin wrote his seminal work on the presidency in 1940 (the 4th edition came in 1957) as "a study in American public law" focusing on the "development and contemporary status of presidential power and of the presidential office under the Constitution."[35] The Constitution and legal developments lie at the heart of Corwin's analysis of presidential power; he scrupulously details the constitutional language and interpretations by presidents and courts over time. It was this emphasis on constitutionalism that caused Neustadt to author his *Presidential Power*[36] as essentially a rebuttal of Corwin's position.

According to Corwin "the history of the presidency is a history of aggrandizement, but the story is a highly discontinuous one." In Corwin's view, force of personality clearly matters in shaping the presidency, not just short-term but also long-term, because a legacy is created: "Precedents established by a forceful or politically successful personality in the office are available to less gifted successors, and permanently so because of the difficulty with which the Constitution is amended."[37]

Throughout his discussion of legal precedents Corwin suggests that the Constitution endows the president with prerogative powers, which often are validated by Supreme Court rulings. As administrative chief "*the Constitution knows only one 'executive power,' that of the President, whose duty to 'take care that the laws be faithfully executed' thus becomes the equivalent of the duty and power to execute them himself according to his own construction of them.*"

Corwin's reading of the Constitution, like Taft's, is very broad when it comes to such matters as removal of executive officers of the government. Jackson's decision to remove his treasury secretary from office was, in Corwin's view "the *sanction provided by the Constitution for his power and duty to control all his subordinates in all their official actions of public consequence.*"[38] Similarly Corwin conceptualizes a far-reaching doctrine of executive privilege that withstands congressional investigation insofar as "this prerogative of Congress has always been regarded as limited by the right of the President to have his subordinates refuse to testify either in court or before a committee of Congress concerning matters of confidence between them and himself."[39]

As to foreign affairs, the constitutional grants of power to the president, the Senate, and the Congress create "an invitation to struggle for the privilege of directing American foreign policy" though the executive, as *The Federalist* tells us, has "certain great advantages" in terms of unity, secrecy, dispatch, and information. The precedents established by President George Washington with respect to the "sole organ" of diplomacy, recognition of foreign governments, a restricted reading of the Senate's advice and consent role in treaty-making, and the use of "personal" agents rather than ambassadors led Corwin to conclude that a Hamiltonian conception of office has prevailed. According to Corwin:

> Definite clauses of the Constitution make the President the organ of communication with foreign governments; and since Hamilton's "Letters of Pacificus," written in 1793 in defense of Washington's Neutrality Proclamation, few have ever ventured to contend that when acting in this capacity the President is the mere mouthpiece of policies determined upon elsewhere. What is more, Hamilton's contention that the "executive power" clause of the Constitution embraces a diplomatic prerogative that is plenary except as it is curtailed by more specific clauses of the Constitution has consistently prospered. The President today is not only the organ of communication of the United States with foreign governments—he is the *only* organ thereof; as such he is entitled to shape the foreign policies of the United States so far as he is actually able to do so within the conditions imposed by the acts of Congress; and more often than not Congress chooses to follow the leadership that his conspicuous advantages of position serve to confer on him.[40]

The bulk of Corwin's analysis is constitutionally grounded, and in these terms Corwin is clearly a champion of a strong presidency. When it comes to the personalization of power in the presidency, however, Corwin is of another mind. The most troubling of developments, in Corwin's judgment, is the widespread acceptance by Congress of the stewardship model of presidential leadership first articulated by Theodore Roosevelt. The stewardship theory "has been proved by events to have been prophetic of developments" mostly because Congress itself has become convinced of the theory. A system of checks and balances will not work where Congress willingly abdicates its basic law-making responsibilities.

The augmentation of presidential authority through the wide acceptance of Roosevelt's stewardship theory has been coupled with the emergence of the president as legislative leader. Corwin chronicles the broad arsenal of highly personalized leadership practices developed by presidents in dealing with Congress, such as the "bully pulpit," executive draftsmanship of bills for Congress, delivery in person of the State of the Union Address, the forging of interest group coalitions, and the use of well-timed veto threats. These techniques, Corwin notes, are dependent not so much on the formal authority of the office as the personality of the president. Hence, Corwin wonders "whether the presidency is a potential matrix of dictatorship [i.e., domination]; and, if it is, whether there is a remedy."[41]

More specifically, Corwin is sympathetic to the view of critics of the presidency who point out that "presidential leadership is discontinuous, not to say spasmodic; that it is too dependent on the personality of the President rather than on the authority of the office; that it is often insufficiently informed, especially as regards the all-important matter of administrative feasibility; and finally, that the contact between the President and Congress is most faulty, being, in fact, at the mercy of either's whim." Thus, at base, this dilemma boils down to two interrelated problems: "First, that of bringing presidential power in *all* its reaches under some kind of institutional control; secondly, that of relieving presidential leadership in the legislative field of its excessive dependence on the accident of personality and the unevenness of performance that this involves."[42] To rectify these problems, Corwin espoused a novel kind of cabinet.

Rather than supplant our presidential system with British-styled cabinet government with a prime ministership of sorts, Corwin advocated a modest reform (though Corwin termed it "a more radical proposal"): "*simply that the President should construct his Cabinet from a joint Legislative Council to be created by the two houses of Congress and to contain its leading members*. Then to this central core of advisers could be added at times such heads of departments and chairmen of independent agencies as the business forward at the moment naturally indicated."[43] This kind of cabinet would "be a body of *advisers*. But there are advisers *and* advisers." By this Corwin reasoned that collective decision-making within the executive would "be a body both capable of *controlling* the President and of *supporting* him; of guaranteeing that the things needing to be done would be done on time, but that, on the other hand, the judgment that they needed to be done represented a wide consensus, a vastly wider consensus that the President can by himself supply."[44]

Corwin was not in agreement with those who thought that "the problem of the 'Personalized Presidency' had already been solved . . . by the 'Institutionalized Presidency.'" President Eisenhower's "unprecedented" use of the cabinet and the executive office of the president was viewed with great favor by Corwin in the 1957 version of his book, but he doubted that the Eisenhower model could survive the 1950s. President Eisenhower's impact on the presidency is apt to be short-lived, Corwin suggested, because "there is a long-term trend at work in the world that consolidates power in the executive departments of all governments, first in the person of one individual, then in an 'administration.' The era of Roosevelt, Churchill, Stalin, Hitler, Mussolini" each, in Corwin's view, marked "a cornerstone of the national 'cult of personality.'"[45]

Corwin concluded that the "great accession to presidential power in recent decades" had been "signalized by the breakdown of the two great structural principles of the American Constitutional System, the doctrine of dual federalism and the doctrine of the Separation of Powers." Going hand-in-hand with these developments was "the replacement of the *laissez-faire* theory of government with the idea that government should make itself an *active, reforming* force" in the private economy. To accomplish their objectives, Corwin noted, presidents "have made themselves spokesmen" for this new outlook. They "have converted their parties to it," and "with the popular support thus obtained, have asserted a powerful legislative initiative." Yet Congress "has found it convenient to aggrandize" the president's new executive role enormously, "by delegating to him the power to supplement its measures by a type of sub-legislation called 'administrative regulations'" to the point of creating "a realm of presidential power of which the Framers had little provision. . . ."[46]

In Corwin's view, the first "exponent" of the aggrandized presidency was Theodore Roosevelt. But it was Franklin Roosevelt, Corwin believed, "who beyond all twentieth-century presidents put the stamp both of *personality* and *crisis* on the presidency. In the solution of the problems of an economic crisis—'a crisis greater than war'—he claimed for the national government in general and for the president in particular powers hitherto exercised only on the justification of war." Corwin ended his treatise on an ominous note: "Does the presidency, then, in the light of these facts, constitute a standing menace to popular government and to those conceptions of personal liberty to which popular government is, in part, traceable?" Corwin's reply is sobering:

> As matters have stood til the other day, presidential power has been at times dangerously *personalized*, and this in two senses: first, that the leadership it affords was dependent altogether on the accident of personality, against which our haphazard method of selecting Presidents offers no guarantee; and, secondly, that there is no governmental body that could be relied on to give the President independent advice and that he was nevertheless bound to consult. As a remedy calculated to meet both phases of the problem I have suggested a new type of Cabinet. At least, if a solution is to be sought in *institutional* terms, it must consist in *stabilizing* in some way or other the relationship between President and Congress.[47]

While Corwin took up the charge for controlling the personal reign of presidents through formal institutional devices, and applauded Eisenhower for his efforts to institutionalize the presidency, Neustadt took up his pen to argue exactly the opposite case. Neustadt urged John F. Kennedy to "deinstitutionalize" and "humanize" the presidency. Garry Wills, in his critique of Neustadt's formula for highly personalized and deinstitutionalized leadership, wrote:

> The Neustadt school maintained that the presidency is only what each President makes it, that the office is defined by the man, not vice versa. This has

led to the intense personalization of the institution. . . . This personalization creates charismatic expectations in noncharismatic times, to be followed by inevitable disappointment.[48]

Hence while Washington's authority "was lent, in diluted and diffused manner, to the constitutional procedures he affirmed by his resignation of power," Wills suggests that modern "charismatic" leaders find it all too easy to attempt to contrive a "crisis" atmosphere even when no crisis exists. And so it is with the Clinton presidency's succession of crises: a "national health care crisis" followed by a "Medicare crisis" and a "social security crisis," and so on.

Corwin was one of the first scholars to express alarm concerning the rise of the personalized presidency, but his commentary seemed mild in comparison to the indictment set forth by another scholar of the pre-1960s era— C. Perry Patterson. Writing some seven years after the first edition of Corwin's book, Patterson charged that the changing complexion of the American presidency had altered the entire political landscape. "We have changed our constitutional democracy into a political democracy," Patterson wrote.

> By this is meant that we have converted a limited into an unlimited democracy and, thereby, substituted an unwritten for a written constitution and a government of laws for a government of men. This means that the principles of the American Revolution, as the foundation of our constitutional system, have been destroyed and that we have returned to the principles of the British system.[49]

In response to the establishment of "the political hegemony of the President," Patterson recommended an institutional solution much like Corwin's. "Government by men, practically without constitutional limitation and primarily by the President (not as constitutional executive but as political executive) requires that the party system be made responsible by the establishment of a modified form of responsible cabinet government." Assessing the implications of the rise of the personalized presidency, Patterson added:

> If the party system has secured control of the Constitution, then the party system should be responsible to the American people through their representatives in the Congress. If party control has superceded constitutional control of the government and unless the American people control the party system, they will have both an unlimited and irresponsible government. Our problem now is to make an unlimited government responsible.

Thus, Patterson concluded, "responsible cabinet government is the best possible means in the absence of constitutional restraint to prevent the permanent establishment of irresponsible executive government in this country in the hands of one man."[50]

Patterson suggested that "the literary theory of the Constitution" had been overthrown by the Supreme Court whose rulings allowed "a fairly consistent nationalistic interpretation of the powers of the national government." Those powers may have originally flowed to Congress, in the first instance, but now resided in the executive. "The nationalization of the presidency has nationalized our governmental system," Patterson wrote. "As head of the nation, head of his party, mouthpiece of the American people, and political executive of the Government of the Day, he is in position to govern the nation. Whether he does or not is not a fault of the system but a matter of the personal capacity of the President."[51]

In reviewing the powers of the constitutional executive, Patterson observed that, beginning with Wilson, the authority to recommend messages came to include "the power to recommend drafted bills and to insist that they be enacted immediately into law without change" just as the veto "has changed from that of merely a constitutional check upon Congress to a positive and controlling agency of legislation." These changes and others led Patterson to conclude that the evolution of party government transformed the kind of political regime desired by the Framers. "The unity of the constitutional and political executive," Patterson observed, "was not provided by the Constitution and was not even anticipated by its Framers. The President envisaged by the Constitution is an exclusively constitutional agent, a nonpartisan adviser of the Congress. He was expected to be a Whig king, and in no sense was he to be the product of the instrument of politics." But party government has transformed the American polity into an "extraconstitutional system of government" marked by three principal ingredients: "(1) that it operates under an unwritten constitution of a strictly national character; (2) that it converts the personnel of all units of our government system into partisans and that as a result it controls the constitutional machinery of our system; (3) that the President is its political executive, and that it is the chief source of his power, adding additional force to his own constitutional powers and giving him a large measure of control over the constitutional powers of the Congress and the judiciary."[52]

In the conclusion to his book, Patterson assesses the impact of Wilson and the two Roosevelts in light of Alexander Hamilton's postulate "that the President has all executive power inherent in the nation subject only to the limitations of the Constitution." Following his review of their presidencies, Patterson observes: "A highly regulated and socialistic type of society forces centralization and requires an executive type of government for its administration. It cannot be operated on any other basis. Under present arrangments the President must be not merely the constitutional but the political head of the government."[53]

He minces no words in his final paragraphs, submitting "that our new constitutionalism dangerously concentrates too much power in the hands of one man, regardless of who the man may be. It is dangerous because no man can exercise this power in person. The most of it must be delegated to subordinates whom he is unable to supervise. This power finally gets so far away from the President that it becomes irresponsible."[54]

Reagan–Era Conservative Scholarship

The Reagan–Bush era spawned three well-known studies of presidential leadership by people associated with conservative and neo-conservative causes, including several members of those Republican administrations. Two were anthologies, *The Imperial Congress*[55] and *The Fettered Presidency*,[56] while the third, *Energy in the Executive*,[57] was authored by Terry Eastland (an official in the Reagan Department of Justice). Curiously, the views expressed in these works have more in common with the liberal textbook studies of the presidency in the 1960s than they do with the conservative views expressed by Taft, Corwin, and Patterson. Indeed, as Robert Spitzer has noted, the views of Reagan era conservatives are in many ways a retake on what liberals complained about forty years earlier. Whereas 1960s liberals objected to the efforts of congressional conservatives "to resist the advance of progressive presidential agendas," the conservatives of the 1980s were "rankled at congressional moves toward reassertion" of authority in the 1970s and 1980s and were frustrated when Democratic Congresses succeeded in amending or thwarting many of Ronald Reagan's initiatives.

Corwin and other mid-twentieth-century conservatives worried about Congress over-delegating power to the executive, and sought means, including the legislative veto, to make the executive responsible. Reagan-era conservatives, on the other hand, attacked the very principle of congressional oversight as meddlesome micromanagement impinging on executive discretion. Reagan-era critics also saw Congress as usurping long-established foreign policy prerogatives, citing the War Powers Resolution of 1973 and the Boland amendment limiting aid to the Nicaraguan Contras as prime examples. In the words of one critic, these acts reflect an implicit "assumption that Congress, as opposed to the Constitution, is the font of presidential power."[58]

Spitzer suggests that Reagan-era conservative writing on the presidency is deeply influenced by "ideology and partisanship." The focus, Spitzer suggests, may be predicated on policy and political expedience:

Liberal-conservative clashes over politics and policy are the legitimate stuff of American politics, but when that debate is cast in abstract, institutional terms involving the possibility of structural shifts between the branches of government, partisan motives must be identified and reconciled with the consequences of proposed changes. (After all, only a fool changes the rules of the game because of losing a contest or two.)[59]

To the extent that conservatives of an earlier era were concerned about actual policy outcomes, such as budgetary or economic issues, the focus was far less on substantive issues per se than on the larger institutional and legal relationships implicit in the separation of powers that impinge on policy. In contrast, modern conservatives like Eastland give more prominent attention to specific policies, as for example, Eastland's arguments against affirmative action.

Gordon Crovitz and Jeremy Rabkin suggest in their American Enterprise Institute volume, which includes essays by former Reagan administration insiders, such as Boyden Gray, that "the best solution," to dealing with a meddlesome Congress "is to build up the political strengths of the presidency, not to litigate the constitutional rights of the office." But Crovitz and Rabkin acknowledge the risks of relying on a politically based rather than a constitutionally based approach to leadership.

> The issue immediately becomes a direct confrontation between rival parties and competing partisan interests. Appeals are made to the cause of the president's followers, not to the prerogatives of office. This strategy looks most attractive to those persuaded that the president and his party can ultimately rally the most popular support; it looks least attractive to those who fear that the president will lose in such confrontations and carry to defeat not just his own policies but also the institutional preconditions for any president successfully implementing his policies; that is, both the president and the presidency will lose.[60]

This caveat notwithstanding, the editors ultimately come down on the side of politics, rather than prerogative. The most pointed defense of a Neustadtian-style politicization of the presidency in the Crovitz and Rabkin volume comes from Irving Kristol. Arguing that the political parties have become "more intensely ideological, more intensely combative," and "more unprincipled in their combativeness," Kristol suggests that the president must take on the Congress, most especially "this Congress," with Rooseveltian means.[61] "The president can learn from the example of Franklin Roosevelt." When faced with congressional resistance to his programs, Kristol notes, FDR "got his program through by defining the presidency not as one branch of the government but as the tribune of the people" and he "got most—not all—of his program through by going to the people and using popular pressure on Congress to achieve his ends. That is the only way that an executive under current circumstances can intimidate Congress." Because "Congress is a bullying institution," Kristol suggests, the president can "cope with this by being what we call populist. Roosevelt set the model for that by going to the people and building popular support."

Gabriel Prosser offers an argument quite similar to that of Kristol's in *The Imperial Congress*, edited by Gordon Jones and John Marini. Taking a page out of the Democratic Party script, Prosser cites Andrew Jackson as the new role model for Republican presidents. The president "must become the tribune of the people," Prosser writes.

> This is the only role that will allow him to effectively counter the enormous institutional clout of Congress. It was the role Andrew Jackson, correctly or not, assumed for himself, thereby drawing such vilification and outrage as would frighten most modern presidents. He did survive it, however, and his place in the history of the presidency might tempt a future chief executive to be as daring.[62]

Eastland's *Energy in the Executive* essentially extends the personal and political formula for power maximizing that Neustadt became famous for. The twist, of course, is that the president must champion conservative causes rather than the social welfare state of the New Deal. Eastland counsels the use of heroic means to achieve the ends of smaller government, suggesting that "Reagan demonstrated that the strong presidency is necessary to effect ends sought by most conservatives." Among those ends were marginal tax rates, tax reform, and an arms race that "exhausted the Soviet economy, hastening the end of the Cold War."

Eastland chides Reagan for signing the Independent Counsel statute, which Republicans (and now most Democrats) opposed. Eastland suggests that Reagan should have held firm in his opposition to the Independent Counsel law by following Jackson's example in his famous veto of the National Bank bill, rather than relying on the courts to defend the president's prerogatives. Jackson, in Eastland's view, was acting wisely and properly when he appealed directly to the people, over the heads of Congress (and the Supreme Court), to defend his position.[63]

Eastland and other Reagan-era conservatives cite two principal lines of argument for justifying political leadership by the president. First, they argue from political necessity. The public itself has come to expect the president to defend his policies and institutional interests with public arguments. Presidents are expected to put forward their "vision" of the public weal; presidents must therefore conform to the Neustadtian model of leadership because the public itself has been convinced of its legitimacy. This expectation has been enshrined in changes in the election laws during the 1970s which encourage candidate-centered campaigns. Failure to adapt to these changes would be political suicide.

Second, the Reagan-era conservatives purport to trace the legitimacy of popular presidential leadership back to the Constitution itself. Eastland, for example, denies that conservatives are merely bending to necessity by accepting strong presidential leadership:

> Cynics will be forgiven for thinking that conservatives have been attracted to a strong executive on purely instrumental grounds, for there have been few efforts on the part of conservatives to discuss the strong presidency in terms other than political self-interest. But if the only explanation conservatives have for their new faith in the presidency is pragmatic, they will find themselves bereft of principle and thus in sync with those many liberals, journalists, and academics who are impatient with governing forms and procedures.
>
> Conservatives definitely should embrace a strong executive, but for the best of reasons: the Constitution. For what the Constitution proposes to establish is limited government that can maintain the conditions of freedom against internal and external threat, administer the nation's laws, and encourage rational deliberation and choice on the part of a self-governing people. And the presidency it regards as necessary for achieving this government . . . is a strong one. Or, as Alexander Hamilton preferred to say in the vocabulary of his time, an energetic one. As Hamilton succinctly stated the matter in the *Federalist Papers*, "energy in the executive is the leading character[istic] of good government."[64]

Like the liberals of the 1960s, Reagan-era conservatives see the need for strong presidential leadership if government is to be effective. The trick is to reconcile the traditional conservative mistrust of the personalization of power, as expressed in the work of Taft and Corwin, with the newfound respect for Jacksonian and Rooseveltian mores of leadership in the writings of Kristol, Eastland, and others.

As recent experience has shown, presidents are at least as likely to consult the sudden breeze of passion reflected in a public opinion poll or focus group as they are to articulate a thoughtful agenda based on the considered interests of the nation. Paradoxically, reliance on presidential leadership as a governing strategy can discourage a president from providing the independent leadership intended by the founders. Acceptance of the premises of poll-driven presidential leadership also adversely affects the deliberative process in Congress. If polls or other immediate manifestations of public opinion are seen as the only legitimate source of public authority, then the rationale for a separated system vanishes. In this light, students of the presidency may want to revisit the old fashioned conservative approach to leadership that Taft envisioned. Too much emphasis on the cult of personality, as writers like Corwin and Patterson suggested nearly a half century ago, is imprudent and unwise.

7

The Formation and Use of the Cabinet

Shirley Anne Warshaw

Perhaps the most intriguing part of the president's advisory structure is the cabinet. Although presidents have turned to personal friends, kitchen cabinets, and more recently to White House staff for policy advice, the cabinet has remained one of the primary sources of policy information for presidents. As presidential scholar Henry Barrett Learned noted in his seminal study of the cabinet, "The Cabinet's usefulness as an advisory board has of course varied from time to time in the past in accordance with the different personal elements of which it has been composed. . . . The Cabinet, however, could not be ignored for long by any of the Presidents."[1] This concept of the cabinet remains somewhat of a dilemma, because the cabinet has traditionally been a highly politicized component of the executive branch and cabinet secretaries are often unknown to the president prior to their appointment as cabinet officers. Some presidents have been more comfortable working with their closest political confidants than relying on their cabinet secretaries. Yet the depth of information that the cabinet officers control is essential to the decision-making capabilities of the president and those around him. Presidents are dependent on the information that the cabinet officers bring to the policymaking process.

This chapter examines the divergent approaches that have been used in appointing and utilizing the cabinet in the two hundred years from George Washington to Bill Clinton. As will be shown, the formation and use of the cabinet has changed significantly. The early practice of appointing individuals of significant political stature and independence to the cabinet corresponded with considerable deference by presidents toward the cabinet's judgment on key issues. In contrast, the modern practice of rewarding the diverse political base within the president's party has been accompanied by less reliance on the cabinet as a deliberative forum for decision-making. Although merit and stature continue to play an important role in the appointment process, political considerations such as loyalty to the president and to the party, geographic balance, reward for political and financial support, and diversity of social background have taken on increased significance over time. As noted below, variations in cabinet building strategy and in the role accorded to the cabinet by the president in the policymaking process have been influenced to a significant degree by the changing relationship of the president to Congress and the political parties, the changes in funding mechanisms for presidential campaigns, the growth in the federal bureaucracy, and the changes in the party structure broadening the base of political power.

Washington's Cabinet

When Washington was elected the nation's first president, he enjoyed considerable freedom in charting the direction of the newly created executive branch of the national government based on the overwhelming support that he maintained in Congress and with the nation as a whole. Throughout the nation's history, Washington remains the only president elected by unanimous vote in the electoral college. The political capital that Washington was afforded during the early years of the republic allowed him to chart the executive branch to his designs, a luxury afforded no other president.

Washington approached the development of his cabinet and the method with which he interacted with his cabinet with great caution. As the nation's first chief executive, Washington knew that he was creating structures and relationships which laid the foundation for future administrations to follow. Writing to a friend, he underscored the care with which he moved: "I walk on untrodden ground. There is scarcely an action the motive of which may not be subjected to a double interpretation. There is scarcely any part of my conduct which may not hereafter be drawn into precedent."[2]

One of the most important decisions that Washington made in his tenure in office was the formation of his cabinet. Washington's primary goal in building his cabinet was to reach out broadly to ensure that individuals of great stature and politically diverse sentiments were involved at the highest level of government. Washington chose Alexander Hamilton, a leading advocate of a strong and energetic national government, as his secretary of the treasury, and Thomas Jefferson, a strict constructionist of the Constitution and a strong proponent of federalism and decentralized governmental power, as his secretary of state. As presidency scholar Sidney Milkis notes:

Recognizing the need to invest his administration with talented and respected leaders whose presence would advance the acceptability of the new government, Washington sought the most admired people available to carry out its functions. Washington's three principal aides—Hamilton, Jefferson, and, in Congress, [James] Madison—formed a remarkable constellation of advisers; indeed, they became the nation's most important political leaders in the generation after Washington. Strong disagreements arose between these men, with Madison and Jefferson often allied against Hamilton. Washington deserves credit not only for recognizing their varied talents but also for yoking three such independent-minded men in a "single harness." His ability to do so and the general success that he achieved as an administrator helped "to plant in the minds of the American people the model of a government which commanded respect by reason of its integrity, energy, and competence."[3]

Whether strictly intentional or not, Washington's cabinet building also included geographic balance. Hamilton represented New York, Jefferson and Attorney General Edmund Randolph represented the Commonwealth of Virginia, and Secretary of War Henry Knox represented Massachusetts. The major regions of the country were thus represented in the Cabinet, ensuring that Washington heard the views of both northern and southern states.

The cabinet operated smoothly in the early months of its existence. "No rigid division of labor was established between the departments, nor were formal rules or strictly defined codes of behavior established to govern their internal operations. In general administration was ad hoc and personal."[4] Though the philosophical differences of Hamilton and Jefferson became more obvious over time, they were able to accommodate one another on important early issues. Hamilton wanted to ensure that Congress passed legislation that allowed the national government to pay the debts incurred by the states to foreign governments and, additionally, to pay the debts incurred by the states during the Revolutionary War. Congress was in full support of Hamilton's efforts to have the national government pay off debts to foreign governments by the states but was split on the legislation to have the national government pay off state debts from the revolutionary war. Southern states in particular opposed the latter. Jefferson proposed accommodation if Hamilton and the Federalists would support legislation allowing creation of the capital city on the banks of the Potomac River, rather than a more northern point. Hamilton agreed and both measures passed. The president's cabinet had worked in harmony to move major measures through Congress.

The harmony that began in the administration, however, failed to last long. When Hamilton wanted to establish a national bank in 1791, Jefferson and Randolph adamantly opposed the bank both within the cabinet meetings and within Congress. Jefferson was so bold as to aggressively lobby against the national bank in Congress, knowing that Hamilton had secured Washington's support for the proposal. In spite of Jefferson's bitter opposition, the bill passed and a national bank was created. The battle between

Hamilton and Jefferson continued throughout the remainder of Washington's first term. Two years later, when France and England exploded in a bitter war, Jefferson sought to have Washington send aid to France. As a former Minister to France, Jefferson implored Washington to support the new French government and return the support that France had given to the revolutionary cause in 1776. Hamilton opposed intercession in a foreign war and secured Washington's backing for a formal "Declaration of Neutrality" by the United States in 1793. Again, Hamilton had won Washington's support for his position, driving a further wedge into the working relationship of the cabinet.

Political tensions came to a head over foreign policy, and near the end of Washington's first term, Jefferson resigned from the cabinet, followed shortly thereafter by Randolph's departure. Washington had tolerated the politically diverse viewpoints in his cabinet, but he never intended to allow his cabinet officers to lobby Congress against his policies or to allow his cabinet officers to publicly argue about administration policies. The grand experiment in political balance was over. Never again would presidents try to create what today would best be described as a "bipartisan" cabinet to enhance their political standing in Congress. Cabinets since the Washington era have been composed overwhelmingly of members of the president's own political party, with few exceptions. Even Warren Harding, who told reporters that the most important criteria for his cabinet members was competence, injected that the cabinet would still "be a Republican cabinet!"[5]

The Jeffersonian Era

Richard Pious, in his discussion of the early cabinet, notes that Madison fought unsuccessfully at the Constitutional Convention of 1787 for a council of state to serve as an "interior check" on the president's exercise of executive power. The evolution of the cabinet in the early nineteenth century, Pious suggests, rendered the cabinet the "functional equivalent" of Madison's council of state. Jefferson, Madison, James Monroe, and John Quincy Adams all instituted forms of "cabinet government." "When an important decision was to be made," Pious observes, "the president would read a state paper outlining his proposed policy to the cabinet: if a majority could not support his policy, it would be modified, deferred, or scrapped."[6] Monroe, for example, used the cabinet as a sounding board for his seventy-page position paper on his opposition to signing laws passed by Congress providing for roads and other internal improvements. "The cabinet was divided" on the issue and "prevailed on Monroe *not* to send the document to Congress as part of his annual message."

Presidents, according to Pious, "did not make or implement policy without full discussion with the cabinet."[7] The "executive power" of the president, was, in effect, exercised "in commission." Jefferson described his utilization of the cabinet in this way:

> All matters of importance or difficulty are submitted to all the heads of departments composing the Cabinet: sometimes by the President consulting them separately and successively, as they happen to call on him; but in the gravest cases, by calling them together, discussing the subject maturely, and finally taking the vote, in which the President counts himself but one.[8]

The boldness of cabinet officers, generally unheard of in modern times, was due to the political independence that most cabinet officers brought to their positions. Presidents in the early Republic tended to choose for their cabinets men of significant public stature, most of whom had distinguished careers in the House and Senate. In policy terms, members of the cabinet often considered themselves co-equals to the president and believed they were free to express their views on issues, whether or not the view coincided with those of their colleagues in the cabinet or the president. Often presidents took no public positions on issues, leaving the cabinet officers free to develop their own positions and to freely express those positions. Cabinet officers rarely solicited the view of the president before expressing their own views or developing departmental policy in accordance with those views.

The independence of the cabinet officers was a product of the cabinet-building strategy of the era, which was predicated on the expectation that the nation's political leaders be included in the cabinet. Indeed, the vast majority of cabinet officers had served in the House or the Senate, and many had been prominent in the Philadelphia convention, or had similarly distinguished political careers. Paradoxically, this strategy led to a cabinet with political bases independent of the president and, therefore, who had the support to move forward in their own directions.[9]

Such was the case during the Monroe administration. General Andrew Jackson began a campaign against the Spanish in Florida in late 1817. Jackson wrote a letter to President Monroe stating, "Let it be signified to me through any channel that the possession of the Floridas would be desirable to the United States and in sixty days it will be accomplished."[10] Monroe failed to answer the letter, leaving Jackson to believe that the president's silence on the matter was a tacit approval to proceed, which he did. As Jackson began his military campaign in Florida, the cabinet soon became deeply divided, with Secretary of State John Quincy Adams supporting General Jackson and Secretary of War John C. Calhoun opposing General Jackson. Both Adams and Calhoun had entered the cabinet with distinguished careers in Congress and served in the cabinet with their own significant followings. Calhoun backed a strongly worded censure message in the House, which would have condemned Jackson's activities. The measure failed, but the Senate reported out a strongly worded report denouncing Jackson. In contrast to Calhoun's stand against Jackson, Adams declared that Jackson had acted in self defense to protect Florida from Spanish incursions. President Monroe allowed the public debate to continue between his cabinet officers, never rebuking either Calhoun or Adams for their positions. Monroe remained silent on the issue throughout the whole affair, allowing Calhoun and Adams to lead their own factions for and against Jackson.

The Age of Jackson and Political Reward

Divisiveness in the cabinet was often repeated during this era, as was vividly displayed during the Jackson administration a dozen years later. The Jackson cabinet was created through political necessity, to mollify the factions of a divided party and to reward political supporters. Unlike cabinets of the past, fewer cabinet officers in the Jackson cabinet were leaders in Congress or longtime leaders of established political dynasties. With the emergence of a new political party, the Jacksonian Democrats, an entirely new generation of political leaders was emerging. The cabinet positions were given to the new political leaders. Only Vice President John C. Calhoun and Secretary of State Martin Van Buren had been major political players in their own right. However, because the cabinet was quite diverse and was marked by fewer long-term political ties than past cabinets, internal wars often exploded within the group.

Both serious and comic examples exist of the public warfare that was waged within the cabinet, particularly during Jackson's first term. On the comic side was the divisiveness even within the social life of the president's cabinet. By tradition, the wives of the cabinet officers held dinner parties for the cabinet, with dinner and dancing followed by a retreat of the men into the library for discussions on matters of state. At one dinner party in 1831, hosted by Van Buren, the wife of Secretary of War John Henry Eaton collided with a general while on the dance floor. Gossip ensued that she was not fit to be a cabinet secretary's wife and did not have the social standing to be included in the traditional cabinet dinners. Mrs. Eaton, the former Peggy O'Neale, had been a barmaid who had become Eaton's second wife in 1829. She was not invited to subsequent cabinet dinners and her husband refused to attend without her. Jackson was forced to call a cabinet meeting, directing his cabinet officers to show greater sensitivity to Mrs. Eaton. "I will not part with Major Eaton," Jackson insisted, "and those of my cabinet who cannot harmonize with him had better withdraw, for harmony I must and will have."[11] Harmony in the cabinet, however, did not become the guiding principle of the Jackson years, as two more serious examples demonstrate.

Within a year after taking office, Jackson learned that Calhoun had opposed Jackson's military role during the Monroe administration. Jackson openly broke with Calhoun as a result of Calhoun's position in 1818 and refused to have further conversations with him. When members of the cabinet began taking sides in the matter, Jackson requested and received in 1831 the resignations of every member of the cabinet in an effort to reduce any allies Calhoun would have within the administration. The April 1831 cabinet changes included a total reorganization, with only the postmaster general retaining his position. The only cabinet member other than the postmaster general to retain a strong relationship with the administration was Secretary of State Van Buren, who was nominated ambassador to Great Britain.

The most severe crisis between Jackson and his cabinet occurred in 1833 when Jackson sought to remove federal funds on deposit in the Second National Bank of the United States and transfer them to a number of state banks in cities across the country. Jackson regarded the Second National Bank as a tool of big business, which had failed to adequately use its financial resources to support smaller business endeavors and to support loans to farmers in the western states. There was, in Jackson's view, a bias by the bank and its director, Nicholas Biddle, in favor of loans to the eastern elite corporations. After the election of 1832, Jackson called a cabinet meeting to discuss removing federal deposits from the bank. The cabinet was split on the issue, with the secretary of the treasury, Louis McLane, opposed to removing the deposits. Undeterred by opposition within his own ranks, Jackson reorganized his cabinet and appointed a new Treasury secretary, William J. Duane. But Duane also opposed removing the deposits and refused to follow Jackson's orders to do so. Duane was then replaced by Attorney General Roger Taney as treasury secretary who announced that public funds would no longer be deposited in the Second Bank of the United States. By the end of 1833 most funds had been transferred to state banks.[12]

Jackson's inability to ensure that the cabinet officers would act according to presidential direction was not unusual during the nineteenth century. There was little harmony within the cabinet and little control over cabinet actions by the president. Arthur M. Schlesinger, Jr. noted in *The Age of Jackson* that the cabinet "far from being an effective instrument of the executive . . . was a group of squabbling men, some in basic disagreement with the President, and one at least intent on defeating his policy."[13]

As executive–legislative relations deteriorated over Jackson's decision to withdraw the federal deposits, the idea of having members of the cabinet also serve in Congress was resurrected. This discussion had originally occurred during the Constitutional Convention but had been rejected as a violation of separation of powers. When the idea was reconsidered during the Jackson administration, some members of Congress argued that the cabinet-in-Congress proposal would ensure that cabinet officers such as McLane and Duane would be protected from abject firing for not acquiescing to unconstitutional presidential demands.[14] Jackson, as had Hamilton, saw the cabinet-in-Congress proposal as a violation of separation of powers and a compromise of executive power vested in Article II of the Constitution. The debate was short-lived and was not resurrected again until the 1880s.

Fence Mending in Lincoln's War Cabinet

Abraham Lincoln's war cabinet faced many of the same problems that Jackson's cabinet had over three decades earlier. Lincoln entered office as the head of a political party barely four years old, a party born of crisis and bitter dispute over the direction the nation should move with regard to slavery and secession. The Republican Party of 1860 was largely composed of factions, described by historian Burton Hendrick as a "party comprised of several groups, under chieftains personally hostile and full of jealousy and rivalry, who had come together upon one question only . . . to check the aggression (of Southern cotton planters to extend slavery into the territories) by political action."[15] To ensure that the leaders of the myriad factions of the party remained loyal to the new administration, Lincoln peppered his cabinet with party leaders and leaders of the antislavery crusade. Nearly all of the members of the cabinet had sought the Republican nomination in Chicago in May 1860 and considered themselves the political, if not intellectual, equals of Lincoln.[16] Senator William H. Seward of New York actually led Lincoln on the first two ballots at the Republican convention but failed to secure a majority of votes. Lincoln won the nomination as a compromise candidate. Once in office, Lincoln named Seward secretary of state, the most prestigious of cabinet appointments, in order to build bridges within the deeply divided Republican Party.

The intraparty wars of the Republican Party were soon eclipsed by the war between the states. Secession by southern states over states' rights and slavery became the central concern for the new administration. In his inaugural address in March 1861, Lincoln directly addressed the issue of secession by the southern states. South Carolina had led a group of southern states in January 1861, three months before Lincoln's inauguration, with the creation of the Confederate States of America. Lincoln resolutely asserted that there would be no compromise, that "we cannot separate. No State, upon its own mere action, can lawfully get out of the union."[17] The members of the cabinet knew at that point of Lincoln's firm commitment to maintaining the Union and ending the separatist movement of the southern states.

Only a month after Lincoln's inauguration the country exploded in civil war. The assault by southern troops on Fort Sumter in South Carolina began the bloodiest, most self-destructive years in American history. In July 1862, after nearly a year of fighting, Lincoln called together his cabinet and sought their approval of an emancipation proclamation for slaves. The cabinet, concerned about military reverses in recent months, persuaded Lincoln to delay the decision, which he did. Six months later, a delegation of radical Republican senators demanded that Lincoln reorganize his cabinet to gain support for more aggressive action in the war, including the issuance of the Emancipation Proclamation. Lincoln refused and assured the senators that the cabinet was behind him. Lincoln then resubmitted his Emancipation Proclamation to the cabinet, who again unanimously opposed it. Lincoln stood up, and announced that the vote was seven against, one for the measure. Because he was in favor of the measure, he pronounced it carried. Unlike Jackson's cabinet, there was little public dissent over presidential policies. All of the cabinet members supported a strong stand against the secessionist states, but differed privately on the strategies that should be employed. When Lincoln finally decided to move forward with the Emancipation Proclamation without his cabinet's approval, no public discourse emerged by the cabinet nor legislative outcries that the views of the cabinet were not fully considered.

The temporary control that Lincoln exerted over his cabinet failed to continue during the Johnson and Grant administrations. Cabinet members returned to the type of fierce independence that had characterized the Jacksonian era. Andrew Johnson, who oversaw the final peace between the Union and Confederate states, had managed to control the cabinet during the war years. But once reconstruction began, the cabinet became deeply divided over administration policies, with Secretary of War Edwin M. Stanton particularly aggressive in opposing Johnson. Stanton opposed Johnson's conciliatory actions against the southern states and refused to support Johnson's directives. Stanton, as did many Republicans in Congress, sought to impose harsh penalties on the southern states. A former New York governor and senator who had led the antislavery movement, Stanton wanted to remain in the cabinet as a voice against Johnson's policies. When fired by Johnson, Stanton refused to go.

Johnson fired Stanton for opposing his reconstruction policies, only to be attacked in Congress by the radical Republicans. Johnson was subsequently impeached (but not convicted) for firing Stanton. Eventually, Stanton resigned when the impeachment process had left Johnson powerless to move forward and Congress gained control of reconstruction. The battles that ensued between the cabinet and Johnson were largely the product of a Republican party that had failed to find common ground and remained splintered in its goals and objectives. The dominant wing of the party,

which included members of the Lincoln war cabinet, did not support Johnson's reluctance to punish southern states.

Managers for Grant's Cabinet

By 1868 the Republican Party had healed many of its wounds and united
behind war hero General Ulysses S. Grant for president. The cabinet that
Grant built reflected the relative harmony within the party and Grant's own
desire for command. Few members of the cabinet had national stature,
such as those in the Lincoln cabinet, and few had experience within their
appointed realms. Most were mid-level political and financial supporters,
rather than the party leaders or corporate giants. The cabinet built by President Grant was one of relative mediocrity, with no individual agendas to
steer public opinion away from the directions set in motion by the White
House. Cabinet choices largely reflected Grant's preference to manage the
government from the top down, as he had commanded the army. Senator
John Sherman, chairman of the Senate Committee on Finance, noted that
"the impression prevailed that the president regarded these heads of departments as mere subordinates whose functions he might assume."[18] Grant
controlled the decision-making structure of government with a small, informal group of advisors. This "kitchen cabinet" was dominated by powerful Republican senators who had moved Grant into politics and through the
nomination process. Policymaking was controlled by the kitchen cabinet
rather than the executive cabinet.

Grant remained involved in many departmental matters and, not surprisingly, had a relatively high turnover in his cabinet. Although cabinet officers
came and went with some regularity during the Grant administration, few
public confrontations occurred over policy differences. In fact, only one major event occurred that threatened stability in the cabinet. In 1876, one of
Grant's cabinet officers, Secretary of War William W. Belknap, was accused
of taking bribes for the sale of trading posts in Indian Territory. The House
of Representatives impeached Belknap but he resigned before the Senate
trial. Belknap was subsequently acquitted in a vote in the Senate, but only
because twenty-three of twenty-five senators who voted not guilty believed
that they could not convict a cabinet officer after resignation.

The Republicans and the Business Community

Administrations during the latter part of the nineteenth century reflected
Grant's view that the cabinet should be administrative rather than policy
leaders. President Benjamin Harrison continued the trend of having cabinet

officers with little or no national stature or congressional experience, and with little expertise in their field. When William McKinley was inaugurated in 1897, he nominated Senator William B. Allison of Iowa, chairman of the Committee on Finance, for his secretary of state in spite of Allison's complete absence of foreign policy experience. Allison's value to the administration was based on his strong alliance with the business community, which McKinley wanted to keep within the administration's fold, rather than his expertise in foreign policy. "In omitting to consider that the tactful financial expert [Allison] was inexperienced in foreign affairs," wrote McKinley's biographer, "McKinley reflected the national disposition to discount the need of special training for the conduct of international relations."[19] Allison, however, decided not to forfeit his Senate seat, which he considered more prestigious, for a cabinet position.

To reward the business community for their strong financial support in the election of 1896, most of McKinley's cabinet appointments came from business, industry, or banking as opposed to careers in the political arena. Even the secretary of war position, which was usually made from among individuals with a military background or from a defense-related congressional oversight committee, was given to Russell Alger, a businessman and financial contributor to the Republican Party. McKinley's secretary of interior, Cornelius B. Bliss, was similarly chosen for his financial contributions to the party. Bliss, a wealthy New Yorker, had served as treasurer of the Republican National Committee and had been a prominent fundraiser for the party. The McKinley era saw cabinet appointments becoming a political reward for financial support during the campaign. In a spoils system reminiscent of the Jackson era, McKinley rewarded financial support with cabinet appointments while Jackson rewarded cabinet appointments for political support.

Following the assassination of William McKinley by an anarchist in 1901, Theodore Roosevelt assured the nation that he did not intend to reshape the cabinet. "I at once announced," said Roosevelt, "that I would continue unchanged McKinley's policies for the honor and prosperity of the country, and I asked all the members of the Cabinet to stay."[20] Roosevelt made few changes in the McKinley spoils system, largely to ensure that the McKinley money tree supported his own presidential campaign in 1904. In keeping his pledge, little restructuring of the cabinet occurred until after the 1904 election, when Roosevelt captured the Oval Office through his own electoral mandate.

The cabinet that Roosevelt assembled continued the trend of having few political leaders and being dominated by business leaders. The most influential member of Roosevelt's cabinet was a McKinley holdover, Secretary of State Elihu Root, a corporate lawyer from New York City. Root had been brought into McKinley's cabinet in 1899 as secretary of war and then

moved to secretary of state by Roosevelt in 1905. As with most of the senior advisors in both the McKinley and Roosevelt cabinets, Root had not
been selected from the halls of Congress but had built a successful career
in the professional world.[21]

The changing climate of the cabinet in the late 1800s and early 1900s reflected the changing character of the political landscape. Presidential
campaigns involved millions of dollars and were dependent on large contributions from the business community. Marcus Hanna, McKinley's campaign manager, had secured contributions from Standard Oil, for example,
of $250,000 in the 1896 and 1900 elections.[22] These were significant sums
of money during this period of time, reflecting the escalating costs of presidential campaigns. The business community was accorded significant access through the cabinet as a reward for its financial support.

The cabinet of William Howard Taft followed the mold set by McKinley and
Roosevelt of incorporating prominent members of the business community
within the cabinet. Few members of the cabinet had direct political connections to the president, with the majority being "well seasoned with corporation
atmosphere," as one scholar described the membership of the Taft group.[23]

Wilson's Cabinet: Diversity Amid Disuse

Although Woodrow Wilson campaigned against the power of big business
in the world of politics, he followed the trend of his recent predecessors by
bringing corporate leaders into the cabinet. The number of corporate leaders, however, was less pronounced than it had been in recent administrations. Two of the wealthier members of the cabinet were William Redfield
and William Gibbs McAdoo. Redfield, the first secretary of the newly created Commerce Department, had built a personal fortune from his holdings
in iron and steel and had a brief career in the House. McAdoo, secretary of
the treasury, owned a company that built the first tunnel under the Hudson
River into New York City.[24] McAdoo later married Wilson's younger daughter, Eleanor, in 1914.

The number of cabinet officers with close political ties to Congress or
the national party was also less pronounced than in previous administrations. With few members of his cabinet to build bridges to Congress, Wilson revived a little used technique and began to deliver his State of the
Union address before a joint session of Congress.[25] Only Washington and
Adams had done so. But Wilson, who needed to forge stronger ties in Congress, saw the State of the Union address as an ideal opportunity to meet
with members of Congress.

The cabinet selection process had been managed by Wilson's campaign
manager, Colonel Edward House, a wealthy Texan who had built a strong

bond with Wilson during the campaign. After the election Wilson went on vacation with his family to Bermuda and gave House the task of assembling the cabinet. House's assignment was to forge a cabinet which would ensure support within political and financial circles, but would not be dominated by those circles. The cabinet that Wilson and House built included representatives from both the political and corporate worlds, but also representatives from academia, the press, and small business. In contrast to the cabinets of his predecessors, Wilson placed strong emphasis on the role of intellectuals in his cabinet. Appointees included Dr. David Houston, president of Washington University in St. Louis, Judge Lindley M. Garrison of the New Jersey chancery court, who was appointed secretary of war, and Josephus Daniels, editor of the *Raleigh News and Observer*, who was appointed secretary of the navy.[26]

Wilson's own insecurities led him to rely more greatly on trusted confidants like Colonel House than on his own cabinet. By 1914, Erwin Hargrove writes, House had become Wilson's "chief adviser and emissary on foreign affairs." Hargrove suggests that "the key to this relationship seems to have been House's understanding of Wilson's need for praise, reassurance, and devotion." Secretary of State Robert Lansing, on the other hand, though superbly trained and qualified, was the subject of Wilson's distrust because he refused "to give the kind of loyalty that Wilson demanded."[27] According to Hargrove, Wilson frequently "bypassed cabinet officials on important matters." Moreover, "he was too fearful of delegation and tried to do too much himself." In matters in which he had a personal interest, Wilson would let members of the cabinet do little. "In matters in which he had no interest," on the other hand, "he would let them do everything." Hargrove adds: "Wilson believed that the President alone must make and control foreign policy, governed only by public opinion and his own conscience. Thus, he often ignored expert advice when it challenged his own intuitive sense." In commenting on Wilson's "temperamental" defect and "one-track mind," Edward House wrote: "No one can see him to explain matters or get his advice. . . . The President does not know what is going on in any of the departments. . . . The President . . . seems incapable of delegating work to others."[28] Ultimately, Wilson made his decisions in seclusion "after lengthy, painstaking, and solitary deliberation."[29]

Roosevelt's Personalization of Leadership

The cabinet had made significant changes since Washington first used the body to bridge the political divisions that had arisen in the country. In the century and a half between Washington and Franklin Delano Roosevelt the cabinet had served various functions for presidents in addition to managing the executive agencies. Perhaps the most striking change that had emerged by 1933 when Roosevelt entered office was the move away from cabinets with strong political ties to Congress to cabinets with strong political ties to business and industry. The composition of the cabinet in the years before Roosevelt took office reflected the changes that had occurred in the political base of the presidency. In the early administrations in which Congress controlled the nomination of the president and the policymaking apparatus of the nation, significant numbers of cabinet members came from Congress. By the latter half of the nineteenth century, with the emergence of national nominating structures for president and a strong corporate influence in the nominating process, individuals from business and industry had gained a majority of the cabinet positions. The pattern of reliance on cabinet officers from corporate America began to subside with the election of Roosevelt.

When Roosevelt entered office in March 1933 he inherited an economic crisis that had plunged the nation into turmoil. The Depression of 1929 left the nation with millions unemployed, factories idle, and long bread lines commonplace. As he campaigned for president, Roosevelt built an elite group from academia and from think tanks to advise him on policy positions. The group became known as "the brains trust." Once in office, he continued to rely on the advice of the brains trust, placing some members of the group into his cabinet, while others remained part of the kitchen cabinet.

Roosevelt's cabinet was significantly different from that of his predecessors, for its dominant feature was political loyalty to the new president. He refused to include anyone in his cabinet that had not supported him during his campaign, including the nomination process. Secretary of the Treasury Will Woodin, for example, had defected from four decades in the Republican Party to support Roosevelt. That support was rewarded with a cabinet position. Each member of the cabinet brought his own strengths to the cabinet, with little commonality in the group except their political loyalty to the president.

Business was represented, but not by the major corporate or industrial leaders of the time. The cabinet included a farmer, a laborer, a social reformer, professionals, and the first woman to hold a cabinet position. Frances Perkins was named secretary of labor. It was also a cabinet that included geographic diversity, with each of the four regions of the country represented. The cabinet was one that Roosevelt "made for his own unique reason, independent of other choices, with no concern for the ease or difficulty with which those chosen could work together, with less concern for political philosophy than might have been expected, and with virtually no concern for the wishes of Democratic city bosses," noted one Roosevelt scholar.[30] Perhaps the best description of Roosevelt's cabinet was that it was built with representation from the heart and soul of the Democratic Party that had propelled Roosevelt into office.

Although cabinet departments retained considerable autonomy over policy, Roosevelt's highly personalized style of leadership, like Wilson's before him, placed the president at the center of all decisions and policies of import. Cabinet meetings "were not an important administrative mechanism" for Roosevelt.[31] "Our Cabinet meetings are pleasant affairs," Secretary of the Interior Harold Ickes commented, "but we only skim the surface of routine affairs."[32]

In essence, Roosevelt ran as much of the government as he could on his own, relying on trusted loyalists rather than his cabinet to get things done. As Hargrove notes, Roosevelt "ran the Departments of State and War through the undersecretaries and ignored his own Cabinet chiefs. He refused to name single heads of programs, for example, Lend Lease, and the War Production Board for a time, for fear that he would not be able to control basic decisions."[33]

Roosevelt had an uncanny ability to stay on top of dozens of important projects at a time, with key aides assigned, often in competition with one another, on the same matter. His administrative approach was, in the words of Stephen Hess, "organized chaos." Hargrove pointedly summarizes some of the key elements of Roosevelt's approach:

> He played Cabinet members and other top officials off against each other. None of them ever felt secure in his service. This insecurity was a function of his view of the Presidency. As he saw it, a President could never put his cards on the table. He had to keep his strategies to himself and leave alternatives of action open. He could never permit a Cabinet officer to commit him to a politically disastrous course of action. . . . He had to protect his Presidential power, even if it meant sacrificing them at times.[34]

Eisenhower and the Revival of Cabinet Government

When Dwight David Eisenhower took the reins of office he brought with him in the cabinet a group of individuals who could manage the burgeoning apparatus of the federal government. The federal government had seen massive changes in the twenty years since Franklin Delano Roosevelt had taken office, with dramatic increases in the size of the federal bureaucracy, federal budget, and federal programs. Eisenhower sought managers for his cabinet, with proven managerial skill over large organizations. Eisenhower biographer Stephen Ambrose describes the decision-making process that Eisenhower employed in choosing his cabinet.

> A major, critical part of presidential leadership, Eisenhower knew, was selecting the right men for the right jobs and working with them. He wanted com-

petent, proven administrators, men who thought big and acted big. Always impressed by successful businessmen who had made it on their own and knew how to run huge organizations, he sought out the high achievers, men he could turn to for advice and with whom he could share both responsibility and praise.[35]

The Eisenhower cabinet was similar to those of Republican presidents of the latter half of the nineteenth century and early twentieth century, such as McKinley, Roosevelt, and Taft, in which the business community dominated the composition. Eisenhower nominated George Humphrey, the head of the Nanna Corporation of Ohio, to serve as secretary of the treasury. Humphrey had been a financial supporter of Taft in 1952 and his selection served as a conciliatory gesture to the Senator Robert Taft wing of the Republican Party.[36]

Eisenhower's connection to corporate America was deeply rooted in his days as president of Columbia University in the late 1940s, when Averell Harriman donated his estate to the university for a think tank on foreign policy known as the American Assembly. Concerned about the direction the nation was moving in the post–World War II era, Eisenhower sought to bring together the leaders of American foreign policy to examine new possibilities in international policy. According to Travis Beal Jacobs, a historian whose father had worked on the American Assembly as a faculty member at Columbia University,

> Eisenhower's determination to launch the American Assembly . . . did have extremely important consequences that would be crucial when he decided to run for the presidency in 1952. Indeed, it is conceivable that his nomination would have been impossible without his assembly friends.[37]

The decision to include primarily wealthy corporate leaders in the cabinet reflected both the relationships that Eisenhower had built in his fundraising for the American Assembly and his belief that corporate leaders were the logical choice to run the multimillion dollar enterprises of the executive departments. Unlike some of his Republican predecessors, Eisenhower brought corporate America into the cabinet because he believed in their competence to run the departments rather than as a reward for political support. Eisenhower's selection for secretary of defense, for example, was Charles E. Wilson, who was chief executive officer of General Motors, the nation's largest corporation. Eisenhower explained his rationale for appointing Wilson in this way:

> He had a reputation as one of the ablest of our executives in big corporations. I sought an experienced man of this kind because of the huge procurement, storage, transportation, distribution, and other logistical functions of the De-

fense Department which, in my opinion, needed to be directed by experts. It seemed to me that a man of such qualifications could team up with professional soldiers to the great advantage of the nation.[38]

The cabinet that Eisenhower selected reflected his proclivity toward self-made men, much as he was.[39] It was, nonetheless, a cabinet weighted heavily in favor of wealth and included eight millionaires and one "plumber," Martin Durkin, the secretary of labor.

Although a career military man, Eisenhower was politically astute, and this adeptness is reflected in his cabinet appointment strategies. Eisenhower's concern for the political ramifications of his decisions is found in a letter that he wrote to Lucius Clay discussing his decision to appoint Douglas McKay as secretary of the interior.

> One of the controlling factors in the selection of McKay involved the matter of geography. It had become customary that the Secretary of the Interior should be appointed from an area west of the Mississippi (Ickes was an exception). Moreover, it was a delicate matter to pick the particular state from which the man should come, one reason being the perennial struggle over water rights between California on the one hand and several of the upper river states on the other. At the time the Hell's Canyon controversy was a bitter one and we felt that about the only states that we could consider were first Oregon or Nebraska, and secondly, the state of Washington or possibly the Dakotas. Since we wanted a man who had a record of political and business accomplishment, we fixed on ex-Governor McKay.[40]

Throughout his presidency, Eisenhower worked well with his cabinet officers, relying on them for the daily administration of the departments and advice on policy matters. The growing White House staff focused less on policy development than on creating internal procedures (Cabinet Secretariat), monitoring paperwork through the Oval Office (Chief of Staff), and dealing with congressional affairs (Office of Congressional Relations).

Eisenhower relied extensively on his cabinet in the development of policy. He believed that frequent meetings of the cabinet offered many advantages, not the least of which was to provide presidential direction in policy development and administration. Eisenhower also used the cabinet as a forum for voicing his own views on policy in order to rally the departments behind his position. Richard Fenno, in describing Eisenhower's use of the cabinet, noted that the president was eager to

> pass problems around for discussion among his advisors, listen carefully to their debates, and use them as a sounding board for his own ideas. He is apt, in other words, to do his thinking in the presence of others, in a group meeting. Most important of all, he frequently if not usually makes his final deci-

sion on the spot. When he wants to act, he wants to make certain that his decision is clear, understood by all and concurred in by all, conditions which are best secured in a meeting rather than afterward.[41]

Eisenhower entrusted his Cabinet with considerable authority for administrative matters while retaining direct control over all major policy decisions. Eisenhower's willingness to delegate was premised on his belief that cabinet members were committed to the administration's principles and would not be tempted by their own political agendas. In a letter to Henry Luce written near the end of his presidency, Eisenhower explained his philosophy of delegation:

> The government of the United States has become too big, too complex, and too pervasive in its influence on all our lives for one individual to pretend to direct the details of its important and critical programming. Competent assistants are mandatory; without them the executive branch would bog down. To command the loyalties and dedication and best efforts of capable and outstanding individuals requires patience, understanding, a readiness to delegate, and an acceptance of responsibility for any honest errors—real or apparent—those associates and subordinates might make.[42]

Kennedy, Johnson, and the American Establishment

When John F. Kennedy captured the White House in 1960, he assembled his cabinet with a broad spectrum of political and corporate leaders. With the exception of his brother, Robert F. Kennedy, who had managed his presidential campaign, Kennedy had few ideas of who to include in his cabinet. He knew he wanted to include several political allies, Stewart Udall of Arizona for interior, Governor Luther Hodges of North Carolina for commerce, and Governor Abraham Ribicoff of Connecticut for health, education, and welfare. After these initial appointments, Kennedy sought to broaden his administration by appointing a wide range of academics, corporate leaders, and members of the "American Establishment." Schlesinger describes the American Establishment as "the New York financial and legal community—that arsenal of talent which had so long furnished a steady supply of always orthodox and often able people to Democratic and Republican administrations."[43]

The cabinet that emerged included few people that knew each other and many who did not know Kennedy. This was quite similar to the Eisenhower cabinet, few of whom had met Eisenhower before their cabinet interviews. Kennedy's cabinet resembled Roosevelt's to a greater degree than Eisenhower's. Like Roosevelt, Kennedy created a somewhat eclectic cabinet, bringing together some of the nation's best minds from disparate backgrounds. Kennedy and Roosevelt also gave a somewhat bipartisan complexion to their cabinet by including Republicans in the mix of cabinet members. Roosevelt appointed two Republicans to his cabinet: Secretary of War Henry L. Stimson and Secretary of the Navy Frank Knox. (Eisenhower had continued the trend toward a bipartisan cabinet with the appointment of a Democrat, Secretary of Labor Martin Durkin.) Kennedy included Republicans C. Douglas Dillon as secretary of the treasury and Robert McNamara as secretary of defense.

Another similarity between the Roosevelt and Kennedy cabinets was their decision to oversee departmental activities from the White House. Once Roosevelt had successfully moved the Reorganization Act through Congress, creating the Executive Office of the President in 1939, he was able to build a White House staff to manage policy development. Cabinet officers often worked in concert with White House staff on policy issues, a practice made possible by the creation of permanent, professional staff in the White House.

Like FDR, Kennedy relegated the role of the cabinet to one of secondary importance in his administration. As his close adviser Theodore Sorensen noted:

> No decisions of importance were made at Kennedy's Cabinet meetings and few subjects of importance, particularly in foreign affairs, were ever seriously discussed. . . . There were no high-level debates, or elaborate presentations, or materials circulated in advance.[44]

By the time Kennedy entered office, the White House staff had grown substantially in size and had become an institutionalized structure for assisting the president. Under Kennedy, the White House staff often eclipsed the role of the cabinet in importance. Kennedy's increased reliance on a growing White House staff with great expertise was based in part on the president's preference for information undiluted by departmental bias. Consequently Kennedy, and Lyndon B. Johnson after him, relied heavily on ad hoc task forces rather than the cabinet for policy development. The primary role of the cabinet in the Kennedy administration centered on day-to-day management of the executive departments.

When Johnson moved into the presidency in November 1963 following Kennedy's assassination in Dallas, he retained Kennedy's entire cabinet. Johnson was following the mold set by other vice presidents who had assumed the mantle of office following the death of the president. But Johnson immediately broke the cordial relationship that Kennedy had built with his cabinet over political goals. As Johnson prepared for the 1964 election, he sought to cut the federal budget as a campaign tool to support his push for a balanced federal budget. Johnson called each cabinet member into his office and demanded that they justify in detail every cost in their budgets.[45] Many argued furtively for their departments, only to anger Johnson who was determined to reduce the budget. In general, Johnson considered members of the Kennedy cabinet committed to public service, able in their jobs, and committed to Johnson's priorities. He did not move to make any changes. Only days before his inauguration, as speculation swirled on new cabinet appointments, Johnson announced that there would be few changes. "One of the great legacies President Kennedy left me," said Johnson, "was the finest cabinet that any president could assemble."[46] Johnson continued to support the Kennedy cabinet even at the end of his administration. In 1967, when the press questioned how well Secretary of State Dean Rusk and Secretary of Defense Robert McNamara, both Kennedy appointments, had served the president, Johnson responded that they were outstanding appointees, "hard working, bright and loyal."[47]

When cabinet vacancies occurred, however, Johnson placed both political loyalists (such as John Connor, president of Merck and Company, who had worked tirelessly for the Johnson/Humphrey ticket) and nationally recognized experts (such as John Gardner on education) to run the departments. Johnson even chose Lawrence O'Brien, a Kennedy White House staff member and former member of Kennedy's Senate staff, to serve as postmaster general.[48] O'Brien had worked tirelessly in support of Johnson's 1964 campaign and delivered what Johnson believed were a considerable number of votes. The Johnson cabinet was not significantly different from the Kennedy cabinet, even with the inevitable changes. Both minimized corporate and political ties in favor of managerial skills, previous commitment to public service, and policy expertise.

The Postmodern Cabinet

The postmodern cabinet that began with Richard Nixon and continues to the present is one which is more cognizant of political considerations than previous cabinets, particularly with respect to building bridges to the president's own party. The choice of a vice president from a different wing of the party had been a frequently used tactic to build bridges within the party. However, as the number of cabinet positions increased with the expansion of cabinet departments in the latter half of the twentieth century, presidents have also used cabinet positions for party building activities. Nixon had George Romney, Jimmy Carter had Cyrus Vance, Ronald Reagan had Andrew Lewis, George Bush had Jack Kemp, and Bill Clinton had Warren Christopher. Each represented a different political wing of the party than the president and served to signal a reconciliation within the party.

The postmodern cabinet is also more cognizant of geographic, ethnic, and gender diversity. If one single description had to be made of the cabinets that have been named since 1968, it would focus on the concerted effort that every president has made to ensure diversity. Geographic diversity has been the most pronounced similarity in modern administrations, with every cabinet ensuring broad geographic representation. Some presidents have tried to reward states that have provided substantial electoral support with at least one cabinet officer, in addition to the normal geographic mix. Several trends have emerged in cabinet placements based on geographic relationship. Certain cabinet posts are essentially guaranteed to geographic regions. For example, the Interior Department traditionally goes to a western state, the Agriculture Department to a midwestern state, and the Treasury Department to a Wall Street banker from New York.

Since Lyndon Johnson named the first African American to the Cabinet with the appointment of Robert Weaver as secretary of housing and urban development, every president has tried to have minority representation in the cabinet. Nixon was the only postmodern president to fail to have a single minority in his cabinet. Although Nixon worked assiduously to bring minorities into the administration, none accepted his offers for a cabinet position. Both Senator Edward Brooke of Massachusetts and Whitney Young of the Urban League were extended offers but declined them.[49] Ford included William Coleman as secretary of transportation, Carter included Patricia Roberts Harris to head first housing and urban development and later health and human services, Reagan had Samuel R. Pierce Jr. at housing and urban development, Bush had Louis W. Sullivan at health and human services, and Clinton had Mike Espy at agriculture, Ron Brown at commerce, and Rodney Slater at transportation. The wheels of diversity that have been set in motion are unlikely to be slowed in future administrations.

Another part of the diversity puzzle that the postmodern administration has focused on has been the inclusion of Hispanic Americans in the cabinet. Reagan began this trend, which has been strongly supported by Bush and Clinton. The inclusion of African American and Hispanic Americans is largely due to the significant role that both groups play in the arena of modern politics. Both groups are mobilized, have influence in the political parties, and sway significant numbers of voters. Presidents are using cabinet positions as a reward for their political support in exactly the same way Jackson rewarded his political supporters and McKinley rewarded his financial supporters. The postmodern cabinet has become a tool for rewarding political support, far more than it had been from 1933 through 1968.

Perhaps the most significant change in the postmodern presidency has been the inclusion of women in the political spectrum of the cabinet. As the economic and political power of women has grown, so too has their influence within the political parties. This has been particularly true since the mid-1970s when the women's movement reached its height with the drive to pass the Equal Rights Amendment. Although the amendment failed to pass, women continue to be a prominent factor in voting behavior, with every presidential candidate courting women's votes. In the 1992 election, Democratic candidate Bill Clinton aggressively sought women's votes, particularly white, middle-class women who had often voted Republican. This group of women, referred to as "soccer moms," was heavily targeted by the Clinton camp. After the 1992 election, Clinton rewarded the solid support that women had provided his campaign with three cabinet positions, including the nation's first female attorney general. In his second term, Clinton continued to reward the women's vote by naming the nation's first female secretary of state.

The postmodern presidency, from Nixon to Clinton, reflects the changing nature of the role of the cabinet. Presidents do not particularly need managers to run their departments, as Eisenhower envisioned, given the strength of a career system within the federal government. Legislative mandates, civil service rules, career staff, and hierarchial structures minimize the need for management expertise as a single criteria for cabinet building. Presidents also do not need to reward large financial contributors, given the passage of campaign finance legislation governing presidential campaigns. The result is that the postmodern cabinet is a blend of highly educated individuals who generally have significant policy expertise in their departmental jurisdiction. Most cabinet officers in the postmodern cabinet have Ph.D.s, law degrees, or MBAs and have been active in policy issues. The postmodern cabinet also is distinguished by the need to reward the diverse political groups that exist under the umbrella of the two main political parties. The new economic and political power of these groups in the election process is keenly understood by presidential candidates. These groups are actively courted by the candidates and rewarded for their support with a cabinet position.

Conclusion

The diversity that dominates the cabinet has precluded the modern cabinet from being a body of great political or policy wisdom for the president. Every modern president has focused his policymaking structure in the White House staff, with staffs often at levels of 400 to 500 without counting the numerous detailees or members of the larger institutional units. The role of the cabinet has become primarily one of administrative management, fiscal control, and programmatic oversight. Policy initiation and development is controlled by the White House with the assistance of the departments. Cabinet members continue to be a central part of the president's advisory structure by virtue of the enormous amount of information that they control for the policy process and the management responsibilities that they direct. But the emergence of the White House staff with its personal and professional expertise has allowed the president to have an independent source of policy advice, similar to the kitchen cabinets of past administrations. Whereas Eisenhower met with his cabinet an average of two to three times a month, President Clinton convened formal meetings of the cabinet only seven times during his first year in office, and only twice in the first eight months of 1998.

The changing character of the cabinet reflects changes in the political structure of the postmodern presidency. Changes in the election laws with the Federal Election Campaign Act of 1972 limited personal contributions and totally banned corporate and labor contributions. This reduced the need to reward major contributors with cabinet positions, and modern cabinets have reflected this change. Changes in voting behavior and economic power within the parties have also created new power structures within the party that are rewarded. Postmodern presidents have built bridges to voting blocs within the party, such as minorities, Hispanics, and women, in the same way that past presidents built bridges to the conservative and liberal wings within the party. This is not to say that bridges are no longer built to such wings of the party, but rather that large voting blocs are considered just as important in cabinet building.

The changes in the finance laws profoundly changed the political landscape, but it ensured a greater role for large, but less wealthy voting blocs in political parties. Every future president will need to reward these voting blocs in the same way that past presidents rewarded political and economic support. Harmony has become less necessary in the cabinet as the White House staff has increasingly controlled policy development and coordination. Presidents do not call their cabinets together for collective decision-making, but rather to announce policy goals established in the White House.

The postmodern presidency is a significantly different institution than existed two hundred years ago or even fifty years ago. The cabinet reflects the changes both in the economic and political structure of the campaign system and in the dominant role that the White House staff plays. The changes that Clinton made in the cabinet structure, reflective of the economic and political relationships of the 1992 and 1996 campaigns, are likely to continue in the future regardless of party. Both Democratic and Republican presidents will likely follow the path that has been set in recent administrations.

8

The Press and the Presidency: Then and Now

Graham G. Dodds and Mark J. Rozell

In the summer of 1998, as reporters relentlessly pursued the details of a presidential sex scandal, the Clinton White House lambasted the media for an obsession with the private lives of public figures. While media coverage tended toward the critical and sensational, opinion polls showed continued high levels of support for President Bill Clinton's leadership and policies. Clinton and his supporters were quick to point out the obvious disparity between the views of reporters and those of the public regarding the importance—or even relevance—of a presidential affair with a young woman.

Clinton's defenders also claimed that by focusing so doggedly on the president's private life, the media were responsible for coarsening the public discourse and diverting attention away from serious public policy issues. The president himself, as well as his most ardent supporters, maintained that the media pursuit of the details of a chief executive's private life was unprecedented and due, in large part, to the competitive pressures of a dramatically changed and fast-paced media environment.

There is much truth to the allegation that media attention to the Clinton sex scandal had squeezed out coverage of many policy issues, and that in earlier periods of U.S. history, reporters had failed to reveal what they knew about the affairs of presidents. Yet criticism of the media for gravitating toward scandal and intrigue over policy substance is nothing new. And certainly there is nothing new about presidential criticism of the media for being unfair or unduly critical.

The new, fast-paced media environment—characterized by a plethora of twenty-four-hour cable television news stations, the internet, talk radio, and tabloid media, as well as the "traditional" media forms—has created a hypercompetitive atmosphere that has altered many of the practices of journalism. Traditional news cycles are gone and public figures complain that they are under siege by an aggressive, attack-oriented media with little regard for the institutional and policy implications of their reporting.

Reporters allege that much of this behavior is necessitated by the modern propensity among public figures to try to manipulate and control the media for self-serving purposes. Most prominently, reporters point out that the White House public relations, speech writing, and press relations staffs have expanded dramatically and that in the modern era, presidents have unparalleled ability to influence their news coverage.

Aspects of the press–presidency relationship widely considered unique to the modern era in fact have a much older pedigree. To be sure, technology has changed dramatically and in the post–Watergate era, in particular, presidential journalism has taken on a more cynical and negative tone. Nonetheless, critical coverage of presidents—including questioning of motives and attacks on character—go back to the earliest years of the Republic, as do presidential efforts to manipulate and control the press. Indeed, much of what some reporters and editors wrote about our chief executives in the early Republic would shock and offend some modern-day sensitivities. And some of the early efforts of presidential press manipulation would be considered outrageous today.

This chapter examines the development of the presidential–press relationship from the early years of the Republic to the present. Presidents and the press have always engaged in bitter battles for control of the public discourse. During all periods of American history presidents have complained about their press coverage and journalists have alleged official efforts to manipulate the news.

The Early Republic

Although George Washington was elected president without the help of the press, newspapers and other forms of political press soon became very important in American politics. Government patronage and the rivalry between Thomas Jefferson and Alexander Hamilton facilitated the development of the partisan press.

In the 1790s, newspaper postage was important, because papers had few subscribers or advertisers. Although low postage helped advance political print journalism, direct patronage was also a factor. From 1790 to 1800, Federalists filled newly formed federal positions with supporters, including twenty printers in ten states who created what amounted to a "Court Press."[1] Of course, Republicans deeply resented this aspect of the Federalist propaganda machine. Federalists also came up with the idea of franking newspapers to facilitate the spread of Federalist views.[2]

However, the main source of patronage for favorable presses was government printing contracts. Congress needed a system to publish its acts and journals. Initially there was no official position of government printer, so Congress selected printers.[3] Within two weeks of becoming Washington's secretary of state, Thomas Jefferson selected John Fenno's semi-weekly *Gazette of the United States* as the official publisher of federal laws.[4] Thereafter, Washington's administration enjoyed highly favorable press through Fenno's paper, for which Secretary of the Treasury Alexander Hamilton often wrote.

When Hamilton and Jefferson began to feud and the Federalist–Republican split developed, Jefferson sought a Republican alternative to Fenno's pro-Federalist paper. Together with James Madison, Jefferson persuaded Philip Freneau in 1791 to set up a rival paper, the *Philadelphia National Gazette.* "Jefferson not only solicited subscriptions for the new paper but also subsidized Freneau with a clerkship in the State Department."[5] Freneau's paper attacked Washington and the Federalists. In response, Hamilton accused Jefferson of being the *National Gazette*'s patron, which he certainly was.[6] The *National Gazette* was the foremost Republican journal until its demise in 1793, at which point the Philadelphia *General Advertiser,* later known as the *Aurora,* occupied that position. The *Aurora* was edited by Benjamin Franklin Bache, the grandson of Benjamin Franklin, and it became a relentless critic of the Federalists in general and Washington in particular.[7]

William David Sloan writes that "because of the American disdain for factionalism, at least a facade of press impartiality was expected during the early part of the period [1788–1812], but by 1800 many editors made no pretense of impartiality." In 1797, for example, William Cobbet, editor of the pro-Federalist *Peter Porcupine's Gazette,* proclaimed, "Professions of impartiality I shall make none." Editors of *The Portfolio* in Philadelphia and the Baltimore *American and Daily Adviser* in 1799 similarly disparaged impartiality.[8] "The Boston *Columbian Centinel,* a Federalist paper with probably the largest circulation of any paper in the country, became so partisan that in 1795 it deleted its motto, 'Uninfluenced by party, we aim only to be just.'"[9]

The press played a major role in the battle for political control between the Federalists and the Republicans. For this reason, "the last decade of the 18th century is well-known for the scurrilous partisanship of the press," with Federalists and Republicans relentlessly attacking one another.[10] Indeed, during Washington's administration, "for every Republican attack there was a defense printed by a Federalist sheet, and some of those replies made the Republican charges of idolatry believable."[11] Harry Ammon writes:

> It was a no-holds-barred form of journalism with personal behavior as well as political views subject to violent abuse. Only a handful of papers devoted to

shipping news and commercial notices were free from the prevailing political bias. . . . Editors had to rely on subscriptions by loyal party members—subscriptions often solicited by major party figures. The more important newspapers also received substantial subsidies on the federal and state level through contracts for public printing. The newspapers, particularly those in the national or state capitals, had an intimate though unacknowledged connection with party leaders who freely used them to defend party positions.[12]

On the Anti-Federalist side, newspapers criticized Washington for the Hamilton fiscal system and Jay's Treaty.[13] One paper derided Washington's use of titles and ceremonies and suggested it amounted to monarchism: "some of us may yet live to behold another George wielding the sceptre of the western world."[14]

Washington was upset by the these attacks. He accused the *Aurora* and other Republican papers of describing him "in such terms as could scarcely be applied to a Nero, to a notorious defaulter, or even to a common pick pocket." Harry M. Ward explains:

> What grated most on Washington's ears were phrases in the *Aurora* claiming that Washington's reputation was due to "the seclusion of a monk and the supercilious distance of a tyrant," his military reputation was owing to luck and he was appointed to command in the Revolution because such a lackluster character would provoke no antagonism from members of Congress, and he was made President because of the "insipid uniformity of a mind which had been happy in proportion to the contracted sphere of its operations."[15]

In 1792, Washington voiced concern that "if the government and Officers of it are to be the constant theme for News-Paper abuse, and this too without condescending to investigate the motives or the facts, it will be impossible, I conceive, for any man living to manage the helm, or to keep the machine together."[16] Yet after Washington, the partisan press increased in number, harshness, and political importance.

Partisan newspapers also attacked John Adams as being aristocratic. "Critics had delightfully ridiculed his parsimoniousness, corpulence, partiality for British 'principles,' vanity, and love of ostentation as Vice-President even in those days when restraint had been felt advisable."[17] During the election of 1796, Republican papers accused Adams of malingering, nepotism, vanity, and senility.[18] After Adams won election, "Benjamin Franklin Bache called the President 'old, querulous, bald, blind, crippled, toothless Adams.'"[19] Bache also accused Adams of trying to "gasconade like a bully, and to swagger as if he were the emperor of all the Russians." Bache furthermore sarcastically referred to Adams as "His Serene Highness" and claimed that Adams was "a man divested of his reason, and wholly under the domination of his passions."[20]

Adams's response to the opposition press was to sign into law the Alien and Sedition Acts of 1798. Rather than silencing the opposition, Adams's attempt at censorship brought even harsher criticism, as the Republican press accused Adams of having a "tyrannical administration."[21] Newspapers denounced him as a "despot" for impinging on their newly won First Amendment liberties.[22] In addition to these charges, Adams was also subject to Republican complaints of corruption. For example, the *Aurora* decried the "public plunder" by Federalist officials and the administration-friendly *National Gazette* charged government figures with corruption.[23]

Politically charged journalism contributed to the crushing Federalist defeat in 1800. According to Stewart, "the incessant newspaper emphasis on betrayal and corruption, in a political party which had become entrenched in power, did much to further the development of our first opposition party—one which was able successfully to convince the electorate that it, rather than the incumbent Federalists, should be entrusted with the direction of national affairs."[24]

The partisan press continued to grow in the 1800s. Indeed, for the first half of the nineteenth century, vituperative, partisan journalism was the norm. The partisan press was marked by "its coarseness and cruelty, its venomous vigor of invective, its contempt for all that should be sacred in political warfare and in private life."[25] Charles Glicksberg characterized the journalism of this period as "neither dignified nor restrained. It was, for the most part, a vehement and envenomed feud, seething with personal controversies and partisan prejudices. Passion ran high and the ethics of the profession sank correspondingly low."[26]

Like Adams, Jefferson expressed a distaste for the partisan press. After leaving Washington's cabinet in 1793, for example, he "was said to have expressed a desire never to see a newspaper again, but such a wish was utterly incompatible with any plan to achieve a change in administrations—and Jefferson realized it."[27] Indeed, Jefferson well understood the importance of the partisan press in helping him gain power.

Accordingly, Jefferson consistently supported Republican presses via printing patronage in his administration. Republican leaders established partisan presses over the course of Jefferson's administration. For example, in 1808, Republican leaders in Newport, Trenton, and Worcester founded new Republican papers.[28] Jefferson also appointed loyal partisan editors as postmasters.[29] Furthermore, Jefferson himself subscribed to and read many different Republican papers, as well as Federalist ones, so as to keep informed about the opposition. He even wrote essays that appeared in Republican papers.[30] Jefferson praised the papers that supported him, especially the *Aurora*, which he claimed had "unquestionably rendered incalculable services to republicanism through all its struggles with the Federalists and has been the rallying point for the orthodoxy of the whole

Union. It was our comfort in the gloomiest days, and is still performing the office of a watchful sentinel."[31]

While the *Aurora* was a key supporter of the Jeffersonians, their most important partisan paper was the *National Intelligencer.* Shortly after taking office, Jefferson gave the government printing jobs previously held by the Federalist press to the *Intelligencer,* in return for which it supported the Republican cause.[32] The *Intelligencer* also served as the authoritative, quasi-official administration spokespiece. Under Jefferson, Noble Cunningham writes, "the *National Intelligencer* as a party organ of nationwide influence gave the Republican party an important advantage over the Federalists, who, though supported by a powerful press, did not have a paper of such national stature and influence."[33]

Jefferson still faced partisan press opposition. Upon his inauguration, the Federalists controlled about four-fifths of the nation's newspapers.[34] The Federalist press accused Jefferson of atheism and of being an "impractical" dreamer, disrespectful toward Washington, and a violent revolutionary, while lesser charges included cowardice, sexual immorality, dishonesty, and political inefficiency. The volume of anti-Jefferson material was enormous and included hundreds of pamphlets, as well as smears in papers such as the *Connecticut Courant,* the *Columbian Centinel,* and the *Virginia Gazette and General Adviser.* The guest editorialist "Brutus" in the *Virginia Gazette and General Adviser* charged Jefferson with "duplicity" and underhandedness and the guest editorialist "Burleigh" in the *Connecticut Courant* charged that Jefferson "and his party have long endeavored to destroy the federal Constitution."[35]

Perhaps stung by these and other criticisms, Jefferson did not protest when several prominent opposition editors were prosecuted for seditious libel, but in 1805 in his Second Inaugural Address, Jefferson expressed regret that the freedom of the press had been much misused. Yet, according to Leonard Levy, "by the time he left the presidency, a much wiser and embittered man, so convinced was he that the press was hopelessly abandoned to licentiousness . . . that he professed to believe that it was doing more harm to the nation than would result from suppression."[36]

Jefferson's reservations about partisan journalism notwithstanding, the Jeffersonian press and the *National Intelligencer* continued to operate and facilitated the presidencies of Jefferson's fellow Virginia Republicans, James Madison and James Monroe. For all three Jeffersonian presidents, the *Intelligencer* was called the "court paper," the "government organ," and the "official gazette."[37] Madison and Monroe had both responded to Hamilton's attacks on Jefferson by publishing a defense of the president in Philadelphia's *American Daily Advertiser.* When Madison became president, he had Monroe draft editorials for the *Intelligencer.*[38]

The Jacksonian Era

The harshness of the partisan press abated with the dissolution of the Federalist Party after the War of 1812 and the "Era of Good Feelings," but it soon increased with the struggle for the presidency in 1824. In 1824 the semi-official congressional caucus for nominating presidential candidates lost its practical effectiveness. Instead, candidates had to appeal more directly to the people, so newspapers became crucial.[39]

John Quincy Adams was at times reluctant to engage in the politics of the partisan press. He claimed that if the Presidency "is to be the prize of cabal and intrigue, of purchasing newspapers, bribing by appointments, or bargaining with foreign missions, I have no ticket in that lottery."[40] Nevertheless, Adams eventually realized that some press support would be required to prevail in the election over Andrew Jackson, Henry Clay, and John C. Calhoun. For this reason, the pro-Adams *National Journal* was established in 1823. The *Journal* proved to be more restrained than the opposition *Gazette* or the *Republican*, but its support of Adams was crucial to his electoral success.[41] The *Journal* consequently replaced the *Intelligencer* as "the semi-official spokesman for the president."[42] Even though Adams used the partisan press, he expressed disdain for it and denounced its practice of pushing particular candidates as "altogether venal."[43]

By the 1828 election, Adams's dislike of the partisan press stood in stark contrast to his Jacksonian opponents, who established pro-Jackson papers in every state. The Jacksonian press's cultivation of mass support played a key role in Adams's defeat.[44] "The presidential campaign of 1828 had been to a large extent a contest among newspapers, with the journalists as much involved as the candidates they championed." Forrest McDonald describes the election coverage as highly "negative." In fact, "nothing at all was said about what the candidates would do if elected."[45]

Adams's backers "characterized Jackson as an uncouth frontier ruffian, a murderer, and an adulterer. They slandered his wife. They charged that his mother had been the concubine of a black man and thus that he was a bastard mulatto." The Raleigh *Register* questioned Jackson's qualifications: "take from General Jackson his military renown, and nothing is left to raise him above the rank of his fellows." Jackson supporters charged Adams with "corruption, with using public funds for private advantage, for having had premarital sex with the woman he later married, and for being involved, while minister to Russia, in facilitating the seduction of an American girl by the tsar."[46]

Jackson used the partisan press more fully than any of his predecessors. When Jackson became president, he changed over 70 percent of the printing patronage arrangements, giving them to pro-Democrat presses. The *National Journal* went from administration organ to leader of the opposition, while Duff Green's *Telegraph* did the opposite.[47] The *Telegraph* remained Jackson's official administration journal until 1830, when Francis Blair's *Washington Globe* took over as the administration's main voice. Blair was "one of President Jackson's confidants, a leading dispenser of the party's patronage, and a principal policy maker in the Executive branch."[48]

Jackson's campaigns in 1828 and 1832 sought to enhance his mass popularity via a complex system of political communication centered on the partisan press. He relied on the strength of a national political machine, now the Democratic Party, the apex of which "was a chain of party newspapers, centered in Washington and extending to all parts of the United States." These papers were organized by then Senator Martin Van Buren, who saw to it that Jacksonian papers like the *Telegraph* went to all parts of the nation "under the franking privileges of friendly Congressmen."[49]

So close was the relation between president and press that Jackson rewarded many supportive newspaper editors with administration positions. This sort of patronage marked an escalation in the quid pro quo between president and press. Whereas Jefferson and others had given printing contacts to favored editors, Jackson actually appointed numerous journalists to government positions. Jackson used the press in exactly the ways that his opponents feared.[50] The partisan press reached what was perhaps its peak of influence in the campaign of 1832. At that time, many of the leaders of the new (second) American party system were newspaper editors.[51]

Having orchestrated Jackson's use of the partisan press, Van Buren was well prepared to use the press for his own purposes upon becoming president in 1837. John Tebbel writes: "More than any president who preceded him, Van Buren appeared to have a natural understanding of the relationship between press and public, and he was the first who knew how to manipulate the press in somewhat the same style that is commonplace today." Van Buren was propelled into presidential politics by the Albany *Argus*, of which he was part owner, and together with the Washington *Globe*, the *Argus* was a primary outlet for pro-Van Buren propaganda to other presses.[52]

As successful as Van Buren was with the Democratic press, he was also vilified by the opposition papers. For example, James Watson Webb's New York *Courier and Enquirer* referred to "the vast machine of intrigue and corruption that [Van Buren] has set in operation in every part of the Union," and the New York *American* noted "the evil we dread, the great and menacing evil, the blighting disgrace of placing Martin Van Buren, illiterate, sycophant, and politically corrupt, at the head of this great republic." Similarly, "a Whig paper in Tennessee characterized him as 'that dandee' who strutted and swaggered 'like a crow in the gutter . . . laced up in corsets such as women in town wear, and if possible, tighter than the best of them.'"[53]

The Decline of the Partisan Press

Shortly after Van Buren, the partisan press began slowly to give way to independent editors. But even though it was declining, the partisan press continued to be important. For example, Horace Greeley began to publish the *Log Cabin* in 1840 simply to get Whig William Henry Harrison elected president. As president, Harrison continued the practice of having a de facto official newspaper, replacing the *Globe* with the *National Intelligencer.*[54]

When John Tyler became president in 1841, the partisan press was increasingly on the decline, and the independent press on the rise. Tyler felt that he had to deal with two very different types of editors, what he referred to as the "affiliated" and the "neutral." Despite some success with the latter, Tyler experienced trouble with the partisan press. Having assumed the presidency when Harrison died after just a month in office, Tyler at first was a relative unknown for the partisan press. However, when Tyler revealed that he was more a states' rights Democrat than a nationalist Whig, the partisan press attacked him relentlessly. Newspapers called Tyler, among other things, an "executive ass," "His Accidency," and "a famished Charles City pettifogger."[55] The Raleigh *Register* called Tyler "a political hypocrite of the first water, and a moral traitor of the deepest dye."[56]

As a vice presidential candidate, Tyler had tried to avoid newspaper politics, and his antipathy toward the partisan press made him poorly prepared to respond to these attacks. He became upset with negative press from the *National Intelligencer* and decided to switch his administration's backing to the *Madisonian.* When Congress balked at his request to grant the executive printing contract to the *Madisonian,* Tyler responded by ordering his postmaster general "to end the long-standing practice of giving appointments as postmasters to editors of political journals."[57]

Franklin Pierce's relationship with the press also demonstrated the decline of the partisan press. According to Michael Birkner: "Prominent Democratic editors were nonplused by the president's failure to take them into his confidence, share tidbits they could use or even to read them regularly."[58] As with his predecessor, however, Pierce's disdain for the political press was also an obstacle to political efficacy. The Raleigh *Register* said that in Pierce's government "we find probably the most feeble Administration that the country has ever seen."[59] Greeley's *Tribune* also "hammered at the president," but Pierce's administration lacked an organized partisan press with which to respond. "The *Union* was not a forceful or effective arm of the White House, in part because Pierce himself provided little access to the editors."[60]

James Buchanan's presidency likewise demonstrated the increasingly independent nature of much of the press. He ended the practice of sending the president's annual message to a select paper and instead made it public through the telegraph, thereby denying any one paper a coup. He also ended the practice of patronage in awarding government contracts to loyal partisan presses, as this function was transferred to the new Government Printing Office in 1860.[61] Yet Buchanan did not ignore the political possibilities of partisan papers, as he courted James Gordon Bennett, the editor of the New York *Herald*, by leaking stories to him to secure more favorable reporting.[62] Abraham Lincoln, like Buchanan, was quick to exploit the press for his purposes. As a former postmaster, he had read the various papers he came across and had developed a keen awareness of the power of the press. He learned to cultivate that power early in his political career. In April 1857, Lincoln met with Frank Blair, editor of the *Missouri Democrat.*

> Exactly what was said in that conference between Blair and Lincoln is not known, but out of it grew two important developments. First, Blair pledged to Lincoln that the *Democrat* would "bloom for Republicanism" in 1860. Second, Lincoln shortly afterward drew up an agreement, signed by him and nine other Illinois Republicans, to furnish five hundred dollars for the promotion of the *Democrat* in Illinois.[63]

Lincoln rewarded the paper's support by naming its editor postmaster of St. Louis: "the best office in my gift within Missouri." Lincoln later even intervened to secure the release of a relative of a proprietor of the *Democrat* who was imprisoned on charges of disloyalty.[64] Although the partisan press was perhaps not as strong as it had once been, it remained a powerful force during Lincoln's administration.

> Politics and journalism were so closely interlocked that it was difficult to tell where one left off and the other began. Loyal editors all over the North felt no hesitancy in dashing off a personal letter to the President when they thought he needed the stimulation of their sage observations or when they had a bone to pick with him over the course of his administration. Letters from editors and publishers piled up in Lincoln's files until they numbered several hundred.[65]

One of Lincoln's most important encounters with the press occurred in New York City in 1860. He had accepted the invitation of a group of lawyers to speak at Cooper Union's Great Hall. He spoke about slavery in front of many of the most important editors of the day, including William Cullen Bryant of the *New York Evening Post* and Greeley of the *Tribune*, who received his speech with great enthusiasm. Greeley wrote: "No man ever before made such an impression on his first appeal to a New York audience." The editor of the *Sacramento Union* said of Lincoln: "He's the greatest man since St. Paul."[66]

Once he was elected president, however, opposition presses harshly attacked Lincoln. In 1861, Joseph Howard of the *New York Times* wrote a story that described how Lincoln traveled in disguise from Harrisburg to Washington because of fears of an attempt on his life. Reprinted throughout the nation, the story described how Lincoln "wore a Scotch plaid cap and a very long military cloak so that he was entirely unrecognizable."[67] Furthermore, "Despite many denials, the story made Lincoln a laughing stock throughout the country. A poetic version of this widely printed ridicule, thirteen stanzas long, called 'Air-Yankee-Doodle,' was reprinted by Democratic newspapers, one verse reading:"

> They went and got a special train
> At midnight's solemn hour,
> And in a cloak and Scotch plaid shawl,
> He dodged from the Slave-Power.[68]

Herbert Mitgang describes the press venom heaped on Lincoln: "In the [Northern] Copperhead press and in the Southern papers, President Lincoln was called, among other things, a Simple Simon, Jack Pudding, Kentucky mule, Illinois beast, not to mention, traitor and dictator." "The Richmond *Examiner* called for the capture of Washington, where lived 'Lincoln the beast' and the 'Illinois ape.'" Even the New York *Daily News* often published anti-Lincoln rhymes.[69] Lincoln was insulted, lied about, and ridiculed by many newspapers, but only the *New York Day Book* tried to involve him in an incident with a sex angle. In the days just before Sumter, it said:

> Some of the newspapers mention with agreeable surprise the fact that the President has appointed a young man keeper of some light house on the sole recommendation of his sweetheart. Old Abe has an eye for a pretty girl, and why should he not have an ear, too? Did he not refuse, while at City Hall in this city, to shake hands with a young man, but said, "if your sister was here, I would shake hands with her."[70]

Some of Lincoln's critics were censored, others imprisoned, while papers such as the New York *Daily News* were forced to suspend publication.[71]

In the years after the Civil War, commercial mass circulation newspapers thrived while the party press was on the decline. The "penny" papers claimed that they were independent of party influence and control, and thus more trustworthy. However, many favored the old-style journalism.[72] James Garfield, for example, said

> The journal should have opinions of its own, and should advocate them. I have no sympathy with the Utopian idea of "Independent Journalism." . . . It is fair to presume that every intelligent man has convictions upon leading

public questions. . . . Let the journalist defend the doctrines of the party
which he approves; let him criticize and condemn the party which he does
not approve, reserving always his right to applaud his opponents or censure
his friends, as the truth will require, and he will be independent enough for
a free country.[73]

Upon election to the presidency in 1884, Grover Cleveland proved hostile to machine politics and ended the practice of giving appointive offices
to loyal party members, further weakening the partisan press. "Even though
many papers retained an official partisan affiliation between 1870 and 1900,
and were often uninhibited in support of their favored candidates, the loos-
ening of the ties between party organizations and the press was an important feature of this period."[74]

The long, slow demise of the partisan press did not mark the end of critical journalism. From the late 1870s through the 1890s, scandals, sensation-
alism, and various crusades marked the "yellow journalism" of Joseph
Pulitzer's St. Louis *Post-Dispatch* and *New York World* and William Randolph Hearst's *San Francisco Examiner* and New York *Morning Journal*,
among other papers. Many historians claim that yellow journalism in 1898
precipitated the Spanish-American War.[75]

But yellow journalism was not traditional partisan journalism. It was
more popularly oriented and enjoyed a broader audience, and it was not as
closely tied to political parties. Richard Rubin explains: "The extraordinary
expansion of newspaper circulation and advertising revenues in just over
three decades following the Civil War effectively broke the press's organizational links to party institutions and established a new relationship between mass media and electoral institutions."[76] American demand for news
grew rapidly in the late 1800s, and "beginning around 1885 Americans were
fed information (or misinformation or disinformation) about their president
on a daily basis."[77]

The Early Twentieth Century

The early twentieth century saw the rise of what Theodore Roosevelt called
the "muckrakers"—journalists who worked to expose corruption in business and government. The "party organ" style of journalism gave way to a
more large-scale and independent press. Popular magazines and mass circulation newspapers flourished during Roosevelt's presidency and he understood the importance of the press in leading the public. Roosevelt
crafted both an "insider" and "outsider" strategy in mobilizing support: he
cultivated support directly with members of Congress while he reached out
to the public to get behind his policies. He held numerous press confer-

ences, had reporters visit him for discussions while he shaved, used reporters to leak information and float "trial balloons," instructed his secretary to feed reporters a steady diet of Roosevelt family stories, and traveled more than any of his predecessors to reach the people directly through speeches.[78]

As a political scientist, Woodrow Wilson theorized that a president who earned the admiration and confidence of the people could be as powerful as he wished. Wilson challenged the wisdom of the constitutional Framers' admiration of separation of powers and checks and balances. To break the debilitating stalemate—or "gridlock"—of the national government, he believed, required the leadership of a strong, popular president.[79]

Wilson's tenure as president certainly revealed the possibilities and limitations of direct popular leadership. Although Wilson was less than cordial with much of the press corps, during a period of war—when the media had customarily softened presidential criticism—he proved to be superbly adept at rallying popular opinion to a common endeavor. Yet even the victorious wartime president could not later rally his people on behalf of his call for Senate ratification of the Treaty of Versailles, which contained provisions for the creation of a League of Nations. The president who had earned the admiration and confidence of the people could not move them to support an unpopular initiative.

Roosevelt: Master of the Media

Perhaps no president has been as adept at news management and popular leadership as Franklin D. Roosevelt. In part, the willingness of reporters to slant coverage in favor of the administration reflected the nature of the times—the nation faced economic calamity at home, then foreign aggression, and reporters did not exhibit the same skepticism of official Washington that is customary today. But none of that detracts from Roosevelt's accomplishment.

Roosevelt captivated reporters and used them with great effect to promote the White House slant on events. For press conferences, reporters abided by White House rules that today would be dismissed as unacceptable: the president determined what information was on-background, off-the-record, or not-for-attribution. Reporters who did not follow the president's rules could be cut off from access to the White House. He requested that reporters who asked what he considered foolish questions figuratively wear a dunce cap. FDR flattered reporters by using their first names, solicited their advice on matters of state, and even invited some to the White House to join the small Roosevelt family dinners.

Press deference to the president was remarkable. Newspapers abided by the White House rule that FDR not be photographed in a wheelchair or when being carried by his aides. When the president fell down face forward in the mud just before he was to deliver his 1936 nomination speech at Philadelphia's Franklin Field, no photographs were taken and no one reported the mishap. James E. Pollard wrote some fifty years ago that,

> In sum, here was an administration with a concept of public relations far beyond that of any predecessor. . . . Much of the early success of the New Deal was undoubtedly due to the constant steady stream of organized information from the White House and to the fact that most of the working correspondents were on the side of Mr. Roosevelt. He played their game and very often they were inclined to play his.[80]

But FDR's New Deal policies were enormously unpopular with newspaper publishers who exerted more control over editorial writers than reporters. Roosevelt maneuvered around the Republican-leaning editorialists and his other critics by reaching out to the people directly through the more liberal-minded reporters. He used the language of class warfare to denounce the "Tory press" that, he claimed, had used its economic power to try to derail the New Deal. He derided editorialists as insignificant, claimed that the vast majority of the people did not read or care about newspaper editorials, and thereby tried to undermine their authority.

His most innovative medium for reaching the people was radio. His performances were masterly. The president's words captivated the public and helped to give to him the political leverage that he needed to take bold action in domestic and foreign policy.

That FDR was liked by reporters and admired by the people redounded to the benefit of his programs. No chief executive since has so succeeded at turning the working press practically into presidential sycophants. And none, with the possible exception of Ronald Reagan, has had FDR's gift of eloquence and ability to lead the people.

Kennedy and the Television Presidency

The powerful medium of television first became a major factor in presidential politics in the 1960 election. Broadcast both by radio and television, the presidential debates between Vice President Richard M. Nixon and Senator John F. Kennedy may well have been decisive to the outcome of that close race. To television viewers, Kennedy—youthful appearing, polished, articulate—bettered Nixon, who had failed to cut such an appealing presence on screen (radio listeners had judged Nixon's performance to be stronger). Kennedy's televised appearances undercut Republican claims that he was not presidential material.

Television gave candidate Kennedy the electoral boost that he needed; he has often been called our "first television president." Indeed, he deftly used the emerging medium of choice as a vehicle to promote himself and his presidency. Kennedy personalized the presidency by allowing television cameras to film him and his family at the White House. Although afflicted with a chronic bad back, the president staged family football games and other outdoor activities to convey to the public an active, energetic, and physically fit chief executive.

More than any other modern president, JFK was adept at off-the-cuff responses that were succinct and often witty. The public relations event that JFK commanded was the televised press conference. His performances were superb, even entertaining, as the president offered just the right mix of serious presentation and humorous bantering with reporters to keep viewers interested and to convey the information that he wanted to reach the public.

Although Kennedy had demonstrated the potential of television as an instrument of persuasion, his presidency also highlighted the independence of the policymaking process to popular leadership by the chief executive. Despite his popularity, JFK had difficulty transferring that support into congressional votes. Many of his most cherished legislative initiatives never made it out of the conservative-led House Rules Committee for a vote.

In part because of his popularity with the press, and in part because of the nature of the times, journalists did not report information that they possessed about JFK that would have destroyed his finely honed image as a vigorous athlete and good family man. They were well aware of his poor health—his chronic bad back and adrenal insufficiency—as well as his many marital infidelities, yet they did not consider such matters of import to the public.

The Impact of Vietnam and Watergate

Journalists who had allowed themselves to get close to FDR or JFK believed that such access was good for their careers. Yet in so doing, many reporters had become conduits for presenting the presidential slant. The revelations of journalist Theodore White's accepting "dictation" from Jackie Kennedy about the "Camelot" image is a case in point. Any reporter today who allowed himself to so lose his objectivity would rightfully be derided by his colleagues. In the 1960s and 1970s, journalists had learned the downside of being seduced by their political leaders: sometimes those leaders concealed information and lied. And nothing so angered the reporters as being turned into unwitting agents of official deception.

The events of the Vietnam war and Watergate resulted in a measure of media cynicism toward official Washington that is still being felt today.

Much of that cynicism has focused on the presidency and the occupants of that office, as reporters, who had for a long time trusted official White House sources, discovered that they had been lied to and deceived. Relations between reporters and the White House broke down.

During the Johnson administration reporters wrote of the "credibility gap"—the distance between reality and government projections about the progress of the Vietnam war. Unlike his predecessor who had charmed the media, Lyndon Johnson was combative with reporters. He was obsessed with the media to the point of having three television screens (one for each major network) and the wire service feeds installed in the Oval Office so that he could monitor his coverage. Johnson felt that the steady drumbeat of media criticism of his wartime policies had undermined public support for U.S. actions and ultimately brought down his presidency.

Antagonism between the White House and the media reached new heights during the Nixon years. Nixon had always believed that the national media were overwhelmingly liberal and that they had despised him for the way that he had run his first campaign for Congress in California and for his vigilant efforts to expose State Department employee Alger Hiss as a communist. Because he believed that he could never get a fair hearing from the press on the merits of his actions, Nixon went to unusual lengths to combat negative national news.

Among the Nixon White House innovations was the creation of the Office of Communications, a unit established to promote the president's actions through letters-to-the-editor campaigns, generating letters to the White House in favor of the president's actions, encouraging favorable editorial essays, and reaching out to the more pro-administration local media. Unlike the White House Press Office, which handles the day-to-day needs of the press corps, the Office of Communications engages in long-term public relations strategies. Although unable to save Nixon from himself or Watergate, the Office of Communications left a lasting imprint on presidential media relations, especially during the Reagan years.

The Nixon White House tried to combat negative news coverage with confrontational tactics. The leading administration spokesman against the press was Vice President Spiro Agnew, who made speeches denouncing reporters as elitist "snobs" and, most memorably, "nattering nabobs of negativism." When Watergate brought down the Nixon presidency, the relationship between the White House and the press corps had deteriorated to the point where the reporters were openly delighted to see the president and his people leave Washington.

Perhaps most galling to the White House press corps was the fact that two young *Washington Post* "Metro" (local affairs) reporters—Bob Woodward and Carl Bernstein—uncovered the Watergate scandal. The White House reporters who had been toiling for years in the press room about thirty feet from the Oval Office had missed the story of a lifetime. Many concluded that their mistake had been that they were too reliant on, and trusting of, official sources of information in the White House.

The White House press corps responded by treating Nixon's immediate successors, Gerald R. Ford and Jimmy Carter, with the skepticism that the reporters wished that they had exhibited toward Nixon. As David Broder reported, "Watergate changed many of the fundamentals in the White House–press relationship." Reporters became more skeptical of official pronouncements and their questioning at White House briefings was "almost more prosecutorial than inquisitive."[81] President Ford explained that, "We inherited a very bad rapport between the White House press corps and the presidency as a result of Watergate and the Vietnam war. It was difficult to quickly change that negative attitude of the White House press corps." As Ford's first press secretary, Jerald F. terHorst, said: "You couldn't talk about policy and the need for continuity without someone questioning whether there was a devious plot behind it all. The press had been feeding on Watergate and Vietnam for so long that it was hard for them to shift gears."[82]

For most of the public, the image of a president, as presented through the media, is reality, whether accurate or not. There is probably no better example of a presidential image at odds with reality than that of Gerald Ford. Perhaps the most athletically gifted man ever to serve in the Oval Office—a former college football All-American drafted by two professional teams, expert skier and swimmer—Ford's image was that of a clumsy, uncoordinated "stumbler." A high academic achiever, Ford graduated from the University of Michigan and Yale Law School, yet he was portrayed as an intellectual lightweight. This image grew out of the media's emphasis on such trivial events as the president losing his footing while exiting an airplane and an oft-repeated story that LBJ had once called Ford too dumb to walk and chew gum at the same time.

Jimmy Carter, too, suffered a press image problem as president, due in part to the post-Watergate cynicism of those covering the White House. Reporters treated allegations of wrongdoing—some petty, some unsubstantiated—with Watergate-like inquisitiveness. And because Carter's election meant that a Democratic president would be working with strong partisan majorities in Congress for the first time since LBJ, press expectations for his leadership were initially very high. Carter's press image suffered irreparably when he battled with congressional Democrats over policy priorities and when his image failed to cut the kind of commanding presence that the media defined as "presidential."

Because media relations are so paramount to presidential leadership in the modern era, journalists often judge a chief executive's leadership acumen according to how well he handles the public presidency. Furthermore, journalists most often view the incumbent administration through the operations of the White House Press Office. When the president's press relations are not smooth and when the Press Office operates chaotically—common complaints during the Ford and Carter years—the White House image is one of poor leadership.

By the late 1970s scholars began to write of the presidency as an "imperiled" rather than "imperial" institution. A succession of "failed" presidencies led some to conclude that public expectations of the office had become so unrealistic and media scrutiny so debilitating that no one could adequately do the job.

The Reagan–Bush Years

Ronald Reagan proved that it is still possible for the modern president to win the battle of imagery with the media. Reagan, a former movie actor, came to the White House with a unique set of skills conducive to image-crafting. His administration gave high priority to the public relations aspects of the presidency.

To a large extent, the president's daily activities were driven by the needs of the news media, especially television. The White House worked hard to stay "on message" by generating its "line of the day" and "theme of the week" and by ensuring that administration spokespersons reinforced one another—a marked contrast to the Carter administration where, for example, White House spokespersons and cabinet officials often contradicted one another.

Also unlike his immediate predecessor, Reagan did not divorce imagery from policy substance. Reagan and his press relations staff understood well the relationship between positive coverage and moving forward a policy agenda. Through the Legislative Strategy Group, the White House coordinated its political and press strategies. As the White House Office of Communications director, David Gergen, explained: "We molded a communications strategy around a legislative strategy. We very carefully thought through what were the legislative goals we were trying to achieve and then formulated a communications strategy which supported them."[83] During crucial periods of his tenure, Reagan consequently was able to sustain enough public support to pressure Congress into approving his agenda and to politically protect himself from the kinds of scandals and investigations that surely would have crippled other presidencies.

Reagan's successor could not match the media and public relations skills of the "Great Communicator." Acutely aware that he lacked Reagan's skills, George Bush downplayed the public relations presidency. According to his press secretary, Marlin Fitzwater, Bush resisted running a Reagan-style, stage-managed presidency.

It represented a kind of phoniness to him, or fakery, that repelled him. There was the basic old-New England, Yankee honesty of spirit about George Bush that made him distrustful of anything that was staged. He used to say to me, "don't tell me what to do Marlin, I'm not a piece of meat. . . ." So he just resisted any efforts to stage manage him or to do the basic public relations things that we wanted him to do.[84]

It is debatable whether better public relations could have saved the Bush presidency. During a period of recession and high public anxiety about the future, few in 1992 were prepared to reward Bush with a second term merely because of his legislative achievements in such areas as clean air and civil rights for the disabled. But it is no small testimony to the importance of press and public relations that Bush received little credit for these domestic accomplishments, and that his reputation for foreign policy acumen was untarnished despite some major setbacks in U.S. policy in Eastern Europe, the Middle East, and Africa.

The Press and the Presidency: Clinton and Beyond

President Clinton often complained that the press denied him the customary "honeymoon" period of positive coverage. He was unarguably correct. Eleven days after his inauguration, the *Washington Post* featured a front-page story entitled "Coverage Quickly Turns Sour as Media Highlight Troubles." The article listed various media descriptions of Clinton that had already been used: "incredibly inept," "slowness and vacillation," "stumbling," and "common sense of a gnat," among others.[85]

From the beginning, the media criticized Clinton for inadequate leadership. At the 100-day juncture, a common media benchmark for sizing up the president, numerous reports and commentaries declared the Clinton presidency in peril. The major criticisms were that Clinton's agenda lacked "focus," that his administration had failed to expediently move much of its policy agenda through Congress and, therefore, "gridlock" still ruled Washington.[86] Just four months into Clinton's term, *Time* magazine featured a cover story, "THE INCREDIBLE SHRINKING PRESIDENT," (with a picture of a miniaturized Clinton) and *Newsweek*'s cover screamed "WHAT'S WRONG?"[87]

Clinton's slights of the media compounded the problem. Journalists complained of not having adequate access to the president and his staff, of being temporarily cut off from the West Wing of the White House, and of not having their inquiries answered in a timely fashion. Reporters began to sense that the new administration did not like them. After a deluge of negative stories about Clinton, *Newsweek* declared: "The press has now had its revenge. Clinton never gets the benefit of the doubt."[88]

Joining the drumbeat of criticism of his actions were an increasingly influential and growing "alternative media" led by the predominantly conservative talk radio format. By the middle of Clinton's second term, both mainstream and alternative media fixated on the presidential sex scandal that drove out almost any coverage of serious policy matters.

What, if anything, can a president do to recover from such media criticism and improve his image? Ford presidential press secretary Ron Nessen claims that "no White House can do much about a president's image." In his view, if the economy is sound and the people feel secure about their future, the president does not need much stage managing or a crafty media strategy to look good. But if the economy falters and people are anxious about the future, the president's image suffers, no matter how articulate he may be, no matter how much he glad-handles the press.[89] Indeed, during a recession in 1982–83, even Reagan, the "Great Communicator," suffered poor press coverage and declining public support. Bush, whose popularity reached an all-time high of 91 percent in early 1991, saw his fortunes plunge during an economic downturn later that year.

Nonetheless, all presidents believe that negative media coverage compounds their problems and makes leading the country unduly difficult. Without a doubt, forces larger than presidential press relations, for example, the inevitable swings of the economy, significantly influence the public's perception of a president's leadership. But the media largely determine the ways in which the public views those larger forces and the adequacy of the president's responses. As Murray Edelman wrote in *The Symbolic Uses of Politics*: "For most people most of the time politics is a series of pictures in the mind, placed there by television news, newspapers, magazines and discussions. . . . Politics for most of us is a passing parade of abstract symbols."[90]

Three decades later this parade of symbols is joined by the cacophonous sound of a larger marching band of computer networks, cable stations, talk radio, town hall meetings, and numerous other means of communications. Presidents cannot control this media environment, but they now have many venues through which they can communicate their messages. Fitzwater believes that, despite all of the complaints of unfair media coverage,

> the president has the upper-hand in press relations. You control the information, you control the time-table, you control the schedule. If the president has bad press relations, he's doing something wrong. . . . The communications tools at the disposal of a president are so immense, that no one can compete with him. When you have 100 to 150 reporters there every day to record everything you say as president, that's an incredible power. . . . A president can get out any message that he wants.[91]

President Clinton tried to get his message to the public in many unconventional ways, including the internet, specialty cable programs, talk shows, and town hall meetings. He moved well beyond his predecessors into innovative areas of communications. But his presidency was testimony to the enduring preeminent importance of the traditional Washington press corps to a White House image. The alternative means of communications have not displaced the White House press corps, and the new means of communications do not appear to have given the president the upper hand in the battle with the media for control of the public dialogue.

Indeed, as interest in a sex scandal dominated coverage of Clinton's presidency, it became clear that his administration was overwhelmed by the multiplicity of media outlets that piled on criticism. New cable news networks saw their program ratings rise substantially the more they emphasized the scandal. Talk radio, the new preferred means of political commentary for many conservatives, relentlessly focused on Clinton's troubles. Even Internet gossip columnists rose in prominence as they reported salacious (if not always or even mostly) accurate details of the scandal and their claims were carried in the mainstream media.

Presidents spend a great deal of time worrying about the press. They employ large numbers of press officers, communications aides, and image makers to try to promote a favorable press. Presidents inevitably are frustrated with the press coverage that they receive, despite all of their efforts to manage the news and project a favorable image. Is the president's image nearly a prisoner to forces over which he has little control? Or, is the president able to control his message and communicate whatever he wants?

The answer is not clear. Often uncontrollable events and circumstances drive the presidential agenda and make it difficult for the White House to stay "on message." Clinton's 1992 campaign boasted the unmistakable message of the candidate's priorities: "It's the economy, stupid." When he entered office, several complex foreign policy crises demanded the president's attention and cluttered his agenda. When the president also tried to move forward his tax and budget policies, the media criticized his leadership, maintaining that he was trying to do "too much, too soon." When the Clinton presidency became mired in scandal, it appeared there was nothing the president could do to change the focus of the media coverage.

Public perceptions of the state of the economy have an enormous impact on the presidential image, as Bush learned. Presidents have little control over the domestic economy, yet they are held accountable for current economic conditions.

The White House also has little control over how journalists define and evaluate leadership. Those who cover the presidency admire the almost larger-than-life image of the activist, visionary leader—an idealized FDR-type figure with an aggressive, hundred-day plan to confront the nation's problems. Yet this standard is almost impossible to achieve.

Presidents nonetheless are able to influence their relationships with the press corps. Although a positive, cordial relationship with the press does not guarantee favorable coverage, White House efforts to accommodate journalists and tend to their needs can help a great deal. Clinton learned that by antagonizing reporters, a president may suffer the press's "revenge."

Presidents are also able to control, to some extent, how they communicate with the public through the media. It is true that the television networks may refuse to carry a presidential speech, or commentators may pan a press conference performance, but there is no excuse for a president failing to communicate a message to the public. As Fitzwater commented, "there is no such thing as the president not getting his message out." The president "may be getting the wrong message out. Or, he may not have a message. But something is being communicated. In our case, it was that President Bush was out of touch with the economy."[92]

Presidents can also lower somewhat the expectations of their performance. Presidents often promise that they will achieve great things and it is reasonable for the press to evaluate whether they have made good on their own promises. Being more realistic about likely achievements can go a long way in breaking the debilitating cycle of promises made, expectations unfulfilled, media criticism, and public cynicism.

For most Americans, understanding the presidency occurs not primarily through textbooks but through the daily reporting and commentary of the media. Most people know the political world only through the messages conveyed to them through the media. For that reason, presidents and their aides are profoundly concerned about what happens in the media. They try to influence their media coverage because, for the public, the image of the president *is* reality. Presidents cannot control how they are viewed through media coverage of their activities, but they have many means by which to influence coverage and to get their message to the public. No president can afford to ignore this powerful force in American politics. Throughout American presidential history, that lesson indeed is clear.

9

Narrative in Presidential Oratory

Stephen J. McKenna

> The events of one year have influence on those of another, and, in like manner, of a preceding on the succeeding administration. The movements of a great nation are connected in all their parts. If errors have been committed, they ought to be corrected; if the policy is sound it ought to be supported. It is by a thorough knowledge of the whole subject that our fellow citizens are enabled to judge correctly of the past and to give a proper direction to the future.
>
> —James Monroe, Second Inaugural Address

Every reader of nineteenth-century American political oratory quickly learns that speakers of that time devoted considerable time and energy to looking backward, to providing an extensive introduction to the issue at hand through historical narrative. James Monroe is a case in point. Believing that direction for the future is unthinkable without due consideration of the past, he provided a four thousand–word account of his previous term in the introduction to his second inaugural address. He fluently recited the events and conditions of his prior term, punctuating the narrative with only a few vague references to policy. Late in the speech he expanded the historical context of these more proximate events to fit within the longer narrative history of the country going back to the Revolution: "It is now rather more than forty-four years since we declared our independence, and thirty-seven since it was acknowledged. The talents and virtues which were displayed in that great struggle were a sure presage of all that has since followed." Though the Revolution is referred to in semi-mythic terms, the "presage" connoted no mystical relation between past and present for Monroe, but a practical one between connected parts: self-government, he argued a sentence later, depends for its success on "the light of experience."

Monroe used his inaugural address not just to make this point but to demonstrate it as well.

One is struck by the narrative quality of older American political rhetoric and the historical outlook it evidences not only because it is so obstinately, often massively *there*—in long periodic sentences and blocky paragraphs— but simply because there is nothing comparable in present day political rhetoric. As Kathleen Hall Jamieson has noted:

> Speakers of earlier ages routinely traced the history of the matter under dis-
> cussion. In the process, they revealed how they saw the world. By contrast,
> history has little place in contemporary discourse except when selectively
> marshalled to argue that a proposed policy is a mistake. . . . In the golden
> ages, speakers lovingly explored the range of available evidence. Today,
> speeches argue by hitting and running.[1]

Jamieson's observation is true in general, but it is particularly descriptive of a shift in the style and structure of presidential rhetoric. Robustly fulfilling the first of the three Ciceronian "offices" of rhetoric—to teach, to move, and to please—earlier presidents took their time drawing the historical and eviden-tiary landscape around them and their audiences. Such narrative has little if any place in contemporary presidential speechmaking. Today, history is more cited than traced; evidence more wielded than explored. Even if a contempo-rary president were to engage in the kind of narrative discourse practiced by nineteenth-century presidents, it would probably never achieve rhetorical im-pact *as* narrative, for inevitably it would be distilled at once by spokespersons, aides, journalists, and spin doctors into its essential policy implications.

It should be noted that narrating broad swaths of history and outlining proximate evidence may seem to be different rhetorical practices, the for-mer often serving epideictic, the latter deliberative, ends. But the fact that both practices were commonplace, conventional, and intermingled in an earlier period of American political discourse, whereas they are rarely used today, suggests fundamental shifts in the way leaders and citizen-audiences have viewed the world, in what they think is reasonable to discuss in the joint exercise of public action in a democracy, and in how they think it should be discussed. Eighteenth- and nineteenth-century speakers gener-ally did not draw a sharp distinction between epideictic uses of history and deliberative summoning of evidence. Evidentiary detail was instructive, but it was also impressive and entertaining; the eloquent display of history was not only impressive and entertaining, it was also instructive. Despite the in-fluences of Enlightenment empiricism, factual evidence in oratory was ex-pected to be historically colored; history, on the other hand, was not mere precedent but one part of what John Quincy Adams called "the prevailing existing state of things."[2] Our tendency to demand a sharp distinction between the rhetorical uses of evidence and history is one measure of what separates us from our forebears.

The decline of narrative in presidential rhetoric has not been studied before, primarily because political scientists and others looking over the full canon of presidential rhetoric tend to focus on the content of arguments rather than on their style and structure. This tendency to isolate content from form is a normal and necessary part of any abstractive process of inquiry, but any such analysis is incomplete if it fails in the end to reconstitute its subject as a unity of form and content. In regard to the presidential uses of rhetorical narrative "then and now," failure to attend to this relation may be critically anachronistic: our modern temptation to read the expansive use of narrative in older presidential oratory as a quaintness or ornament from which the substantive arguments must be extracted may be symptomatic of the very fragmented kind of modern historical consciousness that in part renders the use of historical narrative by contemporary political speakers so unlikely.[3]

Another reason that presidential narrative has not been studied may be that a central concern of those analyzing presidential rhetoric has been with differences in sheer quantity and genre of speeches during different eras.[4] Public rhetoric is a far more prominent aspect of twentieth-century presidencies than it was of earlier ones, and hence comparisons between presidential speechmaking techniques in different times may seem curious, if not entirely moot—"that was then; this is now." Indeed, one of the fundamental difficulties in making such comparisons is deciding to what extent stylistic and structural differences may indeed be accounted to rather arbitrary aspects of discursive convention. But given that nineteenth-century presidents had—or took—far fewer opportunities to conduct their office through the medium of public speech, it is all the more striking that when they did speak, they so often employed lengthy narrative. Correspondingly, the relative absence of such narrative amid the far vaster quantity of twentieth-century presidential rhetoric then seems all the more striking. This chapter is an attempt to describe and diagnose this disappearance: at very nearly the moment that the presidency became the "rhetorical presidency," it vacated one of the main offices of rhetoric as it had been practiced in the prior century.

Narration in the Rhetorical Tradition

Beginning with the West's oldest handbook for political speechmaking, a perennial concern in the theory of rhetoric has been with the placement and function of the different parts of the speech. All that is known of the handbook of Corax of Syracuse (circa 467 B.C.) is that it recommended speeches have an introduction (*proöimion*), a narration of facts (*diêgêsis*), an argument and proof (*pistis*), and a peroration (*epilogos*). Virtually every rhetorical theory since then has in some manner dealt with this matter of *taxis* (or *dispositio* to the Romans). It finds its most elaborate and influential expression in Cicero, who offered the six-part arrangement *exordium* (introduction), *narratio* (statement of facts), *partitio* (preview in outline of the main argument), *confirmatio* (argument), *refutatio* (refutation), and *peroratio* (conclusion).[5] That the history of Western rhetorical practice from Pericles to Martin Luther King demonstrates the pervasiveness of this basic structure should be no surprise, for a moment's consideration suggests that the strategy of introduction, narration, proof, and conclusion meets what seem to be very basic human communication needs: a sender must get the hearer's attention, contextualize the message, deliver the message, and indicate that the message is over.

Perhaps the most elementary of these functions is the narrative one, for narrative in rhetoric draws the connection between any instance of practice, no matter how specialized or conventionalized, and the elemental pull of story, which across time and culture has been the commonest means by which human beings have sought to both understand and relate to the natural and social worlds. In traditional rhetorical education, narration was always valued, not simply as a means of conveying background information about the case at hand (which of course it was, too), but also for its ethical and aesthetic functions. Aristotle attributed particular importance to narration as an element of the speech that not only provides the factual context for political judgment, but that also discloses the moral purpose (*proairêsis*) of the speaker.[6] Cicero likewise closely associated narration with the need of speakers to observe canons of decency and decorum,[7] and he saw narration as equal to introduction in its role as a means of inducing in the audience a state of attentiveness—literally "docility" or teachability.[8] Facts were not just to be laid down, but to be conveyed in a manner respecting the audience's cognitive limitations, prior understandings, and social mores.

In the eighteenth century, Scottish rhetoricians introduced new approaches to rhetoric that variously sought to encompass all forms of human communication under one art of discourse, to accommodate the new epistemological theories of Francis Bacon, John Locke, and David Hume, and to relocate rhetorical practice in closer proximity to aesthetics and literary criticism.[9] But although they dispensed with or radically revised nearly all classical rhetorical doctrine, narration was one element they did not, and indeed could not, entirely give up. Though these new rhetorics of the eighteenth century did not treat narration under the rubric of speech arrangement, they did give prominence to the means and functions of eloquent and vivacious description. Though their approaches differed, they were univocal in treating appropriate narrative description not just as a pragmatic matter but as an ethical one as well. Adam Smith, for example, schematized the impartial method of narrative description in precisely the same way that he theorized the role of appropriate communication in the formation of moral conscience.[10]

These two traditions—the classical rhetorical tradition epitomized in the works of Cicero, and the new psychological and belletristic rhetorics of eighteenth-century Britain—were decisive in shaping attitudes toward rhetorical practice in the early American republic. A good indication of this can be seen in the rhetoric lectures of John Quincy Adams, who, before his political career, held the first Boyleston Professorship of Rhetoric and Oratory at Harvard from 1806–9.[11] While his lectures themselves were not influential, they serve to illustrate, even by their very non-innovative character, the extent to which a neo-Ciceronian model was the dominant paradigm for thinking about public speech and its relation to democratic citizenship at the time. In laying out the classical speech design, Adams differs in no substantive way from classical doctrine save one: he is far more emphatic than his classical sources about the importance of narration in political speechmaking. In their discussions of narration, Cicero and his follower Quintilian had been principally concerned with the statement of facts in judicial settings, and Aristotle before them had likewise remarked that while *diêgêsis* is primarily an element of courtroom speech, it is comparatively rare in political oratory.[12] Adams, on the contrary, has this to say:

> The utility of any measure which is the subject of deliberative discussion generally depends on a prevailing existing state of things; often upon a particular disclosure of facts, which the purpose of the deliberative orator requires him to make before his auditory. No question upon the imposition of a tax, the collection of a revenue, the sale of lands, or the subscription to a loan, a declaration of war, or the ratification of a treaty, can arise, in a public assembly, in a state of abstraction. These great topics of debate must always be connected with a series of great public events; and the expediency, upon which the deliberations will turn, must lean upon the basis of public affairs at the time of deliberation. The policy of the future is interwoven with the history of the past; and every deliberative orator, whose views of a proposed measure are directed by facts within his own knowledge, must lay [them] before his hearers, in justification of his opinions, which he commends or dissuades.[13]

And Adams is equally adamant about the place of narration in epideictic (i.e., ceremonial, display) rhetoric.[14]

For Adams, the purpose of the narration is to "lay the foundation for the speaker's argument;" he refers to as it the very "basis of reasoning." [15] Narration is not, however, simply the recitation of decontextualized information, but has its dramatic purposes as well. Repeating the commonplace classical metaphor that makes every story a road to travel down, Adams advises his students, "As you lead your hearer along, scatter fragrance in his path," and "Spread the smiling landscape around."[16] If one is careful to read Adams in his own idiom, this dramatic recitation of facts is no mere fanciful ornament but is closely tied to the political needs of the audience. He notes, for example, that "There is something in the nature of narrative interesting to all mankind"—where the eighteenth-century meaning of "interesting" primarily denotes not that which diverts or amuses but which draws attention to what is compelling in regard to one's moral, social, or political interests.[17] (In eighteenth- and earlier nineteenth-century presidential annual messages, perhaps no word is used more commonly than "interesting" to describe the facts discussed.) Hence Adams can conclude that while this yen for story explains our appetite for biography, history and novels, nonetheless, ". . . independent of the passion for hearing stories told, the auditory have a further stimulus to attention in the wish to form their own judgment from the facts."[18] By "facts," Adams means something slightly different from purely objective data, for such information would be disinterested rather than "interesting." Adams's narrative facts, which are to be the basis of judgment, include the kind of "smiling" or "fragrant" elements common in the style of eighteenth- and nineteenth-century public speaking. This implies that for Adams, "forming one's own judgment" meant not isolated or alienated calculation on the part of solipsistic and self-interested individuals—persons left "to live and trade each on his own private stock of reason" as Edmund Burke put it—but a more communal kind of prudence, one that respects individual autonomy but also takes into account the way in which individuals are part of a society defined in good measure by its historical tradition.[19]

The same elision of effective democratic judgment and the aesthetics of the rhetorical presentation of these "facts" comes out in a clever way in Adams's closing remarks on narration, wherein he discusses "the power of painting by speech." The phrase "painting by speech" is a commonplace as old as Horace, but it was given new currency in the belletristic rhetorical theory innovated in Britain by Smith and then expanded and enormously popularized in Britain and America in Hugh Blair's *Lectures on Rhetoric and Belles Lettres*, the most influential handbook of rhetoric and composition throughout the century after its publication in 1783.[20] "Painting by speech" was the use of description in the service of the economy, clarity, and plausibility that make a narration effective:

> But as, if attainable at all by exertions of your own, it must be rather by a contemplation of examples, than from the abstraction of precepts, I shall at a future stage of our inquiries invite your attention to some of those imperishable models, which have commanded the admiration of ages, and survived the

revolutions of empires; which may teach you what to do, by showing you what has been done.

The remark about the "revolutions of empires" is "interesting" here. It suggests that the passage be read not solely as a commendation of the ancient rhetorical practice of imitation, but also as sounding a basic assumption about the importance of historical consciousness for effective rhetorical leadership. Eloquent narrative description, Adams seems to suggest, is a rhetorical device that works in the service of political continuity.

Narration in Nineteenth-Century Presidential Speech

The idea that "the policy of the future is interwoven with the history of the past" is evident in the earliest presidential speechmaking, playing itself out as a regular recourse to narrative that would strike modern audiences as fairly peculiar. George Washington is not the best exemplar of this tendency, but given his place in the country's immediately preceding history and his stature among his countrymen, this is perhaps not surprising. It simply was not necessary nor would it be particularly in character for the man who had done so much to shape and execute the American founding to refer to that history with much regularity in his speeches. Washington was himself a piece of the well-known revolutionary narrative in his audiences' imaginations, and for him to recite any part of it would have been superfluous and contrary to his known public modesty. Nonetheless, in the first inaugural address, Washington did pay an implicit tribute to the *need* for a narrative presentation of historical circumstances surrounding the moment. His speech begins not with historical narrative but with a personal narrative of the wrenching mental process by which he decided to accept the office.

> . . . it has been my faithful study to collect my duty from a just apprehension of every circumstance by which it might be affected. All I dare hope is that if, in executing this task, I have been too much swayed by a grateful remembrance of former instances, or by an affectionate sensibility to this transcendent proof of the confidence of my fellow citizens . . . my error will be palliated by the motives which mislead me.

In keeping with the ethic according to which offices were to seek men and not the other way around, Washington avoided any grandiose reference to recent history, and yet he still managed subtly to summon history ("former instances") in a way that humbly acknowledged its interweaving with his own personal narrative.

In most of his annual messages, too, Washington avoided narrative, instead referring to his audiences' own acquaintance with the surrounding facts and circumstances and taking that to suffice for a more elaborate recitation, as he does here, in his third annual message:

> Your own observations in your respective situations will have satisfied you of the progressive state of agriculture, manufactures, commerce and navigation. In tracing their causes you will have remarked, with particular pleasure the happy effects of that revival of confidence, public as well as private, to which the constitution and laws of the United States have so eminently contributed; and you will have observed, with no less interest, new and decisive proofs of the increasing reputation and credit of the nation.[21]

While this passage is not particularly eloquent as narrative, its mere appearance strongly indicates that Washington felt that the kind of contemplation invoked by narrative—even when audiences were cued to present it to themselves—was an important duty of his rhetoric.

On one occasion, Washington did make use of extensive narrative, and it is particularly noteworthy because he made explicit connections between that use of narrative and the nature of the new form of government over which he presided. When crisis loomed in the form of the Whiskey Rebellion, Washington responded in his fifth annual message with a lengthy summary and interpretation of events. The speech is typically seen as exemplifying Washington's abhorrence of factionalism and his use of the rebellion's failure as a vindication of the new nation's system of government.[22] While these are of course important aspects of the speech, the most striking formal rhetorical quality of the speech is the sheer length of Washington's narrative summary: some fifteen hundred words, more than half of the entire message.

Washington provided an explanation for this seeming imbalance. After opening with a simple announcement of the rebellion, but before launching into his narrative, he paused to note that, "It is due . . . to the character of our government, and to its stability, which cannot be shaken by the enemies of order, freely to unfold the course of this event."[23] The word "unfold," commonly used in eighteenth-century English to mean "to disclose through description," is a telling word choice. Clearly Washington saw the narrative recreation of the event here not only as practical but as politically fitting.[24] From a practical viewpoint, Washington's factual exposition can be seen as already serving in a small way the advancement of public education that he would ever more strongly advocate later in his presidency.[25] And, of course, the narrative also supplies the evidence undergirding his arguments for garrisoning troops in western Pennsylvania and initiating better regulation of the militia. But in view of Washington's almost apologetic remark, his use of narrative must be understood in yet a broader sense. Such freely unfolded story has a quality that might be called discursive generosity, and as such it betokens the merits of citizenship in a democratic republic. In Washington's mind there is a dialectical relationship between the knowledge-giving role of narrative and the character of the American government: each is in some measure the product of the other, with the government defending liberty in speech and thought, and narrative dissemination of information helping stabilize the government by enabling reasonable civic discourse. Washington's statement, then, is in keeping with the anti-factionalism animating his policies in response to the rebellion and his Federalist position generally. It argues that narrative is a device for holistically capturing events in a way that both fosters a unified political vision resistant to hostile partisan interpretation, and, far from foreclosing debate in some antidemocratic way, sets the terms for further civic discourse on the matter.[26]

An impression of this stabilizing function of narrative may help assuage the sense of disorientation likely to come over late twentieth-century readers of John Adams's inaugural address, which at first blush may seem more like a nineteenth-century Independence Day speech. Even at this very early moment in the life of the nation, the President already felt it necessary to distinguish the first transfer of executive power and inaugurate his term in office with a lengthy narrative interpretation of the well-known events of two prior decades.

> When it was first perceived, in early times, that no middle course for America remained between unlimited submission to a foreign legislature and a total independence of its claims, men of reflection were less apprehensive of danger from the formidable power of fleets and armies they must determine to resist than from those contests and dissensions which would certainly arise concerning the forms of government to be instituted over the whole and over the parts of this extensive country. Relying, however, on the purity of their intentions, the justice of their cause, and the integrity and intelligence of the people, under an overruling Providence which had so signally protected this country from the first, the representatives of this nation, then consisting of little more than half its present number, not only broke to pieces the chains which were forging and the rod of iron that was being lifted up, but frankly cut asunder the ties which had bound them and launched into an ocean of uncertainty.[27]

The passage is quoted at length here because it epitomizes the stylistic tendencies of rhetorical narrative at the time: long and intricately hypotactic sentences, metaphorical coloring, encompassing generalities, and tonal solemnity. Adams took up roughly a quarter of the speech with this narration, moving through the Revolution, the framing of the Constitution, and the two terms of the prior executive. He paused only once for an aside reflecting on the nature of the government, thus bearing out by example Washington's correlation of narrative rhetoric and democratic political character. Although Adams was well-known and respected, he lacked Washington's mighty stature, and consequently this luminous historical narration, drawn in an overtly mythologizing mode ("in early times . . ."), was a rhetorically strategic way for Adams to help convey his own worthiness for the office.

When his chronology reached the Constitution, Adams interlaced his own personal narration, noting that he had first read and approved of the Constitution in a foreign country (i.e., France, where he had served as Washington's foreign minister). As one commentator has summarized:

> In the [personal] narrative, Adams was not an agent but a spectator. He situated himself on the margins where he observed and approved the great experiment. The narrative was Adams' way of expressing his purchase in a constitution drafted without his participation while he was away in Europe. The story also contributed to the cultivation of a national mythology, rehearsing historical events that would necessarily become the foundation for the American identity.[28]

This apt characterization needs but one clarification: Adams is not simply a lone spectator in his narrative, but a co-spectator, and this is an important distinction. He is simultaneously an oracle of history and a model witness to history. Adams's rhetoric, like that of Washington before him, yet in a more explicit way, shows a conviction that civic fitness requires a historical view of the world, that leadership will be conducted in part through recourse to a contemplation of history in public speech, and that the rhetoric of republican democracy entails such free unfolding of events in public discourse. Later in the speech, he noted (as so many writers and speakers of the day were apt to do) that the persistence of the democratic political system depends upon "a general dissemination of knowledge and virtue throughout the whole body of the people" and that the only justifiable national pride is based on "innocence, information, and benevolence." In eighteenth-century usage, the word "information" did not yet fully bear its contemporary arhetorical meaning of context-free data. Instead, it was apt to connote ideas still cognate with "informing [against]" and, more fundamentally, "formation." Hence "information" could be listed quite harmoniously with more subjective notions like "innocence" and "benevolence." It could easily accommodate rhetorical recitation of history and circumstance.

Not all nineteenth-century presidents would make as extensive use of narrative as Adams did in his inaugural address, but most did show a strong bent for narrative in their discourse. Whether it was used or not, substantial evidentiary and historical narrative was always an available means of presidential persuasion. Even when it was not used, a certain historical air was often explicitly summoned in a manner that was designed to inscribe more abstract statements of principle into the known narrative of American history.

Thomas Jefferson, for example, is one president whose rhetoric often lacked a strong narrative quality, a circumstance that can perhaps be attributed to his empiricist cast of mind. His first inaugural address is generally noted for its meliorative tone ("We are all Republicans, we are all Federalists") and most importantly for its famous statement of guiding principles. His statement of principles was not, however, a set of future-oriented policy directives, nor was it a summoning of completely abstract ideas or radically isolated axioms. One strong indication of this is that Jefferson hastened to contextualize his principles historically. Immediately following his litany of principles, he noted:

> These principles form the bright constellation which has gone before us and guided our steps through an age of revolution and reformation. The wisdom of our sages and the blood of our heroes have been devoted to their attainment.

A few lines later he repeated the "steps" metaphor in a manner suggesting that he wished the enumerated principles to be thought of as providing a kind of experiential prudence equivalent to that found in historical knowledge: ". . . should we wander from [these principles], let us hasten to retrace our steps and to regain the road which alone leads to peace, liberty, and safety."[29] At other moments in his rhetorical practice, Jefferson was more conventionally narrative in his approach. All of his annual messages were typical narrative reports of the year's events and circumstances. (Virtually all nineteenth-century annual messages were highly narrative in character; keeping in mind the older connotations of "information," which is what Article II, Section 3 of the Constitution requires the president to provide concerning the state of the union, this was surely seen as the most appropriate practice.) Jefferson's second inaugural address reads much like those messages, providing "outlines," as he calls them, of his first term. The one pointedly argumentative section of the second inaugural address was an endorsement of freedom of the press, which Jefferson gave in a passage narratively recollecting his own re-election as a refutation not only of his critics' partisanship and "licentiousness" but of those skeptical of press freedom:

> The experiment has been tried; you have witnessed the scene; our fellow-citizens looked on, cool and collected; they saw the latent source from which these outrages proceeded; they gathered around their public functionaries, and when the Constitution called them to the decision by suffrage, they pronounced their verdict, honorable to those who have served them and consolatory to the friend of man who believes that he may be trusted with the control of his own affairs.[30]

It was not enough for Jefferson to simply make the argument for press free-dom; he also presented this mini-narrative, which gave the argument a kind of finality by reenacting for the audience their own witnessing of the events and circumstances.

To thus pointedly make witnesses out of the audience seems to be the function of much nineteenth-century rhetorical narrative, and as such it was a tribute to the basic rationality of the American rhetorical audience. The same device is notable in James Madison's war message, an address of some three thousand words, of which all but some two hundred are de-voted to a broad narrative description, or "view" as Madison refers to it, of Britain's offenses.[31] In his second inaugural, he asserted the justice of Amer-ica's actions in the war, then again provided an extensive narrative recita-tion of the conduct of the war. In a telling remark, he spoke of the rhetorical purpose of such narrative as calling into "view" its subject and "painting" a picture of events:

> I need not call into view the unlawfulness of the practice by which our mariners are forced at the will of every cruising officer from their own vessels into foreign ones, nor paint the outrages inseparable from it. The proofs are in the records of each successive Administration of our Government, and the cruel sufferings of that portion of the American people have found their way to every bosom not dead to the sympathies of human nature.[32]

Feigning to eschew narrative, Madison actually expanded the historical context within which he wished his audience to consider the more proxi-mate events of the war.

Few nineteenth-century presidents diverged from the general pattern of using extensive rhetorical narrative. A significant exception is Andrew Jack-son, whose eloquence was carried mostly by his revered ethos and general popularity as a war hero. Otherwise, as presidents taking office were fur-ther and further from the founding generation, the use of extensive narra-tive summary generally continued. John Quincy Adams applied narrative in ways consistent with his teaching as a rhetoric professor, giving an inau-gural address, for example, that expressed his devotion to the Constitution, but that also painted the Constitution at some length as an historical achievement of the previous generation. Martin Van Buren did much the same, seeking to counterbalance his admission that "I belong to a later age" (than that of the founders) with an inaugural address that is little other than a four-thousand–word panoramic view of the nation's history and progress. He explained the strategy:

> . . . to me, my fellow citizens, looking forward to the far-distant future with ardent prayers and confiding hopes, this retrospect presents a ground for still deeper delight. It impresses on my mind a firm belief that the perpetuity of our institutions depends upon ourselves . . .[33]

It may well seem that Van Buren's sentiment evinces a certain contradiction: how is "delight" in "retrospect" commensurate with self-reliance? The answer can only be that to Van Buren, "self" connoted the individual as richly infused with knowledge of and therefore connections to the past.

Even Abraham Lincoln, with his reticence to engage in public rhetoric once he became president, made regular and compelling use of narrative in his formal public orations. It may even be said that the most powerful arguments of his greatest speeches were crucially buttressed by narrative presentation—albeit in somewhat truncated form—of relevant history. Fully half of his second inaugural address was a biblically toned narrative review and interpretation of the prior four years' events, a summary without which his concluding call for national reconciliation would likely have fallen flat. Lincoln's words at Gettysburg, though brief, were powerfully driven by their historical resonance as a narrative linking the events of "fourscore and seven years ago" with those of the cemetery dedication. Without this connection, the speech could not have achieved its hortatory aim of rededicating Americans to the cause of union, nor could it have achieved its hermeneutic aim of foregrounding equality for all as the true nature of that cause. The address's success at reinterpreting the founding did inaugurate a "revolution in thought," as Garry Wills has put it, but not quite a "revolution in style," as Wills also has claimed.[34] The former was possible only because the speech was, at least in its use of narrative, stylistically conservative. Even what it achieved in its brevity was made possible precisely because the address followed Edward Everett's very lengthy narrative exposition of the battle of Gettysburg.

Perhaps Lincoln's most telling use of narrative was in his first inaugural address, which was rather uncharacteristically argumentative and policy-heavy for presidential orations at the time. In it, Lincoln noted that he was taking office "under great and peculiar difficulty" of a sort not met in the "scope of precedent" spanning fifteen prior executives.[35] Far from taking this as grounds for claiming some new paradigm obsoleting the past and calling for any equally "peculiar" measures in the present, however, Lincoln reached back to root the perpetuity of the Union first in the 1774 Articles of Association, then in the 1776 Declaration of Independence, then in the 1778 Articles of Confederation, and only then in the Constitution. Hence he could argue that this perpetuity was "confirmed by the history of the Union itself." Even where the speech did not trace history, it carefully surveyed the situation of the moment, always disclosing circumstances from the vantage point of this perpetuity. The opening line of his justly famous peroration—"I am loath to close"—should be understood as expressing a disinclination to stop the tightly woven narrative flow of the discourse because to Lincoln it metonymically indexed the very fabric of national unity. To relinquish control over the speech was to give that fabric a chance to unravel.

Narration in Twentieth-Century Presidential Speech

It is difficult to document an absence. Perhaps the quickest way to recognize the near absence of traditional narrative in contemporary presidential speaking is to look at—literally *see*—the text of Jimmy Carter's speeches as they are printed in his *Public Papers*. Gazing upon their fragmented appearance on the page—many short sentences, many one- or two- sentence paragraphs, many inset, bulleted policy lists—one can quickly grasp that by the late twentieth-century the narrative quality of presidential rhetoric had drastically changed.

The change appears to have originated in what has become known, after Jeffrey Tulis's work, as the "rhetorical presidency"; that is, the transformation of the presidency near the beginning of the twentieth-century into an office of popular leadership. The shift away from narrative can readily be seen—which is to say, *not* seen—in the rhetoric of Theodore Roosevelt. A telling artifact in respect to this is not any particular speech but the first printed collection of Roosevelt's speeches, suggestively enough entitled, *The Roosevelt Policy*, which was published while Roosevelt was still in office. Edited by Andrew Carnegie, the book collects all of Roosevelt's main speeches on government's relation to corporate wealth, the subject that most precipitated Roosevelt's rhetorical innovations in the presidential office, yet it offers many of the speeches in excerpted form.[36] The editorial decision to excerpt many of the speeches suggests several interrelated sociopolitical conditions: a shift in audience expectations toward a policy-oriented presidential rhetoric, a concomitant shift in that oratory away from tight narrative coherence in rhetorical form (hence the ease of excerpting parts of speeches), and a diminished concern with displaying and weaving narrative connections to broad historical context. As for the last of these conditions, Roosevelt consistently espoused the view, here represented in his 1905 inaugural address, that the past was *not* prologue:

> Our forefathers faced certain perils which we have outgrown. We now face other perils, the very existence of which it was impossible that they should foresee. Modern life is both complex and intense, and the tremendous changes wrought by the extraordinary industrial development of the last half century are felt in every fiber of our social and political being. Never before have men tried so vast and formidable an experiment as that of administering the affairs of a continent under the forms of a Democratic Republic.[37]

Such a view is self-fulfilling, obviating any need for narrative review of the past. Later in the speech, he did note that the "spirit" of the forefathers remained a salient example, he referred to the "mighty past" as a memory to which his audience should remain true, and he praised Washington and Lincoln in his closing; but the problems of the moment and the means of solving them were represented as completely novel. Of course the problems were new, and so would be the means of dealing with them; most immediately evident among these was Roosevelt's rhetorical treatment of history, which is neither presented nor thought of as a narrative, but as a monument. The great men of the past "did their work," he said, and "they left us the splendid heritage we now enjoy."[38] In this speech, the past is less something the audience is intricately connected to and hence still living and thinking with; rather it is reified as an object that is pleasing and beneficial, all the more so because it is superannuated.

This was not the first time that a president had tried to articulate the present moment as unprecedented—Lincoln, quite justly, had done as much—but it is the first time that a president had sought so keenly to sever the present from the past in the national imagination. Compare Roosevelt's approach to that of Benjamin Harrison, who, just sixteen years earlier, had similarly claimed that there were "marvelous and in great part happy contrasts" between the nation's past and present. Though Harrison claimed that he would "not attempt to note" these contrasts, note them he did—in a thousand-word narrative beginning with the institution of the government under the Constitution and describing serially the enormous growth in the nation's prosperity and population through the Civil War and beyond.[39] Over that time, he said, the "suggestions of reason" embodied in the Constitution were "strongly reinforced by the more imperative voice of experience," which had stood as the warrant for, among other things, a federal government strong enough to impose and maintain the tariff. Within this context, ably constructed in a narrative that does more to tie together than cleave apart the "happy contrasts," Harrison characterized his day's revived national enthusiasm for a high tariff (which he supported) as "not a departure but a return that we have witnessed."[40]

The turn away from such nineteenth-century narrative rhetorical practices was graduated but unmistakable. Roosevelt's own calls for greater federal "sovereignty" as a means of dealing with corporate power were not always presented in a historical or narrative vacuum. Though generally he did not survey the causes and development of the growth in corporate wealth and industrial expansion in his many speeches on the subject, on some occasions he did. But even where he did so, the effect was usually to stress the discontinuity of history and the ineluctable dominance of present and future exigency over any considerations framed from the perspective of the past. In tracing the recent expansion of the American industrial economy, he was apt to relegate all preceding time to *ancient* history. He did this in one or another version of a set-piece he used often, such as here, in a 1902 speech in Wheeling, West Virginia:

> A century and a quarter ago . . . commerce was carried on by packtrain, by wagon, by boat. That was the way it was carried on throughout the whole

civilized world—oars and sails, wheeled vehicles and beasts of burden—those were the means of carrying on commerce at the end of the eighteenth century, when this country became a nation. There had been no radical change, no essential change, in the means of carrying on commerce from the days in when the Phoenician galleys plowed the waters of the Mediterranean. For four or five thousand years, perhaps longer, from the immemorial past when Babylon and Nineveh stood in Mesopotamia, when Thebes and Memphis were mighty in the valley of the Nile—from that time on through the supremacy of Greece and Rome, [and so on at length though the Italian and northern European Renaissance, the discovery of the new world, to the founding of the United States] . . . the means of commercial intercourse remained substantially unchanged.[41]

This passage is a kind of anti-narrative: it has the structure and styling of historical narrative and thus borrows in some measure its rhetorical grandeur, but its purpose is to cleave the past from the present rather than to provide a "view," as Madison had put it, providing a context for the moment. In the eighteenth-century idiom, the past here has become "uninteresting."

In place of a political prudence that could operate with the benefit of a full historical consciousness, Roosevelt urged the necessity of the personal integrity of citizens as individuals: ". . . we must never forget [that] the determining factor in every kind of work, of head or hand, must be the man's own good sense, courage, and kindliness."[42] Or: "If there is not this condition of individual character in the average citizenship of the country, all effort to supply its place by the wisest legislation and administration will in the end prove futile."[43] At times, he was apt to discourse at great length upon the qualities of the "average American," and at such times his rhetoric subtly took on the dilatory and expansive tone of an older narrative oratorical style: "He knows, whether he be business man, professional man, farmer, mechanic, employer or wage-worker, that the welfare of each of these men is bound up with the welfare of all the others; that each is neighbor to the other, is actuated by the same hopes, and fears, has fundamentally the same ideals, and that all alike have much the same virtues and the same faults."[44]

For the nation, as for its citizens, all that was needed to deal with new problems were "prudence, self-knowledge, and self-restraint."[45] But self-knowledge, among these attributes, is a somewhat problematic idea in Roosevelt's rhetoric, for his "self"—either national or individual—is nearly bereft of a sense of continuity with its own history; certainly it is a quite different self than that entertained by Van Buren. Thus Roosevelt's rhetoric worked subtly to construct the audience not as a polity by whose consent the government operates, but as a more fragmented, atomistic collection of people nearly at the mercy of one another—and, implicitly, in need of government protection. It proved a useful strategy to a president proposing large-scale changes in the scope and function of federal power. Nonetheless, Roosevelt's inauguration of the rhetorical presidency was measured: his actual recommendations were often more cautious than some of his bolder pronouncements would suggest; he often counseled moderation and restraint in the solutions he posed, and he warned his audiences not to expect miracles. Yet his revision of presidential rhetoric to monumentalize and hence distance the past was decisive for future rhetorical presidents, who would, in the absence of stronger narrative connections to the nation's history, not always proceed with Roosevelt's circumspection.

Woodrow Wilson seemed to understand that a dependence on the integrity of atomized individuals to see the safest course through change was problematic: in his inaugural address he argued that the philosophy of "Let every man look out for himself; let every generation look out for itself" presupposed political self-alienation, and consequently that there was a need to "square every process of our national life again with the standards we so proudly set up at the beginning and have always claimed at heart."[46] Yet in the same address Wilson articulated a disrupted national narrative that surely would frustrate any such squaring, for in Wilson's rhetoric, past and present were not just different, but inverted opposites:

> Some old things with which we had grown familiar, and which had begun to creep into the very habit of our thought and of our lives have altered their aspect as we have latterly looked critically upon them, with fresh, awakened eyes; have dropped their disguises and shown themselves alien and sinister. Some new things, as we look frankly upon them willing to comprehend their real character, have come to assume the aspect of things long believed in and familiar, stuff of our own convictions.[47]

Suggesting as it does that any broader historical context of understanding was essentially void, this view tends to vex the basis for sound political judgment by an audience. Even the vagueness of Wilson's language and his confusing antitheses—multiple interchanging "aspects" and "things"—are disorienting. Thus does Wilson exemplify in this speech one of the central paradoxes of the modern presidency: at the moment the office became "rhetorical," it essentially vacated one of the traditional functions of presidential rhetoric, which had usually involved defining through narrative review of historical and circumstantial evidence a context within which political judgment should be made. The new context is rather like what George W. S. Trow once referred to as the chief cultural product of commercial media: "the context of no context."[48]

Not all twentieth-century presidents would so diminish the place of rhetorical narrative in their oratory. Calvin Coolidge inaugurated his presidency with a speech that ran counter to the approaches of Roosevelt and

Wilson. In contemplating the generally encouraging conditions of the nation, Coolidge was quick to point out that they were the results of generations of effort and sacrifice; nor did he merely mention this in passing.
Instead, he argued that, "It is necessary to keep the former experiences of
our country both at home and abroad continually before us, if we are to
have any science of government. If we wish to erect new structures, we
must have a definite knowledge of the old foundations."[49] Accordingly, he
offered a traditional narrative beginning with the nation's founding, then
traced for several hundred words the main course of events up to the present. Only after this careful recreation did he venture any policy positions,
and even in doing so, he repeatedly buttressed his hopes for what could be
with a view to what had been. But Coolidge's speech is a rare exception.

Another exception is presidential war rhetoric, wherein twentieth-
century presidents have all continued in some measure the narrative practices of nineteenth-century oratory. Karlyn Kohrs Campbell and Kathleen
Jamieson have noted this in their treatment of war rhetoric: they list the presentation of "a chronicle or narrative from which argumentative claims are
drawn" among five key characteristics of presidential war rhetoric.[50] In fact,
the function of narrative in war rhetoric goes beyond merely stating the
facts on which later arguments rest. Wilson opened his war message by
saying that there were "serious, very serious, choices of policy to be made,"
but the address was relatively short on policy—some four hundred out of
thirty-six hundred words.[51] It was long, however, on narrative recreation of
the events and circumstances leading up to the moment. The duration and
vividness of his narrative and analysis were not simply a buttress to Wilson's call for war; they were a dramatization of one of his central arguments—namely, that the "deception" and "aggression" of Germany were a
function of despotic rule, and that such behavior was "happily impossible
where public opinion commands and insists upon full information concerning all the nation's affairs."[52] In a manner that similarly echoed Washington's view that such information was "due to the character of our
government," Harry S. Truman was careful to note in his first radio and TV
address on Korea that "It is important for all of us to understand the essential facts as to how the situation in Korea came about."[53] He then gave
lengthy narration of those facts going back more than a decade, and summarized them again two months later in the second radio and TV address.
Although none of these addresses reaches far back into history for context,
it is significant that in those rhetorical moments most dreadfully charged
with forging popular consensus, presidents do typically trace, paint, and
contemplate the surrounding situation at some length, and not simply as a
warrant for argument but as a means of enacting executive power.

By and large, however, rhetorical presidents have made scant use of historical narrative as a significant means of persuasion in their most visible

speeches. History, when it is mentioned, is generally cited, or simply referred to as our "heritage" rather than followed or recreated. A case in point is John F. Kennedy's much admired inaugural address, which drew heftily on history but did so in a remarkably fragmentary and oscillating way. In his opening, Kennedy consecutively referred to "the same oath our forebears prescribed nearly a century and three quarters ago" (distant past), then flatly announced that "The world is very different now" (urgent present), veered back again to the "revolutionary beliefs for which our forebears fought" (past), which were now being fought for elsewhere in the world (present), then reminded his audience that they were "heirs to that first revolution" (past), but that "the torch has been passed to a new generation" (present), a generation "proud of our ancient heritage" (present fused to distant past).[54] Near the end of the address, he again spoke of his generation as being one of the few "in the long history of the world" charged with "defending freedom in its hour of maximum danger." He then made the famous appeal—"And so, my fellow Americans: ask not what your country can do for you—ask what you can do for your country."[55] The antimetabole is memorable, but it is the conjunctive "and so" that is the most crucial part of his plea. "And so" explicitly meant "because we are a generation uniquely charged with a grave duty"; but in the wake of the speech's preceding historical disjunctures, it also meant "because we are an *unprecedented* generation charged with a grave duty." It is partly in consequence of this latter meaning that Kennedy strove to remind his audience that they needed to think of themselves not as customers or clients but as citizens. In the absence of strong narrative connections to the past, so it seems, such reminders are needed.

More recent presidential rhetoric shows a similar deemphasis on history as narrative. Ronald Reagan's first inaugural address, held on the west steps of the capitol so that the television cameras could pan over the national mall, quite literally monumentalized history. In the close of his second inaugural address, he followed a similarly cinematic strategy. Noting that "history is a ribbon, always unfurling; history is a journey," he asked his audience to recall "those who traveled before us." In keeping with the metaphor, one might reasonably have expected a connected itinerary in narrative form. Instead—after cracking a joke about the weather—Reagan drew a melodramatic montage of disparate images: ". . . a general falls to his knees in the hard snow of Valley Forge; a lonely president paces the darkened halls, and ponders his struggle to preserve the Union; the men of the Alamo call out encouragement to each other; a settler pushes west and sings a song, and the song echoes out forever and fills the unknowing air." Here was history as a Hollywood production, complete with swelling soundtrack.

George Bush, in his inaugural address, atavistically summoned the "memory of Washington," whose hand, Bush reminded his audience, had also touched the Bible on which Bush laid his; then he noted on that bi-centennial of the presidency that "our continuity these two hundred years since our government began" was a "stunning fact."[56] So stunning was it, in fact, that that was the end of the matter. The only other mention of history in the speech was a potentially salient one—namely, the still-potent effects of the Vietnam War—but Bush simply declared that "the statute of limita-tions has been reached," as if history had timed out.[57] On another occasion, there was momentary cause for hope that Bush would revive the old nar-rative office of presidential rhetoric. He began his first State of the Union address auspiciously:

> Tonight, I come not to speak about the "state of the Government"—not to de-tail every new initiative we plan for the coming year, nor to describe every line in the budget. I'm here to speak to you about and to the American Peo-ple about the State of the Union—about our world—the changes we've seen, the challenges we face. And what that means for America.[58]

This was an altogether fitting beginning for a speech that is required by the Constitution to "give to the Congress information on the State of the Union," especially when the eighteenth-century connotations of "informa-tion" are kept in mind. But Bush failed to follow through on his promise. After mentioning World War II and then the fall of the Berlin Wall as events that divided present from past, he followed the pattern of virtually all late twentieth-century State of the Union addresses, which have become almost solely vehicles for announcing policy.

Bill Clinton's rhetoric fares no better where narrative use of history is concerned. Early in his first inaugural address, he remarked that "Though we march to the music of time, our mission is timeless. Each generation of Americans must define what it means to be an American."[59] These two statements can be simultaneously true only under the condition that "what it means to be an American" has nothing to do with "our mission." In keep-ing with this fragmentation of the generations, Clinton gave what may be one the most scattered of any inaugural addresses. Like Teddy Roosevelt, he presented the past as obsolete: "When George Washington first took the oath I have just sworn to uphold, news traveled slowly across the land by horseback and across the ocean by boat." The speech made frequent his-torical references, but chronologically the references are jumbled: from the Founders, to the Cold War, to George Washington, to global communica-tions, back to a one-sentence survey of the "pillars" of our history (or three of them: The Revolution, the Civil War, the Great Depression), then back to Thomas Jefferson. Such disordered references read more like hypertext than narrative, which is inherently linear. Echoing Kennedy, Clinton an-nounced, "We must do what no generation has had to do before." Then once again he went back to the Founders, who "saw themselves in the light of posterity," to which Clinton added: "We can do no less." Until one recalls that the Founders did not see themselves *only* in the light of posterity, the statement could almost mean, "We are *able* to do no less." In his 1996 State of the Union address, Clinton showed promise in asking perhaps the most crucial of all political questions in a democracy: "How do we preserve our old and enduring values as we move into the future?" But he gave no real answer. Instead, he offered digested sentiments like this one: "We live in an age of possibility. A hundred years ago, we moved from farm to factory. Now we move to an age of technology, information, and global competition."[60] The ages of "technology, information, and global competition" have been dawning for quite some time, of course, but audiences listening to Clinton's oratory would never know it, because in Clinton's hands both rhetoric and history have themselves been reduced to information in its raw, decontextualized, "information-age" sense.

Causes, Consequences

The reasons for the de-narratization of presidential rhetoric are multiple and interrelated in complex ways that can only be suggested here. The most obvious reason is quite natural: the historical age of the country. As the nation simply had more history to it—a history punctuated with transforming events such as the major wars—it became more difficult (though not impossible) to survey the past in a practical narrative span. The development of the presidential office as a rhetorical platform for popular leadership is probably the most profound cause. This shift meant that presidents would deliver a far greater number of speeches than they once did, often several a day, and it is probable that the rhetorical effectiveness of historical narrative would be diminished were it to become a routine occurrence. The increased reliance on the speechwriting apparatus, which has come to mean that most speeches are now crafted by committee to send a particular policy "message," also militates against the use of narrative, for narrative, as a story, tends to presuppose a single author.

The proliferation of electronic media as the main channel for presidential communication has vastly extended the distribution and replayability of speeches, thus adding to these problems. Seeking to use the media for their own purposes, rhetorical presidents have come to understand that speeches are to be pruned for easy quotability, thus also militating against the use of narrative, which is inherently unfit for the sound bite. The electronic mass media have also enabled rhetorical presidents to speak more directly to a vast audience. (Some of the rare instances of historical narrative in recent presidencies have come before smaller audiences where media attention was scant: Ronald Reagan at a Constitution bicentennial celebration in Philadelphia, reminding his audience in an eloquent historical narration that political divisiveness is hardly a recent phenomenon in American politics;[61] George Bush tracing the history of the Civil Rights Act at a commemorative gathering in 1989, weaving it into the narrative fabric of the nation's history;[62] or Bill Clinton offering a historical overview of Youngstown, Ohio and its contribution to the nation's progress in a Fourth of July speech there in 1996.[63]) The vastness and diversity of the mass media audience makes the use of narrative problematic. In the age of postmodernism, political correctness, and identity politics, history has become a "contested site," the mention of which is as likely to fragment the mass audience as it is to summon grounds for consensus. Yet another problem for the orator who would employ historical narrative is, sadly, that he or she might just lose the audience. The state of pre-college history education in America is poor at best, while the most pervasive form of rhetoric to which Americans are exposed—advertising—relentlessly propagandizes for an eternal present.[64]

Nearly half a century ago, the renowned rhetorical theorist and critic Richard Weaver lamented the disappearance of what he referred to as the "spaciousness" of nineteenth-century political rhetoric.[65] By "spaciousness," Weaver meant that the old rhetoric relied on a high degree of resonant generality, applied historical and literary reference with regularity, and operated under a quasi-judicial "right of assumption" that "precedents are valid, that forms will persist, and that in general one may build today on what was created yesterday."[66] This assumption, upon which the use of rhetorical narrative depends, was possible because the American audience shared to a far greater degree than it does today a basic consensus of belief. Notes Weaver, "The object of an oration a hundred years ago was not so much to 'make people think' as to remind them of what they already thought."[67] Given this, we might be quick to assume that the relegation of rhetorical narrative in presidential rhetoric is a measure of democratic progress. Weaver quite persuasively held that the inability or unwillingness of contemporary orators to call on narrative spaciousness was not a good thing. For one, such narrative is essential for establishing contextual grounds whereon political discourse may be reasonably conducted. Second, Weaver explains, such spaciousness was critical for maintaining an "aesthetic distance" neither too close nor too far between audiences and speakers, and between audiences and the subject matter of speeches.[68] Spacious, narrative political speech consequently transcended what Weaver terms the "impertinence of singularity"—the central indecorum committed by speakers who use excessive policy detail and fragmentary historical citation. Weaver's notion of aesthetic distance is useful, because it adds a dimension to the notion of "political distance" often cited as a prerequisite for healthy

presidential leadership. But rather than rooting the collapse of proper distance in the practices of the media, Weaver's idea suggests that the collapse
is promoted by what many take to be a normal part of official presidential
conduct.[69]

The gravest consequence of the loss of proper distance is that speakers
who fail to maintain such distance denature, even corrupt, their audiences.
Hearers are thus conditioned to abdicate the role of participants in a polity
that obligates them to take account of one another not just as individuals
but as citizen-actors in a great and very real historical drama. Presidents
who eschew narrative and offer little but policy in their speeches treat the
public as a *populace*: in effect, they train their audiences to think in terms
that are prone to be less civic than utilitarian—to ask not what they can do
for their country, but what their country can do for them.

10

The Rise of the Rhetorical Candidate

Richard J. Ellis and Mark Dedrick

Twud be inth'restin' . . . if th' fathers iv th' counthry cud come back an' see what has happened while they've been away. In time past whin ye voted f'r prisidint ye didn't vote f'r a man. Ye voted f'r a kind iv a statue that ye'd put up in ye'er own mind on a marble pidistal. Ye nivir heerd iv George Wash'nton goin' around th' counthry distrributin' five cint see-gars.

—Mr. Dooley

Nothing seems more unremarkable than a presidential candidate delivering a speech before a large, enthusiastic crowd. We expect those who would be president to come to us, the people of the United States, and solicit our votes. We expect them to explain their positions on the issues, to mobilize the faithful, and to persuade the wavering. Every presidential candidate is expected to criss-cross this vast country in pursuit of votes. Would-be presidents do not stand for office, they run for it.

Although we take this sort of behavior for granted today, it represents a radical departure from the behavior Americans used to expect and generally get from their presidential aspirants. For close to a century, the prevailing norm was that "the office of president of the United States should neither be sought nor declined."[1] So hardy was this norm that it survived, though not unscathed, the emergence of organized, mass-based political parties, the adoption of universal white male suffrage, and even the breakdown of the congressional nominating caucus. Andrew Jackson himself, even as he revolutionized the basis of presidential authority,[2] dutifully upheld this norm. As he explained to a friend, "I meddle not with elections, I leave the people to make their own President."[3]

Of course, nineteenth-century presidential candidates, Jackson very much included, were rarely as disinterested or as passive as they claimed. President

Abraham Lincoln, for instance, while striking a statesmanlike pose, worked behind the scenes to ensure his reelection. Indeed, according to his Secretary of the Treasury, William Pitt Fessenden, Lincoln was "too busy looking after the election to think of anything else."[4] Yet in "feigning disinterest," Jeffrey Tulis points out, "candidates exemplified a public teaching that political campaigns were beneath the dignity of men suited for governance, that honor attended more important activities than campaigns." According to Tulis, in the nineteenth-century "the tone of campaigns was set by that of governance." Presidents generally did not give partisan or policy-oriented speeches and so presidential candidates were expected to refrain from such undignified behaviors as well. Today, Tulis observes, "in a striking reversal, campaigns are becoming the model for governing." Those responsible for crafting the electoral strategy are brought in to shape governing strategy. Governance becomes an extension of the campaign. Governing, like campaigning, becomes a perpetual quest for popular support.[5]

Tulis traces this seismic shift in American politics to Woodrow Wilson. Wilson, Tulis notes, was "the first victorious presidential candidate to have engaged in a full-scale speaking tour during the campaign." Wilson, according to Tulis, brought us not only "the rhetorical presidency" but also "the rhetorical campaign." Indeed for Wilson, the two phenomena were necessarily related. "In Wilson's view," Tulis tells us, "the rhetorical campaign was intended . . . to prepare the people for a new kind of governance—the rhetorical presidency." Wilson revolutionized not just presidential governance but presidential campaigns.[6]

The stark contrast in candidate behaviors between a Bill Clinton and an Andrew Jackson or a Bob Dole and an Abraham Lincoln reveals the dramatic, revolutionary changes that have occurred in American presidential campaigns. Yet the dichotomy between a nineteenth-century "old way" and a twentieth-century "new way" obscures as much as it reveals. It relies on an overly unified and static version of nineteenth-century presidential history. Moreover, focusing on a single, pivotal presidency, whether that president is Wilson or, alternatively, Theodore Roosevelt, slights the gradual evolution in candidate behaviors and expectations that occurred in the latter third of the nineteenth century and the opening third of the twentieth century. Finally, by treating all presidential candidates of a given era as essentially the same, it ignores the quite different norms that attached to incumbent presidents and challengers.

The Nineteenth-Century Presidency

The nineteenth-century presidency was not simply a logical extension of the Founders' original constitutional design. Writing in 1881, William Graham Sumner suggested that in fact "the intention of the constitution-makers has gone for very little in the historical development of the presidency." Instead, he believed, "the office has been moulded by the tastes and faiths of the people."[7] Sumner overstated his case, but he provides a useful reminder of the dynamism of the nineteenth-century presidency, buffeted as it was between venerable republican traditions and an emergent mass democracy, between a search for leaders of dignity and self-restraint and a fiercely competitive party system that relentlessly organized and mobilized the American voter. In nineteenth-century presidential campaigns, there was no single norm, no constitutional "old way," but rather contested, rival norms, derived from divergent political cultures.

As historian Gil Troy has shown, the norm proscribing candidate speech coexisted uneasily with the parties' and candidates' own political interests as well as with the people's growing demand to know, as one voter wrote to Lincoln in 1860, "exactly every inch of ground you stand upon." That expectation had been stoked by Jackson's bold declaration in 1824 that it "is incumbent on me, when asked, frankly to declare my opinions upon any political or national question pending before and about which the country feels an interest." Believing that voters had a right to know where he stood on the leading issues of the day, Jackson penned a numbers of letters designed for publication that laid out his position on the issues. In the 1828 campaign, Jackson was constantly badgered by his advisers to refrain from declaring his opinions or answering attacks. Such behaviors, Jackson was repeatedly told, violated presidential decorum and would only hurt the candidate. James Polk, for instance, bluntly warned:

> the ground taken for you by your friends . . . that you live in retirement on your farm, calm and unmoved by the excitement around you, taking no part in the pending canvass for the Presidency, but committing yourself into the hands of your country, would seem to superficial observers to be inconsistent with any appeal to the public made by you at this juncture.

"Our people," Martin Van Buren advised Jackson, "do not like to see publications from candidates." Jackson largely heeded this advice, explaining to one disappointed correspondent that were he to state his opinions he "would be charged with electioneering views for selfish purposes." As an incumbent, in 1832, Jackson needed no prompting from his advisers to tell him that the proper course was to remain silent during the campaign.[8]

Not everyone, though, was persuaded that a candidate for president should remain mute. In 1836, Kentucky Congressman Sherrod Williams announced that it was "the right of every citizen of the United States to ask and demand and be fully informed of the political principles . . . of those who are candidates for the various offices in the gift of the people." This was no less true of candidates for president than it was for any other candidates for public office. Insisting that each presidential candidate "has the imperious duty to frankly and fully . . . disclose the opinions which he entertains," Williams posed five political questions to each of the presidential candidates running for office.[9] Presidential candidates in the middle of the nineteenth-century found themselves whipsawed between contradictory expectations. On the one hand, they were not supposed to seek the presidential office; on the other, they were supposed to engage in a direct and honest dialogue with the people about the issues.

William Henry Harrison's 1840 campaign vividly illustrates the dynamic interplay of conflicting norms. Throughout 1839 and the first part of 1840 Harrison made no public appearances, largely remaining at home and modeling his behavior on George Washington. The dignity of the presidency, he insisted, prevented any man from actively seeking the office. To those who inquired about his views, Harrison referred them to his record or to specific letters he had written prior to his nomination, most especially the detailed response he had made to Williams's inquiry in 1836.[10] Early in the spring, Whig operatives announced that since Harrison's views had already "been given to the public," the General would make no further statements, leaving the task of answering mail to a three-man "correspondence committee." Democrats immediately seized upon this as a violation of democracy. Jackson's old organ, the *Washington Globe*, countered that in a democracy a candidate "must give direct answers to all reasonable inquiries [concerning] character and principles." Harrison was ridiculed as "General Mum," a "caged" simpleton, an "Old Granny" too feeble to leave home. Against such charges, Harrison's defenders countered, "There is not a man in the United States who has more frankly and distinctly expressed his opinions upon questions involving matters of public policy than General Harrison."[11]

As the Democratic attacks on Harrison intensified, the General decided to reverse course and go public, making a three-week tour in June and a month-long trip in September. Such behavior, he told one crowd, violated his own "sense of propriety," and he worried aloud that he might be "establishing a dangerous precedent." Yet though he preferred to "remain at the domestic fireside," he felt impelled to show the people that he was not the "caged," decrepit man depicted by Democrats. In his speeches, Harrison insisted he was not electioneering: "I do not come here to ask your sympathy or to excite your feelings in my behalf," he told one crowd in Cincinnati. Though he generally avoided issues, he did not shrink from attacking the Democrats. And, as Troy points out, on occasion Harrison did make policy pronouncements: "'Methinks I hear a soft voice asking: Are you in favor of paper money? I AM,' Harrison shouted to the 'ten acres of Whigs' gathered at Dayton, Ohio." Showing little concern for consistency,

Whig newspapers praised the size and enthusiasm of the crowds that came to see and hear Harrison. Democrats also subordinated consistency to partisanship, now condemning Harrison for vulgarly begging for votes as if he were running for local sheriff.[12]

Taking to the stump as Harrison did remained the exception rather than rule, but the notion that the people had a right to know where a presidential nominee stood on the issues was rapidly becoming a widely accepted norm, much to the chagrin of one well-to-do Whig who complained to Henry Clay that "since the categories of Sherrod Williams set the precedent, every one claims to question the candidate of his life, opinion and general conduct." Van Buren, Harrison's opponent in 1840, refrained from taking the stump, but wrote long, frank letters that explained his position on important issues. As Van Buren explained, responding to "interrogatories from my fellow Citizens upon public questions" was a presidential candidate's democratic duty, and quite different from soliciting support. After being nominated by the Whig Party in 1844, Clay initially vowed that he would retire quietly to his home since the people "should be free, impartial and wholly unbiased by the conduct of a candidate himself," but he soon broke his pledge of silence, penning several public letters that attempted to clarify his position on the annexation of Texas. Clay's opponent in 1844, James Polk, tried to say as little as possible for fear of alienating key constituencies but even he agreed that it was a presidential candidate's "imperative duty" to address "NEW QUESTIONS, or old questions upon which he had not been sufficiently explicit." Democracy demanded that voters know where their candidates stood on the issues.

By the 1840s and 1850s, then, presidential candidates were no longer expected to remain silent, though some, like Polk, found it politically advantageous to say as little as possible. Writing issue-oriented public letters was becoming relatively routine, but public speaking was quite a different matter. Harrison's departure from the republican taboo in 1840 was not repeated again until 1852 when another Whig general, Winfield Scott, took to the stump in a five-week railroad tour. Scott believed, as one supporter put it, that "a live lion in good voice, will produce . . . a far greater and more lasting effect by being *seen* and *heard*, than all the [campaign biographies] which can be written." Democrats lambasted Scott, who in choosing to "beg . . . for votes" had violated the venerated traditions set down by the "wise and patriotic Fathers." Scott's speeches avoided all issues, but this, too, brought him criticism from Democrats who felt that his speeches insulted the people's intelligence and encouraged "man-worship." Whigs, meanwhile, denied that Scott was electioneering and pointed to the spontaneous enthusiasm that everywhere greeted the candidate's appearances. After Scott's defeat, many Whigs as well as Democrats blamed the loss on Scott's "stumping tour," which they contrasted unfavorably with Pierce's "talent for silence."[13]

Party elites' post hoc analysis of the electoral consequences of Scott's speaking tour helped to solidify the old proscription. Speaking was not just bad form but might actually be electorally costly. Even in the wake of Scott's debacle, however, the injunction against speaking remained anything but absolute. In fact between 1860 and 1872, three of the four Democratic presidential nominees—Stephen Douglas, Horatio Seymour, and Horace Greeley—took to the stump. Douglas began the 1860 presidential campaign expecting "to look on and see a fight without taking a hand in it," but repeated entreaties from local Democrats together with his own concerns about the country's perilous situation led him to launch a speaking campaign that directly addressed the divisive issues confronting the nation. To those opponents who criticized his unseemly behavior, Douglas retorted: "What a pity it would be if a man, by the honest expression of an honest sentiment, should lose anybody's vote." In 1868, Seymour, another accomplished Democratic orator, bucked convention. Like Douglas, Seymour initially vowed not to take "an active part" in the campaign, but then bowed to the "universal sentiment" among his friends that he take the stump. As the Democratic *New York World* insisted, the taboo against presidential candidates' speaking "has no foundation in reason." Given the Republicans' tremendous financial and organizational advantages, why should Democrats deny themselves their one asset, "the most powerful and impressive speaker in the United States?" In 1872, Greeley was also persuaded to take the stump. As a Democratic congressman explained: "Things are proper now . . . that never were before."[14]

Traditional rhetorical norms, however, remained a powerful constraint on candidate behavior. Even as Greeley became the third Democratic candidate in four elections to break with convention, he acknowledged "the unwritten law of our country that a candidate for President may not make speeches." For defying the norm, Greeley, much like Douglas and Seymour before him, was denounced as the "great American office beggar" who believed the "man should seek office rather than the office the man."[15] Greeley, like Douglas, Seymour, and Scott, was beaten badly, which only helped to drive home the lesson that the stump was for losers. Staying home was now not only good form but good strategy.

The 1876 contest affirmed both the power of the old norm and the gulf separating the presidency envisioned by the Framers and the presidency as it had come to exist in the mid-nineteenth century. Democrat Samuel Tilden, who had managed Seymour's campaign for the presidency in 1868, decided he could not wait for the presidency to seek him out. Instead he established a "literary bureau" that circulated his speeches and other documents intended to advertise his candidacy and create a "Tilden Boom."[16] Upon his nomination, moreover, Tilden wrote an acceptance letter of unprecedented length that spelled out in excruciating detail his position upon virtually every issue mentioned in the party's platform. Tilden's Republican opponent, Rutherford Hayes, was more concise but still devoted close to fifteen hundred words to a discussion of what he deemed the central campaign issues. Hayes's issue-oriented letter was a dramatic departure from the practice of his Republican predecessors, Lincoln and Grant, neither of whom had gone beyond 250 words.[17]

Though Hayes and especially Tilden were innovators in certain respects,[18] their behavior as candidates remained powerfully shaped by traditional norms. Both candidates went to great lengths to avoid the appearance of electioneering. "Silence," Hayes told his campaign biographer, "is the only safety." As a symbolic display of restraint, Hayes refused even to vote for himself on election day. Tilden, too, publicly professed disinterest and, like Hayes, retreated to the governor's mansion to await "the call of the people." Both Tilden and Hayes largely followed the accepted practice of leaving the job of promoting their candidacy to the legions of party orators who fanned out across the country. Not everyone was happy with the "customary" reserve displayed by the candidates. When it appeared that Hayes had lost, Republicans groused about the candidate's studied silence. Democrats, meanwhile, complained about Tilden's refusal to answer Republican charges. And to those who believed that the vital function of a presidential campaign was to scrutinize the candidates' views on the "vital and fundamental questions" or even just to "sift a man's character," the candidates' insistence on remaining in the background seemed irrational and even undemocratic.[19]

Candidates in the late nineteenth century continued to be buffeted by conflicting expectations. On the one hand, they were not supposed to solicit votes or display unseemly ambition; on the other hand, they were expected to communicate their views on the issues to voters. People wanted their presidential candidates to be dignified, but they also wanted to be able to scrutinize the candidates. James Garfield, the Republican nominee in 1880, struggled to carve out a role that would satisfy these contradictory norms. Invited to New York to soothe a party rift, he at first resisted for fear such a trip would appear undignified, but ultimately relented. On route to and from New York he greeted enthusiastic crowds at virtually every stop. His speeches never went "beyond thanks & an occasional remark on the localities through which [he] passed," but the success of the trip brought Republican calls for Garfield to take the stump. "If I could take the stump," Garfield confided, "I should feel much happier," but President Hayes and other Republicans urged him to "sit cross legged and look wise until after the election." In the face of conflicting advice, Garfield hit upon an innovative arrangement that in 1896 would come to be dubbed the "front-porch" campaign. By remaining on his Ohio farm, he placated the traditionalists who believed candidates should await the people's call, but by greeting swarms of visitors at his home he "played the good democrat, addressing

the people as equals in his own home." In speaking to the people he de-
fied "the foolish custom which seals a presidential candidate's lips," and yet
at the same time his speeches respected convention by avoiding issues or
policy stands.[20]

In 1884, a quite different, more modern tack was taken by the Republican nominee, James Blaine, who launched an extensive tour in which he
made more than four hundred short speeches, mostly praising the protective tariff. Blaine made no apologies for his popular appeals: "I am a profound believer in a popular government," he explained, "and I know no
reason why I should not face the American people." Republicans praised
his "bold and brilliant" efforts while Democrats, predictably, charged him
with "vote-begging." Blaine's opponent, Grover Cleveland, opted for a
more dignified pose, remaining for most of the campaign at the governor's
office in Albany, just as Tilden had done in 1876. Yet even Cleveland, who
was never one for public speaking, did give two substantive if brief
speeches (one in Connecticut, the other in New Jersey) on civil service reform, tax reduction, and the conditions of labor. Policy-oriented speech
was clearly no longer proscribed though taking to the stump, in the fashion of Blaine, was still to open oneself up to criticism for demeaning the office.[21]

Wishing to avoid the fate that had befallen Blaine, Benjamin Harrison in
1888 chose instead to stay at home and emulate Garfield's "front-porch"
strategy. But unlike Garfield, who had carefully avoided issues in his addresses, Harrison spoke often on the virtues of the protective tariff as well
as on the need for increased veterans' pensions and civil service reform.
Harrison's front-porch campaign was also much better organized and more
carefully scripted:

> a committee arranged the visits and reviewed proposed introductory
> speeches—twice. Two to three times a day, at the appointed hour, Harrison
> would stride from his house in Indianapolis to nearby University Park, listen
> to the greetings, and respond. Afterward, Harrison edited these speeches and
> sent them out on the Associated Press wires for publication the next day.

All told, Harrison gave ninety-four speeches to 300,000 people in 110 del-
egations, going in the course of a few months from a relatively unknown
ex-senator from Indiana to the principal spokesman for the Republican
Party. Most indicative of all, few people questioned the propriety of Harrison's behavior.[22]

The reaction to Harrison's speaking in the 1888 campaign signaled the
shift that had taken place in the nation's expectations of candidate behavior.
Yet at the same time, President Cleveland's behavior in 1888 as well as President Harrison's own actions in 1892 (the first incumbents to be renominated

by their party since Ulysses Grant in 1872) show that the norms for sitting presidents were different than those for challengers. The thought of a president campaigning, the *New York Times* pronounced in the summer of 1892, "disgusts the people." Conscious of the dignity of the office, neither Presidents Cleveland nor Harrison took an active public role in their campaigns.[23]

Few candidates for the presidency disliked stump speaking as much as Cleveland. Yet in 1892, Cleveland, now a challenger once again, was persuaded to turn his speech accepting the nomination into a massive political rally. In 1884 and again in 1888 Cleveland had given traditional acceptance speeches. In 1884, for instance, a short, dignified, and private ceremony was held at the Governor's residence, where Cleveland gave a short speech that by his own admission was filled with little but "trite [and] . . . simple truths." This time, though, Cleveland agreed to accept the nomination at Madison Square Garden. Unlike the private ceremonies of the past, the public was let in this time. As the *Times* reported, "The doors of the Madison Avenue entrance were now like a dam holding back a vast reservoir. From without there came a hoarse, rumbling sound; the doors were quickly thrown wide open and a sea of human beings came pouring in." Roughly fifteen thousand people rushed into the Garden, filling every spare inch, cheering madly, and chanting loudly, "four—four—four years more." Large pictures of Cleveland and the vice presidential candidate Adlai Stevenson hung over the entrance, and behind the speakers' platform were "the words 'Cleveland and Stevenson' in huge electric-lighted letters." The event was, as the *Times* pointed out, "without precedent in political annals." So raucous was the crowd that Cleveland found it impossible to speak; returning to his chair did not restore quiet and so he was "obliged to speak without waiting for order." Only then did the shouting and cheering subside.[24] A more dramatic contrast with the stately, stiff acceptance ceremonies of the previous years would be hard to imagine.

It was not the setting and ceremony alone that broke new ground, but the speech itself, which was far more issue-oriented and partisan than any previous acceptance speech. Cleveland aggressively attacked the Republican tariff system as bad for "the plain people," consumers, farmers, and even the working man. In rousing Jacksonian tones, the ex-president condemned "unjust Governmental favoritism" and "the accumulations of a favored few" that invariably resulted from such favoritism. He tore into the Republicans, reminding his audience of the "saturnalia of theft and brutal control" that took place during Republican Reconstruction and of how Republican party managers robbed the people of their duly elected president in 1876. Cleveland made no apologies for his "tone of partisanship" which, he explained, "befits the occasion." He instructed the crowd on the paramount importance of party unity, and of the disastrous consequences that would result from a Democratic defeat in the coming campaign. "Let us tell the people," he urged his followers, "plainly and honestly what we believe and how we propose to serve the interests of the entire country." Cleveland's break with tradition brought a predictable outcry from Republicans, who complained that Cleveland had behaved like "a hired orator before a district meeting." "No Presidential candidate in the course of American history," complained one Republican partisan, "ever before made a speech so unworthy of his dignity." Democrats, however, loved the public spectacle; it showed, said the Democratic National Chairman, "that the candidates were in touch with the people."[25]

After his dramatic acceptance speech, Cleveland returned to his summer home on Buzzard's Bay where, against the strong urgings of his de facto campaign manager, he reverted to a more conventional campaign of letter writing: "I have never been a stump speaker and do not think I should be a success in that role," Cleveland explained.[26] Still Cleveland did not avoid public speaking altogether. He moved to New York in mid-October and in the weeks leading up to the election made several speeches at campaign rallies in New York City. On the Saturday before the election he traveled to New Jersey to deliver a blistering attack on the Republicans' tariff policy before a huge and enthusiastic crowd of Democratic partisans.[27] Republicans might not have liked what Cleveland said, but few if any believed Cleveland's speech was improper. Cleveland's relative inactivity during the bulk of the 1892 campaign had more to do with his own proclivities than it did with any norms of the day. A different candidate, with a different temperament and skills, could expect to find little resistance to taking a prominent speaking role in the campaign. In 1896 that candidate came along in the person of William Jennings Bryan.

From Bryan to FDR

The 1896 campaign is probably the most famous in American history. It is remembered for Bryan's precedent-shattering speaking tour as well as for the carefully orchestrated and impressive front-porch campaign of William McKinley. An estimated five million Americans across twenty-seven states heard one of the six hundred passionate and substantive speeches Bryan gave during the campaign. McKinley stayed home but still managed to speak to 750,000 people in the three hundred or so speeches he gave.[28] Neither Bryan nor McKinley shied away from issues, the former focusing almost exclusively on free silver while the latter preferred to harp on the virtues of the protective tariff.

Bryan's herculean speaking tours and McKinley's slick front-porch campaign marked a giant step in the direction of the modern candidate-centered campaign. Yet to focus on the revolution made is to miss the evolutionary changes that had laid the foundations for such behavior. The term "front-porch campaign" may have been coined in 1896, but there was nothing particularly novel about McKinley's behavior. McKinley certainly gave more speeches than Harrison had (three times as many in fact) and to more people, but the basic campaign design was clearly derivative. Bryan's behavior, too, had precedents (in Cleveland's 1892 acceptance speech, as well as in Blaine's ill-fated tour in 1884, not to mention Douglas, Seymour, and Greeley), but more important was the gradual change in expectations and incentives that encouraged Bryan to make such a tour. By 1896 the nominee was expected to be the primary spokesman and central figure of the campaign.[29]

To be sure, the immense scale of Bryan's stumping did bring partisan criticism. Republican John Hay, who in 1884 had praised Blaine's speaking tour as "bold" and "brilliant," now condemned Bryan for "begging for the Presidency as a tramp might beg for a pie." Most Republicans, though, seemed more disturbed by the "reckless" policies Bryan advocated and the emotions he played upon than they were by the act of stumping itself. Indeed a number of worried Republicans, Mark Hanna included, urged McKinley to join Bryan on the stump. McKinley rejected their pleas, explaining that "I might just as well put up a trapeze on my front lawn and compete with some professional athlete as go out speaking against Bryan."[30]

The 1900 rematch between Bryan and McKinley provides further evidence of the different constraints felt by challengers and incumbents at this time. Bryan essentially reprised his performance from 1896, but McKinley's behavior changed radically. "The proprieties," McKinley reasoned, "demand that the President should refrain from making a political canvass on his own behalf."[31] In 1904, the same "proprieties" constrained the far more garrulous incumbent, Theodore Roosevelt. During his first term in office, Roosevelt had not hesitated to go to the people,[32] but after his nomination, Roosevelt went almost completely silent. The strain on him was terrible. "I could cut [Alton Parker, the Democratic nominee] into ribbons if I could get at him in the open," Roosevelt told his son. "But of course a President can't go on the stump . . . and so I have to sit still and abide by the result." A sympathetic Henry Cabot Lodge wrote to Roosevelt: "I think it depresses you a little to be the only man in the country who cannot take part in the campaign for the presidency."[33]

The behavior of Judge Parker showed how radically different the norms were for challengers. Unlike Roosevelt, who longed to be on the stump, Parker would have preferred to maintain a dignified silence. Parker initially tried to adopt a low-key, front-porch campaign, but amidst continual rumors that Parker would take the stump he was eventually dragged out on to the stump by Republican criticisms of the "Mummy" and by Democrats urging him to speak to the people. "The one thing more than anything else that the people of the country want to see," party leaders informed Parker, "is the candidate and hear him speak on the issues."[34] During the last week of the campaign, Parker spoke in public every evening, before large crowds in New York, New Jersey, and Connecticut

The 1908 campaign began with both candidates, William Howard Taft as well as Bryan, intent on conducting a front-porch campaign reminiscent of McKinley's 1896 campaign. By the end of summer, though, Bryan had reverted to his old ways. Taft, concerned with Bryan's popularity as well as by the paucity of people visiting his Cincinnati front stoop, decided that he, too, needed to take to the stump. The *Washington Times* assured the candidates: "It is not undignified, it is not improper. The people want to see and listen to the men asking their votes." Taft could not match Bryan's eloquence, but he came close in quantity, delivering four hundred speeches over an 18,000 mile tour.[35] For the first time in the nation's history, both major party presidential nominees had criss-crossed the nation in search of votes. Taft (not Wilson) became the first victorious presidential candidate to mount a full-scale speaking tour, and in doing so helped erase the association between stumping and losing. That Taft, who neither enjoyed public speaking nor was good at it, took to the stump testifies to how completely expectations of candidates had changed. At the same time, Roosevelt, who loved speaking to large crowds, remained silent in 1904, showing that incumbent presidents still operated under a different set of expectations.

In 1912, Taft found himself the incumbent while Roosevelt, the nominee of the Progressive party, was now a challenger. Free of all constraints, Roosevelt immediately hit the hustings, denouncing Taft, speaking early and often until an assassin's bullet in mid-October temporarily slowed the Bull Moose. The incumbent Taft meanwhile raced for the protective cover of the norm that had so tormented Roosevelt in 1904. Invoking "the dignity of his office," Taft fell almost completely silent after his acceptance speech, except during the week leading up to the election when he wrote "a few dignified letters for publication."[36]

Woodrow Wilson, the other major candidate in the historic 1912 election, disliked the emotionalism of the "extended stumping tours" that he associated with Bryan and Roosevelt. Respectful of the "old-fashioned" proprieties, Wilson emphasized that "people . . . look for dignity in high office." He initially refused to mount a demeaning "rear-platform" campaign of the sort that Taft and Bryan had engaged in 1908. "I don't mind talking, but I do mind being dragged over half a continent," he explained to a friend. The telegraph, he pointed out, was a far more effective means of communicating his message than trying to cross the nation by train. Wilson's view was untenable and outmoded, and he was quickly compelled to stump, at least across the Midwest and Northeast (the South he took for granted and the West he left to Bryan). In the modern campaign the candidate's persona increasingly was the issue; people wanted to know not just where Wilson stood on the issues but what sort of a person he was. Wilson himself acknowledged this demand in a speech in Indiana. "It is a great pleasure for me to . . . greet . . . my fellow countrymen in this way," he told the assembled crowd, "because I know they want to see what I look like, at least; not for the sake of my beauty, but for the sake of forming their own opinion as to what sort of chap I seem to be."[37]

As president, Wilson remained wary of campaigning, which he viewed as "a great interruption to the rational consideration of public questions." While Wilson's Republican opponent, Supreme Court Justice Charles Evans Hughes, traversed the country attacking the Wilson administration, Wilson refused to take to the stump. "Bad taste is always bad judgment," Wilson reasoned. At a press conference at the end of September, he was asked repeatedly about his reluctance to campaign. He was too busy with the real work of governing to campaign, he explained. Moreover, he felt that "it is a sort of impropriety for the President to campaign, not because of the dignity of the office, merely, but because, after he has served for four years, the record is there, and he can't change it." Wilson, though, was feeling the heat from Democrats worried by the recent Republican victory in Maine, which was among the many states Hughes had already visited in his tour. A few days before the press conference, Wilson had already delivered his first campaign speech from his estate at Shadow Lawn, the first of seven campaign addresses he would eventually deliver from his summer home. Democrats were not satisfied though. "A stump, my Kingdom for a stump," implored one Democratic Senator. Wilson consented to appear before the country but refused to turn his travels into what he derisively termed a "speech-making campaign." In early October, for instance, he traveled to Omaha, Nebraska, to speak at festivities celebrating Nebraska's semi-centennial, en route making no less than fourteen stops in the critical state of Ohio. At none of the stops, though, did Wilson go beyond expressing his gratification at the reception. Compared to his opponent Wilson was a model of traditional restraint. But the campaign speeches he delivered at Shadow Lawn and in New York as well as the more nonpolitical speeches in Baltimore, Omaha, Indianapolis, Chicago, and Cincinnati represented a far more active postnomination campaign than any previous incumbent had attempted. Wilson's contribution to the modern presidential campaign was incremental, though, not foundational. In some ways in fact Wilson acted as a brake on emerging public expectations of candidate behavior, particularly in his reluctance to reveal his personal life to the press or the public. Like many of his contemporaries, Wilson continued to feel conflicted, caught, as Troy notes, "between traditional sensibilities and modern demands."[38]

One such conflicted contemporary was Warren Harding, the Republican nominee in 1920. Harding vowed to emulate McKinley and stick to his front porch; "this method of campaigning," he explained, "conforms to my own conception of the dignity of the office." But like Parker and Taft before him, Harding was pushed onto the stump by opposition charges that he was violating his "clear duty" as a candidate and pulled there by local Republicans insisting on the candidate's presence. Democrats, on the other hand, showed none of Harding's (or Wilson's) ambivalence. Their model was not McKinley but the hard-charging, aggressive campaigning of Bryan. Harding's opponent, James Cox, was "perpetually in motion," outdoing even the Great Commoner by traveling 22,000 miles and speaking to over 2 million people. Subsequent Democratic nominees behaved similarly. Even John Davis, the gentlemanly former ambassador that the Democrats nominated in 1924, covered 12,000 miles in order to speak to the people.[39] Both Al Smith in 1928 and Franklin Roosevelt in 1932 relished taking their case to the people and campaigned extensively across the country. But what of incumbents?

The Republican nominee in 1924, incumbent Calvin Coolidge, was famous for his silence, but he was no traditional candidate. Coolidge liked to tell people that "no Presidential candidate was ever injured by not talking too much," but "Silent Cal" was far from mute during the 1924 campaign. Indeed, by nineteenth-century standards he was almost verbose. He talked far more than Theodore Roosevelt had in the 1904 campaign, for instance. After the now obligatory lengthy acceptance speech in mid-August, Coolidge used the occasion of a visit of labor leaders on Labor Day to defend his administration's policies and to attack the "radicalism and paternalism" of Senator Robert La Follette, the Progressive Party nominee. Later that week he traveled to Baltimore for the unveiling of a monument to Lafayette and again attacked La Follette. Two weeks later Coolidge spoke to 100,000 Catholics in Washington, D.C., and vigorously upheld the principles of religious liberty, which in 1924 was far from a nonpartisan gesture. That same week, before several thousand members of the National Association of Retail Druggists, Coolidge pledged lower taxes and less interference with business. The following day he traveled to Philadelphia to speak at a ceremony commemorating the 150th anniversary of the Continental Congress, and used the nonpartisan occasion to criticize key planks of the Progressive Party platform. And that was just in September. Moreover, a number of Coolidge's speeches were transmitted via radio to larger audiences. The most important of these was a detailed, issue-specific speech before the United States Chamber of Commerce that was broadcast via radio to the entire nation just two weeks before the election.[40] Coolidge could, of course, have spoken much more. In the second week of September, the *Times* reported that Coolidge had on his desk sixty-five speaking invitations from organizations across the country, and the president considered embarking on a western tour if a trend to La Follette developed. All indications, though, were that even with the La Follette challenge Coolidge was safe.[41] Coolidge's decision not to tour reflected political strategy (as well as his own taciturn personality), not the constraint of norms.

Strategy and personality had become more important than traditional norms of presidential dignity in explaining candidate behavior, as is evident from Herbert Hoover's behavior in the 1928 and in the 1932 elections. Previous presidents had always campaigned dramatically less in their reelection bids than they had in their first run for office. Hoover was the first president of which this was not true. In 1928, Hoover, confident of his lead and uncomfortable with public speaking, campaigned as little as possible, delivering seven carefully crafted speeches but little else. In 1932, Hoover hoped to remain similarly inactive, and announced at the beginning of the summer that "except for a few major addresses expounding policies of the administration I will not take part in the forthcoming campaign." But 1932 was not 1928, and the Republicans' defeat in the Maine election finally brought Hoover out onto the stump. Hoover now threw himself into "the rough and tumble" of partisan campaigning, traveling across the midwest, excoriating Roosevelt for lying, evasiveness, and even profiteering. For the first time, a president was campaigning as actively as a challenger, giving as good as he got, trading partisan barbs before partisan crowds across the nation. The president as campaigner had arrived.[42]

The emergence of the modern president as campaigner was confirmed in the 1936 election. While Hoover had swung uncontrollably between dignified passivity and frenetic partisan campaigning, Roosevelt devised a campaign that deftly wove together the dignified and nonpolitical with the partisan campaigning. Roosevelt made a series of "nonpolitical" trips throughout the summer that enabled him to appear as "President of the whole people." As aide Samuel Rosenman observed, these nonpolitical trips, to a drought-stricken area of the midwest or a part of the northeast working on flood control, were "the most effective political trips a President can make." Unlike Hoover who was forced onto the stump by political events and partisan attacks, Roosevelt from the outset planned to reserve his explicitly political stumping for October. During the five weeks leading up to the election, Roosevelt took to the stump like a duck to water. In speeches across the nation, in auditoriums as well as from the rear platform of a train, the president vigorously defended New Deal programs and his administration and attacked the Republican party leadership.[43]

On election day, Roosevelt was reelected to the presidency in a historic landslide that buried not only his opponent, Alf Landon, but the traditional proscription against presidential stumping. Future incumbents would, of course, continue to capitalize on the president's nonpolitical duties and status. And presidents on the stump would still often try to take the "high road," leaving the harsher partisan or personal attacks to the vice president or the national party chairman.[44] But the question of whether it was dignified or acceptable for a president to travel the country and actively solicit the people's vote had been settled for good. The president was no longer to be fixed on a "marble pidistal" but was now expected to speak with the American people just like any other candidate for elected office.

11

The Rhetorical Presidency, Presidential Authority, and Bill Clinton

Keith E. Whittington

Bill Clinton is unlikely to ever be known as the "Great Communicator." His speeches, even on formal occasions, are often of inordinately long duration. His instincts are "wonkish," favoring policy details over political vision. But Clinton is deservedly known as the "Great Campaigner." His favored discursive style is personal and intimate. With the benefit of television, those personal moments can be vicariously enjoyed by large audiences. Like Ronald Reagan, Clinton has used his rhetorical skills to achieve political success, surviving in office despite legislative defeat and personal scandal. The Clinton presidency both diverges from and recalls that of Reagan, raising questions as to whether Clinton marks the full realization of what has been called the "rhetorical presidency" or its transcendence.

This chapter is concerned with clarifying the concept of the rhetorical presidency and its political development, and with exploring some aspects of that concept as applied to the Clinton presidency. Analysis of the rhetorical presidency is too often divorced from the broader institutional and political context of the presidency, which has particular implications for understanding the Clinton presidency. Some have suggested that Clinton has altered the form of the rhetorical presidency so as to avoid many of its difficulties. But Clinton's particular deviations from the Reagan model have done less to transform the rhetorical presidency as previously understood than to bring it to fruition. I will begin with a reconsideration of the rhetorical presidency and its link to the rise of the "modern presidency." The Clinton administration serves to underscore the perils posed by the modern rhetorical presidency, notably its manipulation of legislative policymaking, its propensity toward demagoguery, and its de-emphasis of deliberation.

The Traditional Rhetorical Presidency

The concept of the rhetorical presidency has been rendered somewhat ambiguous by its use to refer to both the practices and ideals governing presidential communications generally and the specific set of practices followed
by twentieth-century presidents.[1] I distinguish here between the "traditional" rhetorical presidency of the nineteenth century and the "modern" or
"new" rhetorical presidency of the twentieth century. Both are specifica-
tions of the general concept of what Jeffrey Tulis has called the "second
constitution" that governs with whom presidents communicate and how.[2]
Moreover, the study of the rhetorical presidency must be distinguished
from the study of presidential rhetoric, which is generally less concerned
with questions of institutional practice and political authority than with
forms of communication.[3]

Presidents have always used rhetoric to communicate to the public and
politicians and to structure their political environment. In the nineteenth-
century, however, there were tight restrictions on presidential communication and a sharp division between how presidents related to the public and
the political elite. At the core of traditional practice was the limitation of
spoken addresses to the people to an essentially ceremonial and educative
function. Presidents did not often venture into the public arena, and when
they did it was for such formal occasions as inaugural addresses or memorial dedications. On those occasions, the presidential role was specific. The
president was to mark the solemnity of the moment, help draw the nation
together by an appeal to common principle and experience, and offer a lesson in true constitutional values. Presidents appeared before the public as
representatives of its best ideals, and their function was as much symbolic
as governmental. The presidential bearing was to be dignified, the message
uncontroversial, the rhetoric principled.

Traditional presidents were not above politics, but politics had its place.
Presidential communications about substantive policy were either informal
or written, and were directed to members of the political class. Thomas Jefferson initiated the practice of sending only a written text of his State of the
Union address to Congress. The custom was maintained throughout the
nineteenth century.[4] Such practices helped give meaning to the idea of representative government. Government officials were representatives of the
people, sent to deliberate on the public business. Popular authority was
recognized through the electoral elevation of a particular set of individual
representatives, but the public did not have a direct role in making policy.
Constant appeals to the people to determine government policy bore too
many risks.[5] Public favor could be won by demagogues appealing to mere
self-interest or transitory emotions. Necessary compromises could not be
made by those with longer experience and a broader perspective. Modera-

tion would be lost to divisive appeals to popular prejudice. Partisan behavior by the president, for example, threatened to undermine the sense of the presidency as a national representative. A partisan president was necessarily a partial president, elevating a faction over the whole. The inaugural address was a ritual moment of national reconciliation after a bitter campaign, in which the president laid aside the trappings of a candidate to take on the mantle of a popular representative.[6]

Presidential authority in this model is derived above all from the constitutional office. The Founders had sought to replace informal power based on individual charisma with formal power based on impersonal law.[7] When the president went to the nation at large, he was to be clothed in the mantle of office to impart constitutional wisdom, not to pursue power. Andrew Johnson's national speaking tour seeking to rally support for the 1866 congressional midterm elections provoked outrage and eventually played into his impeachment, even in the midst of one of the most partisan periods in American history. Johnson was charged not only with degrading the presidency with his public appeals, but also with threatening the stability of the Republic.[8] A public presidency subverted the constitutional checks and balances, as it traded the limited authority of a particular office for the broader authority of popularity. Popular appeals by the president were necessarily self-aggrandizing, coming at the expense of the popular credentials of other government officials. The strictures of the traditional rhetorical presidency further served to reinforce the significance of constitutional office by specifying the mode of presidential communication. The president's right to speak came from his official duty, and it was limited by that duty. Public presidential intervention in the legislative process was rare. Presidents could advise Congress in their annual messages or challenge Congress in their veto messages, but presidents were to recognize congressional independence as bills were being considered.

The Rhetorical Presidency and the Modern Presidency

The traditional rhetorical presidency was gradually abandoned in the twentieth century. Beginning with Theodore Roosevelt's "bully pulpit," twentieth-century presidents have increasingly been willing to use their office to rally public support behind their policy positions. Although Roosevelt initiated the practice, Woodrow Wilson gave it a coherent vision. For Wilson, the Constitution was an evolving organism, not a machine to be maintained. As a scholar, Wilson was among a growing number of writers who took a more "realistic" view of presidential power, emphasizing public support and informal leadership over constitutional authority and legal powers. Moreover, the presidency held the key to potential governmental beneficence. Decisive energy and unity of purpose were cardinal virtues for Wilson that only the president could provide. The presidency was a prime repository of those virtues, and the old constitutional understandings merely hampered their exercise.

The Wilsonian president was to take a leading role in the political system, which required modifying presidential practices and inherited constitutional understandings. The president could take such a role by shedding the presidency's specifically executive character and undertaking a distinctly more political function in a revised democracy. The reformed president was to be less concerned with administering congressional policy than with the "interpretation" of public opinion.[9] The president's new constitutional task was to provide the vision for future policy and to rally public support around that vision. The president was to lead through an interaction with the people, not merely to execute government policy.

This reconceptualization of the presidential role was accompanied by and partially achieved through an alteration in the practices of the rhetorical presidency. The new rhetorical presidency was less formal and more popular, less argumentative and more assertive. The characteristic presidential speech in the twentieth century has been directed at popular rather than congressional audiences and has been oral rather than written.[10] Presidents shed their inhibitions about commenting on pending legislation and began to "go public" in order to appeal "over the heads" of congressmen to their constituents for support in current legislative battles.[11] Confidential negotiations among elites were increasingly supplemented or replaced in legislative efforts with public displays of political force. If presidents could not effectively cajole or purchase support through personal contact and political promises, they could coerce the compliance of legislators by threatening electoral repercussions for intransigence. Public presidential discourse became less concerned with reaffirming consensual values and more concerned with identifying and rallying partisans. The distinction between governing and campaigning was gradually blurred.[12]

This evolution of the rhetorical presidency is closely related to changes in the political system more broadly. Yet examination of the rhetorical presidency is often separated from the study of other aspects of the presidency and American politics. This division is reinforced by a tendency to evaluate the rhetorical presidency in the same terms as political scientists evaluate other aspects of the modern presidency—notably, in the language of power. Does presidential rhetoric "persuade" politically relevant audiences? Can rhetoric be separated as a distinct explanatory variable in legislative accomplishments?[13] But such questions are misplaced, and the distinction between the rhetorical presidency and the modern presidency is artificial. The concept of the rhetorical presidency is less concerned with power than with authority, less concerned with distinguishing instruments of power than with characterizing the exercise of presidential power and influence.

The new rhetorical presidency is intimately related to the changes in the party system and presidential selection and to the institutional and ideological features of the modern presidency, narrowly defined.[14] Wilson's reconceptualization of the presidential role was a particular manifestation of Progressive thinking about U.S. parties and political system. The nineteenth-century inheritance of "congressional government" was seen as regressive and corrupt. Presidents, in Wilson's view, had become mere pawns of party factions entrenched in Congress, and the parties themselves had ceased to be representative of popular desires. The revaluation of constitutional structures would provide the president with a direct relationship to the American people, and the old party apparatus would be transcended by presidential interpretation of the popular will. Parties were no longer necessary as intermediaries between the president and the people, and by speaking directly to the public presidents built support for their individual political agendas and identity rather than the concerns of a political party more broadly. This new model of presidential leadership implied that presidents were personally responsible for social and political outcomes. Presidential candidates were to be selected on the basis of their issue advocacy rather than their party services. Presidents were themselves to develop and articulate the political agenda.[15] Presidents were to circumvent or overcome legislative intransigence to realize their mandates. Although Wilson provided the theoretical justification for presidential leadership, Franklin Roosevelt provided the institutional structure to support such leadership. If presidents bore a direct responsibility for articulating and achieving political goals, then the presidential office required the resources to draft and implement the means for achieving those goals. Moreover, whereas Wilson thought of the reformed president as a party leader, Roosevelt was forced by party resistance to his agenda to establish the power of the presidency as an independent force in American politics.[16] As presidential activity and independence became paramount requirements of the office, the method of presidential selection was adjusted to emphasize the required skills. The party reforms of the 1960s and 1970s were implicit in the transformation of the office in the early decades of the century. Presidential candidates were now evaluated on their media savvy and public persona, not their bargaining skills or legislative reputation.[17] Ronald Reagan and Bill Clinton possessed the qualities most suited to the modern presidency. Such unsuccessful challengers as Walter Mondale and Bob Dole were more akin to such successful nineteenth-century candidates as Martin Van Buren and James Polk. They were successful party and political "insiders," but had no mass following and little popular charisma with which to build electoral support based on their personal identity.

Clinton and the Rhetorical Presidency

The Clinton presidency offers an opportunity to revisit the characteristics of the modern rhetorical presidency and particularly Jeffrey Tulis's original concerns about its development. The rhetorical presidency scholarship took root during the Reagan era, and although there was a longer lineage of modern rhetorical presidents, Reagan quickly became the exemplar. This had great benefits and costs. The obvious importance of public rhetoric to the Reagan presidency propelled an interest in the topic, but Reagan's image tended to overshadow the details of the theoretical and historical model. Reagan simply was the rhetorical presidency. Once that assumption is made, the rhetorical presidency model becomes excessively brittle. The Reagan presidency may have stood at the end of a long historical development, but Reagan himself was unique. Although Clinton is quite different from Reagan, he embodies many of the characteristics of the new rhetorical presidency. Unlike Reagan, Clinton is not prone to televised addresses from the Oval Office inviting voters to call their congressmen.[18] In contrast to Reagan, Clinton offers no grand vision of politics.[19] In place of Reagan's grandfatherly image that deflected criticism, Clinton appears more in the guise of a salesman who survives despite criticism.[20] But in shedding such particulars of Reagan's performance, Clinton highlights more central features of the modern rhetorical presidency.

For Clinton, the task of governance is seamlessly linked to a permanent electoral campaign. Although this approach to government appears consistent with Clinton's personal experience and character, it is also the consequence of his political situation. Modern congressional parties remain quite weak, and there are few mechanisms for gaining a legislative majority other than winning one vote at a time. As a "New Democrat," Clinton also faced some difficulty in mustering party loyalty for a legislative program that was constantly shifting and ideologically incoherent. The president initially attempted a mix of legislative strategies, ranging from party appeals, to individual negotiations, to televised speeches, to speaking tours. Nonetheless, his first budget battle unfolded as a parody of the classic Neustadtian bargaining strategy, with the president forced to publicly buy (and sometimes buy again) the votes of individual backbench congressmen with specific promises for parochial interests.[21] The eventual failure of Clinton's health care proposal and the Republican takeover of Congress freed the president from his relationship with congressional Democrats. Clinton has relied heavily on a strategy of "campaigning to govern" in order to prove himself still relevant.[22] No longer the putative head of a legislative majority, Clinton has been freed to concentrate on building public support for his programs and trying to influence legislative outcomes by altering the political agenda. The 1995 government shutdown highlighted this strategy as the president used his veto power to hold off Republican budgets while using his public platform to frame the debate in a manner most favorable to him. Ultimately, the president proved far more adept at capturing the public mind than did the Republican leadership, who were forced to absorb the blame for the impasse.

Although the pathologies of this style of governing are many, they are difficult to escape in the modern context. Beyond any personal failings of management, style, or substance, Clinton has also suffered the consequences of his situation and exemplifies the qualities, tendencies, and risks of the modern rhetorical presidency. It should not be surprising that the greatest crisis of the Clinton administration was also deeply personal. When presidential authority is built on the qualities of the individual, then the most sensitive and the most relevant aspect of a president will be his personal character. The Clinton presidency has been highly personal from its beginnings in the campaign film, "The Man from Hope," to the Lewinsky saga as Clinton continued to trade on his personal connection with the voters. Such an immediate relationship between the president and the people left Clinton no choice but to publicly deny any inappropriate relationship with Monica Lewinsky. No longer primarily a constitutional officer or party representative, the modern president is nothing but a charismatic individual leader. As a consequence, individual personality becomes the most relevant feature of presidential politics. The remainder of this chapter briefly considers three particular illustrations of this in the areas of legislation, public leadership, and deliberation.

Presidential Leadership and the Health Care "Crisis"

A major drawback of the modern rhetorical presidency, as developed in the earlier literature, is the increasing presidential reliance on public speaking to coerce Congress into passing hastily drafted presidential initiatives. Presidential rhetoric created a legislative imperative arising from some identified crisis, which supplanted both the need for and possibility of the type of legislative deliberation desired by the Founders. The discourse surrounding policy proposals increasingly emphasized impending crisis and the need for haste, qualities that have traditionally favored executive power within the constitutional system. Policy problems were characterized by the president as "crises"; policy responses became "wars," whether the target of the moment was poverty, inflation, energy, drugs, or crime. Legislative measures were more likely to be drafted within the executive branch and then rushed through Congress, avoiding the detached consideration and exposure to multiple interests that were central to the Founders' constitutionalism.[23]

Jeffrey Tulis has recently argued that Clinton provided the possibility of moving beyond the modern rhetorical presidency, especially in his handling of the health care issue. Indeed, Tulis argued, Clinton's failure in the health care debate derives in part from the inability of others to perceive his constitutional innovation and the president's unwillingness to explain it. Tulis finds certain presidential speeches highly significant in their effort to build public support for an agenda rather than for a specific piece of legislation. As a consequence, presidential rhetoric could help create the context for legislative deliberation, rather than substituting for it.[24] Consideration of this example, however, indicates that though Clinton may have revised the rhetorical presidency of his immediate predecessors, he did not transcend it. Indeed, much of the administration's behavior in this area fell into precisely the pattern seen as most problematic in the modern presidency. Further examination of this case emphasizes that presidential rhetoric cannot be separated from its institutional and political context. Although the language of some of Clinton's speeches may have departed from that of his recent predecessors, his institutional and political effort closely adhered to the standard script of the modern presidency.

This political genesis of the Clinton health care plan indicates the continuing operation of the modern rhetorical presidency model and the implausibility of a later Clinton revision of that model. Significantly, although various health care reforms had been under consideration for decades, the health care debate of Clinton's first term began as a campaign issue. Its elevation onto the national political agenda was a function of the efforts of candidate Clinton's campaign advisors to secure electoral support in first the primary and then the general campaign. Consistent with the Wilsonian model of politics, health care policymaking was driven by the imperatives of a political campaign, rather than by party or legislative deliberation. Such results are structurally reinforced in the context of candidate-centered campaigns, in which candidates prevail on the basis of personal issue advocacy and elections serve as plebiscites.[25] Given the intimate connection between Clinton's campaign and the health care issue, proposed reforms were necessarily personalized. Modern campaigning and its role in agenda setting extend the logic of the modern presidency itself, which emphasizes presidential leadership of the polity. Clinton's particular commitment to government activism merely highlights this relationship, leading him to embrace explicitly such Rooseveltian imagery as the "100 days" time frame.[26] Health care reform was necessarily presidential policy.

Having placed health care reform on the national political agenda, Clinton went to extremes to personalize the debate over the particular reforms. The appointment of his wife to head the health care task force symbolized the president's personal stake in the debate over legislation. In its reliance on presidentially designated policy experts, its carefully maintained secrecy from congressional and party leaders, and its ambitious comprehensiveness and complexity, the presidential effort to draft health care reforms identified Clinton not only with reform generally but with a very particular reform program. The administration's unintended delay in presenting its legislation allowed alternative reform proposals to be offered and derailed efforts to force a dichotomous choice between comprehensive reform and the status quo. Nonetheless, the task force's product necessarily dominated the eventual debate, and its flaws could be readily attributed to all reform proposals. Moreover, the president was unavoidably identified with the task force's effort. There could be only one "Clinton plan" once the task force was constituted. The process was wholly inconsistent with the type of deliberation favored by critics of the modern rhetorical presidency such as Tulis. The health care proposal represented the presidential absorption of legislative tasks. The task force bypassed congressional deliberation in favor of an insulated, hierarchical process. Meanwhile, Clinton sought to foreclose debate and highlight presidential qualities of energy with a rhetoric of crisis.

Clinton did suggest a different approach in some speeches to Congress on the health care issue, which some have taken as a beginning of a transformation of the rhetorical presidency. This rhetorical effort was limited, however, and at odds with his institutional efforts. Specifically, in a September 1993 address to Congress, Clinton identified five principles that must be met by reform legislation in order to be accepted by him.[27] At this point, Clinton did not detail his own legislative proposal and invited Congress to offer its own specific proposals. The speech did not attempt to box Congress out of the deliberative process but rather seemed to invite congressional initiative in developing the reforms. Moreover, the speech suggested that the presidential role was to rally support behind basic principles rather than to dictate specific policy. Although suggestive, this rhetorical effort was ultimately disingenuous and futile. At the same time that the president was inviting congressional deliberation, the first lady was presiding over a task force designed to minimize congressional participation. Given the complexity and comprehensiveness of the administration's own eventual proposal, the room for presidential compromise was necessarily limited. The task force's work was designed to be accepted as a whole, as the fulfillment of the president's electoral mandate. Once the administration's proposal was made public a month later, the president could not maintain a stance of neutrality toward competing plans or suggest that other plans were equally capable of realizing his stated goals.

The weakness of the president's position was made clear by the time of his January 1994 State of the Union address. The introduction of the administration's plan pushed the debate from one of vague goals to one of specific costs and benefits, and momentum on the health care issue stalled. The 1994 message to Congress was to reinvigorate the debate on the president's terms. Clinton again made the case for the existence of a crisis, supporting both his own authority and the need for reform. The president concluded by reiterating, "I am open . . . to the best ideas of concerned members of both parties. I have no special brief for any specific approach, even in our own bill," except that any acceptable proposal must guarantee "universal" health insurance.[28] How Clinton could give no priority of place to his own proposal, even after the dedication of substantial administration resources to its development, the president did not explain. Senator Robert Dole's televised response demonstrated how far the field had shifted from the fall. Dole denied that there was a health care "crisis," though he admitted that there were problems. In that context, incremental reform under congressional direction was most appropriate. Moreover, Dole crystallized the president's comprehensive reform plan in a complex chart detailing the "mountain of bureaucracy between you and your doctor" that would be created by the administration's proposal.[29] Dole's speech eliminated the distance between the president and the administration's proposal, while mortally wounding Clinton's specific plan. Later presidential efforts to create room for compromise in his requirement for guaranteed universal coverage quickly brought charges of administration waffling and political confusion.[30] The reform effort was abandoned by the end of the summer.

The fate of Clinton's health care effort illustrates an administration torn by the tensions inherent in the modern rhetorical presidency. Health care reform emerged out of a presidential campaign as a central political issue, yet there was little political or policy preparation within Congress to develop or act on a unified program of reform. The president played the now-routine trump card of "crisis," yet the lengthy process of developing a legislative proposal sapped the persuasiveness of that claim. The administration sought to offer a single comprehensive package, but in doing so it blurred the goals of reform and highlighted the limits of the electoral mandate. The president sought to present himself as open to compromise, even as the administration inevitably committed the president to a single course of action. By allowing friends and foes alike to define the content of the president's various principles of reform, the administration found itself unable to adjust its public posture to respond to legislative developments. Although Clinton's failure was exaggerated in its scope, it was prefigured in the historical political situation that he entered and the limited political resources available to his administration. This example indicates not only the continuing significance of the developments associated with the modern rhetorical presidency, but also the dangers of attempting to separate presidential rhetoric from its institutional context. Twentieth-century developments incorporate both a discursive style and a set of institutional and ideological practices that are mutually reinforcing. Clinton's brief efforts to alter his discursive strategy were pursued along with a highly stylized adherence to the familiar script of the modern presidency.

The "Medi-scare" Strategy

A second and related peril explicated in the rhetorical presidency literature is the fear of demagoguery. According to early proponents of the idea of the rhetorical presidency, demagoguery was a major concern of the Founders.[31] In its softer form, demagoguery pandered to transitory public opinion, flattering the citizenry rather than enlightening it. Popularity rather than the public good became the driving force of politics. In its more immediately subversive form, demagogues manufactured or exploited divisions within society to enhance their own position and that of their supporters. The practices associated with the classic rhetorical presidency of the nineteenth century were integral to a constitutional effort to minimize the opportunities for and dangers of demagoguery in a popular government.

In this context, demagoguery is not only a discursive strategy but also a perversion of constitutional forms. The original conception of the rhetorical presidency emphasized the distinction between the founding and normal politics. The founding was an extraordinary event of directly pursuing the consent of the people to the principles of good government. The appropriate political task of normal politics was one of preservation.[32] Rhetorical efforts were to educate the people in the principles of true republican government, reinforcing inherited constitutional forms. If elected government officials were to appeal directly to the people for support in daily legislative struggles, then the struggles of the founding would be effectively perpetuated. The populace would be aroused and divided in constant contests over the future of American government, placing the political edifice at risk.[33] The turbulence of genuinely popular politics could not be indefinitely maintained without frequent mishap and eventual disaster. Republican constitutionalism would be replaced by plebiscitary democracy.

The safeguards against demagoguery have been removed in the twentieth century, according to the rhetorical presidency scholarship, and as a consequence, demagogues have become more common and deliberative government has been made more difficult. The modern rhetorical presidency minimizes the dangers of demagoguery and dismisses the significance of the founding as a historical event. For Woodrow Wilson, the basic task of political leadership is to interpret public opinion and struggle over fundamental principle, not merely to conserve inherited commitments and execute government policy. In contrast to the Founders, who thought that true political leadership was rare, Wilson had more faith in the capacities of politicians and their publics. Wilsonian presidents are regularly called on to be the public leaders that the Founders did not expect to be readily available. Clinton's strategy in his battle with the Republican Congress over the federal budget illustrates this continuing tendency.

After the 1994 midterm election, power seemed to slip even further from the White House to the Congress and in particular from the president to the Speaker of the House. The Republican takeover of Congress placed Clinton in a difficult position. On the one hand, it freed Clinton from managing uncooperative congressional Democrats in a superficially unified government. On the other hand, the surprising Republican occupation of Congress seemed to render the Democratic president an early lame duck. The president felt compelled to announce at a press conference that he was still relevant.[34] Clinton's political problem was determining how to make that assertion a reality. A central element, though hardly the only one, of the president's strategy to regain political influence and position himself for ultimate reelection was his handling of the Medicare issue in the budget debates of 1995.

Serious efforts to achieve long-term fiscal balance would necessarily require some reform of entitlement spending. Both the president and the Congress were at least nominally committed to a hawkish position on the deficit. Nonetheless, the administration decided to avoid any potentially politically damaging fiscal decisions in its 1995 budget proposal to force the Republicans in Congress to initiate cuts in Medicare spending and absorb the expected constituency backlash alone. The administration then led attacks on the Republicans for planning those cuts. The attacks were particularly noteworthy given the close similarity between the Republicans' proposed spending on Medicare and Clinton's own previous proposals. There were significant structural differences between the plans, but the administration chose to emphasize the cuts rather than the restructuring.[35] White House policy advisors urged Clinton to exploit the opportunity to make real reforms in entitlement spending. Political advisors urged Clinton to exploit Republican vulnerability on Medicare to recover the support of senior citizens and increase his standing in the polls. The president took the political advice.[36]

The president's subsequent attack on the Republicans' proposed budget for Medicare was widely reviled among opinion leaders. Although the Republican plan was criticized in the press on various structural grounds, the administration did not pursue such critiques.[37] The administration's focus on spending cuts was more readily conducive to a public campaign than a more limited and arcane debate over programmatic reforms. This focus was also more divisive and more capable of mobilizing support for the administration among those threatened with cuts. The strategy was successful, and the president's approval ratings rose during the controversy, fed by large gains in support among the elderly.[38] The administration maintained this line of attack through the general election the following fall, defeating not only the Republican budget but also Republican candidates. Officials in both parties have since refrained from pursuing significant reforms in entitlement spending, directly attributing their hesitancy to the president's earlier use of the issue.[39] Unusually worried about his place in history, the president once identified entitlement reform as the key to his legacy. Unfortunately, the needs and instruments of modern presidential power undermined that effort as soon as an opportunity presented itself.

This episode illustrates an ever-present temptation in modern American politics and a central tendency in the new rhetorical presidency. As public opinion has increasingly become a crucial determinant of presidential success, the pursuit of public opinion has become the foremost goal of the American presidency.[40] Issue advocacy is tailored to enhance the electoral fortunes of the president, even to the detriment of previously held policy commitments and widely accepted beliefs about the public good. Resisting the urge to do whatever is necessary to gain immediate public favor becomes untenable when presidential authority relies on public favor. Even beyond conscious exploitation of public fears on controversial issues, simplification and rigidity are persistent problems when policy debates are primarily conducted in public campaigns. Polarizing the electorate around health care spending on senior citizens is hardly the worst case of political demonization, even in contemporary American politics.[41] The case is valuable, however, in the transparency of its motivations and the height of its success. This example indicates the persistence of the tendencies described in the rhetorical presidency literature and the manner in which the modern rhetorical presidency facilitates demagoguery even in the face of severe criticism by the political elite.

Emotionalism and Public Deliberation

A final troubling aspect of the Clinton presidency anticipated in the literature on the rhetorical presidency is the derogation of reasoned public deliberation. Specifically, Clinton as candidate and president has broken new ground in contributing to a shift in political discourse away from reasoned deliberation and toward emotional reaction. This transition is not simply an aberration or a function of Clinton's personal style but rather is consistent with long-term trends in the rhetorical presidency. To the extent that modern practice valorizes public approval as the primary source of presidential authority, a shift in how presidents relate to technology, media outlets, and constituencies is to be expected.

Emotionalism per se has not been a primary theme of the rhetorical presidency literature, but it is a specific elaboration of twentieth-century practices. As noted above, "soft" demagoguery has been defined within this literature as efforts by politicians to flatter and ingratiate themselves with the public. The legitimization of such tactics has accompanied the rise of public opinion as the key component of presidential political capital. In addition, analysts of the rhetorical presidency have emphasized the tradeoff between popular politics and policy deliberation. As presidents increasingly spoke to popular audiences and increasingly spoke to them on policy issues, presidential speeches relied more heavily on assertion and position taking rather than argumentation. Television has merely amplified the "sound bite" that has dominated throughout the twentieth century. Campaigns have always emphasized emotional appeals and sloganeering in order to reach a popular audience and mobilize public support. The modern rhetorical presidency highlights the extent to which governing has been given over to campaigning. With the decline of party and office as sources of presidential authority and the breakdown of congressional institutions that fostered presidential bargaining, presidents have relied upon intra-election campaigns to put public pressure on individual legislators and coerce their support.

These problems of modern governance were well established by the time of the Clinton presidency, but Clinton is adept at precisely this form of modern campaigning, emphasizing media skills and developing the direct connection between the crowd and the president that nineteenth-century customs were designed to prevent. The 1992 presidential campaign established Clinton's approach to the presidency. Upon securing a clear lead for the Democratic nomination, the candidate began to turn his attention to the broader audience that would be decisive in the general campaign by making an appearance on the *Arsenio Hall Show*. On Hall's celebrity talk show, Clinton made his bid for the presidency by playing the saxophone and casually chatting with the host. Clinton's appearance on *Arsenio Hall* was not unique in the 1992 campaign season, but it marked a turning point in conventional campaign practices.[42] Forums that had previously been shunned as below the dignity of a presidential campaign were now viewed as highly desirable for their large audiences and their mostly risk-free environment. Candidates had long engaged in such standard "baby kissing" campaign rituals, but Clinton's appearance on a celebrity talk show was seen as setting a new tone for presidential campaigns, in which media appearances were pitched as entertainment rather than as news. The privileged location of "serious" discussion in the television age had been transformed into photo opportunities. Such alterations in campaign practice were perceived not only as damaging public deliberation on issues of government but also as undermining the stature of an eventually successful candidate. One of George Washington's primary concerns as president was to establish the correct demeanor for the office.[43] As the basis of presidential authority is shifted from constitutional office to personal popularity, the nineteenth-century ideal of presidential stature has little meaning. In minimizing the distance between the president and the populace, the modern rhetorical presidency has minimized the significance of stature. Presidents are merely popular individuals whose particular arena of celebrity is political. Although congressional Democrats complained that Clinton was undermining his stature as president by appearing on *Larry King Live* during his standoff with the Republicans over the federal budget, the president recognized that popularity was a greater political asset than stature.[44] Clinton made no sharp distinction between the forums appropriate for a candidate's appearance and those appropriate for a president's, and at the same time redefined them. Clinton's personal skills enabled him to make the leap to more popular and less political arenas toward which the modern rhetorical presidency has been moving for the past several decades.

A somewhat more dramatic example of this aspect of the Clinton presidency is the use of the so-called electronic town hall format for candidate and presidential discourse. These televised events feature politicians answering questions posed directly by a studio audience of relatively average citizens. This format favored Clinton's own speaking style, which works better in small-scale, interactive settings than in set speeches, and his aides pushed for its inclusion in the candidate debates in 1992. Similar events were staged after Clinton reached the White House, whether in support of specific initiatives such as health care reform or of the general standing of the administration. Like appearances on talk shows, the town halls tend to reduce the space between government officials and the citizenry. Individual citizens enjoy unmediated access to the president, whom they can interrogate about topics ranging from fiscal policy to personal scandal to underwear preference. Both the interactive form of questioning and the arrangement of sets and camera angles emphasize the conversational nature of presidential speech. The president is immediately responsive to the demands of "representative" citizens.

A particularly striking feature of this format for present purposes is the degree to which it elevates empathy as a political virtue. At least symbolically, traditional debate, question-and-answer formats, and set speeches emphasize the authority of politicians and government officials. Presidential candidates establish their qualifications for office by displaying their knowledge of "the issues" by responding to challenges from other members of the political elite. Successful candidates demonstrate their expertise under pressure. Significantly, incumbent presidents have traditionally avoided such exchanges except in the context of electoral campaigns. The town hall format dispenses with these protections to presidential authority, traditionally conceived. The consequence, however, is not a more extensive challenge to presidential policy expertise. Rather, presidential authority is reconceptualized within the context of the town hall meeting in such a way that dialogue with the president reinforces rather than challenges authority. The president is tested in the town hall on a new standard of responsiveness. The image that Clinton created through the town hall was not primarily of adept policy leadership but rather of boundless empathy. The cliched portrait of the president gazing into the eyes of a citizen and intoning that he feels their pain is the source of Clinton's authority, as well as a wellspring of parody. The effect was heightened after the election when the administration employed the town hall format to feature tales of personal misfortune and failed health insurance. Such forums offer little in the way of useful policy information or debate[45]; they are primarily stages for the display of appropriate emotional responses.[46] Those emotions, however, are meant to determine policy outcomes. The town hall format offers a veneer of public deliberation on political affairs but in fact circumvents it.

The Problem of Governing

The rhetorical presidency offers one mechanism for characterizing presidential practice and the sources of presidential authority. It does not offer a complete model for explaining presidential behavior. The flaws in U.S. politics identified in the rhetorical presidency literature are not the only problems in American governance, and the practices making up the modern rhetorical presidency are not the only sources of those failings. The rhetorical presidency is simply one approach to understanding how and why presidents conduct their office and how presidents relate to the larger constitutional structure.

The rhetorical presidency does, however, exist within a particular ideological and institutional context that helps explain both why presidents behave the way they do and how the rhetorical presidency plays out in practice. Presidential rhetoric not only persuades but also constructs a political world within which various political actors operate; it is itself fertile ground for interpreting and understanding the modern presidency. The Clinton presidency both shapes and is shaped by this broader constitutional context, as the president attempts to use the tools available to him to enhance his own authority and achieve his political goals. The practices of the modern rhetorical presidency are both empowering and constraining. They are also flexible, and Clinton has been particularly innovative in further developing the logic of transformations initiated early in the century.

Clinton's innovativeness should not be mistaken for an escape from the dilemmas of the twentieth-century rhetorical presidency. Although the president has translated changes within the television entertainment industry into viable political tools for both campaigning and governing, he remains rooted in the authority structures and political necessities that have grown around his predecessors. If Reagan played on the grand stage of political drama and ideology, Clinton has played on the small stage of call-in talk shows and personal charisma. Both are products of the type of political system envisioned by Wilson early in this century. Presidents must "stay in touch" with the voters throughout their term of office, and their authority for action is dependent on the fluctuations of the opinion polls. Presidential speech is geared toward identifying and mobilizing supporters to achieve particular legislative results. Presidents make less effort to reason with political elites and more effort to move mass audiences. Presidents are less concerned with persuasion and more concerned with political coercion. Ultimately, the Clinton presidency is a product of a constitutional system that increasingly identifies the presidential office with democracy rather than as a potential check on democratic ambitions and failings.

12

Technocratic Leadership: The Policy Wonk Presidencies of Jimmy Carter and Bill Clinton

Phillip G. Henderson

One of the most ominous trends in presidential leadership during the last quarter of the twentieth century has been the resurgence, in theory and in practice, of the dictum first popularized by Woodrow Wilson, that there is a science of policy and administration that is separate and distinct from politics and political statecraft. Consistent with Wilson's famous dichotomy between politics and administration, modern presidents, with the notable exception of Ronald Reagan, have become more technocratic, more visionless, and more obsessed with minutiae in the policymaking process. Even George Bush, despite a long career of service in the federal government, was not immune from the tendency toward a technical and somewhat bureaucratic approach to presidential leadership. As Ann Reilly Dowd wrote in *Fortune* magazine, Bush "dives into the nitty-gritty of policymaking. And yes, he likes to check who's playing on the White House tennis court and horseshoe pit, who's flying on Air Force One, and who's sitting next to whom at White House dinners."[1] During an abortive coup attempt against Panamanian Manuel Noriega in 1989, Bush became paralyzed by his own overimmersion in raw intelligence reports from the CIA and other sources. Taking calls directly from the field, President Bush "turned the Oval Office into a military operations center replete with maps and raw intelligence data that he personally ordered from the CIA. Buried in unfiltered and often contradictory information, the President hesitated and the coup fizzled."[2] Significantly, Bush learned some early lessons about micromanagement and political decisiveness that he later applied to his leadership in the Persian

Gulf War. Namely, he granted broad authority over the conduct of the war to his commanders in the field. Bush concentrated his energies on masterfully building a broad coalition of support with leaders in Britain, France, Egypt, Jordan, Yemen, and Saudi Arabia, among others. And as Joseph Avella notes in chapter 4 of this book, Bush also spelled out clear, achievable goals in the Gulf War, and provided the force levels necessary to accomplish these objectives. His strategic vision, at least in this important instance, contributed to the overwhelming success of the mission.

Bill Clinton and Jimmy Carter were not as fortunate as Bush when it came to overcoming the urge to lead through sheer mastery of information rather than through the art of consensus building and political statecraft. Rather, they came to embody the highly technical approach to leadership that may fittingly be called the "policy wonk" presidency. Below I offer a point-by-point analysis of the Carter and Clinton administrations in an effort to define more clearly the common characteristics of the policy wonk presidency. These traits include, among others, the inability to set and articulate clear priorities with the type of compelling logic that can be readily construed as a "sense of vision"; the immersion of the president in policy minutiae and the corresponding tendency toward micromanagement; a marked propensity to elevate White House–centered policy development above legislative debate and purposeful deliberation by attempting to depoliticize the policy process; and finally, a lack of strategic vision (especially in foreign affairs) resulting in vacillation and indecision. The policy wonk presidency provides powerful evidence that mastery of information and policy mechanics is far less consequential in shaping leadership than good judgment and a set of clear guiding principles. No matter how good a president or presidential candidate may be at advocating policies or showing good intentions, the lack of a clear vision and a sense of strategy and purpose severely limits the capacity to lead and inspire.

The Policy Wonk Presidency

In *The Comeback Kid*, Charles Allen and Jonathan Portis note that during the 1992 presidential campaign, Clinton "became known as a 'policy wonk,' a politician who could spout data and statistics nonstop, a man with a quick answer for every question. Members of the national press were amazed at his ability to formulate answers to complicated questions, seemingly without thinking."[3] Clinton continued to impress reporters and the general public after his presidential election victory in 1992. The president-elect organized an economic summit to display his mastery of economic issues publicly in a setting that was "structured to be supportive of ideas he had presented during the campaign."[4] As journalist Elizabeth Drew notes, "Clinton got to do what he loves most: talk policy and show off his knowledge."[5] The summit, Stanley Renshon adds, gave Clinton a chance to showcase a "mastery of facts" that resulted from "decades of immersion in policy."[6]

Although many in the press were in awe of Clinton's almost computer-like capacity to articulate a highly intricate command of policy, not all observers were convinced of the benefits of the policy wonk approach to leadership. Princeton professor Fred Greenstein, for example, noted that Clinton "finds it all too easy to deluge the public with details," with no clear facility for transcending "policy mechanics" to convey a broader vision or focus.[7] Greenstein drew a distinction between Clinton's obvious "verbal intelligence" and his somewhat less crisp "analytical intelligence."

As will be shown below, Clinton's highly detailed and technical discussion of issues is not new. Indeed, Clinton's Democratic predecessor in the White House and fellow Southerner—Jimmy Carter—was strikingly similar to Clinton in his style and approach to leadership. By systematically juxtaposing the Carter and Clinton presidencies, the potential perils and pitfalls of the policy wonk presidency become readily apparent.

The Absence of Coherence and Cogency

One problem that impedes the Clinton presidency in much the same way that it affected Carter's is the inability to set and articulate clear priorities and to follow through on these objectives with a clear strategy for governance. James Fallows, who served as President Carter's chief speech writer, concluded that Carter's inability to set a clear course in Washington was rooted in the president's lack of a guiding ideology. "I came to think," Fallows observed, "that Carter believes fifty things, but no one thing. He holds explicit, thorough positions on every issue under the sun, but he has no large view of the relations between them."[8] Carter found it easy to take positions on issues, but he had difficulty synthesizing ideas and filtering tough choices through a unifying framework. The lack of a guiding vision made Carter inclined to alter positions (as with the neutron bomb) or tolerate inconsistencies in policy (as in the acceptance of divergent views between his secretary of state and national security adviser on U.S.–Soviet relations).

Clinton, like Carter before him, has had a problem with coherence and consistency. He sees essentially no inconsistency between proposing new multibillion dollar government programs while proclaiming that "the era of big government is over"; or in saying that the Bush administration's extension of Most Favored Nation (MFN) trade status to China was a shameful act, but later granting the same MFN status on the basis of economic practicality; or in saying that U.S. troops would be in Bosnia for only one year—"date certain"—only to say later that the American people in voting for his reelection tacitly approved of an indefinite extension of the troop commitment. [9]

A scatter-gun approach to policy initiatives in the Carter and Clinton presidencies is reflective of the underlying absence of a clear philosophy of government. Carter proposed an ambitious agenda early in his administration that was strikingly similar to Clinton's vast array of proposals sixteen years later: an economic stimulus package, campaign finance reform, extensive reorganization of the federal government ("Reinvention" in the Clinton era), hospital cost containment, and new energy taxes. Political scientist Erwin Hargrove notes that Carter's proposals "produced a 'monstrous jam up,' and most of them went nowhere."[10]

Clinton's agenda met a similar fate. His $16 billion pork barrel–laden stimulus package and his BTU energy tax proposals were gutted by the Senate; his sweeping health care reform proposals were pronounced dead on arrival (after a drawn-out and highly secretive planning process nullified the sense of urgency that the president had attached to the health care "crisis"); and the administration's campaign finance reform proposals languished six years into his presidency as the president unabashedly solicited the very type of soft-money campaign contributions that the reform bill he endorsed would have outlawed.

Both Carter and Clinton proposed massive policy agendas that were simply inconsistent with the self-imposed fiscal restraint that they had promised in their campaigns as "new" Democrats. Stuart Eizenstat, Carter's top domestic policy adviser, acknowledged that there was a fundamental tension between Carter's grandiose proposals, on the one hand, and his desire to be perceived as a fiscal conservative, not a "tax and spend" Democrat.

> One always knew that he wanted to spend as little money as possible and yet at the same time he wanted welfare reform, he wanted national health care insurance, he wanted an urban policy, he wanted job training programs. And I think that that tended to lead to some of the clearest internal conflicts . . . perhaps led to the public perception of an administration without the clearest of courses. You know the question of where are you taking the country . . . You can't keep a foot in each path without severe cost.[11]

Like Carter, Clinton wanted to be known as a new kind of Democrat and pronounced in his 1996 State of the Union address that "the era of big government is over." Yet he proceeded to set forth a multitude of proposals for costly government programs in the same speech. As Renshon notes, it is difficult to reconcile the president's promise of an end to big government with the administration's earlier proposal for a sweeping and costly overhaul of the nation's health care system, much less the plethora of additional proposals for new and costly federal programs. In 1998 alone, Clinton called for significant expansion of federal responsibilities in areas that were traditionally taken care of by the states, including regulating private health care insurance and the nation's child care arrangements at an estimated cost of $20 billion over five years,[12] and using federal funds to hire 100,000 new school teachers. Even proposals that were thought to save money, such as Clinton's promise of "ending welfare as we know it," included the inconsistent proviso that the federal government would serve as the employer of last resort for those who could not find a job after their welfare ended.[13]

The evidence suggests that Clinton, like Carter before him, entered office with no coherent ideology and no clear strategy for governance. Indeed, Clinton shares with Carter the propensity to think in terms of "lists not arguments."[14] Fallows observed that when Carter presented an outline for a speech, "it would consist of six or seven subjects rather than a theme or tone." There was no sense of hierarchy or unity. Likewise, Clinton has a history of pursuing long lists of goals without an overarching theme or vision. As a top official in the Clinton administration put it: "The President has a very long list of goals. Instead of having three big goals and taking lots of time to fight for them over many months, he has more. Managing such a long list of goals is his big challenge."[15] *Time* magazine White House correspondent Michael Duffy concluded that Clinton's appetite for "policies and ideas of all kinds—often make it hard for him to organize his time and sort out his priorities."[16]

The precedence of long lists of policy proposals over a clear-cut philosophy of governance dates back to the earliest stages of Clinton's career in politics. As a first-term governor in Arkansas, Clinton had his pollster and adviser, Dick Morris, conduct a survey of Arkansas voters to rank the popularity of dozens of ideas that Clinton had discussed in his budget. Morris then had the unenviable task of finding a theme to weave these ideas together. Morris concluded that Clinton had left a program that "was thoroughly admirable but indescribable." Foreshadowing Clinton's massive presidential agendas, Morris notes that Clinton's program as governor had "a bit of everything. Like a kid in a candy store, he wanted to do it all."[17]

After losing his reelection bid for the governorship in 1980, Clinton had Morris conduct another poll to see why he had lost. Morris constructed a family parable out of the poll results. "The citizens of Arkansas viewed Clinton as a prodigal son who had grown too big for his britches, who had thought that he knew everything and had tried to tell the other family members what was best for them rather than listening to their suggestions."[18] Clinton had a different interpretation of the election. Rather than seeing himself as too arrogant and too hasty in trying to impose his way of doing

things on the citizens of Arkansas, Clinton viewed the loss as a consequence of overextending himself. "I made a young man's mistake. I had an
agenda a mile long. . . . I was so busy doing what I wanted to do I didn't
have time to correct mistakes."[19] Yet, despite this acknowledgment, Clinton
continued to flood the Arkansas legislature with legislative requests after
his political comeback in 1982. A 312-page booklet was submitted to the
legislature in 1983 that included eighty bills that the governor was proposing. Clinton submitted proposals for over ninety new bills in his 1989 report
to the legislature.[20]

Edith Efron, in her careful analysis of Clinton's career in politics, notes
that the problem (or excuse) for having disjointed, "mile-long" agendas is
repeated time and again by Clinton. During the 1992 presidential campaign,
Clinton, in an interview on the *Arsenio Hall Show*, provided a glimpse of
introspective analysis:

> Even now, after all these years, I still sometimes work hard instead of smart.
> I'm a workaholic, I'm always churning and doing things, and sometimes
> I lose the forest for the trees. Sometimes you can do so many things that you
> don't do enough . . . You've got to really focus and have that kind of men-
> tal discipline that sometimes my workaholic tendencies don't permit me to
> have. . . .[21]

Clinton at least showed awareness of his problem. The dual tendencies
of taking on too much, on the one hand, and not communicating objectives
effectively, on the other, find expression over and over again in Clinton's
comments. Predictably, Clinton's tendency toward circuit overload carried
over into his presidency. As Drew notes, Treasury Secretary Lloyd Bentsen
was so troubled by the overload of policy proposals early in the administration that he told the president in a private meeting in the Oval Office:
"You have too many issues out there, and the public is losing focus on what
you're trying to do." But, according to Drew, "nothing much changed" after that.[22] As Renshon suggests, Clinton's massive policy agendas are not
without costs.

> Persistence and determination in the service of a large agenda can function to
> wear down opposition. A president's persistence, however, can turn from a
> leadership asset to a public liability. While Clinton himself has enormous en-
> ergy, *he often exhausts public understanding.* This strategy may be effective
> in the short term to get policies passed, but it does not provide a firm foun-
> dation for public acceptance. Thus, while Clinton has been successful in get-
> ting a number of his policies enacted, it is much less clear that he has made
> progress in resolving the basic public dilemma his presidency faces. A presi-
> dent must be able to educate the public if he wishes to gain its trust. An am-
> bitious agenda may not leave much time for public education because

citizens are struggling to keep up with all the implications of what they are asked to judge.[23]

In September 1995, three years into his presidency, Clinton continued to express concern that he was spreading himself too thin with his broad agenda and detailed focus on policies. In an impromptu meeting with a group of reporters on Air Force One, the president noted that he was "still grappling with a way to communicate in a crisp and compelling way."[24] Recalling his performance on a radio call-in show with Larry King the week before, Clinton said: "I thought it was good, I loved doing it, but I [found] myself . . . doing too much of the, you know, details of the specific issue they're asking without trying to keep putting it into larger contexts."[25] The president acknowledged that he had not done a good job of focusing on the "big picture" because of his tendency to dwell too much on details. "I would have been better served," he said, "and the country probably would have been better served, if maybe we'd done, even if we'd done just slightly less, if people had understood some of the big picture more."[26] Curiously, the president in these comments tends to shift the inability to focus onto the American people, who need help understanding "the big picture more."

By 1995 Clinton was no longer a naive newcomer to politics. Yet even as a seasoned politician, fully aware of his destructive tendency to build "mile-long" agendas without providing a clear rationale, he remained seemingly incapable of rectifying the problem. After reelection to the presidency in 1996, the "lists" of ideas repeatedly grew to unmanageable size. In 1997 the president circulated an internal document listing fourteen "pillars," or goals for the administration in its second term. According to *Boston Globe* reporter David Shribman, "Key White House aides were allowed to read the memorandum but not to keep it." Shribman notes that the items on the president's list were so numerous, and in some cases so insignificant, that some top officials could not even remember what was on the list.[27] Some of Clinton's disparate second-term initiatives included proposals for restrictions on teenage smoking, national testing of high school students, a Hollywood ratings system, and the V-chip for television sets.

Compounding the problems posed by large, unmanageable agendas is the president's tendency to focus on items that are, at best, peripheral to his stated objectives. The president's self-proclaimed first-term emphasis on economic issues, for example, was sidetracked almost immediately by his attempts to forge a new policy on gays in the military. Similarly, the president's second-term agenda, hardly cohesive to begin with, was wait-listed while the president pushed forward with what appeared to be a hastily contrived public relations initiative on race. Clinton pledged to use a series of "town hall" meetings to promote community dialogue about race relations and to recommend concrete solutions to racial problems. But as Renee Smith notes, instead of generating dialogue about racial issues, "these town meetings produced discussions about Clinton's performance during them and about his willingness to listen to all points of view."[28] Smith concludes that "the President's Initiative on Race was over almost as soon as it began."[29] One reason for the failure was the "lack of focus by Clinton and the advisory board." Clinton's town hall meetings on race amounted to little more than forums in which participants talked "about talking bluntly about race."[30]

As with the ad hoc nature of the administration's initiative on race, the wandering quality of Clinton's second-term agenda was self-evident in a speech that the president delivered at the Massachusetts Institute of Technology in June 1998. Without pinpointing any clear priorities, much less any overriding theme or any particular course of action, Clinton said:

> Last month I went to the Naval Academy to talk about the new security challenges of the twenty-first century—terrorism, organized crime and drug trafficking, global climate change, the spread of weapons of mass destruction. Next week at Portland State in Oregon I will discuss how our nation's third wave of immigration can either strengthen and unite America or weaken and divide it. . . . Today I ask you to focus on the challenges of the information Revolution . . . and its limitless possibilities.[31]

Hence, six years into his presidency, Clinton continued to wander between disparate objectives seeking a theme. While Clinton is a classic overachiever, the net result of endless lists of policies which lack cohesion and a clear-cut focus is, arguably, underachievement.

The Rhetorical Dimension

In a sense, the antecedents for the policy wonk presidency, particularly its rhetorical dimension, can be traced back to the turn of the century. Jeffrey Tulis notes, for example, that William Howard Taft "became the first president to regularly build his messages around 'laundry lists' of legislative initiatives."[32] Woodrow Wilson continued with the policy specificity of Taft, but he also adopted the "inspirational" form of speech-making that Theodore Roosevelt had popularized. Wilson recognized that the two purposes of speeches were best achieved separately. Hence, "he sought to establish two ideal types of popular address." The first form—the "'visionary speech' would articulate a picture of the future and impel a populace toward it."[33] The second form of speech, which Tulis labels the "policy-stand" speech, aimed at specificity. This type of speech would ideally indicate "where the president stood or what he would do regarding the issues of the day." Wilson, Tulis notes, "often referred to these stands as 'definite poli-cies,' and his insistence upon them grew out of his concern for greater ac-countability."[34]

The Carter- and Clinton-era speeches are not noted for success in achiev-ing the type of accountability that Wilson sought. In part this is because of a failure in both administrations to separate the "visionary" form of speech from the "policy-stand" genre. Indeed, the lists of policy specifics have be-come so extensive that they have often overshadowed the visionary aspira-tions of presidential addresses. Moreover, the visionary elements have often been so platitudinous and disparate that the speeches of the Carter and Clin-ton eras have done little to inspire. As Tulis notes, "it is difficult in practice for a single speech to be inspirational and highly specific at the same time. Consider, for example, President Carter's 'moral malaise' speech. Beginning with an analysis that pointed to a deep sickness in the American soul, it ends with a call to conserve energy and tax oil companies."[35]

Clinton's State of the Union messages have been remarkably similar to Carter's speeches in attempting "with predictable difficulty, to be both in-spirational and exhaustive as to specific legislative initiatives."[36] Often de-void of ordered argument or reasoned analysis, the Carter- and Clinton-era speeches are heavily weighted in the direction of "laundry lists" rather than conveying an underlying sense of conviction or direction. As such, Clin-ton's State of the Union addresses are largely symptomatic of the problem that the president has had in focusing his policy agenda. His 1994 State of the Union address was described by one correspondent as an "ungainly, of-ten messy affair that moves in many directions," and "is impervious to or-der."[37] Clinton's speech listed seven major initiatives, but the president "couldn't resist adding a dozen or so secondary and tertiary items, amount-ing to an enormously ambitious and detailed to-do list by any standard."[38] Despite clear recognition within the administration of the need for a clearer focus, Clinton's 1995 State of the Union address was not only longer (over eighty minutes), but arguably more ungainly than his 1994 speech had been. Carl Cannon, Washington bureau chief of the *Baltimore Sun*, noted that Clinton "touched on all the great problems of our age from teenage pregnancy to television violence." The President "took time to debate whether the government ought to be studying tick infestations, told us how much he liked to hunt, promised to get tough on terrorists' bank accounts and railed at Congress for accepting free football tickets from lobbyists."[39]

Fresh from reelection, Clinton's 1997 State of the Union address pro-vided a familiar refrain. The *St. Louis Post-Dispatch* highlighted the absence of a unifying theme or vision in the 1997 speech with the headline: "Clin-ton Covers The Waterfront, Seeking A Theme."[40] The *Post-Dispatch* analy-sis of the speech provided a sharply worded review of the president's performance.

The problem with President Bill Clinton's declaration of education as his "number one priority" is that this is a president who has already declared several top priorities. . . .

. . . Clinton devoted nearly a quarter of his speech to a litany of initiatives on education, from college tuition tax grants to new national achievement standards. He promised everything from expanded "flex time" and family leave to a space probe of Mars. . . .

. . . Clinton's rhetoric on education and other proposals was more inflated than bold.[41]

All told, Clinton's list of educational initiatives alone amounted to ten separate and mostly distinct programs. Chester Finn, a former assistant secretary at the Department of Education, suggested that Clinton's education proposals were "not a unified 'plan' at all, but rather a collection of loosely related programs which the president happened to throw together in the same speech."[42] It is "pointless," Finn added, "to search for coherence—and meaningless to be 'for' or 'against' the lot of them. Instead, they are rather like a list of unrelated courses offered by a brainy but undisciplined student to fulfill 'distribution' requirements."[43]

What is missing from Clinton's and Carter's speeches is a unifying framework with clear and readily discernible underlying principles. On this count, both Carter and Clinton would have been well served to study the example of Theodore Roosevelt's presidency. As Tulis notes, Roosevelt took care "to state his case in terms of principle, not detailed policy; to repeat principles often; and to moderate public expectations of the success of the policy."[44] In addressing the Hepburn Act on railroad regulation, a major accomplishment of his administration, Roosevelt said:

I believe [the Hepburn Act] will work a measurable betterment for the public. Listen to what I say—a measurable benefit for the public. I do not believe that it will produce the millennium, or anything approaching it; and I am quite certain that some of its most ardent advocates will be disappointed with the results.[45]

The contrast between Roosevelt's rhetoric and Clinton's is striking. Note, for example, Clinton's inflated rhetoric about technology and particularly regarding the role of the Internet as a panacea for the major problems facing the nation. In his 1997 State of the Union address, the president promised eventual access to the Internet for every classroom in America. In so doing, he reiterated one of the ideas enunciated with exuberance in his first inaugural; that is, "Technology is almost magical."[46] In his commencement address at the Massachusetts Institute of Technology on June 9, 1998, the president's utopian faith in technology was stated with even more force. With the rise of the "Information Age," Clinton observed, "there will be a cure for cancer; a flourishing economy that will produce much less pollution and move back from the brink of potentially devastating global warming. High-speed wireless networks that bring distance learning, Tele-medicine and economic opportunity to every rural community." The president then told the MIT audience of the "revolutionary" educational and "democratizing potential" of new information technologies.

> Before too long, our children will be able to stretch a hand across a keyboard and reach every book ever written, every painting ever painted, every symphony ever composed.
>
> For the first time in our history, it is now possible for a child in the most isolated inner-city neighborhood or rural community to have access to the same world of knowledge at the same instant as the child in the most affluent suburb. Imagine the revolutionary democratizing potential this can bring. . . .
> . . . First graders are producing small books on computers. Sixth graders are producing documentaries. . . .

Hence, in contrast to Roosevelt's caution in telling his audience about the "measurable betterment" that a major legislative accomplishment of his administration would bring and his distaste for millennial assertions, Clinton conveys to his audience the awesome expectation that access to the Internet in every classroom in America will somehow make the child in the "most isolated inner-city" equal in skill and accomplishment to the child in the "most affluent suburb." The implication is that computers can give children the skills to read and write, add and subtract, and become playwrights and authors. Technology is the teacher. And the government's stake in seeing to it that "every child has a computer in the classroom" is no less than the revolutionary democratization of society itself.

The president concluded his speech with an impassioned plea for a technology literacy requirement in middle schools throughout the nation. "All students should feel as comfortable with a keyboard as a chalkboard; as comfortable with a laptop as a textbook." Ironically, the president himself apparently has very little aptitude for the keyboards and laptops that he so eloquently embraces as the lifeline to the twenty-first century. According to former presidential aide Dick Morris, the president has never even learned how to type, much less master the Internet. Indeed, the first lady remarked that daughter Chelsea was going to teach the president "how to do e-mail" before departing for Stanford University. The president's limited understanding of the very technology that he was trumpeting as the bridge to the twenty-first century was perceptively noted by Brian Hecht in the *New Republic,* who wrote: "merely wiring the classrooms does not guarantee that students, even when guided by teachers, will find their way through the clutter of Internet schlock. The first president in American history to actively promote an agenda for cyberspace is largely ignorant, overly optimistic and naive in his view of computer based education."

Micromanagement in the Oval Office

It is not surprising that Clinton's rhetoric places so much emphasis on information and the technical means of amassing information while giving so little emphasis to philosophy and wisdom, virtue and discernment. Consistent with this technocratic orientation, the inclination toward "information overload" is one of the dominant characteristics of the policy wonk presidency. Clinton, like Carter before him, has shown a propensity to be needlessly sidetracked by a compulsion for micromanagement of policy. The presumption that inheres in the policy wonk is that mastery of information ensures good results. While this proposition may hold true for high school debate teams, it does not ring true for American presidents.

Early in his career, Carter believed that mastery of detail would foster good decisions. As a state senator he "pledged to read every bill before he voted on it and did so."[47] This pattern of meticulous study carried over into the governorship and the presidency. Carter, by his own admission, "spent hour after hour studying the structure of the federal government in preparation of the budgets."[48] Fallows noted Carter's proclivity to immerse himself in detail in 1979 when he wrote that Carter "would pore over budget tables [from OMB] to check the arithmetic, and during his first six months in office would personally review all requests to use the White House tennis court."[49] Fallows likened Carter's behavior to that of a "perfectionist accustomed to thinking that to do a job right you must do it yourself."[50] Noting that Carter "read hundreds of pages of material on welfare programs and did almost everything but draft the legislation," Joseph Califano, Secretary of Health, Education and Welfare, said somewhat ruefully that Carter was "the highest paid assistant secretary for planning that ever put a reform proposal together."[51] Attorney General Griffin Bell added that Carter was "about as good a president as an engineer could be."[52] Carter's obsession with detail not only bogged him down in unnecessary tasks; it also hampered his ability to see the forest for the trees. Over time, countless examples have surfaced concerning Carter's tendency to take in detail at almost intoxicating levels. Hugh Sidey of *Time* provided one of the more notable illustrations of Carter's micromanagement of a decision. In reviewing plans for the Iran hostage rescue attempt, Sidey revealed, "the president asked about the Iranian guards stationed inside the embassy, near the wall that the commandos intended to scale. Were they volunteers or conscripts? he wondered. If they were radicals, Carter explained, he could go along with killing them, but if they were only peasant conscripts, he wanted them knocked out temporarily."[53] Carter's decision-making, Sidey concluded, was gripped by the "tyranny of the trivial."

Like Carter, Clinton "loves immersing himself in minutiae."[54] As one White House aide put it: "We've had a hard time deciding what *not* to take to him because he wants to do everything."[55] Another member of the administration noted that Clinton "is reluctant to let even minor White House proclamations go out without review."[56] Whereas Carter inspected the presidential seal on White House stationery, Clinton "pores over the Agriculture Department's 'acreage planted' reports."[57] As chief executive, Clinton has closely paralleled Carter's habit of wanting to do everything himself, without delegating authority to others. As Bert Rockman suggests, however, there are pitfalls inherent in Clinton's micromanagement in the White House. "Bill Clinton, by his nature, wants to be involved with everything, but, of course, he cannot be. A system that brings everything to him will assure a greater than average number of foul-ups that are purely a function of the inability of the White House to work properly."[58]

In *The Agenda*, Bob Woodward draws a portrait of Clinton that reinforces the image of a micromanager reluctant to delegate. Treasury Secretary Bentsen recalled saying to President Clinton: "Mr. President, you want to make every decision. You can't. You've got to delegate more."[59] Bentsen advised the president that what really mattered was the quality of his decisions, not the quantity. Bentsen's observation brings to mind earlier accounts concerning Carter's presidency. According to National Security Adviser Zbigniew Brzezinski, Carter was intent on maintaining complete control over the direction of policy and resisted the attempts by top aides to lighten his workload. "Whenever I tried to relieve him of excessive detail," noted Brzezinski, "Carter would show real uneasiness, and I even felt some suspicion, that I was usurping authority."[60]

In his memoirs, Carter wrote that he came into office believing that "my ability to govern well would depend upon my mastery of the extremely important issues I faced."[61] Notwithstanding Carter's intentions, one of the lessons that the Carter experience demonstrates is that detailed knowledge and mastery of policy do not ensure good decisions or enlightened leadership. Indeed, too much emphasis on the details of policy may well detract from leadership. Drawing on several case studies from the Carter and Reagan years, Matthew Kerbel concluded that "technical expertise, or facility with information and detail, is unrelated to success. President Carter was perceived to hold a greater command of detail than President Reagan, but his expertise was at its greatest during his failed initiatives."[62]

Political scientist Bert Rockman reached a similar conclusion with regard to the Clinton presidency. "Ironically," Rockman wrote:

> Bill Clinton seems to leave everyone in doubt when he is greatly engaged, . . .
> or minimally engaged. . . . When he is highly engaged, he often leaves it un-
> clear as to where he has drawn his line and whether that will prove to be
> changeable or not. When he is disengaged, those acting in his name are left
> unsure as to what he wants or at least will settle for.[63]

Clinton's level of involvement in policy was so deep and so nuanced "that
he could argue both sides of any issue" before him. "Even when a decision
had been made," James Pfiffner noted, "it was subject to revision upon further reflection."[64]

Woodward's account of the administration's development of an economic program underscores the degree to which "presidential ambivalence reverberated through the administration" and the difficulty insiders
had in pinpointing the direction that the president wished to go. At a meeting in the Oval Office with Vice President Al Gore, chief of staff "Mack"
McLarty, and congressional liaison director Howard Paster, Clinton "ram-
bled on inconclusively about the endless compromises and delays on investments and health care" and turned to Gore, asking "What can I do?"
The vice president responded: "You can get with the ___ damn program!"
The president, after a long pause, laughed and said "Okay."[65] This episode
illustrates the apparent difficulty that even the president's closest advisers
have in discerning where the president stands on key issues. As Renshon
notes: "The fact that there is apparently as much debate within Clinton's
inner circle about where he stands as there is outside it does not suggest
that Clinton has a clear, relatively consistent set of core ideals, values or
principles."[66] George Stephanopoulos, one of the president's closest advisors in the first term, compared Clinton with a kaleidoscope. "What you
see is where you stand," Stephanopoulos explained. "He will put one facet
toward you, but that is only one facet. . . . Every person would see a different pattern. It was real, but it could change in an instant, as soon as
Clinton turned."[67]

As with Clinton, Carter was capable of great ambivalence and vacillation,
despite extraordinarily detailed knowledge of the issues at hand. As
Richard Neustadt and Ernest May note, Carter "had a capacity for intense
concentration on detail combined with a curious flightiness, which could
carry him from subject to subject or, on a given subject, to one conviction
one day and an opposite the next."[68] Carter's complete about-face on the
decision to deploy the neutron bomb in Europe is a case in point. Initially,
Carter insisted that NATO equip itself with the new enhanced radiation
"tactical" nuclear weapons known as neutron bombs. After German Chan-
cellor Helmut Schmidt put his prestige on the line by building support in
Bonn for deploying the weapons, "Carter announced out of the blue that
he had changed his mind."[69] Press accounts suggested that Carter's immer-

sion in the details of how the neutron bomb operated fostered moral concerns in the president's mind and led to equivocation on whether it was justifiable to deploy an advanced radiation weapon, despite the need to offset a huge tank advantage of Warsaw Pact forces in Europe. In the aftermath of Carter's decision, Schmidt suggested that Europeans faced a Soviet threat they might have to meet on their own.

The Policy/Politics Dichotomy

Although Clinton is clearly more politically adept than Carter, he often seems to share Carter's affinity for pristine problem solving removed from the murky waters of politics. Indeed, a troubling aspect of the policy wonk approach to governance is the tendency of its practitioners to become so confident in the correctness of their policies that deliberation and compromise are viewed disdainfully as "politics as usual," with little or no room for purposeful accommodation. In broaching President Clinton's certitude in the correctness of his policies, Greenstein observed: "like many bright, self-confident people, he is impatient with those who do not share his views and not likely to take them seriously."[70] Not only is the president impatient with those who do not share his views; he has devised strategies aimed at stifling opposition. Drew reports that the president and First Lady Hillary Clinton pushed forth their health care reform proposals on a "fifty-one vote" strategy in the Senate so that they would not have to compromise in order to pick up Republican votes.[71] Drew suggests that the Clintons operated in this manner because they felt "that they were smarter than anyone else."[72] But in the end the Clintons were too smart for their own good. As Drew puts it: "For people who considered themselves masterly politicians with a fine feel for the public, and people who were of considerable political talents, they misjudged probable public reaction."[73]

Clinton's aura of policy superiority continued to create problems for him in his second term when he made similar miscalculations in his efforts to secure passage of fast-track negotiating authority on trade agreements in 1997. But this time, it was the president's own party that was being snubbed. According to *Baltimore Sun* Washington Bureau Chief Carl Cannon, Clinton's smugness and insistence that his own views on free trade were more important than the concerns of organized labor and environmentalists had the effect of eroding support within the Democratic party for fast-track legislation. Cannon reports that the president "alienated Democrats when he characterized a vote for fast-track as a 'no-brainer.' And in a dig at labor's financial support for members opposed to fast-track, Clinton said that if the vote could be done secretly, it would pass easily."[74] Representative Benjamin Cardin of Maryland, a prominent Democrat, lamented the frustration felt by many of his colleagues in the House of Representatives in dealing with the president. Cardin observed that even though he had received five calls from the White House on fast-track, he felt that none of the president's people were listening to his concerns. "Cardin was offered presidential visits to his district for fund-raisers or other events but not what he really desired: stronger environmental and labor standards. 'Why not talk to your own party,' Cardin asked."[75] In the end, fast-track, which had been one of the president's top priorities in his second term, was defeated. Fewer than fifty Democrats in the House supported the president's position.

Clinton's failures in securing health care and fast-track legislation bring to mind comparable traits in Carter's approach to policy. A former White House aide said of Carter: "his notion that he was the smartest person made him not want to horse trade."[76] A member of Congress recalled after a White House meeting with President Carter: "We had barely got seated and Carter started lecturing us about the problems he had with one of the sections of the bill. He knew the details better than most of us, but somehow that caused more resentment than if he had left the specifics to us."[77] When Carter decided to target nineteen water projects for elimination in the 1978 budget without consulting members of Congress, Senator Gary Hart of Colorado said: "I don't think we were dealt candidly with. . . . It's known as being blind-sided."[78]

To a considerable degree, Carter broke ground for Clinton by practicing a form of leadership that often dichotomized policy and politics. Carter viewed policy, especially when the policy is crafted by the White House, as standing above politics. In his book *The Trusteeship Presidency,* Charles Jones suggests that Carter "judged it important that representatives separate electoral politics from policy-making."[79] In a telling revelation of the unresolved tension arising from the policy/politics dichotomy, one Carter aide said:

> I always had the sense of a man who was an engineer, who truly believed that if he knew enough about details of a subject, he could make a decision that was in the public interest rather than in the interest of particular groups. Therefore, you needed a lot of information; therefore, you needed substance; therefore, don't bother me about politics. But then suddenly, he would be forcibly jerked back from this position . . . into a sort of purely political context in which a decision had to be made and I don't think it was ever integrated. I had the feeling of moving between the two [policy and politics] but never of pulling it together.[80]

Clinton does not share Carter's background in science and engineering, but he does share Carter's technocratic faith in the "science" of policy. He is so preoccupied with the study of policy that he, like Carter before him, thinks that choosing the "best policy" is an end in itself. And like Carter,

Clinton studies and masters the details of the policies that he proposes so thoroughly that he tends to become self-righteous about the correctness and desirability of his positions. He appears to share with Carter considerable difficulty in accepting the notion that policies drafted in the White House can be legitimately perceived as flawed or incomplete. The inflexibility and lack of consultation that characterized the development of Clinton's health care reform program is consistent with the notion that policy is best drafted in the White House and then given to Congress for ratification. Indeed, the Clinton administration's approach to health care reform is nearly identical to the Carter administration's efforts to pass a comprehensive energy program in 1977 and 1978. As with the Clinton health care proposals, Carter's energy proposals were "conceived in secret [and] presented to the country as a fait accompli without the consultation of interested parties."[81] A Carter administration official described the process of preparing the energy program as "vintage Carter." "The assignment to prepare a plan was given to the [person] responsible for policy. It dealt with a national problem requiring a comprehensive solution, so there was no need to compromise or consult."[82]

Even more so than Carter, Clinton has attempted to elevate presidential omniscience over political deliberation by depoliticizing the policy process. Indeed, Clinton's rhetoric is often carefully crafted to preempt dialogue, negotiation, and compromise. Those who agree with White House policies are hailed as statesmen, while those who disagree are "just playing politics." With regard to health care reform, for example, Clinton remarked: "Folks, all over America the airwaves are full of a lot of rhetoric. This has gotten to be about politics. . . . This is not a political issue. This is a practical problem."[83] While the White House health care proposals were viewed by the President as standing above politics, alternative proposals were, in the eyes of the administration, nothing but politics. Responding to the Republican alternative offered by Senator Bob Dole, the President stated: "Unlike our proposal, his idea of reform is really more politics as usual."[84] Curiously, the president considered his own proposal, which called for a complete retreat from the medical profession's emphasis on specialization, as somehow rising above politics. Yet, the Republican alternative of modest reform was "more politics as usual." In pressing his agenda, the President said: "all I ask of any of you is to ask the members of Congress to put aside partisanship, rhetoric, and this sort of word-throwing, and let's just think about the people of America. . . ."[85]

Clinton's efforts to depoliticize the policy environment persisted well into his second term. In his 1997 State of the Union address, for example, Clinton moved to preempt political opposition to his proposals for tuition tax credits and national education testing by saying emphatically that "politics must stop at the classroom door."[86] The president elaborated on the danger that "politics" posed for his educational proposals in a speech to Education International in July 1998, stating:

> There are some in the other party who don't see eye to eye with me on what we should be doing for our public schools. . . . There are those who would actually prohibit the development of national tests for our schools. . . . What seems so self-evident to you and me is still not entirely clear to all decision makers. . . .
>
> . . . You must not stop until every political leader with any political influence, in any political party knows that this is something that has to be lifted above partisanship. This is something that ought to be beyond all debate.[87]

"Beyond all debate" seems to be precisely the standard that Clinton wishes to apply to the most controversial legislative initiatives of his administration.

Clinton's comments on the budget impasse with Congress in October 1988 represent yet another example of the president's eagerness to place White House proposals on a pedestal rising above politics. The president applauded congressional leaders of the Democratic Party for their "constant efforts to elevate progress over partisanship." Republicans in Congress, on the other hand, were rebuked by the president for challenging some of the more controversial provisions of the administration's proposals, including significant new funding for the International Monetary Fund, federal funds for 100,000 new school teachers (even though teachers' salaries have traditionally been a concern of local government), appropriations for "commonsense efforts to address global warming," and additional funding for U.S. troops stationed in Bosnia a year after their scheduled withdrawal—all items that many Republicans opposed in principle. The president questioned the motives of Republicans who were opposed to passing appropriations bills with these measures fully funded at the levels of the administration's request, saying:

> There is still time for real achievement, still time for progress over partisanship. Troops in the field and citizens in crisis should never be subject to partisan wrangling. . . . There is still time for us to put the people of our country ahead of politics. . . .
>
> . . . So Republicans need to get to work in the seven days that remain, stop playing politics, pass legislation, and let's make some progress.[88]

Clinton's rhetoric on his proposals for a national health care program, national high school testing, and the 1998 budget illustrates that the president is predisposed to use his formidable public relations skills to preempt or undermine principled disagreement with White House proposals by labeling such disagreement as "politics as usual" rather than pursuing strategies based on purposeful compromise and earnest accommodation. As

Renshon notes, Clinton's tendencies "to market and sell his policies rather than deal with their costs and implications honestly, and his rages at those who don't share his view of the virtues of his plans, and especially his views of himself, suggest that he doesn't trust others to respond on the basis of substance or hard work to find common ground."[89] Clinton's behavior fits the general trend discussed by Gary Gregg in chapter 5 of this book, in which the purportedly superior judgment of the president is extolled while political deliberation in the Congress is demeaned.

There is no question that the aura of invincibility that characterized the positions that Carter and Clinton held on various policy proposals of national import was shaped in part by the broad leeway that they were accustomed to as governors of their respective states. Over time, both Carter and Clinton acknowledged difficulty in making the transition from being state governors in relatively homogeneous one-party states to being president. In a *New York Times* interview, Carter said, "We had an overly optimistic impression that I could present a bill to Congress that seemed patently in the best interest of the country and the Congress would take it and pretty well pass it. I have been disabused of that expectation."[90] Clinton's transition to the presidency was similarly affected by the magnitude of change of going from Arkansas to Washington. As Clinton himself acknowledged: "Arkansas was a small state and I could run the place like a country store—open house. But here, with this many people in the country, you are always being interpreted through filters. So, you have to be much more careful. And this has been a problem."[91]

Foreign and National Security Policy in Disarray

Nowhere are the pitfalls of the policy wonk presidency as pronounced or as debilitating as in the realm of foreign and national security policy. The paucity of a strategic vision and the ad hoc nature of policymaking processes in both the Carter and Clinton administrations has left a legacy of vacillation and uncertainty. The Clinton administration's prolonged and tortuous decision-making on whether or not to intervene in Haiti or Bosnia, and whether or not to bomb strategic targets in Iraq and Serbian targets in Kosovo, or whether to link human rights in China to MFN trade status, are reminiscent of the Carter administration's vacillation on deployment of the neutron bomb in Europe and on questions of U.S. policy toward Iran, and whether or not to link Soviet adventurism in Angola with arms control talks with the Soviets.

The Panama Canal treaties and the Camp David agreement between Israel and Egypt were notable accomplishments of the Carter presidency. But the failure to ratify a strategic arms limitation accord with the Soviet

Union and the inability to provide a clear direction in U.S.–Soviet relations did much to overshadow these accomplishments even before the Iran hostage crisis began to cast a pall over the administration's foreign policy. Carter's general ambivalence in superpower relations prior to the Soviet invasion of Afghanistan, and his unwillingness or inability to resolve the deep philosophical schism between National Security Adviser Brzezinski and Secretary of State Cyrus Vance on linkage between Soviet adventurism and U.S. foreign policy, led to the perception of indecision and disarray. Carter unwittingly exacerbated the contradictions inherent in the public pronouncements of his two top foreign policy advisers in a speech delivered to the Naval Academy graduating class on June 7, 1978. According to speech writer James Fallows, Carter prepared for the Naval Academy address by soliciting memos from both Vance and Brzezinski. He then "assembled the speech essentially by stapling Vance's memo to Brzezinski's without examining the tensions between them." When Carter finished the speech there was "an obvious break in the middle, like the splice in a film."[92] _The Washington Post_'s account the next morning was titled "Two Different Speeches," which in Fallows's view was "an accurate and obvious interpretation."

Part of Carter's problem was procedural. Instead of focused meetings of the National Security Council with clear agendas and issue papers, Carter preferred making decisions informally with a small group of core advisers. A commission on "National Security Policy Integration," chaired by Philip Odeen and appointed by President Carter in August 1977, cited "weaknesses in organization and procedures" in the Carter White House's national security advisory apparatus as an instrumental cause of the "widespread perception that the administration lacks coherence in policy and action."[93] The Odeen report suggested that Brzezinski and his NSC staff had failed to strike a balance between their "personal advisory role" to the president and their less glamorous "institutional responsibilities" in helping the president in crisis planning and in following up on policies at the implementation stage.[94]

The Odeen report underscored the point that beneath the surface appearance of a formal national security apparatus, important decisions were frequently made in an ad hoc manner by a small group of Carter administration officials who met at breakfast or lunch. These informal get togethers, such as the Vance, Brzezinski, and Brown (VB&B) breakfast meetings on Fridays, were not unlike the famous Tuesday Luncheons used by Lyndon Johnson to shape strategy during the Vietnam War. The result of such informality, the Odeen commission concluded, is that officials came away "with differing perceptions of just what the agreement was." In assessing the impact of Carter's undisciplined approach to foreign policy, former _Foreign Affairs_ editor William Bundy wrote: "It is unlikely that historians or fu-

ture practitioners of foreign policy will find the Carter administration anything but a negative example of method and process."[95]

Like Carter before him, Clinton has not been noted for consistency, vision, or disciplined process in foreign and national security policy. When
Clinton met with his top aides to discuss his policy agenda for his first one
hundred days in office he made no mention whatsoever of foreign policy.
The primacy of domestic economic policy in the early months of the Clinton presidency was not lost on observers. In a perceptive essay in the *New
Republic*, John Judis wrote:

> Clinton has placed short-term American economic interests ahead of any
> broader issues of foreign policy. In Asia trade has taken precedence over se-
> curity. Relations with Europe have been dominated by economic concerns.
> After the Bosnian Serbs rejected a peace plan [in May 1993], the president
> lamented, "I felt really badly because I don't want to have to spend more time
> on [Bosnia] than is absolutely necessary, because what I got elected to do was
> to get Americans to look at our own problems."[96]

Though Clinton was inevitably drawn into the realm of foreign affairs by
events beyond his control, his administration has been plagued by the
same indecisive and wandering quality that impeded policymaking during
the Carter years. In organizing the White House for decision-making, Clinton's approach is reminiscent of Jimmy Carter's for its lack of insight and
sophistication. As Greenstein put it: "He is said to be a student of the presidency and of American history, but he shows little awareness of the uses
some presidents have made of well designed formal organization. Indeed,
he entered the White House with no plan for White House organization,
whether at the informal or the formal level."[97]

Though he was the first Democratic president to formally appoint a chief
of staff at the onset of his presidency, Clinton's White House has been far
less structured and less systematic in decision-making than the appearance
of a formal chief of staff system would suggest. In a comment that could
easily have been made in the Carter administration, a top White House aide
said that Clinton "wants to be his own Chief of Staff, his own legislative director and his own National Security Advisor."[98] There is little room for advance planning or strategic thinking in the Clinton White House. One
Clinton associate noted that the president's difficulty in making decisions
can be attributed in part to the lack of a system to focus the president's attention. "There is no system. He has a decision making method which is a
postponement process."[99]

As was the case in the Carter administration, formal meetings of the National Security Council and of the cabinet are few and far between. The full
cabinet met only seven times during Clinton's first year in office and was
convened just twice in the first nine months of 1998. One participant ob-

served that a deliberative or policymaking focus was distinctly absent from most meetings of the Cabinet.[100] On the rare occasions that formal meetings of the cabinet or National Security Council are convened, they often lack a clear agenda and a clear focus, and can quickly take on a rambling and digressive quality. One participant described a Clinton cabinet meeting as "all talk, no deliberation." There was "no agenda to act on, no policy or political strategies were set."[101] The story has been much the same on the national security side of policymaking. When Jim Hoagland of the *Washington Post* asked a top national security aide who had attended many of the administration's most important foreign policy meetings what surprised him most about the meetings, the aide responded without hesitation that he was struck by "how much of the meeting was not about the meeting. What gets brought into the meeting often has very little to do with the issue under discussion."[102]

As with the Carter administration, disorganization has had clear consequences for Clinton's foreign policy. Hoagland notes, for example, that the administration simultaneously gave its support to two *substantially different* peace proposals to settle the conflict in Bosnia. One proposal called for giving the Serbs 49 percent of Bosnian territory; the other proposal, being negotiated at the same time, called for giving the Serbs only 42 percent of the land. The State Department could not explain to Paris or London how the United States had given its endorsement to two different proposals at the same time. One British official said: "This is either completely amateurish or extremely cynical. . . . The lack of comprehension that now exists between us and Washington is greater than at any time in my experience." [103]

This was not the first time that the Clinton administration had contradicted itself on Bosnia. Early in the administration Secretary of State Warren Christopher described the Bosnian War as "a conflagration that could envelop all of Southern Europe and perhaps rage beyond." Yet, in the summer of 1993 Christopher remarked that Bosnia "does not affect our vital national interests." As Richard Cohen noted in the *Washington Post,* "these inconsistent statements cannot both be right."[104]

Clinton's reversals and missteps in foreign policy have not been confined to Bosnia. During the campaign of 1992, candidate Clinton condemned the Bush administration policy of shipping Haitian refugees back to Haiti as "heartless and immoral." As president-elect, Clinton shifted positions and declared that Haitian refugees had to be shipped back "because it was too dangerous for them to be at sea 'in homemade boats made from wood they take off the roofs of their house.'"[105] Clinton's ad hoc policy stance on Haiti was not settled, however. "After he became president and activist Randall Robinson went on a hunger strike to protest the repatriation of Haitians who had fled their county, Clinton sided with Robinson as though his administration's policy had been none of his doing."[106]

A more costly flip-flop occurred regarding Somalia, where eighteen American soldiers were killed after the administration reshaped a humanitarian mission into active pursuit of a leading warlord. In June 1993, the president announced that the goal of the U.S.-led U.N. operation was "to make sure that the United Nations can fulfill its mission there and continue to work with the Somalis toward *nation building* [emphasis added]." Yet, in October of that year, Clinton reported to Congress: "The U.S. military mission is not now nor was it ever one of 'nation building.' "[107] Clinton's flip-flops prompted Joe Klein of *Newsweek* to conclude: "With the Clintons, the story always is subject to further revision." Clinton's "rhetorical promiscuity" is predicated on a "reckless belief that he can talk his way out of anything."[108] Writing in the *New York Times*, Michael Kelly sounded a similar theme: "It isn't that Clinton means to say things that are not true, or that he cannot make true, but that everything is true for him when he says it." Kelly added, "He is the existential President, living with absolute sincerity in the passing moment."[109] Interestingly, Klein and Kelly made these observations years before Clinton's Grand Jury testimony in the Monica Lewinsky case, where the president gave new meaning to verbal gymnastics by splitting hairs over the meaning of the word "alone" and ruminating on what the meaning of "is" really "is."

A sampling of opinion of prominent foreign policy analysts conducted by the Carnegie Endowment for International Peace indicates that the improvisational nature of Clinton's foreign policy and the lack of a strategic vision have not been lost on observers from afar. Rupert Pennant-Rea, editor of the *Economist* from 1986 until 1993, commented in 1997: "It is surely fair to be disappointed by Clinton's foreign policy record: relentlessly tactical and never in the cause of strategy."[110] Nayan Chanda, editor of the *Far Eastern Economic Review*, observed: "The image of Clinton in Asia is that of an indecisive president so preoccupied with domestic scandals that he has allowed special interest groups to drive U.S. foreign policy." Chanda voiced concern that "On the few occasions when Clinton did choose to comment on Asia, such as the case of an American youth caned in Singapore, it only underlined the casualness of his interest in the region. The president's flip-flops highlight how Asia is merely a matter of tactics in his domestic policy wrangles, not of foreign policy strategy."[111]

One of the biggest "flip-flops" in Clinton's foreign policy toward Asia involved his position on extending Most Favored Nation trade status to China. In the days leading up to his election to the presidency in 1992, candidate Clinton excoriated Bush for his passive stance on human rights violations in China, saying:

> When China cracked down on pro-democracy demonstrators, exported advanced weapons to radical regimes, and suppressed Tibet, this administration

and this president failed to stand up for our values. Instead, he sent secret emissaries to China signaling that we would do business as usual with those who murdered freedom in Tiananmen Square.[112]

Yet, as president, Clinton not only decided to extend MFN status to China, but also agreed to meet the Chinese leadership in Tiananmen Square during his June 1998 visit. The dramatic turnabout in Clinton's views on policy toward China led NBC's Tim Russert to comment: "The Chinese are still cracking down on democracy, still trading nuclear weapons, still not recognizing the freedom of Tibet, exactly what candidate Clinton denounced George Bush for, and now he's journeying to Tiananmen Square and toasting the Chinese leadership."[113]

Yoichi Funabashi, chief diplomatic correspondent for the *Asahi Shimbun,* suggests that the Clinton administration's lapses in foreign policy are not limited to Bosnia, Haiti, Somalia, and China.

> Asians . . . learned quickly that domestic politics always come first for this president. Two years after trumpeting his commitment to building an Asia-Pacific "community," Clinton canceled his visit to the APEC meeting in Osaka, Japan, because of the budget crisis with the newly elected Republican majority in Congress—adding insult to injury in Asian eyes by choosing to go ahead with a subsequent trip to Ireland under similar circumstances.[114]

Foreign policy analysts in Europe expressed similar frustration with American foreign policy during the Clinton years. In 1997, Christoph Bertram, Hamburg-based diplomatic correspondent for *Die Zeit,* wrote: "The only unambiguous indication that Clinton has given of his international agenda is that he wants to make the world safe for U.S. exports and investments. For the rest, the president has failed to formulate any hierarchy of priorities."[115] Jacques Attali, former special adviser to president François Mitterrand, had perhaps the most telling assessment of Clinton's foreign policy:

> Of course, strong leadership is not just about vision. To be truly effective, a leader must seek the views and win the support of allies and partners. But under Clinton, this process of consultation is not taking place. Lacking a long-term vision, his administration seeks to impose its fancied solutions on an ad hoc basis, dictating policy and using boycott diplomacy to get its way. Today, just under one-third of the world's population lives under the cloud of an American embargo. Blackmail is becoming a surrogate for negotiation; boycott a substitute for compromise.
>
> . . . International law should be the product of consensus, not dictat. If the Clinton administration does not put its diplomacy in the context of a well-thought-out global vision and show a willingness to discuss that vision in the relevant international forums, then relations between Europe and the United States are destined to enter a very dark age.[116]

In the sixth year of the Clinton administration, the story had not changed with regard to the disjointed nature of the Clinton administration's approach to foreign and national security policy. Three days after his grand jury testimony in the Monica Lewinsky matter, the president ordered a Tomahawk cruise missile attack on a Sudanese pharmaceutical factory in Khartoum and on selected targets in Afghanistan that were thought to be training camps for Osama bin Laden and his terrorist organization. The administration justified the attacks as retaliation for the terrorist truck bombings of the American embassies in Nairobi, Kenya and Dar es Salaam, Tanzania, and as a preemptive strike against the "imminent danger" of more terrorist attacks on U.S. targets.[117]

According to a published account in the *New Yorker*, the decision to bomb alleged terrorist installations was made hastily without broad consultation or careful analysis. The Joint Chiefs of Staff were not briefed on the attack until the day before the raids. The veil of secrecy and lack of consultation surrounding the missions appears to have closely paralleled the Carter administration's decision-making in the Iran-hostage rescue attempt where the "need to know" standard was so rigorously enforced that even the Pentagon had an incomplete picture of the overall plan. The chairman of the Joint Chiefs was instructed by the Clinton White House not to discuss the operation with other members of the Joint Chiefs or to involve senior officers of the Defense Intelligence Agency.[118] Moreover, FBI Director Louis Freeh was kept out of the planning even though the FBI had played a key role in investigating the bombings in Kenya and Tanzania. Attorney General Janet Reno requested, to no avail, that a decision to use force against targets in Afghanistan be delayed until solid evidence could be assembled to link Saudi extremist bin Laden to the attacks on American embassies. A Justice Department official added that the evidence tying bin Laden to the U.S. embassy bombings did not meet the "Tripoli Standard" used to justify the Reagan administration's decision to bomb targets in Libya after incontrovertible evidence showed a link between Libya and a terrorist attack on a West Berlin nightclub that killed several American soldiers.

The Clinton administration insisted that the Sudanese pharmaceutical plant destroyed in the air attack had been producing VX nerve gas, but sources in the Directorate of Science and Technology at the Central Intelligence Agency purportedly believed that evidence of past activity did not represent reliable evidence concerning conditions at the plant at the time of the U.S. attack.[119] Jimmy Carter and Clinton congressional ally Barney Frank were among those who said that the raid in Sudan was "a mistake."[120] In assessing the cruise missile attacks, a top Pentagon official commented that the Clinton administration does not have a national security policy. "It's all ad hoc. All off the shelf. Decisions are random."[121]

The Clinton administration's ad hoc and unsystematic approach to foreign policy continued unabated in the spring of 1999 when the White House pushed for U.S.-led NATO airstrikes to show the determination of the West to put an end to Serbian "ethnic cleansing" of Albanians in the province of Kosovo. Weeks before the NATO air campaign against Serb President Slobodan Milosevic began, however, CIA Director George J. Tenet "had been forecasting that Serb-led Yugoslav forces might respond by accelerating their campaign of ethnic cleansing in the province of Kosovo," precisely the outcome that came to fruition.[122] According to the *Washington Post*, U.S. military leaders had advised Clinton that if the Serbs did launch such an assault, "air power alone would not be sufficient to stop it."[123] Despite this advice, the *Post* reported, "Clinton and his senior White House advisers pressed on with their planning for an air campaign." The White House "never reassessed the fundamental judgment they had reached the previous fall, which ruled out the use of ground troops as a way of protecting Kosovo's majority Albanian population from a brutal crackdown by the Serbs." With more than a hundred thousand Albanians already driven out of Kosovo, and an unknown number killed, the central question confronting Clinton, according to the *Washington Post*, was this: "Why were his foreign policy aims not more closely matched with the military means necessary to achieve them?"[124]

Conclusion

The Carter and Clinton presidencies had their bright moments. The Camp David Accord between Israel and Egypt and the Civil Service Reform Act of 1978 are lasting legacies of the Carter years. And even though NAFTA and welfare reform were Republican bills (Clinton withdrew his own welfare reform bill after Republicans took control of Congress in 1994), and even though the accomplishment of a balanced budget was not achieved until the Republican Congress was in place to check some of the extravagance in the president's multifaceted proposals for new federal programs, the fact is that these accomplishments did occur on Clinton's watch. Moreover, Clinton's intervention in the Northern Ireland peace agreement and his personal role in negotiating the Wye Accord between Israel and the Palestinian Authority offset to some degree the erratic and unfocused nature of America's foreign policy in the rest of the world during the Clinton years.

Carter and Clinton will both be remembered as exceptionally bright and hard-working presidents, each possessing many gifts, not least of which are the ability to empathize (Clinton appropriated Carter's promise to be a president "who feels your pain"),[125] the ability to recite endless arguments in support of their policies, and especially in Clinton's case, the ability to charm supporters and adversaries alike. The question that arises is how men of such talent could leave legacies that are so lacking in the type of inspiration that Franklin D. Roosevelt and John F. Kennedy are remembered for, or in the common-sense pragmatism and decisiveness that we associate with Harry S. Truman and Dwight D. Eisenhower? To the extent that FDR and JFK were more inspirational and far-reaching, and to the degree that Truman and Ike were more plain-spoken, pragmatic, and decisive, their backgrounds and life experiences seem to have better prepared them for leadership and statesmanship on the national and international stage than the more limited experiences of Carter and Clinton. Whether it was Truman's experience as an artillery commander, Roosevelt's challenges as a New York Assemblyman battling Tammany Hall or as Assistant Secretary of the Navy and governor of New York, Kennedy's PT109 heroism, or Eisenhower's job as Supreme Allied Commander, there was something tangible about the leadership qualities that these individuals brought to bear in the White House. As Kennedy biographer Richard Reeves notes, Clinton "is not, by any measure, wise beyond his years, possibly because he has had such limited life experience—school and politics, that's about it. He was never in the armed services or Peace Corps; he's never really held a job in the private sector."[126] Carter at least had a noteworthy career in the Navy prior to his career in politics, but his background in engineering with its emphasis on discrete problem solving and detailed knowledge may have hindered the development of a broader perspective in approaching national and international problems.

What distinguishes the policy wonk presidencies of Clinton and Carter is the complete preoccupation with policy as an end in itself. A broad sense of history, statesmanship, and a sense of vision based on broad experience were not an integral part of the makeup that these men brought with them to the Oval Office. The narrowness of Carter's focus led Fallows to conclude that Carter's approach to problems was "technical, not historical." Indeed, the elevation of the mechanics of policy over political statesmanship represents one of the most obvious flaws of the policy wonk presidency.

The record of the Carter years indicates that an insatiable appetite for detailed knowledge in numerous policy areas and an impressive command of information was of limited use when it came to leadership. "For the part of his job that involves leadership," Fallows suggested, "Carter's style of thought cripples him. He thinks he 'leads' by choosing the correct policy; but he fails to project a vision larger than the problem he is tackling at the moment."[127] Ultimately, Fallows concluded, "Carter often seemed more concerned with taking the correct position than with learning how to turn that position into results."[128]

A similar conclusion can be rendered regarding Bill Clinton's presidency. The president's stand on gays in the military and his second-term initiative on race reflect a tendency by Clinton to let ideas and good intentions overtake action and accomplishment. As Efron has noted, Clinton "fails to distinguish between having an idea and taking an action, between thinking and doing; he gets lost in details, so he cannot retain his abstract purposes; and he has great difficulty in reaching conclusions or making decisions."[129] Clinton's well-documented early delays in filling top appointments in the executive branch, his almost complete failure in the health care and fast-track episodes, his waffling in putting together the administration's early economic program, and his erratic foreign policy toward Haiti, Somalia, China, Bosnia, and Iraq all suggest that the president has great difficulty reaching closure on key issues. Moreover, as Greenstein notes, "Clinton is a devotee of policy *qua* policy and not just the policies of his own administration, so much so that his rhetoric on the stump sometimes has more of the ring of the public policy school than of the political arena."[130]

Clinton's exaggerated sense of the primacy of policy over statesmanship came to the fore at a meeting of the cabinet on September 10, 1998. Some three weeks after admitting that he had misled the nation regarding an "inappropriate" relationship with a White House aide and former intern, the president invited the cabinet to his private residence to apologize for his personal behavior. In what one participant described as a "convoluted" speech punctuated with tears in the president's eyes, "Clinton pleaded for forgiveness and implored Cabinet members to give him their support."[131] The *Washington Post* indicated that not all cabinet members were mollified by the president's impassioned plea. Participants observed that Donna E. Shalala, secretary of health and human services, was visibly upset with the president's insinuation that his policies and programs were ultimately more important than the moral tone of his leadership. According to the *Post*, Shalala said to the president: "I can't believe that is what you're telling us, that is what you believe, that you don't have an obligation to provide moral leadership."[132] Shalala's candid exchange with the president captured in microcosm the essence of Clinton's notion that policies and programs are synonymous with leadership. Conservative critic William J. Bennett was even more blunt than Shalala in his appraisal of Clinton's "policy" defense. "It is said that private character has virtually no impact on governing character; that what matters above all is a healthy economy; that moral authority is defined solely by how well a president deals with policy matters . . . that we shouldn't be judgmental." Even as the president was formally impeached by the House of Representatives on December 19, 1998, the administration's defenders continued to cite the president's positions on issues and his policy accomplishments as the central reason for not holding an impeachment trial in the U.S. Senate. Yet a good many Democrats in the House of Representatives, in an effort to forestall impeachment, were prepared to support a censure resolution stating that Clinton had brought "dishonor" to the office of president.

Although Carter shared Clinton's propensity for elevating the mechanics of policy over the broad contours of statesmanship, a fundamental distinction must be drawn with regard to Carter's conception of moral leadership in public office. Throughout his years in public service, Carter never lost sight of the importance of setting a high moral standard in leadership. As Carter himself put it in his autobiography:

> Public officials, the President, the Vice-President, Members of Congress, Attorneys General, federal judges, the head of the CIA, the head of the FBI and otherwise, ought to set a standard that is absolutely exemplary. We ought to be like Caesar's wife. We ought to be free of any criticism or allegation. We ought to be open about mistakes that we make, not try to hide from the public what is done. . . . In that way, mistakes can be more quickly corrected.[133]

Whatever similarities and shortcomings Carter may have shared with Clinton in his approach to leadership, from a moral perspective Carter's leadership was clearly exemplary. The Clinton presidency gives more force than ever to the example set by Jimmy Carter. The Clinton legacy also reinforces the judgment that David McCullough rendered shortly after completing his Pulitzer Prize–winning biography of Harry Truman, when he said: "Character counts in the presidency more than any other single quality. It is more important than how much the President knows of foreign policy, or economics, or even about politics."[134] Indeed, presidential leadership involves much more than the mastery of the details of policy, or the ability to charm the voters, or the compassion to empathize with their pain. A president must hold deep and abiding principles, a clear and compelling vision, and a commitment to uphold the constitutional order and the dignity of office.

Notes

Chapter 1

1. The facts of Washington's life are well known and noncontroversial. This essay is the author's interpretation of those facts. For these reasons, no notes will be offered except to document quotations. The fullest biographies, in which the factual data are found, are Douglas Southall Freeman's *George Washington*, 6 vols.; seventh and last volume by John A. Carroll and Mary A. Ashworth (New York: Scribner's, 1948–57); and James Thomas Flexner's George Washington, 4 vols. (Boston: Little, Brown, 1965–72). Flexner also published a one-volume condensation, *Washington: The Indispensable Man* (Boston: Little, Brown, 1974). Neither succeeds in depicting the inner man. Two extremely valuable works that attempt, with considerable success, to do so are Paul K. Longmore, *The Invention of George Washington* (Berkeley: University of California Press, 1988) and Richard Brookhiser, *Founding Father: Rediscovering George Washington* (New York: Free Press, 1996). Washington's correspondence is contained in John C. Fitzpatrick, ed., *Writings of George Washington*, 31 vols. (Washington, D.C.: U.S. Government Printing Office, 1931–39). A new edition, which includes letters sent to as well as from Washington, is W. W. Abbot et al., eds., *The Papers of George Washington* (Charlottesville: University Press of Virginia, 1983–). An excellent anthology is William B. Allen, ed., *George Washington: A Collection* (Indianapolis: Liberty Press, 1988).

2. Quoted in Flexner, *Washington: The Indispensable Man*, 16.

3. Washington to Benjamin Harrison, 22 January 1785, in Allen, *George Washington: A Collection*, 295.

4. Washington to Congress, 23 December 1783, ibid., 273.

5. Washington to Hamilton, 3 October 1788, ibid., 422.

6. Hamilton to Washington, 13 August 1788, in Harold C. Syrett et al., eds., *The Papers of Alexander Hamilton*, 27 vols. (New York: Columbia University Press, 1961–79), 5:202.

7. Hamilton to Washington, September 1788, ibid., 5:221.

8. Both quotations cited in Longmore, *The Invention of George Washington*, 181.

9. Gouverneur Morris to John Marshall, 26 June 1807, in Anne Carey Morris, ed., *The Diary and Letters of Gouverneur Morris*, 2 vols. (New York: Scribner's, 1888), 2:492.

10. Kenneth R. Bowling and Helen E. Veit, eds., *The Diary of William Maclay and Other Notes on Senate Debates* (Baltimore: Johns Hopkins University Press, 1988), notes of 22 August 1789, 128–30.

11. Washington to Edward Rutledge, 5 May 1789, in Fitzpatrick, *Writings of George Washington,* 30:309.

12. Quoted in Brookhiser, *Founding Father,* 5.

13. Ibid., 109; Flexner, *Washington: The Indispensable Man,* 69; Forrest McDonald, *The Presidency of George Washington* (Lawrence: University Press of Kansas, 1974), 26.

14. Washington to David Stuart, 26 July 1789, in Fitzpatrick, *Writings of George Washington,* 30:360–62.

15. Queries on a Line of Conduct to be Pursued by the President, 10 May 1789; Washington to Madison, 11 May 1789, and to David Stuart, 26 July 1789. All in Fitzpatrick, *Writings of George Washington,* 30:319–22, 361–62.

16. Washington to the Hebrew Congregations, January 1790, in Allen, *George Washington: A Collection,* 546.

17. Washington to the United Baptist Churches in Virginia, 10 May 1789, 532.

18. General Orders, 4 July 1775, ibid., 43.

19. Farewell Address, 19 September 1796, ibid., 521.

20. Washington to George Mason, 3 October 1785, ibid., 312.

21. Washington to Edward Carrington, 28 September 1795, in Fitzpatrick, *Writings of George Washington,* 34:317.

Chapter 2

1. Thomas Jefferson, "Fair Copy" of the Kentucky Resolutions [Nov. 1798], in Paul L. Ford, ed., *The Writings of Thomas Jefferson,* 10 vols. (New York: Putnam's, 1892–99) 7:304 (Eighth Resolution).

2. David N. Mayer, *The Constitutional Thought of Thomas Jefferson* (Charlottesville: University Press of Virginia, 1994), 129–30, 320–21.

3. For a discussion of the radical Whig tradition and its relevance to early American constitutional theory, see David N. Mayer, "The English Radical Whig Origins of American Constitutionalism," *Washington University Law Quarterly* 70 (1992): 131–208.

4. Other "chains of the Constitution" that were important to Jefferson were federalism, strict interpretation of enumerated powers, broad interpretation of the guarantees provided by the Bill of Rights, and, ultimately the power of the people to amend the Constitution.

5. M. J. C. Vile, *Constitutionalism and the Separation of Powers* (Oxford: Clarendon, 1967), 13.

6. Ibid., 33.

7. Jefferson, *Notes on the State of Virginia* [1784], in Ford, *Writings of Thomas Jefferson,* 3:223–24.

8. Jefferson to John Adams, 28 September 1787, in Julian P. Boyd, et al., eds, *The Papers of Thomas Jefferson,* 26 vols. (to date) (Princeton: Princeton University Press, 1950–) 12:189.

9. Taylor's *Inquiry into the Principles and Policy of the Government of the United States* (1814), written in response to John Adams's *Defence,* embodied what Vile regards as the "high water mark" of separation of powers theory; Taylor envisioned political power flowing in "distinct channels" directly from the people to

each of the three branches of government. Vile, *Constitutionalism and Separation of Powers*, 166. During his retirement years, in a series of letters he wrote in 1816—at about the same time he read Taylor's book—Jefferson too expounded such a pure separation of powers theory, linked to his concept of republicanism as a form of government in which each branch is directly accountable to the people. See Mayer, *Constitutional Thought of Jefferson*, 130–35, 141–44.

10. Madison, *Federalist* 51 [6 February 1788], in Jacob E. Cooke, ed., *The Federalist* (Middletown, Conn.: Wesleyan University Press, 1961), 347–48.

11. Jefferson to Edward Carrington, 21 December 1787, in Boyd, *Papers*, 12:445.

12. Jefferson to Madison, 20 December 1787, in Boyd, *Papers*, 12:439. With regard to the veto power, however, he added that he "should have liked it better had the Judiciary" been associated or "invested with a similar and separate power," thus anticipating his view, discussed below, that the veto power ought to be confined to constitutional matters.

13. Ibid., 440–41. Jefferson also feared that European nations would attempt to influence the election of American presidents, and he concluded that the "incapacity to be elected a second time" was "the only effectual preventative" to the disorder and danger of foreign intrigue which would attend elections.

14. Jefferson to Edward Carrington, 27 May 1788, in Boyd, *Papers*, 13:208–9. The tradition set by Washington lasted until the presidency of Franklin D. Roosevelt; after Roosevelt's death, the Twenty-second Amendment was added to the Constitution.

15. Jefferson to Madison, 15 March 1789, in Boyd, *Papers*, 14:661.

16. Jefferson's functions of the secretary of state are discussed more fully in Dumas Malone, *Jefferson and the Rights of Man* (Boston: Little, Brown, 1951), 269–85.

17. Dumas Malone, *Jefferson the President: Second Term, 1805–1809* (Boston: Little, Brown, 1974), xii; James Sterling Young, *The Washington Community, 1800–1828* (New York: Columbia University Press, 1966), 78.

18. Jefferson to Nathaniel Macon, 14 May 1801, in Ford, *Writings of Thomas Jefferson*, 8:51.

19. Jefferson was writing to his good friend, Dr. Benjamin Rush, explaining why he had appointed someone else as director of the mint in Philadelphia. Hence, he wrote, one of the "laws of action" that governed his exercise of the appointments power was to "anatomize the living man as the Surgeon does his dead subject, view him also as a machine & employ him for what he is fit for, unblinded by the mist of friendship." Jefferson to Dr. Benjamin Rush, 13 June 1805, quoted in Malone, *Jefferson the President: Second Term*, 20.

20. Jefferson to Nehemiah Dodge and others, A Committee of the Danbury Baptist Association in the State of Connecticut, 1 January 1802 (draft), *Jefferson Papers*, Manuscripts Division, Library of Congress.

21. Jefferson to Rev. Samuel Miller, 23 January 1808, in Ford, *Writings of Thomas Jefferson*, 9:175.

22. Jefferson, Opinion on the Constitutionality of the Bill for Establishing a National Bank, 15 February 1791, in Boyd, *Papers*, 19:279–80. For a discussion of Jefferson's and Hamilton's contrasting opinions on the merits of the bank bill, see Mayer, *Constitutional Thought of Jefferson*, 189–97.

23. Jefferson, Opinion on the Bill Apportioning Representation, 4 April 1792, in Boyd, *Papers*, 23:370–76; Malone, *Jefferson and the Rights of Man*, 441. Washington exercised his second and final veto on 28 February 1797, of a bill relating to the military establishment of the United States. He did so largely on policy, not constitutional grounds; and this was long after Jefferson had left the cabinet.

24. Richard A. Watson, "Origins and Early Development of the Veto Power," *Presidential Studies Quarterly* 17 (1987): 407–8.

25. Ibid., 409.

26. Forrest McDonald, *The American Presidency: An Intellectual History* (Lawrence: University Press of Kansas, 1994), 351–52.

27. Ibid., 353–54.

28. Without the veto, the president "would be absolutely unable to defend himself against the depredations" of Congress, Hamilton argued. *Federalist* 73, in Cooke, *The Federalist*, 494.

29. See Noble E. Cunningham Jr., *The Process of Government under Jefferson* (Princeton: Princeton University Press, 1978), 322.

30. For example, in his Fourth Annual Message of 8 November 1804, Jefferson observed to Congress: "Whether the great interests of agriculture, manufacturing, commerce, or navigation, can, within the pale of your constitutional powers, be aided in any of their relations; whether laws are provided in all cases where they are wanting . . . in fine, whether anything can be done to advance the general good, are questions within the limits of your functions which will necessarily occupy your attentions." Ford, *Writings of Thomas Jefferson*, 8:332.

31. For example, during his tenure as secretary of state, Jefferson advised Washington that the Senate's confirmation powers did not give it the authority to negative the *grade* of a diplomatic appointment as well as the *person* to be appointed. Reasoning that "the transaction of business with foreign nations is Executive altogether" and accordingly belongs to the President, "*except* as to such portions of it as are specially submitted to the Senate" by the Constitution, he concluded that exceptions such as the Senate's "advise and consent" power "are to be construed strictly" (Jefferson, Opinion on Powers of the Senate Respecting Diplomatic Appointments, in Boyd, *Papers*, 16:378–80). Similarly, when upon the death of Benjamin Franklin, the French National Assembly sent a message of condolences to the Congress, Jefferson through the American minister in Paris instructed the French that "Congress can only correspond through the Executive, whose organ in the case of foreign nations is the Secretary of State. The President of the U.S. being coordinate with Congress, cannot personally be their scribe" (Jefferson to William Short, 8 March 1791, in Boyd, *Papers*, 19:424–25, 102 [editorial note]).

32. Jefferson to James Madison, 6 September 1789, in Boyd, *Papers*, 15:397.

33. See Jefferson to James Madison, 23 June and 29 June 1793, in Ford, *Writings of Thomas Jefferson*, 6:315, 327.

34. Robert F. Turner, *The War Powers Resolution: Its Implementation in Theory and Practice* (Philadelphia: Foreign Policy Research Institute, 1983), 20.

35. See, for example, Robert Scigliano, "The War Powers Resolution and the War Powers," in Joseph M. Bessette and Jeffrey Tulis, *The Presidency in the Constitutional Order* (Baton Rouge: Louisiana State University Press, 1981), 138. ("Advocates of the War Powers Resolution [of 1973] turn to [Jefferson] perhaps more often than

to any other founder as authority for their opinion that the president's war power was limited to meeting attack."), cited in Turner, *War Powers Resolution*, 40 n.61.

36. See Jefferson, "Anas," [Report of Cabinet meeting of 15 May 1801], in Ford, *Writings of Thomas Jefferson*, 1:293–94.

37. Jefferson, First Annual Message, 8 December 1801, ibid., 8:118–19.

38. Dumas Malone, *Jefferson the President: First Term, 1801–1805* (Boston: Little, Brown, 1970), 98. With regard to Hamilton's argument, Malone observes that "if President Franklin D. Roosevelt had believed that, he would not have needed to go to Congress after Pearl Harbor." Roosevelt's motivations in 1941, however, were more complicated, as is the full story of other presidents' understanding of the nature of war powers. See Harold M. Hyman, *Quiet Past and Stormy Present? War Powers in American History* (Washington, D.C.: American Historical Association, 1986).

39. The War Powers Act requires congressional action after sixty days to authorize the introduction of U.S. armed forces into foreign territory or into "hostilities or . . . situations where imminent involvement in hostilities is clearly indicated by the circumstances." War Powers Act, 87 Statutes at Large 55 (1973), in Melvin I. Urofsky, ed., *Documents of American Constitutional & Legal History* (New York: Knopf, 1989), 2:449–50.

40. See, e.g., Thomas M. Franck, "Declare War? Congress Can't," *New York Times*, December, 1990. Franck, director of the Center for International Studies at NYU School of Law, argues that in ratifying the U.N. Charter, the United States "became a part of a new order," one which "does not leave room" for constitutional checks on presidential power.

41. See *United States v. Curtiss-Wright Export Corporation*, 299 U.S. 304 (1936). (In an opinion by Justice Sutherland, the Court held that "the very delicate, plenary and exclusive power of the President as the sole organ of the federal government in the field of international relations" gives the president "a degree of discretion and freedom from statutory restriction which would not be admissible were domestic affairs alone involved").

42. Jefferson to Abigail Adams, 11 September 1804, in Lester J. Cappon, ed., *The Adams-Jefferson Letters*, (New York: Clarion, 1971 reprint of 1959 edition), 279–80.

43. Jefferson, First Annual Message to Congress (draft), 8 December 1801, *Jefferson Papers*.

44. Jefferson to Samuel Kercheval, 12 July 1816, in Ford, *Writings of Thomas Jefferson*, 10:39.

45. This was a campaign of rhetoric conducted by a group of Virginia "Old Republicans" in response to a series of decisions handed down by the Supreme Court, including *McCulloch v. Maryland* (1819) and, most importantly, *Cohens v. Virginia* (1821). The Virginia campaign, and Jefferson's involvement in it, are discussed in Mayer, *Constitutional Thought of Jefferson*, chapter 9.

46. Jefferson to William Charles Jarvis, 28 September 1820, in Andrew A. Lipscomb and Albert Ellery Bergh, eds, *The Writings of Thomas Jefferson*, 20 vols. (Washington, D.C.: Thomas Jefferson Memorial Association, 1904), 15:277–78.

47. For a discussion of the Louisiana Purchase and Jefferson's doubts about its constitutionality, see Mayer, *Constitutional Thought of Jefferson*, 215–16, 244–51.

48. Jefferson to Wilson Cary Nicholas, 7 September 1803, in Ford, *Writings of Thomas Jefferson*, 8:247–48.

49. Thomas Paine to Jefferson, 23 September 1803, quoted in Malone, *Jefferson the President: First Term*, 321.

50. Jefferson to John C. Breckinridge, 13 August 1803, in Ford, *Writings of Thomas Jefferson*, 8:244n.

51. Jefferson to J. B. Colvin, 20 September 1810, in Lipscomb and Berg, *Writings of Thomas Jefferson*, 12:418, 421–22. The examples he cites include the destruction of property during the Revolutionary War, a "hypothetical case" involving the acquisition of Florida (which presented constitutional questions analogous to those that troubled Jefferson about the Louisiana Purchase), and the illegal arrests of participants in the Burr Conspiracy by General James Wilkinson, governor of the Louisiana Territory.

52. John Locke, ed, Peter Laslett, in *Two Treatises of Government* (New York: Cambridge University Press, 1960), 421–22.

53. An exception that possibly proves the rule is the Korean War steel seizure case, where the Supreme Court held that President Truman's commander in chief power did not authorize him to seize control of the nation's steel mills to forestall a strike. As broad as the president's war power may be, the Court determined, it did not give him the power to flout the law within the United States. *Youngstown Sheet & Tube Co. v. Sawyer*, 343 U.S. 579 (1952).

Chapter 3

1. See "White House Motion Seeking Privilege," filed March 17, 1998, and unsealed May 27, 1998 (www.washingtonpost.com/wp-srv/politics/special/clinton/stories/whitehouse052898.htm).

2. Ruff declared that because Judge Norma Holloway Johnson had given credibility to some of the arguments in the White House filings on the legitimacy of executive privilege, the White House had achieved its goal of ensuring the viability of this presidential power for future administrations.

3. The phrase "executive privilege" did not exist at the time of the founding and, in fact, did not become a part of the common language of U.S. politics until coined by the Eisenhower administration.

4. John Locke, *Second Treatise of Government*, chapter 12, sections 143–148 (New York: Cambridge University Press, 1960).

5. Ibid., sections 146–148.

6. Ibid., chapter 14, section 166.

7. Baron de Montesquieu, *The Spirit of the Laws*, Book II (New York: Hafner Press, 1966).

8. Quoted in Daniel Hoffman, *Governmental Secrecy and the Founding Fathers* (Westport, Conn.: Greenwood Press, 1981), 21.

9. *U.S. v. Nixon* 418 U.S. 683, 705 (1974).

10. J.W. Peltason, *Corwin and Peltason's Understanding the Constitution*, 11th ed. (New York: Holt, Rinehart, and Winston, 1988), 84.

11. Quoted in Robert Green McCloskey, ed., *The Works of James Wilson* (Cambridge: Harvard University Press, 1967), I: 294, 296.

12. *Marbury v. Madison* 1 Cranch 137, 166 (1803).

13. Quoted in Daniel L. Feldman, *The Logic of American Government: Applying the Constitution to the Contemporary World* (New York: William Morrow, 1990), 82.

14. Quoted in George B. Galloway, *History of the House of Representatives* (New York: Thomas Y. Crowell, 1961), 236–37.

15. Raoul Berger, "Executive Privilege v. Congressional Inquiry," *UCLA Law Review* 12 (1965): 1060, 1117.

16. Ibid., 1117.

17. Raoul Berger, *Executive Privilege: A Constitutional Myth* (Cambridge: Harvard University Press), 1974, 10–11.

18. James W. Ceaser, "In Defense of Separation of Powers," in Robert Goldwin and Art Kaufman, eds., *Separation of Powers—Does It Still Work?* (Washington: American Enterprise Institute, 1986), p 171.

19. *Watkins v. U.S.* 354 U.S. 178 (1957); *Wilkinson v. U.S.* 365 U.S. 399 (1961).

20. *U.S. v. Nixon* 418 U.S. 683 (1974).

21. Quoted in Glenn A. Phelps, "George Washington and the Founding of the Presidency," *Presidential Studies Quarterly* 17 (Spring 1987): 345.

22. *3 Annals of Congress* (1792): 493.

23. Paul L. Ford, ed., *The Writings of Thomas Jefferson*, 10 vols. (New York: Putnam's, 1892–99) 1:189–190.

24. Abraham Sofaer, "Executive Privilege: An Historical Note," *Columbia Law Review* 74 (1975): 1319.

25. Ibid.

26. Ibid.

27. Ibid., 1320.

28. Ibid., 1321; Abraham Sofaer, "Executive Power and Control Over Information: The Practice Under the Framers," *Duke Law Journal* 1977 (March 1977): 8.

29. James Richardson, *A Compilation of the Messages and Papers of the Presidents* (New York: Bureau of National Literature, 1897), 1: 186–187.

30. *5 Annals of Congress* (1796):771, 782–83.

31. Ibid., 773.

32. Quoted in Gary Schmitt, "Executive Privilege," in Joseph Bessette and Jeffrey Tulis, eds., *The Presidency in the Constitutional Order* (Baton Rouge: Louisiana State University Press, 1981), 188n.

33. Ibid., 187n.

34. Sofaer, "Executive Power and Control Over Information," 16–17.

35. Thomas P. Abernathy, *The Burr Conspiracy* (New York: Oxford University Press, 1954).

36. *16 Annals of Congress* (1806–1807): 336.

37. Richardson, *Messages and Papers of the Presidents*, 400.

38. Ford, p. 55.

39. Sofaer, "Executive Power and Control Over Information," pp. 19–24.

40. Ibid., pp. 28–45.

41. Quoted in Schmitt, "Executive Privilege," 169.

42. A detailed coverage of the extensive uses of executive privilege is contained in Mark J. Rozell, *Executive Privilege: The Dilemma of Secrecy and Democratic Accountability* (Baltimore: The Johns Hopkins University Press), 1994.

43. *Public Papers of the Presidents of the United States: Dwight D. Eisenhower, 1954* (Washington, D.C.: U.S. Government Printing Office, 1955) 483–484.

44. Quoted in Fred I. Greenstein, *The Hidden-Hand Presidency* (New York: Basic Books, 1982), 204.

45. Ibid., 205–7.

46. *Washington Post*, 18 May 1954: 14.

47. Letter from Nixon to Rep. John E. Moss, 7 April 1969, Folder: "Executive Privilege (2)," Box 13, Edward Schmults Files, Gerald R. Ford Library, Ann Arbor, Michigan; Memorandum from President Nixon to Executive Department Heads, 24 March 1969, Folder: "Executive Privilege [1973]," White House Staff Files, Ronald Ziegler Alphabetical Subject File, Nixon Presidential Materials Project, Alexandria, Virginia.

48. "Nixon: A President May Violate the Law," *U.S. News & World Report*, 30 May 1977: 65.

49. For an earlier study, the author examined White House and congressional documents on executive privilege from the Ford, Carter, Reagan, and Bush years and discovered a common thread: the effort to avoid executive privilege and instead use other justifications—statutory, national security directives, other forms of privilege or secrecy policies—for withholding information. See Rozell, *Executive Privilege,* chapters 4 and 5.

50. "Ruff's Argument for Executive Privilege," unsealed 27 May, 1998 (www.washingtonpost.com/wp-srv/politics/special/clinton/stories/ruff052898.htm).

51. "White House Motion Seeking Privilege," filed 17 March, 1998 (www.washingtonpost.com/wp-srv/politics/special/clinton/stories/whitehouse052898.htm).

52. "Judge Johnson's Order on Executive Privilege," issued 26 May, 1998 (www.washingtonpost.com/wp-srv/politics/special/clinton/stories/order052898.htm).

Chapter 4

1. From "The Use of Military Force: The President's Difficult Choice." Address by President George Bush to the Corps of Cadets, U.S. Military Academy, West Point, NY, 5 January 1993.

2. Colin Powell, "US Forces: Challenges ahead," *Foreign Affairs* 71 (1992/93): 36.

3. In a letter to the author dated 1 May, 1990, Weinberger stated: "They represented pretty much the conclusion I had formed following considerable thought as to why we had such a difficult time in Vietnam. My principal conclusion was that our problems stemmed from the fact that we entered a conflict we never intended to win. The six tests were formulated by me as a guide or yardstick to help us decide what I knew would be many requests that we use our Armed Forces in various ways."

4. Portions of this section were extracted from Joseph R. Avella, "Whose Decision to Use Force?" *Presidential Studies Quarterly* (Spring 1996).

5. William P. Rogers, "Congress, The President, and the War Powers," *California Law Review* 59 (1971): 1209–10.

6. Alexander Hamilton, *Federalist* 69, in Clinton Rossiter, ed., *The Federalist Papers* (New York: Penguin Books, 1961), 418.

7. Donald L. Robinson, *"To the Best of My Ability" The Presidency and the Constitution* (New York: Norton, 1987), 121.

8. *Notes of Debates in the Federal Convention of 1787*, reported by James Madison (New York: Norton, 1987), 476.

9. Clinton Rossiter, *1787: The Grand Convention* (New York: Norton, 1987), 221.

10. Alexander Hamilton, *Federalist* 23, in Rossiter, *The Federalist*, 155.

11. Under international law, a quarantine is considered an act of war. In the 1990s, the United States has conducted quarantine operations in the Persian Gulf and in the Adriatic Sea, both without specific congressional authorization.

12. Hugo Grotius, *The Rights of War and Peace* (Westport, Conn.: Hyperion, 1993), In its original form, *De Jure Belli ac Pacis* was first printed in 1625.

13. Letters of marque and reprisal authorized private citizens to prey upon shipping and property of enemy nations without being labeled pirates. This practice was banned by international treaty in 1856, but the United States never signed the protocol.

14. Ancient Rome and Roman society were also referenced in *Federalist* 5, 6, 18, 34, 38, 41, 63, 70, and 75.

15. Arthur Schlesinger, Jr., "Congress and the making of American foreign policy," *Foreign Affairs* 51 (1972): 83.

16. Willard Sterne Randall, *Thomas Jefferson—A Life* (New York: Henry Holt, 1993), 45.

17. Jacob E. Cooke, *The Federalist* (Middletown, Conn.: Wesleyan University Press, 1961), ix.

18. William W. Bishop, *International Law: Cases and Materials* (Boston: Little, Brown, 1962), 744.

19. Ibid., 784-85.

20. Grotius, *The Rights of War and Peace*, 18.

21. *Supreme Court Reporter*, 57, 299 U.S. 304 (St. Paul: West Publishing, 1937), 216-27.

22. Ibid., 220.

23. "Authority of the President to Repel the Attack in Korea," Department of State Memorandum, 3 July, 1950, 23 *Department of State Bulletin*, No. 173, 173-78.

24. 50 USC § 1541(c), in Public Law 93-148, § 2, November 7, 1973, 87 Stat. 555. *United States Code Annotated*, "Title 50: War and National Defense" (St. Paul: West Publishing, 1991), 530.

25. Alfred P. Rubin, "War Powers and the Constitution," *Foreign Service Journal*, February (1991): 20.

26. Albert Lakeland, "War Powers: A Source of Presidential Strength," *Foreign Service Journal,* February (1991): 24.

27. This provision of the resolution is a legislative veto, which was declared unconstitutional by the Supreme Court in *Immigration and Naturalization Service v. Chadha*, 1983, 103 S.Ct. 2764, 462 US 919, 77 L.Ed. 2 317.

28. In 1987, some members of the House of Representatives sought to enforce the resolution and require the Reagan administration to submit reports to Congress concerning U.S. forces in the Persian Gulf during the Iran–Iraq War. The court declined to rule, noting that if it were to decide whether the president was required to submit a report, it would also have to decide whether forces were engaged in hostilities or whether hostilities were imminent. See *Lowry v. Reagan*, D.D.C. 1987, 676 F.Supp. 333.

29. *The Uses of Military Power.* Remarks prepared for delivery by Secretary of Defense Caspar W. Weinberger to the National Press Club, Washington, D.C., 28 November, 1984.

30. Colin Powell, "U.S. Forces: Challenges Ahead," *Foreign Affairs* 71 (Winter 1992/93): 32–45.

31. "The Use of Military Force: The President's Difficult Choice." Address by President George Bush to the Corps of Cadets, U.S. Military Academy, West Point, NY, 5 January 1993.

32. *Conduct of the Persian Gulf War,* Final report to Congress, Department of Defense (April 1992): 19. (Hereafter "Gulf War Report.")

33. The increased revenue from Kuwaiti oil would provide funding support for continuing ballistic missile research and the production of weapons of mass destruction, however.

34. *Gulf War Report,* 33.

35. Military theorists typically postulate a ratio of three attackers to one defender.

36. Oval Office remarks by President Bush, 16 January, 1991.

37. See Catherine Kelleher, "Security in the New Order: Presidents, Polls, and the Use of Force," in Daniel Yankelovich and I. M. Destler, eds., *Beyond the Beltway* (New York: Norton, 1994), 227–28.

38. A poll conducted by Hart and Teeter on 18–19 August 1990 revealed that 70 percent of Americans supported military intervention. When the war actually commenced, the U.S. action gained 85 percent approval in an ABC/*Washington Post* poll taken 24 February 1991. Yankelovich and Destler, *Beyond the Beltway,* 244.

39. Networks included in the count were ABC, CBS, CNN, and NBC. Not added were multiple appearances on different networks on the same day.

40. *Gulf War Report,* 4.

41. Attributed to Colin Powell by Rick Atkinson in *Crusade* (Boston: Houghton Mifflin, 1993), 452.

42. See Joseph Avella, "Evaluating Criteria for Military Force," *Comparative Strategy* 10 (July–September 1991): 217–40.

Chapter 5

1. For other considerations of our ambivalence, see Harvey C. Mansfield, Jr., *Taming the Prince: The Ambivalence of Modern Executive Power* (New York: The Free Press, 1989); and Richard M. Pious, *The American Presidency* (New York: Basic Books, 1979).

2. Barbara Hinckley, *The Symbolic Presidency: How Presidents Portray Themselves* (New York: Routledge, 1990), 9.

3. As Robert Remini has put it, "Both parties accepted the principle that the great masses of plain people throughout the United States should rule. Whereas, thirty years earlier, Alexander Hamilton had called the people a 'beast' and John Adams and other Founding Fathers expressed fears that anarchy was the natural consequence of democracy, in the Age of Jackson these fears evaporated in a cele-

bration of the mass electorate." *The Revolutionary Age of Andrew Jackson* (New York: Harper & Row, 1976), 147.

4. Wilfred E. Binkley, *The Powers of the President: Problems of American Democracy* (Garden City, N.Y.: Doubleday, Doran, 1937), 68.

5. "To the people belongs the right of electing their Chief Magistrate. . . . Experience proves that in proportion as agents to execute the will of the people are multiplied there is danger of their wishes being frustrated. Some may be unfaithful; all are liable to err. So far, therefore, as the people can with convenience speak, it is safer for them to express their own will." Indeed it is most interesting here to note that Jackson makes his assumptions explicit—that even in the popularly elected House of Representatives, "the will of the people is still constantly liable to be misrepresented." Andrew Jackson, "First Annual Message," in James Richardson, *A Compilation of Messages and Papers of the Presidents* (New York: Bureau of National Literature, 1897), 2:447–8.

6. Roger Remini, *Andrew Jackson and the Course of American Freedom, 1822–1832* (New York: Harper & Row, 1981), 369.

7. Jackson vetoed twelve bills during his administration while all previous presidents had only vetoed ten acts of Congress. Jackson also put the "pocket veto" into use for the first time. Sidney M. Milkis and Michael Nelson, *The American Presidency: Origins and Development, 1776–1990* (Washington, D.C.: CQ Press, 1990), 122.

8. Here I give but a sampling of the arguments and sentiments on either side. This is not the forum for a more detailed exegesis of this important historical moment.

9. All further citations from Jackson's "Protest" and the Senatorial responses are from *Register of Debates in Congress*, 1st Session of 23rd Congress, 1833–1834, Part 2 (Washington, D.C.: Gales and Seaton, 1834), 1318.

10. *Debates in Congress*, Jackson, 17 April 1834, 1318.

11. Ibid., 1324.

12. Ibid., 1325.

13. Ibid., 1333.

14. Ibid., 1334.

15. Ibid., 1322.

16. Ibid., 1329.

17. Ibid., 1333.

18. *Debates in Congress*, Poindexter, 17 April 1834, 1336.

19. *Debates in Congress*, Preston, 6 May 1834, 1658. On that same date Calhoun called Jackson's protest "the war message," 1645. Clay put it like this on 30 April: "Already has the President singled out and designated, in the Senate of the United States, the new object of his hostile pursuit; and the protest, which I am now to consider, is his declaration of war.", 1564.

20. *Debates in Congress*, Webster, 7 May 1834, 1681.

21. Ibid., 1681.

22. Ibid., 1685.

23. Ibid., 1672.

24. *Debates in Congress*, Calhoun, 1645–46.

25. See James Madison, Alexander Hamilton, and John Jay, in Isaac Kramnick,

ed., *The Federalist Papers,* Paper Number 47 (England: Penguin Books, 1987), 303.

26. See, for instance, Calhoun's discussion of the solely legislative nature of all "implied" powers in the Constitution and the need to preserve the balance between the institutions of government, in *Debates in Congress,* Calhoun, 1642.

27. *Debates in Congress,* Webster, 1674.

28. *Debates in Congress,* Jackson, 1333.

29. *Debates in Congress,* Calhoun, 1648.

30. *Debates in Congress,* Webster, 1684.

31. Ibid., 1684.

32. Ibid., 1684.

33. Ibid., 1677.

34. Ibid., 1677.

35. *Debates in Congress,* Calhoun, 1645.

36. Ibid., 1646.

37. See Wilfred E. Binkley, "The Jacksonian View of the Presidency Prevails," chapter 5 in *President and Congress,* 3rd ed. (New York: Vintage Books, 1962), 105–32.

38. The term *plebiscitary presidency* was originally used by Theodore J. Lowi in his *The Personal President: Power Invested Promise Unfulfilled* (Ithaca, N.Y.: Cornell University Press, 1985). I use the term here, not because I mean to endorse his thesis in any way, but because the term really best captures the spirit of the presidency that followed Wilson's example and writings.

39. Quoted in James MacGregor Burns, *Presidential Government: The Crucible of Leadership* (New York: Avon Books, 1965), 50.

40. For an examination of this charge against Lincoln's presidency, see Herman Belz, *Lincoln and the Constitution: The Dictatorship Question Reconsidered* (Fort Wayne, Ind.: Louis A. Warren Lincoln Library and Museum, 1984).

41. For example, Lincoln in his speech at Gettysburg appeals not to the Constitution as the founding document of a transcendent people but to the Declaration of Independence. He seems to give representation to that constituting people that he imagined to be "conceived in Liberty, and dedicated to the proposition that all men are created equal." This is the people of 1776, not 1787. On Lincoln's constitutionally revolutionary rhetoric at Gettysburg, see Gary Wills, *Lincoln at Gettysburg: The Words that Remade America* (New York: Simon & Schuster, 1992); and Willmoore Kendall, "Equality: Commitment or Ideal?" in *The Intercollegiate Review* (Spring, 1989), 25–33.

42. Richard Loss, *The Modern Theory of Presidential Power: Alexander Hamilton and the Corwin Thesis* (Westport Conn.: Greenwood Press, 1990), 89.

43. Abraham Lincoln, *Speeches and Writings,* 1859–1865, ed. Don E. Fehrenbacker (New York: The Library of America, 1989), 585.

44. Ibid., 585. Indeed, Lincoln here makes it absolutely clear that the president is so empowered only when the constitutional order is seriously threatened and not merely when his "abstract judgment" might dictate that he act. Less so, even, it would seem, on the grounds of ordinary public policy.

45. Woodrow Wilson, *Congressional Government* (New York: World Publishing, 1967; originally published in 1885).

46. All subsequent quotations of *Constitutional Government* are from Arthur Link, ed., *The Papers of Woodrow Wilson,* vol. 18 (Princeton: Princeton University Press, 1974).

47. Ibid., 107.

48. Harvey C. Mansfield, Jr., *America's Constitutional Soul* (Baltimore: The Johns Hopkins University Press, 1991), 5.

49. Wilson, in fact, acknowledges that all governments, not just the American system of government, are ruled by the evolutionary process and change with the ages. See Link, *The Papers of Wilson*, 104–05.

50. Ibid., 105.

51. Ibid., 106.

52. Ibid., 106.

53. Ibid., 115.

54. Ibid., 107.

55. Ibid., 108.

56. Ibid., 113.

57. Ibid., 141.

58. Ibid., 114.

59. Ibid., 114.

60. Ibid., 141.

61. Ibid., 116.

62. Ibid., 115.

63. Ibid., 141.

64. Quoted in Charles R. Kesler, "Woodrow Wilson and the statesmanship of Progress," in Thomas R. Silver and Peter W. Schramm, eds., *Natural Right and Political Right* (Durham, N.C.: Carolina Academic Press, 1984), 123.

65. Clinton Rossiter, *The American Presidency*, Rev. ed. (New York: Mentor, 1960; first published in 1956).

66. Richard E. Neustadt, *Presidential Power and the Modern Presidency* (New York: Free Press, 1990; originally published in 1960).

67. Neustadt nowhere makes his understanding of presidential representation explicit. Nevertheless, it is my contention that his presidocentric understanding of the system is built around the implicit assumption that the presidency is the one legitimate representative in the American political system. Hence, as he believes, the public good can be equated with that of the presidency. There being no presidency that can be differentiated from the individual incumbent, what is good for the individual power seeker is good for the public. Presidential representation could hardly be expressed in a clearer relationship.

68. Neustadt, *Presidential Power and the Modern Presidency*, 29.

69. Terry Eastland, *Energy in the Executive: The Case for the Strong Presidency* (New York: Free Press, 1992), 8.

70. Joseph Bessette quoted in Eastland, *Energy in the Executive*, 8.

71. Neustadt, *Presidential Power and the Modern Presidency*, xix.

72. Ibid., 155.

73. Ibid., 156.

74. Ibid., 40.

75. Ibid., 32.

76. Ibid., 55.

77. I contend that Neustadt's lack of concern with presidential rhetoric is not simply a misunderstanding on his part. Rather, it demonstrates that the Wilsonian

revolution in the presidency had much wider consequences than simply the legitimation of a "rhetorical presidency," though this was a crucial change. A presidentially centered plebiscitary system of representation is what links the modern presidency to Wilson, Neustadt, and others who have praised active presidential government over the past few decades.

78. See, for instance, Neustadt, *Presidential Power and the Modern Presidency*, 1990, xvi; Garry Wills, *The Kennedy Imprisonment: A Meditation on Power* (New York: Pocket Books, 1981), 182–94.

79. As William Andrews put it, "In summary then, the 1960 writers glorified the presidency, especially in foreign and defense affairs. That institution incarnated governmental virtue. If only it could be made virtually omnipotent through institutional reforms and by electing men with enough will power and skill, the presidency could solve as many of our problems as is humanly possible." William G. Andrews, "The Presidency, Congress, and Constitutional Theory," in Aaron Wildavsky, ed., *Perspectives on the Presidency* (Boston: Little, Brown, 1975), 27.

80. Thomas E. Cronin, "The Textbook and Prime-Time Presidency," in *The State of the Presidency*, 2nd ed., (Boston: Little, Brown, 1980), 76.

81. James W. Ceaser, Glen E. Thurow, Jeffrey Tulis, and Joseph M. Bessette, "The Rise of the Rhetorical Presidency," *Presidential Studies Quarterly* 2 (1981).

82. See Ceaser, et al., 1981, and Tulis, 1987, and Jeffrey K. Tulis, *The Rhetorical Presidency* (Princeton: Princeton University Press, 1987).

83. Ryan J. Barilleaux, *The Post-Modern Presidency* (New York: Praeger, 1988), 61–64.

84. Cronin, *State of the Presidency*, 88.

85. I use the word "conservative" as a generic term for those of the right who were intellectually and politically active during the middle decades of the twentieth century. I include under the term "conservative" both the traditional/cultural conservatives of the "Old Right" as well as their libertarian cousins. Though they differed fundamentally on key values and ideas, on their opposition to presidential power they were soulmates. For a good sampling of the intellectual disagreements between these two groups, see George W. Carey, ed., *Freedom and Virtue: The Conservative/Libertarian Debate* (Lanham, Md.: University Press of America and The Intercollegiate Studies Institute, 1984).

86. For an example of how these two phenomena were connected in the minds of conservatives, see Barry Goldwater, *Where I Stand* (New York: McGraw-Hill, 1964), 88–93.

87. Russell Kirk, *A Program for Conservatives* (Chicago: Henry Regnery Company, 1954), 251.

88. James Burnham, *Congress and the American Tradition* (Chicago: Henry Regnery Company, 1965), 321.

89. See, for instance, Alfred de Grazia, *Republic in Crisis* (New York: Federal Legal Publications, 1965); Burnham, *Congress and American Tradition*; Kirk, *Program for Conservatives*, 263.

90. Willmoore Kendall, "The Two Majorities in American Politics," chapter 2 in *The Conservative Affirmation in America* (Chicago: Gateway Editions, 1985). This essay was originally published in *Midwest Journal of Political Science* (November 1960): 317–45.

91. On this point see, J. Richard Piper, "Presidential-Congressional Power Prescriptions in Conservative Political Thought Since 1933," *Presidential Studies Quarterly*, 21 (Winter 1991): 35–54.

92. On the change in conservative foreign policy prescriptions from isolationism to interventionist anti-communism during the 1950s and 1960s, see chapter 4 in George H. Nash, *The Conservative Intellectual Movement in America Since 1945* (New York: Basic Books, 1976), 84–130.

93. Capturing this sentiment concerning the relationship between foreign policy adventures, increasing democratization, and the concentration of power in the executive was the conservative Frenchman Amaury de Riencourt in his *The Coming Caesars* (New York: Coward-McCann, 1957), 5. "Our Western world, America and Europe, is threatened with Caesarism on a scale unknown since the dawn of the Roman Empire. . . . [E]xpanding democracy leads unintentionally to imperialism and that imperialism inevitably ends in destroying the republican institutions of earlier days; further, . . . the greater the social equality, the dimmer the prospects of liberty, and . . . as society becomes more equalitarian, it tends increasingly to concentrate absolute power in the hands of one single man."

94. For a critical rendition of this history of changing liberal power prescriptions during the 1960s and 1970s, see M. Stanton Evans, *Clear and Present Dangers: A Conservative View of America's Government* (New York: Harcourt Brace Jovanovich, 1975).

95. Arthur M. Schlesinger, Jr., *The Imperial Presidency* (New York: Popular Library, 1974).

96. George E. Reedy, *The Twilight of the Presidency* (New York: Mentor, 1970).

97. Marcus Cunliffe, "A Defective Institution?" *Commentary* (February 1968): 28.

98. Schlesinger, *Imperial Presidency*, 11.

99. Saul K. Padover, "The Power of the President," *Commonweal* (August 9, 1968): 575.

100. James W. Ceaser, *Liberal Democracy & Political Science* (Baltimore: Johns Hopkins University Press, 1990), 210.

101. "Swing of the Pendulum," *The New Republic* (27 March, 1971).

102. For a solid evaluation of the recent "institutional partisanship" of both conservatives and liberals, see Ryan J. Barilleaux, "Liberals, Conservatives, and the Presidency," *Congress & The Presidency* 20, (Spring 1993): 75–82.

103. Jeffrey Hart, "The Presidency: Shifting Conservative Perspectives," *National Review* (November 22, 1974), 1351–55.

104. See Gordon S. Jones and John A. Marini, eds., *The Imperial Congress: Crisis in the Separation of Powers* (New York: Pharos Books, 1988); L. Gordon Crovitz and Jeremy A. Rabkin, eds., *The Fettered Presidency: Legal Constraints on the Executive Branch* (Washington, D.C.: American Enterprise Institute Press, 1989); Terry Eastland, *Energy in the Executive: The Case for the Strong Presidency* (New York: Free Press, 1992). Some conservatives did maintain a more traditional caution against such a one-sided institutional embrace. See Samuel Francis, "Imperial Conservatives?" *National Review* (4 August, 1989): 37–38; Mickey Edwards, "Of Conservatives and Kings," *Policy Review* 48 (Spring 1989); William F. Buckley, Jr., "Agenda for the Nineties," *National Review* (19 February, 1990): 39–40.

Chapter 6

1. William G. Andrews, "The Presidency, Congress, and Constitutional Theory," in Aaron Wildavsky, ed., *Perspectives on the Presidency* (Boston: Little, Brown, 1975), 24. See also our discussion of liberal/progressive dogma on the presidency in Scott Yenor, Travis Cook, and Raymond Tatalovich, "The Normative Study of the Presidency," in Ryan J. Barilleaux, ed., *Presidential Frontiers: Underexplored Issues in White House Politics* (Westport, Conn.: Praeger, 1998).

2. Andrews, "Presidency, Congress, and Constitutional Theory," 24.

3. Ibid., 26.

4. Ibid., 25.

5. Ibid., 26.

6. Quoted in ibid., 26.

7. Quoted in ibid., 27.

8. Ibid., 30.

9. Ibid., 35.

10. Donald F. Anderson, "The Legacy of William Howard Taft," *Presidential Studies Quarterly* 12 (Winter 1982): 27.

11. Ibid.

12. Ibid.

13. Ibid., 28.

14. Ibid.

15. Ibid.

16. Ibid.

17. William Howard Taft, *Our Chief Magistrate and His Powers* (New York: Columbia University Press, 1916), 5–6.

18. Ibid., 76.

19. Ibid., 94–95.

20. Ibid., 112–13.

21. Anderson, "Legacy of William Howard Taft," 29.

22. Quoted in ibid., 29.

23. Ibid.

24. Theodore Roosevelt, *Theodore Roosevelt: An Autobiography* (New York: Macmillan, 1913), 388–89.

25. Taft, *Our Chief Magistrate*, 139–40.

26. Barbara Hinckley, *The Symbolic Presidency* (New York: Routledge, 1990), 110.

27. Ibid.

28. William Manners, *TR and Will* (New York: Harcourt, Brace, Jovanovich, 1969), 175.

29. Calvin Coolidge, *The Autobiography of Calvin Coolidge* (New York: Cosmopolitan Book Corporation, 1929), 198–99.

30. Ibid.

31. Hinckley, *The Symbolic Presidency*, 110–11.

32. Ibid., 111.

33. Ibid.

34. Edward S. Corwin, *The President: Office and Powers* (New York: New York University Press, 1957), p. 14.

35. Ibid., vii.

36. Richard E. Neustadt, *Presidential Power* (New York: Wiley, 1960).

37. Corwin, *The President: Office and Powers*, 30.

38. Ibid., 84.

39. Ibid., 116.

40. Ibid., 226.

41. Ibid., 294.

42. Ibid., 294–95.

43. Ibid., 297.

44. Ibid., 299.

45. Ibid., 304.

46. Ibid., 310–11.

47. Ibid., 311–12.

48. Garry Wills, *The Kennedy Imprisonment: A Meditation on Power* (New York: Pocket Books, 1981), 209.

49. C. Perry Patterson, *Presidential Government in the United States: The Unwritten Constitution* (Chapel Hill: The University of North Carolina Press, 1947), v.

50. Ibid., vi.

51. Ibid., 14, 38.

52. Ibid., 84, 94–95.

53. Ibid., 132, 133, 142.

54. Ibid., 237.

55. Gordon S. Jones and John A. Marini, eds., *The Imperial Congress: Crisis in the Separation of Powers* (New York: Pharos Books, 1988).

56. L. Gordon Crovitz and Jeremy A. Rabkin, eds., *The Fettered Presidency: Legal Constraints on the Executive Branch* (Washington, D.C.: American Enterprise Institute for Public Policy Research, 1989).

57. Terry Eastland, *Energy in the Executive: The Case for the Strong Presidency* (New York: The Free Press, 1992).

58. Douglas A. Jeffrey, "Executive Authority Under the Separation of Powers," in Jones and Marini, *The Imperial Congress*, 49.

59. Ibid., 252.

60. Crovitz and Rabkin, *The Fettered Presidency*, 11.

61. Irving Kristol, "Commentary and Exchanges on Politics and Public Debate," in Crovitz and Rabkin, *The Fettered Presidency*, 315–16.

62. Gabriel Prosser, "Comes the Revolution," in Gordon S. Jones and John A. Marini, *The Imperial Congress: Crisis in the Separation of Powers* (New York: Pharos Books, 1988), 331.

63. Eastland, *Energy in the Executive*, 71.

64. Ibid., 2–3.

Chapter 7

1. Henry Barrett Learned, *The President's's Cabinet: Studies in the Origin, Formation, and Structure of an American Institution* (New York: Burt Franklin, 1912), 393.

2. Woodrow Wilson, *George Washington* (New York: Schocken Books, 1969, first published 1896), 273.

3. Sidney M. Milkis and Michael Nelson, *The American Presidency: Origins And Development* (Washington, D.C. : Congressional Quarterly Press, 1990), 75.

4. Ibid., 74.

5. Quoted in Eugene P. Trani and David L. Wilson, *The Presidency of Warren G. Harding* (Lawrence: University of Kansas, 1977), 38.

6. Richard M. Pious, *The Presidency* (Needham Heights, Mass.: Allyn & Bacon, 1996), 51–52.

7. Ibid., 52.

8. Ibid.

9. Such independence was not unique to the early Republic. Modern presidents have faced conflict with independent cabinet members as well. Richard Nixon's uneasy relationship with his Secretary of Housing and Urban Development, George Romney, and his Secretary of Interior, Walter Hickle, stemmed in part from their own political independence as former Governors of Michigan and Alaska, respectively.

10. Richard B. Morris, *Encyclopedia of American History* (New York: Harper, 1953), 156.

11. Marquis James, *The Life of Andrew Jackson* (New York: Bobbs-Merrill, 1938), 231.

12. Congress was so outraged that Jackson would transfer the federal funds that the Republican-dominated Senate passed a censure motion. The Senate motion was expunged from the annals of the Senate Journal in 1837 when the Jacksonian Democrats gained control of Congress.

13. Arthur M. Schlesinger, Jr., *The Age of Jackson* (Boston: Little, Brown, 1945), 66.

14. Stephen Horn, *The Cabinet and Congress* (New York: Columbia University Press, 1960), 32.

15. Burton J. Hendrick, *Lincoln's War Cabinet* (Boston: Little, Brown, 1946), 4.

16. Ibid., 4.

17. Morris, *Encyclopedia of American History*, 229.

18. John Sherman, *Recollections of Forty Years in the House, Senate and Cabinet: An Autobiography* (Chicago: Werner, 1895), 447.

19. Margaret Leech, *In the Days of McKinley* (New York: Harper and Brothers, 1959), 99.

20. Theodore Roosevelt, *An Autobiography* (New York: Macmillan, 1913), 380.

21. Lewis L. Gould, *The Presidency of Theodore Roosevelt* (Lawrence: University of Kansas Press, 1991), 154.

22. The Tilman Act of 1907 banned corporate contributions from presidential campaigns, but was easily evaded by corporations funneling funding through their executives to the campaigns.

23. Paole E. Coletta, *The Presidency of William Howard Taft* (Lawrence: University of Kansas Press, 1973), 50.

24. Kendrick A. Clements, *The Presidency of Woodrow Wilson* (Lawrence: University of Kansas Press, 1992), 32.

25. Jan Willem Schulte Nordholt, *Woodrow Wilson: A Life for World Peace* (Berkeley: University of California Press, 1991), 95.

26. Arthur S. Link, *Woodrow Wilson and the Progressive Era* (New York: Harper and Row, 1954), 30.

27. Erwin Hargrove, *Presidential Leadership: Personality and Political Style* (London: Macmillan, 1966), 48.

28. Ibid., 49–50.

29. Ibid.

30. Kenneth S. Davis, *FDR: The New York Years: 1928–1933* (New York: Random House, 1979), 422.

31. Stephen Hess, *Organizing the Presidency* (Washington, D.C.: Brookings Institution, 1988), 31–32.

32. Ibid., 32.

33. Hargrove, *Presidential Leadership*, 71.

34. Ibid., 71–72.

35. Stephen Ambrose, *Eisenhower: Soldier and President* (New York: Simon & Schuster, 1990), 288.

36. Herbert Brownell with John P. Burke, *Advising Ike* (Lawrence: University of Kansas Press, 1993), 134.

37. Travis Jacobs Beal, "The American Assembly," in Shirley Anne Warshaw, ed., *Reexamining the Eisenhower Presidency* (Westport, Conn.: Greenwood Press, 1993), 25.

38. Dwight D. Eisenhower, *Mandate for Change: The White House Years* (New York: Doubleday, 1963), 86.

39. Ambrose, *Eisenhower: Soldier and President*, 291.

40. Dwight D. Eisenhower to General Lucius D. Clay, 18 December 1958, Folder: DDE Dictation, December 1958, Papers of Dwight D. Eisenhower as President of the United States, Ann Whitman file, Dwight D. Eisenhower Diary Series, Box 37, Eisenhower Library.

41. Richard Fenno, *The President's Cabinet* (Cambridge, Mass.: Harvard University Press, 1959), 41.

42. Dwight D. Eisenhower to Henry Luce, 8 August 1960, Folder: Luce Harry (1), Papers of Dwight D. Eisenhower as President of the United States, 1953–1961, Ann Whitman File, Letter Series, Box 5, Eisenhower Library.

43. Arthur M. Schlesinger, Jr., *A Thousand Days: John F. Kennedy in the White House* (Boston: Houghton Mifflin, 1965), 128.

44. Theodore Sorensen, *Kennedy* (New York: Harper and Row, 1965) 283.

45. William S. White, *The Professional: Lyndon B. Johnson* (Boston: Houghton Mifflin, 1964), 39–40.

46. Quoted in Vaughn David Bornet, *The Presidency of Lyndon B. Johnson* (Lawrence: University of Kansas Press, 1983), 27.

47. Ibid., 28.

48. Eric F. Goldman, *The Tragedy of Lyndon Johnson* (New York: Knopf, 1969), 265.

49. Richard M. Nixon, *R.N.: The Memoirs of Richard Nixon* (New York: Grosset and Dunlap, 1978), 338–39.

Chapter 8

1. Carl E. Prince, "The Federalist Party and the Creation of a Court Press," *Journalism Quarterly* 53 (1976): 238.

2. Ibid., 240.

3. William E. Ames, "Federal Patronage and the Washington, D.C. Press," *Journalism Quarterly* 49 (1972), 22.

4. Ibid., 23.

5. Harry Ammon, "Monroe: The Fifth President and the Media," *Media History Digest* 3 (1983): 22.

6. Culver H. Smith, *The Press, Politics, and Patronage* (Athens: University of Georgia Press, 1977), 16.

7. Donald Stewart, *The Opposition Press of the Federalist Period* (Albany: State University of New York Press, 1969), 609; Harry M. Ward, "George Washington and the Media," *Media History Digest* 7 (1987): 26.

8. William David Sloan, "The Early Party Press: The Newspaper Role in American Politics, 1788–1812," *Journalism History* 9 (1982): 18–19.

9. Kent R. Middleton, "The Partisan Press and the Rejection of a Chief Justice," *Journalism Quarterly* 53 (1976): 106.

10. Ibid., 106.

11. Walt Brown, *John Adams and the American Press: Politics and Journalism at the Birth of the Republic* (Jefferson City, N.C.: McFarland, 1995), 51.

12. Ammon, "Monroe and the Media," 22.

13. Ward, "Washington and the Media," 2–5.

14. *The Boston Herald Freedom* (31 July 1789), quoted in Stewart, *Opposition Press*, 488.

15. Ward, "Washington and the Media," 27.

16. Ibid., 25.

17. Stewart, *Opposition Press*, 535.

18. Peter Shaw, "The Second President and the Press," *Media History Digest* 1 (1981): 15.

19. Ibid., 15.

20. Brown, *Adams and the American Press*, 25, 90.

21. Noble E. Cunningham, Jr., *The Jeffersonian Republicans in Power: Party Operations, 1801–1809* (Chapel Hill: University of North Carolina Press, 1963), 238–48.

22. Shaw, "Second President and the Press," 12.

23. Stewart, *Opposition Press*, 462, 439, 429.

24. Ibid., 450.

25. Benjamin Ellis Martin, "Transition Period of the American Press—Leading Editors in This Century," *Magazine of American History* 17 (April 1887): 273.

26. Charles I. Glicksberg, "William Cullen Bryant and the American Press," *Journalism Quarterly* 16 (1939), 53.

27. Stewart, *Opposition Press*, 12.

28. *Lexington Kentucky Gazette*, (12 June 1804), quoted in Cunningham, 194.

29. Smith, *The Press, Politics, and Patronage*, 10.

30. Cunningham, *Jeffersonian Republications in Power*, 253–57.

31. Jerry W. Knudson, "Political Journalism in the Age of Jefferson," *Journalism History* 1 (1974): 21.

32. Cunningham, *Jeffersonian Republicans in Power*, 247, 271.

33. Ibid., 267.

34. Knudson, "Political Journalism in the Age of Jefferson," 20.

35. Charles O. Lerche, Jr., "Jefferson and the Election of 1800: A Case Study in the Political Smear," *William and Mary Quarterly* 3 (1948): 470–82.

36. Levy, 23, 26.

37. Smith, *The Press, Politics, and Patronage*, 24.

38. Ammon, "Monroe and the Media," 24, 27.

39. William E. Ames and Dean S. Olson, "Washington's Political Press and the Election of 1824," *Journalism Quarterly* 40 (1963).

40. Lynn H. Parsons, "John Quincy Adams: Sixth President and the Press," *Media History Digest* 4 (1984): 26.

41. Ames and Olson, "Washington's Political Press," 346.

42. William E. Ames, "A History of the National *Intelligencer*." (Ph.D. dissertation, University of Minnesota, 1962), 187.

43. Parsons, "John Quincy Adams," 26–27.

44. Parsons, "Adams and the Press," 26–27.

45. Forrest McDonald, *The American Presidency: An Intellectual History* (Lawrence: University Press of Kansas, 1994), 430.

46. Ibid., 430; Robert Neal Eliot, Jr., *The Raleigh Register, 1799–1863* (Chapel Hill: University of North Carolina Press, 1955), 50.

47. Smith, *The Press, Politics, and Patronage*, 100, 114.

48. Richard B. Kielbowicz, "Party Cohesiveness: Jacksonian Newspapers, 1832," *Journalism Quarterly* 60 (1983): 518.

49. Herbert Ershkowitz, "Millard Fillmore: Crises and Compromise," *Media History Digest* (Spring–Summer 1990): 10, 12.

50. Ibid., 12, 14.

51. Gerald J. Baldasty, "The Press and Politics in the Age of Jackson," *Journalism Monographs* (1984).

52. John Tebbel, "Van Buren: The 'Little Magician' and the Press," *Media History Digest* 6 (1986): 41–42.

53. Ibid., 43.

54. Kenneth Lee John Hawkins, "Forgettable Chester Arthur: A Politician Who Changed," *Media History Digest* (Spring–Summer 1991): 4; Smith, *The Press, Politics, and Patronage*, 163.

55. Judith Serrin, "President Tyler and the Press," *Media History Digest* (Fall–Winter 1988): 41.

56. Raleigh *Register*, 26 August 1842, quoted in Elliot, *The Raleigh Register, 1799–1863*, 77.

57. Serrin, *Tyler and the Press*, 44–45.

58. Michael J. Birkner, "Handsome Franklin Pierce: At Sea in Eye of A Storm," *Media History Digest* (Fall–Winter 1990): 29.

59. Raleigh *Register*, (9 March 1853), quoted in Elliot, *The Raleigh Register*, 1799–1863, 97.

60. Birkner, "Handsome Franklin Pierce," 30.

61. Ames, "Federal Patronage and the Press," 22; Smith, *The Press, Politics, and Patronage*, 206.

62. James Feister, " 'Old Buck' Buchanan Steers Down Middle Before War," *Media History Digest* (Spring–Summer 1991): 54.

63. Jim Alee Hart, *A History of the St. Louis Globe-Democrat* (Columbia, Missouri: University of Missouri Press, 1961), 69.

64. Ibid., 77, 80.

65. Robert S. Harper, *Lincoln and the Press* (New York: McGraw-Hill, 1951), 184.

66. Robin Fisher Larsen, "Cooper Union Speech: New York Media Launch a Candidate," *Media History Digest* (Fall–Winter 1986): 3.

67. Alan Metcalf, "How the Press Made Fun of Ol' Abe," *Media History Digest* (Fall–Winter 1986): 23.

68. Ibid., 23.

69. Herbert Mitgang, "From New Salem to the White House: Friend of the Press," *Media History Digest* Fall-Winter, 1986; Mitgang, 10; *Richmond Examiner* (23 April 1861), quoted in Harper, *Lincoln and the Press*, 92; McDonald, *The American Presidency*, 117.

70. *New York Day Book*, (6 April 1881), quoted in Harper, *Lincoln and the Press*, 121.

71. Milwaukee *News* (24 December 1874), quoted in Summers, p. 55; Harper, *Lincoln and the Press*, 116–117.

72. Joseph McKerns, "Short-term James Garfield Favored Old Style Ways," *Media History Digest* (Fall-Winter, 1993): 27–31, 64.

73. Ibid.

74. Richard L. Rubin, *Press, Party, and Presidency* (New York: Norton, 1981), 56.

75. William E. Matsen, "How the Media Drummed Up War Fever in World War I," *Media History Digest* (Fall–Winter 1992): 57.

76. Rubin, *Press, Party, and Presidency*, 3.

77. McDonald, *The American Presidency*, 435.

78. Mark J. Rozell, "The Press and the Presidency," in James P. Pfiffner and Roger Davidson, *Understanding the Presidency* (New York: Longman, 1997), 89–90.

79. Wilson, *Constitutional Government*, in Arthur Link, ed. *The Papers of Woodrow Wilson*, vol. 18 (Princeton: Princeton University Press, 1974).

80. James E. Pollard, *Presidents and the Press* (New York: MacMillan, 1947), 774.

81. Quoted in David S. Broder, *Behind the Front Page: A Candid Look at How the News is Made* (New York: Simon and Schuster, 1987), 167.

82. Author interviews with Gerald R. Ford (13 December 1989) and Jerald F. ter-Horst (27 June 1990).

83. Quoted in Mark Hertsgaard, *On Bended Knee: The Press and the Reagan Presidency* (New York: Farrar Straus Giroux, 1988), 108.

84. Author interview with Marlin Fitzwater, 9 July 1994.

85. Howard Kurtz, "Coverage Quickly Turns Sour as Media Highlight Troubles," *Washington Post*, (31 January 1993): A1.

86. Rozell, "The Press and the Presidency," 96.

87. Both issues were 7 June 1993.

88. Joe Klein, "What's Wrong?" *Newsweek*, (7 June 1993): 19.

89. Author interview with Ron Nessen, 5 July 1990.

90. Murray Edelman, *The Symbolic Uses of Politics* (Urbana: University of Illinois Press, 1967), 5.

91. Fitzwater interview.

92. Ibid.

Chapter 9

1. Kathleen Hall Jamieson, *Eloquence in an Electronic Age: The Transformation of Political Speechmaking* (New York: Oxford University Press, 1988), 11.

2. John Quincy Adams, in J. Jeffrey Auer and Jerald L. Banninga, eds., *Lectures on Rhetoric and Orators*, 2 vols. (New York: Russell & Russell, 1962).

3. Tulis cites this kind of historical incongruity in the works of twentieth-century scholars who have measured nineteenth-century presidential oratory by twentieth-century criteria. See Jeffrey K. Tulis, *The Rhetorical Presidency* (Princeton: Princeton University Press, 1987), 63, 72.

4. This is a significant aspect of Tulis's approach; generic comparisons comprise the basis of Karlyn Kohrs Campbell and Kathleen Hall Jamieson, *Deeds Done in Words: Presidential Rhetoric and the Genres of Governance* (Chicago: University of Chicago Press, 1990).

5. Marcus Tullius Cicero, *De Inventione*, H. M. Hubbell, trans. (Cambridge: Harvard University Press, 1977), 1.15.20–1.53.100.

6. Aristotle, *The "Art" of Rhetoric*, J. H. Freese, trans. (Cambridge: Harvard University Press, 1926), 3.16.8.

7. Marcus Tullius Cicero, *Orator*, H. M. Hubbell, trans. (Cambridge: Harvard University Press, 1962), 26:123–4.

8. Marcus Tullius Cicero, *De Oratore*, 2 vols., H. Rackham, trans. (Cambridge: Harvard University Press, 1968), 1:2.19.80.

9. Adam Smith, Hugh Blair, and George Campbell are chief among these. See Adam Smith in *Lectures on Rhetoric and Belles Lettres*, J. C. Bryce, ed. (Oxford: Oxford University Press, 1985); Hugh Blair in *Lectures on Rhetoric and Belles Lettres*, 2 vols., Harold F. Harding, ed. (Carbondale: Southern Illinois University Press, 1965); George Campbell, in Lloyd F. Bitzer, ed., *The Philosophy of Rhetoric* (Carbondale: Southern Illinois University Press, 1988).

10. See Stephen J. McKenna, "Fitting Words: Propriety in Adam Smith's Rhetoric and Ethics," in Lynee Lewis Gaillet, ed., *Scottish Rhetoric and its Influences* (Mahwah, NJ: Hermagoras Press, 1998), 57–65.

11. For a history of the Boyleston chair and Adams's contribution to it, see Ronald Reid, "The Boyleston Professorship of Rhetoric and Oratory, 1806–1904: A Case Study of Changing Concepts of Rhetoric and Pedagogy," in Edward P. J. Corbett, James L. Golden, and Goodwin F. Berquist, eds., *Essays on the Rhetoric of the Western World* (Dubuque, Iowa: Kendall Hunt, 1990), 261–82.

12. Aristotle, *"Art" of Rhetoric*, 3.16.11.

13. Auer and Banninga, *Lectures on Rhetoric and Oratory.* 1: 412-13.

14. Ibid.

15. Ibid., 1:417.

16. Ibid., 1:423.

17. In Adams's own concluding lecture, for example, he characterizes the moment of graduating from the study to the practice of rhetoric as an "interesting" one. Ibid., 2:394.

18. Ibid., 1:428.

19. Edmund Burke, in J. G. A. Pocock, ed., *Reflections on the Revolution in France* (Indianapolis: Hackett, 1987), 76.

20. See Robert M. Schmitz, *Hugh Blair* (New York: Kings' Crown Press, 1948). Schmitz counts over one hundred full and abridged editions of Blair's lectures in the century following its first publication; thirty-seven of the full editions appeared in America.

21. W.B Allen, ed., *George Washington: A Collection* (Indianapolis: Liberty Classics, 1988), 474–75.

22. This is the emphasis of Stephen E. Lucas and Susan Zaeske, "George Washington," in Halford Ryan, ed., *U.S. Presidents as Orators: A Bio-Critical Sourcebook* (Westport, Conn.: Greenwood, 1995), 9.

23. Allen, *Washington*, 492.

24. See, for example, Adam Smith's discussion of "unfold" in *Lectures*, 4.

25. "Knowledge is, in every country, the surest basis of public happiness," he would say in his third annual message. Allen, *Washington*, 468.

26. See Michael Warner, *The Letters of the Republic: Publication and the Public Sphere in Eighteenth-Century America* (Cambridge: Harvard University Press, 1990), 46: "Antiparty rhetoric appears to . . . oppose the existence of the debate itself. In actuality, however, it sustains the debate by providing the categories that would make an ongoing public debate thinkable. The language of resistance to controversy articulates a norm for controversy. It silently transforms the ideal of a social order free from conflictual debate into an ideal of debate free from social conflict."

27. John Adams, "Inaugural Address," in James D. Richardson, ed., *A Compilation of the Messages and Papers of the Presidents*, 10 vols. (Washington, D.C.: U.S. Congress, 1899) 1:218.

28. James M. Farrell, "John Adams," in Ryan, *Presidents as Orators*, 24.

29. Andrew A. Lipscomb, ed., *The Writings of Thomas Jefferson*, 20 vols., (Washington, D.C.: The Thomas Jefferson Memorial Association, 1903), 3:312.

30. Ibid., 369.

31. James Madison, "To the Senate and House of Representatives of the United States, 1 June, 1812," in Richardson, *Messages and Papers of the Presidents*, 1:490.

32. Ibid., 509.

33. Martin Van Buren, "Inaugural Address," in John Gabriel Hunt, ed., *The Inaugural Addresses of the Presidents* (New York: Gramercy, 1995), 100.

34. See Garry Wills, *Lincoln at Gettysburg: The Words that Remade America* (New York: Simon and Schuster, 1992), especially chapters 4, "Revolution in Thought," and 5, "Revolution in Style."

35. Marion Mills Miller, ed., *Life and Works of Abraham Lincoln*, 10 vols., (New York: Current Literature Publishing Co., 1907), 6:138.

36. Theodore Roosevelt, in Andrew Carnegie, ed., *The Roosevelt Policy*, 2 vols. (New York: Current Literature Publishing Co., 1908).

37. Theodore Roosevelt, *The Works of Theodore Roosevelt: The National Edition*, 22 vols. (New York: Scribner's, 1926), 15:268. Roosevelt often made this point, for example, in a 1903 speech at a banquet in Milwaukee: ". . . we are confronted with problems which in their present shape were unknown to our forefathers" (Carnegie, *Roosevelt Policy*, 110); and in an address in Minneapolis the same year: "We are now in a condition of prosperity unparalleled not merely in our own history but in the history of any other nation" (Ibid, 122).

38. Roosevelt, *Works*, 15:269.

39. Benjamin Harrison, "Inaugural Address," in *Inaugural Addresses of the Presidents*, Hunt, 252.

40. Ibid., 253–54.

41. Roosevelt, *Roosevelt Policy*, 62. See other examples of this dissociative device at ibid., 45, 76.

42. Ibid., 233. This was one of Roosevelt's most frequent appeals. See, for example, his "Labor Day address," of 1903, 144–58.

43. Ibid., 240.

44. Ibid., 150.

45. Ibid., 32.

46. Arthur S. Link, ed., *The Papers of Woodrow Wilson*, 68 vols. (Princeton: Princeton University Press) 27:150.

47. Ibid., 148.

48. George W. S. Trow, *Within the Context of No Context* (Boston: Little, Brown, 1981).

49. Calvin Coolidge, "Inaugural Address," in Hunt, *Inaugural Addresses of the Presidents*, 350–51.

50. Campbell and Jamieson, *Deeds Done in Words*, 105.

51. Link, *Wilson*, 41:519.

52. Ibid., 41:523.

53. "Radio and TV Address to the American People on the Situation in Korea, 19 July, 1950," in *The Public Papers of the Presidents: Harry S. Truman*, 8 vols. (Washington, D.C.: Government Printing Office, 1961–66), 6:537.

54. "Inaugural Address," in Bernard Boutin, ed., *The Public Papers of the President of the United States: John F. Kennedy*, 3 vols. (Washington, D.C.: U.S. Government Printing Office, 1962–64) 1:1.

55. Ibid., 1:2–3.

56. "Inaugural Address, January 20, 1989," in *The Public Papers of the Presidents: George Bush* (Washington D.C.: Government Printing Office, 1991–3), 1:1.

57. Ibid., 1:3.

58. "Address before a Joint Session of Congress of the State of the Union, 31 January, 1990," in *Bush*, 1: 129–30.

59. "Inaugural Address, January 20, 1993," *The Public Papers of the Presidents: William J. Clinton*, 8 vols. to date (Washington D.C.: Government Printing Office 1993–98 to date), 1:1.

60. "Address before a Joint Session of Congress of the State of the Union, 23 January, 1996," in *Clinton*, 7: 79.

61. "Remarks at the 'We the People' Bicentennial Celebration in Philadelphia, Pennsylvania, Sept. 17, 1987," in *The Public Papers of the Presidents: Ronald Reagan*, 15 vols. (Washington D.C.: Government Printing Office, 1982–91), 13:1040.

62. "Remarks at a White House Ceremony Commemorating the Twenty-Fifth Anniversary of the Civil Rights Act, 30 June 1989," in *Bush*, 1:834–36.

63. "Remarks at an Independence Day Celebration in Youngstown, Ohio, 4 July 1996," in *Clinton*, 8:1074.

64. For a troubling assessment of the state of historical knowledge in the American public, see Christopher Hitchens: "Goodbye to All That: Why Americans are not Taught History," *Harper's Magazine* (November 1998): 37–47.

65. Richard Weaver, *The Ethics of Rhetoric* (South Bend, Ind.: Regnery/Gateway, 1953), 164.

66. Ibid., 169.

67. Ibid., 172.

68. Ibid., 175.

69. For a discussion of political distance and the presidency, see Bruce E. Gronbeck, "The Presidency in the Age of Secondary Orality," in Martin J. Medhurst, ed., *Beyond the Rhetorical Presidency* (College Station: Texas A & M University Press, 1996), 39–40.

Chapter 10

1. "Mr Polk's Acceptance of the Nomination," *Niles's National Register* (6 July, 1844), 294. Also see *New York Times* (18 June, 1876), 1.

2. Richard J. Ellis and Stephen Kirk, "Presidential Mandates in the Nineteenth Century: Conceptual Change and Institutional Development," *Studies in American Political Development* 9 (Spring 1995): 117–86.

3. Jackson to David Burford, 28 July, 1831, as quoted in Gil Troy, *See How They Ran: The Changing Role of the Presidential Candidate* (New York: Free Press, 1991), 16.

4. Troy, *See How They Run*, 69.

5. Jeffrey K. Tulis, *The Rhetorical Presidency* (Princeton: Princeton University Press, 1987), 183–84.

6. Ibid., 182–83.

7. William Graham Sumner, "Presidential Elections and Civil-Service Reform," in Robert C. Bannister, ed., *On Liberty, Society, and Politics: The Essential Essays of William Graham Sumner* (Indianapolis: Liberty Fund, 1992), 95.

8. Troy, *See How They Ran*, 62; Ellis and Kirk, "Presidential Mandates," 128; Richard P. McCormick, *The Presidential Game: The Origins of American Presidential Politics* (New York: Oxford University Press, 1982), 145.

9. Troy, *See How They Ran*, 16.

10. Harrison's response can be found in William Ogden Niles, ed., *The Tippecanoe Textbook* (Baltimore: Cushing, 1840), 77–82.

11. Troy, *See How They Ran*, 23–24.

12. Ibid., 25–26.

13. Ibid., 51, 53, 56.

14. Ibid., 62, 65, 70, 75.

15. Ibid., 75–76.

16. Michael McGerr, *The Decline of Popular Politics: The American North, 1865–1928* (New York: Oxford University Press, 1986), 73; Troy, *See How They Ran*, 79; Shelly Strong, "The Rhetorical Presidency: Rethinking Democrats in the Late Nineteenth Century," typescript, December 1995, Willamette University.

17. Richard J. Ellis, "Accepting the Nomination: From Martin Van Buren to Franklin Delano Roosevelt," in Richard J. Ellis, ed., *Speaking to the People: The Rhetorical Presidency in Historical Perspective* (Amherst: University of Massachusetts Press, 1998), 115. The Tilden and Hayes acceptance letters can be found in the *New York Times*, (5 August 1876), 1, and (10 July 1876), 1, respectively.

18. On Tilden's important role in the rise of "educational politics," see McGerr, *Decline of Popular Politics*, 72–74.

19. Ari Hoogenboom, *The Presidency of Rutherford B. Hayes* (Lawrence: University Press of Kansas, 1988), 17–18; Troy, *See How They Ran*, 78–81.

20. Troy, *See How They Ran*, 89–90; Leonard Dinnerstein, "Election of 1880," in Arthur M. Schlesinger, Jr., *History of American Presidential Elections, 1789–1968*, (New York: Chelsea House, 1985), 1506–07.

21. Troy, *See How They Ran*, 92–93; Mark D. Hirsch, "Election of 1884," in Schlesinger, *History of American Presidential Elections*, 1573.

22. Troy, *See How They Ran*, 95–96; Robert F. Wesser, "Election of 1888," in Schlesinger, *History of American Presidential Elections*, 1638–39.

23. Troy, *See How They Ran*, 97; Wesser, "Election of 1888," 1640. President Harrison, having alienated many in the Republican Party, had planned initially to take the stump. His plan was to avoid talking politics and instead to capitalize on the "non-partisan attention" a president could attract. His wife's illness (she died two weeks before election day), however, led him to cancel the proposed tour (Troy, *See How They Ran*, 97–98).

24. *New York Times* (30 July 1884), 1; (21 July 1892), 1. Also see Ellis, "Accepting the Nomination," 118–19.

25. *New York Times* (21 July 1892), 2; Troy, *See How They Ran*, 99.

26. H. Wayne Morgan, "Election of 1892," in Schlesinger, *History of American Presidential Elections*, 1711; George Harmon Knoles, *The Presidential Campaign and Election of 1892* (Stanford: Stanford University Press, 1942), 175–76, 154–60; Troy, *See How They Ran*, 100. The illness of President Harrison's wife gave Cleveland further cause to avoid stumping.

27. *New York Times* (27 October 1892), 1–2; (2 November 1892), 1–2; (5 November 1892), 1–2; also see (5 October 1892), 1–2; (26 October 1892), 1. Also see Knoles, *Presidential Campaign and Election of 1892*, 207–08.

28. Troy, *See How They Ran*, 104–05.

29. Ibid., 102.

30. Ibid., 93, 104; Gilbert C. Fite, "Election of 1896," in Schlesinger, *History of American Presidential Elections*, 1816.

31. Troy, *See How They Ran*, 109.

32. Gerald Gamm and Renee M. Smith, "Presidents, Parties, and the Public: Evolving Patterns of Interaction, 1877–1929," in Ellis, *Speaking to the People*, 87–111.

33. McGerr, *Decline of Popular Politics*, 171–72; Troy, *See How They Ran*, 114.

34. Troy, *See How They Ran*, 116–17; "Leaders Urge Parker to Take the Stump," *New York Times*, (10 September 1904), 1.

35. Troy, *See How They Ran*, 121; Paolo E. Coletta, "Election of 1908," in Schlesinger, *History of American Presidential Elections*, 2086.

36. Troy, *See How They Ran*, 127–28; George E. Mowry, "Election of 1912," in Schlesinger, *History of American Presidential Elections*, 2156.

37. Troy, *See How They Ran*, 128–29.

38. Arthur Link et al., *The Papers of Woodrow Wilson* (Princeton: Princeton University Press, 1982), 38:475, 8, 287; for his campaign speeches at Shadow Lawn see 38:212–19, 301–12, 362–68, 430–38, 500–09, 549–59, 608–15. "Big Crowds Cheer Wilson on His Trip," *New York Times* (5 October 1916), 1; Troy, *See How They Ran*, 138–41, 132.

39. Troy, *See How They Ran*, 143–45, 150.

40. *New York Times* (17 September 1924), 2; (15 August 1924), 1; (2 September 1924), 1; (7 September 1924), 1; (22 September 1924), 1; (25 September 1924), 1; (26 September 1924), 1; (14 October 1924), 1.

41. *New York Times* (12 September 1924), 1; (13 September 1924), 3. Also see (3 September 1924), 1; (14 September 1924), 1; (17 September 1924), 2; and (8 October 1924), 1.

42. Troy, *See How They Ran*, 156, 161, 165.

43. Ibid., 168–69.

44. See Richard J. Ellis, *Presidential Lightning Rods: The Politics of Blame Avoidance* (Lawrence: University Press of Kansas, 1994), esp. chapter 4.

Chapter 11

1. Jeffrey K. Tulis, "Revising the Rhetorical Presidency," in Martin Medhurst, ed., *Beyond the Rhetorical Presidency* (College Station: Texas A&M University Press, 1996), 3–4. The term was initiated in James W. Ceaser, Glen E. Thurow, Jeffrey Tulis, and Joseph M. Bessette, "The Rise of the Rhetorical Presidency," *Presidential Studies Quarterly* 2 (1981): 158.

2. Jeffrey K. Tulis, *The Rhetorical Presidency* (Princeton: Princeton University Press, 1987), 17.

3. Martin J. Medhurst, "A Tale of Two Constructs: The Rhetorical Presidency Versus Presidential Rhetoric," in Medhurst, *Beyond the Rhetorical Presidency*, xi–xx.

4. Tulis, *Rhetorical Presidency*, 56.

5. For example, Alexander Hamilton, James Madison, and John Jay, in Clinton Rossiter, ed., *The Federalist Papers* (New York: Mentor, 1961), No. 10, 81–84; No. 49, 314–17.

6. See also Karlyn Kohrs Campbell and Kathleen Hall Jamieson, *Deeds Done in Words: Presidential Rhetoric and the Genres of Governance* (Chicago: University of Chicago Press, 1990), 14–36.

7. See also James W. Ceaser, *Presidential Selection: Theory and Development* (Princeton: Princeton University Press, 1979), 52–61; Harvey C. Mansfield, Jr., *America's Constitutional Soul* (Baltimore: Johns Hopkins University Press, 1991), 137–62.

8. Tulis, *Rhetorical Presidency*, 87–93; Eric L. McKitrick, *Andrew Johnson and Reconstruction* (Chicago: University of Chicago Press, 1960), 421–47.

9. See especially Tulis, *Rhetorical Presidency*, 118–32; Ceaser, *Presidential Selection*, 175–97; John A. Rohr, *To Run a Constitution: The Legitimacy of the Administrative State* (Lawrence: University Press of Kansas, 1986), 55–75; Robert Eden, "The Rhetorical Presidency and the Eclipse of Executive Power: Woodrow Wilson's *Constitutional Government in the United States*," Polity 18 (Spring 1996): 357.

10. Tulis, *Rhetorical Presidency*, 138, 140. Meanwhile, presidential communications shifted away from developed arguments and toward mere statements of position. Ibid., 143.

11. For example, Samuel Kernell, *Going Public: New Strategies of Presidential Leadership* (Washington, D.C.: CQ Press, 1986).

12. See also Sidney Blumenthal, *The Permanent Campaign* (New York: Simon and Schuster, 1980); Anthony King, *Running Scared: Why America's Politicians Campaign Too Much and Govern Too Little* (New York: Martin Kessler, 1997).

13. For example, George C. Edwards III, "Presidential Rhetoric: What Difference Does It Make?," in Medhurst, *Beyond the Rhetorical Presidency.*

14. For defining statements of the modern presidency, see Fred I. Greenstein, "Change and Continuity in the Modern Presidency," in Anthony King, ed., *The New American Political System* (Washington, D.C.: American Enterprise Institute, 1978); Richard E. Neustadt, *Presidential Power and the Modern Presidents: The Politics of Leadership from Roosevelt to Reagan* (New York: Free Press, 1990); Clinton Rossiter, *The American Presidency* (New York: Harcourt, Brace, and World, 1960).

15. See also James W. Ceaser, "The Rhetorical Presidency Revisited," in Marc Landy, ed., *Modern Presidents and the Presidency* (Lexington, Mass: Lexington Books, 1983).

16. For example, Sidney M. Milkis, *The President and the Parties: The Transformation of the American Party System Since the New Deal* (New York: Oxford University Press, 1993), 23–146; Theodore Lowi, *The Personal President: Power Invested Promise Unfulfilled* (Ithaca: Cornell University), 44–96.

17. For example, Ceaser, *Presidential Selection,* 170–259.

18. See also, Craig Allen Smith, "'Rough Stretches and Honest Disagreements': Is Bill Clinton Redefining the Rhetorical Presidency?" in Robert E. Denton, Jr. and Rachel L. Holloway, eds., *The Clinton Presidency: Images, Issues and Communication Strategies* (Westport, Conn: Praeger, 1996).

19. Clinton's historic position would make such a grand vision untenable. The "New Democrat" survives by being a pragmatist in a post-Reagan era. See especially Stephen Skowronek, *The Politics Presidents Make: Leadership from John Adams to George Bush* (Cambridge: Harvard University Press, 1993).

20. Clinton's image as unprincipled and duplicitous, both politically and personally, is recurrent among presidents in his historic position. Stephen Skowronek, "President Clinton and the Risks of 'Third-Way' Politics," *Extensions* (Spring 1996): 10.

21. For a more general, and somewhat more optimistic, assessment, see Leroy N. Rieselbach, "One Vote at a Time: Building Presidential Coalitions in Congress," in James A. Thurber, ed., *Rivals for Power: Presidential-Congressional Relations* (Washington, D.C.: CQ Press, 1996).

22. For example, Charles O. Jones, "Campaigning to Govern: The Clinton Style," in Colin Campbell and Bert Rockman, eds., *The Clinton Presidency: First Appraisals* (Chatham, NJ: Chatham House, 1996).

23. For example, Tulis, *Rhetorical Presidency,* 161–204; Lowi, *The Personal President,* 134–75.

24. Tulis, "Revising the Rhetorical Presidency," 7–10; Jeffrey K. Tulis, "The Two Constitutional Presidencies," in Michael Nelson, ed., *The Presidency in the Political System,* 4th ed. (Washington, D.C.: CQ Press, 1995), 117–18.

25. Martin P. Wattenberg, *The Rise of Candidate-Centered Politics* (Cambridge: Harvard University Press, 1991).

26. Elizabeth Drew, *On the Edge: The Clinton Presidency* (New York: Simon and Schuster, 1994), 189–197; Rachel L. Holloway, "The Clintons and the Health Care Crisis: Opportunity Lost, Promise Unfulfilled," in Denton and Holloway, *The Clinton Presidency,* 163–68.

27. "Address to the Joint Session of Congress on Health Care Reform, 22 September, 1993," in *Public Papers of the Presidents of the United States: William J. Clinton, 1993* (Washington, D.C.: U.S. Government Printing Office, 1994), 1556.

28. "Address Before a Joint Session of Congress on the State of the Union, January 25, 1994," in *Public Papers of the Presidents of the United States: William J. Clinton, 1994*, 126.

29. Quoted in Holloway, "Clintons and the Health Care Crisis," 173.

30. Ibid., 176–82; Drew, *On the Edge*, 303–11, 434–47. See also Theda Skocpol, *Boomerang: Clinton's Health Security Effort and the Turn Against Government in U.S. Politics* (New York: Norton, 1996), 107–72.

31. See especially, Tulis, *Rhetorical Presidency*, 27–33; Ceaser, *Presidential Selection*, 318–27.

32. See also Michael Lienesch, *New Order of the Ages: Time, the Constitution, and the Making of Modern American Political Thought* (Princeton: Princeton University Press, 1988), 159–83.

33. Clinton's investiture of moral significance to his 1996 presidential campaign in defense of his campaign's fundraising practices is consistent with this Wilsonian view of elections.

34. "The President's News Conference, April 18, 1995," *Weekly Compilation of Presidential Documents* 31 (24 April, 1995), 657.

35. Robert Pear, "Familiar Ring to the GOP Medicare Plan? It's What Clinton Talked About," *New York Times* (26 September 1995), A20; Christopher Connell, "GOP Medicare Increase Put at $4 More than Clinton Plan," *Boston Globe*, (5 October 1995) 11; Elizabeth Drew, *Showdown: The Struggle Between the Gingrich Congress and the Clinton White House* (New York: Simon and Schuster, 1996), 316–17.

36. William Booth, "Clinton Stumps Fla. For Himself, Medicare Reform," *Washington Post* (20 September 1995), A4; Todd Purdum, "Desperately in Need of Winning Streak, Clinton Finds One," *New York Times*, (7 May 1995), 1.

37. For example, David S. Broder, "Scare Politics of Medicare," *Washington Post*, (26 July 1995), A23; "Medagogues," *Washington Post*, (15 September 1995), A24; "Scaring the Elderly," *Wall Street Journal* (14 November 1995), A14.

38. "Washington Wire: The Wall Street Journal/NBC News Poll: Age Matters," *Wall Street Journal* (3 November, 1995), A1.

39. For example, Jackie Calmes, "Angry GOP Isn't in the Mood to Talk Medicare Deal," *Wall Street Journal*, (11 November 1996), A18; "The Medicare Argument," *New York Times*, (4 July 1996), A14; Gerald F. Seib, "Medicare Scare: It's a Fun Game, But Risky Too," *Wall Street Journal*, (17 July 1996), A15; Steven Pearlstein and Clay Chandler, "Medicare: After the Rhetoric, A Reality Check," *Washington Post*, (3 November 1996), p. H1.

40. Consistent with recent practice, Clinton has fully integrated political and media advisors into his administration. The president is not the only politician to be guided by the polls, of course. The alterations in governing norms highlighted by the rhetorical presidency literature are pervasive throughout the American political system. The restructuring of the presidency, however, is more extensive, and perhaps more damaging, than the evolution of the more popular branch of the federal government.

41. See generally, Michael Rogin, *Ronald Reagan, The Movie, and Other Episodes in Political Demonology* (Berkeley: University of California Press, 1987), 272–300.

42. Denton and Holloway, *The Clinton Presidency*, 17; Smith, "Rough Sketches and Honest Disagreements," 237.

43. Forrest McDonald, "Presidential Character: The Case of George Washington," in this volume.

44. Drew, *Showdown*, 236–37, 54, 95.

45. Clinton did briefly introduce a potentially more significant device that could address the concerns surrounding the modern rhetorical presidency in the form of the "policy conference." Although more demonstrative than deliberative, the conferences did at least reintroduce reasoned discussion into presidential public discourse.

46. Denton and Holloway, *The Clinton Presidency*, 23–37.

Chapter 12

1. Ann Riley Dowd, "How Bush Manages the Presidency," *Fortune* (27 August, 1990), 68.

2. Ibid., 68–69.

3. Charles F. Allen and Jonathan Portis, *The Comeback Kid: The Life and Career of Bill Clinton* (New York: Birch Lane Press, 1992), 168.

4. Stanley A. Renshon, *High Hopes: The Clinton Presidency and the Politics of Ambition* (New York: New York University Press, 1996), 129.

5. Drew quoted in Renshon, *High Hopes,*129.

6. Renshon, *High Hopes*, 128–29.

7. Fred Greenstein, "The Presidential Leadership Style of Bill Clinton: An Early Appraisal," *Political Science Quarterly* 108 (1993–94): 595.

8. James Fallows, "The Passionless Presidency: The Trouble With Jimmy Carter's Administration," *Atlantic Monthly* (May 1979): 42.

9. Stanley A. Renshon, *High Hopes: The Clinton Presidency and the Politics of Ambition* (New York: Routledge, 1998), ix, 80.

10. Erwin Hargrove, *Jimmy Carter as President:Leadership and the Politics of the Public Good* (Baton Rouge: Louisiana State University Press, 1988), 179.

11. Ibid., 36.

12. Renshon, *High Hopes*, 1998 ed., xii.

13. Ibid., 84.

14. Fallows, "The Passionless Presidency," 42.

15. Michael Duffy, "The State of Bill Clinton," *Time* (7 February 1994), 24.

16. Ibid.

17. Quoted in David Maraniss, *First in His Class* (New York: Simon and Schuster, 1995), 360.

18. Ibid., 397.

19. Ibid., 27.

20. Renshon, *High Hopes*, 268.

21. Quoted in Edith Efron, "Can the President Think?" *Reason* (November 1994): 26.

22. Drew, quoted in Renshon, *High Hopes*, 267.

23. Renshon, *High Hopes*.

24. John F. Harris, "After Season of Doubt, Clinton Says He's Charging Up for '96 campaign," *Washington Post* (24 September 1995), A9.

25. Ibid.

26. Paul Bedard, "Dr. Clinton, National Therapist," *Washington Times* (24 September 1995), A1, A6.

27. David Shribman, "With End in Sight, Clinton Works on Modest Legacy," reprinted in *Baltimore Sun* (9 July 1998), 15A.

28. Renee M. Smith, "The Public Presidency Hits the Wall: Clinton's Presidential Initiative on Race," *Presidential Studies Quarterly*, 28, (Fall 1998).

29. Ibid., 784.

30. Ibid., 783.

31. President William Jefferson Clinton, "Remarks to the Graduating Class of the Massachusetts Institute of Technology," 9 June, 1998.

32. Jeffrey K. Tulis, *The Rhetorical Presidency* (Princeton: Princeton University Press, 1987), 118.

33. Ibid., 135.

34. Ibid., 136.

35. Ibid.

36. Ibid.

37. Duffy, "The State of Bill Clinton," 24.

38. Ibid.

39. Carl M. Cannon, "Clinton's Tune: 'Yakety Yak,'?" *Baltimore Sun* (29 January 1995), F1.

40. Jon Sawyer, "Clinton Covers the Waterfront, Seeking a Theme," *St. Louis Post-Dispatch* (5 February 1997).

41. Ibid.

42. Chester E. Finn, Jr., "C For Effort," *National Review* (7 April 1997): 34.

43. Ibid.

44. Tulis, *The Rhetorical Presidency*, 108–09.

45. Ibid.

46. President William Jefferson Clinton, Inaugural Address, 1993.

47. Hargrove, *Jimmy Carter as President*, 4.

48. Ibid., 25.

49. Fallows, "The Passionless Presidency," 38.

50. Ibid.

51. Quoted in Stephen Hess, *Organizing the Presidency*, 2nd ed. (Washington, D.C.: Brookings, 1988), 142.

52. Ibid.

53. Hugh Sidey, "Assessing a Presidency," *Time*, (18 August 1980), 14.

54. Kenneth Walsh and Matthew Cooper, "Disaster in Waiting," *U.S. News and World Report* (25 October 1993), 29.

55. Duffy, "The State of Bill Clinton," 28.

56. Ibid., 26.

57. Ibid., 29.

58. Bert A. Rockman, "Leadership Style and the Clinton Presidency," in Colin Campbell and Bert Rockman, eds., *The Clinton Presidency* (Chatham, N.J.: Chatham House, 1996), 352.

59. Bob Woodward, *The Agenda* (New York: Simon & Schuster, 1994), 329.

60. Quoted in Hess, *Organizing the Presidency*, 142.

61. Ibid.

62. Matthew Kerbel, *Beyond Persuasion: Organizational Efficiency and Presidential Power* (Albany: SUNY Press, 1991), 128.

63. Rockman, "Leadership and the Clinton Presidency," 353.

64. James P. Pfiffner, *The Strategic Presidency: Hitting the Ground Running* (Lawrence: University Press of Kansas, 1996), 149.

65. Woodward, *The Agenda*, 280.

66. Renshon, *High Hopes*, 82.

67. Ibid.

68. Richard E. Neustadt and Ernest R. May, *Thinking In Time: The Uses of History for Decision Makers* (New York: Free Press, 1986), 68.

69. Ibid., 187.

70. Greenstein, "Presidential Leadership Style of Clinton," 595.

71. Elizabeth Drew, *On The Edge: The Clinton Presidency* (New York: Simon & Schuster, 1994) 434.

72. Ibid., 305.

73. Ibid.

74. Carl Cannon, "Clinton Pledges to Continue Fight for Fast-Track," *Baltimore Sun*, (11 November 1997), A1.

75. Ibid.

76. Quoted in Hargrove, *Jimmy Carter as President*, 20.

77. Quoted in Fred I. Greenstein, "Reagan and the Lore of the Modern Presidency: What Have We Learned?" in Fred I. Greenstein, ed., *The Reagan Presidency: An Early Assessment* (Baltimore: Johns Hopkins University Press, 1983), 170.

78. Quoted in Betty Glad, *Jimmy Carter: In Search of the Great White House* (New York: Norton, 1980), 419.

79. Charles Jones, *The Trusteeship Presidency: Jimmy Carter and the United States Congress* (Baton Rouge: Louisiana State University Press, 1988), 6.

80. Quoted in ibid., 7.

81. Ibid., 94.

82. Quoted in Hargrove, *Jimmy Carter as President*, 49.

83. Remarks of the President to the People of Greensburg, Pennsylvania (15 July 1994), White House Press Release.

84. President's Radio Address to the Nation, 2 July 1994, White House Press Release.

85. President William J. Clinton, "Remarks on the Anniversary of the Passage of the Economic Program, August 5 1994", *The Public Papers of the President of the United States: William J. Clinton, 1994*, book 2 (Washington, D.C.: U.S. Government Printing Office, 1995), 1435.

86. Clinton's address quoted in *The St. Louis Post-Dispatch* (5 February 1997), A1.

87. Remarks by the President to Education International World Congress, Washington Hilton, 29 July 1998, White House Press Release.

88. Remarks by the President, Senator Tom Daschle, and Representative Dick Gephardt on Legislative Priorities, 5 October 1998, White House Press Release.

89. Renshon, *High Hopes*, 105.

90. Quoted in James David Barber, *The Presidential Character*, 3rd ed. (Englewood Cliffs, N.J.: Prentice Hall, 1985), 441.

91. Clinton quoted in Nancy Collins, "A Legacy of Strength and Love," *Good Housekeeping* (November 1995), 200.

92. Fallows, "The Passionless Presidency," 43.

93. Dick Kirschten, "Beyond the Vance–Brzezinski Clash Lurks an NSC under Fire," *National Journal* (17 May 1980), 814.

94. Ibid.

95. William P. Bundy, "The National Security Process," *International Security*, 7 (Winter 1982–1983): 104.

96. John Judis, "Clinton's Foreign UnPolicy," *The New Republic* (12 July 1993), 18.

97. Greenstein, "Presidential Leadership Style of Clinton," 595.

98. Quoted in Duffy, "The State of Bill Clinton," 26.

99. Quoted in Renshon, *High Hopes*, 82–83.

100. Fred Barnes, "Cabinet Losers," *The New Republic* (28 February 1994), 23.

101. Ibid.

102. Jim Hoagland, "Image Isn't Everything," *Washington Post* (31 May 1994), A17.

103. Ibid.

104. Richard Cohen, *Washington Post*, September 1993.

105. Press Conference in Little Rock, 14 January 1993, quoted in Lynne V. Cheney, *Telling the Truth* (New York: Simon & Schuster, 1995), 187.

106. Ibid.

107. Remarks at White House Briefing With President of Namibia Sam Nujoma, 16 June 1993, and Somalia Message to Congress from President Clinton, 13 October 1993, quoted in Cheney, *Telling the Truth*, 187.

108. Quoted in Cheney, *Telling the Truth*, 188.

109. Quoted in ibid.

110. Quoted in Moises Naim, "Clinton's Foreign Policy: A Victim of Globalization?" *Foreign Policy*, 109 (Winter 1997–98): 49.

111. Nayan Chanda, "A View From Asia II," *Foreign Policy* 109 (Winter 1997–98), 67.

112. Remarks of Bill Clinton, 13 August, 1992, replayed on NBC News, *Meet the Press*, 14 June, 1998.

113. Ibid.

114. Yoichi Funabashi, "A View From Asia II," *Foreign Policy* (Winter 1997–98): 51.

115. Christoph Bertram, "A View From Europe (I)," *Foreign Policy* (Winter 1997–98): 46.

116. Jacques Attali, "A View From Europe (II)," *Foreign Policy* 109 (Winter 1997–98).

117. Seymour Hersh, "The Missiles of August," *The New Yorker* (12 October 1998), 37.

118. Ibid., 35.

119. The evidence cited here is taken from Hersh, "The Missiles of August," 34–41.

120. Quoted in "Consequences of a Languishing CIA," *Baltimore Sun* (8 October 1998).

121. Quoted in Hersh, "The Missiles of August," 37.

122. John F. Harris, "Advice Didn't Sway Clinton on Airstrikes," *The Washington Post* (1 April 1999), A1.

123. Ibid.

124. Ibid.

125. Jimmy Carter, in his "Energy and National Goals" speech of 15 July, 1979, better known as the "Malaise" speech, said: "I promised you a President who is not isolated from the people, who feels your pain, and who shares your dreams. . . ."

126. Richard Reeves, *Running in Place* (Kansas City, MO.: Andrews and McMeel, 1996), 87.

127. Fallows, "The Passionless Presidency," 42–43.

128. Ibid., 35.

129. Efron, "Can the President Think?", 26.

130. Greenstein, "Presidential Leadership Style of Clinton," 593.

131. Robert Kaiser and John Harris, *Washington Post* (11 September 1998), A1.

132. Ibid.

133. Carter quoted in Glad, *Jimmy Carter*, 477.

134. David McCullough, "Harry S. Truman 1945–1953," in Robert A. Wilson, ed., *Character Above All* (New York: Simon and Schuster, 1995), 41–42.

Index

About the Editor

Phillip G. Henderson (Ph.D., University of Michigan) is Associate Professor of Politics at The Catholic University of America and author of *Managing the Presidency: The Eisenhower Legacy* (Westview 1988) and of numerous articles on White House organization, presidential leadership, and national security advisory processes.

About the Contributors

(In Order of Appearance)

Forrest McDonald (Ph.D., University of Texas) is Distinguished Professor of History at the University of Alabama and the author of sixteen books, including *The American Presidency: An Intellectual History* (Kansas 1994), *The Presidency of George Washington* (Kansas 1974), and *Novus Ordo Seclorum: The Intellectual Origins of the Constitution* (Kansas 1985).

David N. Mayer (Ph.D., University of Virginia; J.D., University of Michigan) is Professor of Law and History at Capital University Law School in Columbus, Ohio, and the author of *The Constitutional Thought of Thomas Jefferson* (Virginia 1994).

Mark J. Rozell (Ph.D., University of Virginia) is Associate Professor of Politics at The Catholic University of America and the author of eight books, including *Executive Privilege* (Johns Hopkins 1994), *The Press and the Ford Presidency* (Michigan 1992), and *Interest Groups in American Campaigns* (Congressional Quarterly 1999). He is the editor, with William Pederson, of *George Washington and the Origins of the Presidency* (Praeger 1999), and of *The New Politics of the Old South* (Rowman & Littlefield 1998).

Joseph R. Avella (Ph.D. The Catholic University of America; Captain (Ret.) U.S. Navy) was assigned to the Crisis Management Group in the Office of the Secretary of Defense during the Persian Gulf War. He serves as Executive Vice President of Capella University in Minneapolis, Minnesota, and has written extensively on military decision-making and national security policy.

Gary L. Gregg II (Ph.D., Miami University of Ohio) is Mitch McConnell Chair in Political Leadership at the University of Louisville and Director of the McConnell Center for the Study of Leadership. He is the author of *The Presidential Republic* (Rowman & Littlefield 1997) and the editor of *Vital Remnants: America's Founding and the Western Tradition* (Intercollegiate Studies Institute 1999).

Raymond Tatalovich (Ph.D., University of Chicago) is Professor of Political Science at Loyola University, Chicago, and author of numerous books and articles on the presidency, including *To Govern A Nation: Presidential Power and Politics* (St. Martin's 1998) and *Presidential Power in the United States* (Brooks Cole 1984).

Travis Cook (Ph.D. candidate, Loyola University, Chicago) is Director of the Integritas Institute for Business and Professional Ethics at the University of Illinois—Chicago.

Scott Yenor (Ph.D., Loyola University, Chicago) is Assistant Professor of Political Science at Gustavus Aldophus College.

Shirley Anne Warshaw (Ph.D., Johns Hopkins University) is Professor of Political Science at Gettysburg College and the author of *The Domestic Presidency* (Allyn & Bacon 1997), *Powersharing: White House-Cabinet Relations in the Modern Presidency* (SUNY Press 1996), and editor of *The Eisenhower Legacy* (Bartleby Press 1992).

Graham G. Dodds is a Ph.D. candidate in political science at the University of Pennsylvania.

Stephen J. McKenna (Ph.D., The Catholic University of America) is Assistant Professor of English at The Catholic University of America and author of articles on eighteenth-century rhetorical history and the rhetoric of advertising.

Richard J.Ellis (Ph.D., University of California, Berkeley) is Mark O. Hatfield Professor of Politics at Willamette University and the author and editor of several books, including *Founding the American Presidency* (Rowman & Littlefield 1999), *Presidential Lightning Rods* (Kansas 1994), and *The Dark Side of the Left: Illiberal Egalitarianism* (Kansas 1998).

Keith E. Whittington (Ph.D., Yale University) is Assistant Professor of Politics at Princeton University and the author of *Constitutional Construction: Divided Powers and Constitutional Meaning* (Harvard 1999) and *Constitutional Interpretation: Textual Meaning, Original Intent, and Judicial Review* (Kansas 1999).